Lecture Notes
in Economics and
Mathematical Systems

Managing Editors: M. Beckmann and W. Krelle

229

Interactive Decision Analysis

Proceedings, Laxenburg, Austria, 1983

Edited by M. Grauer and A. P. Wierzbicki

Springer-Verlag
Berlin Heidelberg New York Tokyo

Lecture Notes in Economics and Mathematical Systems

For information about Vols. 1–100, please contact your bookseller or Springer-Verlag

Vol. 101: W. M. Wonham, Linear Multivariable Control. A Geometric Approach. X, 344 pages. 1974.

Vol. 102: Analyse Convexe et Ses Applications. Comptes Rendus, Janvier 1974. Edited by J.-P. Aubin. IV, 244 pages. 1974.

Vol. 103: D. E. Boyce, A. Farhi, R. Weischedel, Optimal Subset Selection. Multiple Regression, Interdependence and Optimal Network Algorithms. XIII, 187 pages. 1974.

Vol. 104: S. Fujino, A Neo-Keynesian Theory of Inflation and Economic Growth. V, 96 pages. 1974.

Vol. 105: Optimal Control Theory and its Applications. Part I. Proceedings 1973. Edited by B. J. Kirby. VI, 425 pages. 1974.

Vol. 106: Optimal Control Theory and its Applications. Part II. Proceedings 1973. Edited by B. J. Kirby. VI, 403 pages. 1974.

Vol. 107: Control Theory, Numerical Methods and Computer Systems Modeling. International Symposium, Rocquencourt, June 17–21, 1974. Edited by A. Bensoussan and J. L. Lions. VIII, 757 pages. 1975.

Vol. 108: F. Bauer et al., Supercritical Wing Sections II. A Handbook. V, 296 pages. 1975.

Vol. 109: R. von Randow, Introduction to the Theory of Matroids. IX, 102 pages. 1975.

Vol. 110: C. Striebel, Optimal Control of Discrete Time Stochastic Systems. III. 208 pages. 1975.

Vol. 111: Variable Structure Systems with Application to Economics and Biology. Proceedings 1974. Edited by A. Ruberti and R. R. Mohler. VI, 321 pages. 1975.

Vol. 112: J. Wilhelm, Objectives and Multi-Objective Decision Making Under Uncertainty. IV, 111 pages. 1975.

Vol. 113: G. A. Aschinger, Stabilitätsaussagen über Klassen von Matrizen mit verschwindenden Zeilensummen. V, 102 Seiten. 1975.

Vol. 114: G. Uebe, Produktionstheorie. XVII, 301 Seiten. 1976.

Vol. 115: Anderson et al., Foundations of System Theory: Finitary and Infinitary Conditions. VII, 93 pages. 1976

Vol. 116: K. Miyazawa, Input-Output Analysis and the Structure of Income Distribution. IX, 135 pages. 1976.

Vol. 117: Optimization and Operations Research. Proceedings 1975. Edited by W. Oettli and K. Ritter. IV, 316 pages. 1976.

Vol. 118: Traffic Equilibrium Methods, Proceedings 1974. Edited by M. A. Florian. XXIII, 432 pages. 1976.

Vol. 119: Inflation in Small Countries. Proceedings 1974. Edited by H. Frisch. VI, 356 pages. 1976.

Vol. 120: G. Hasenkamp, Specification and Estimation of Multiple-Output Production Functions. VII, 151 pages. 1976.

Vol. 121: J. W. Cohen, On Regenerative Processes in Queueing Theory. IX, 93 pages. 1976.

Vol. 122: M. S. Bazaraa, and C. M. Shetty, Foundations of Optimization VI. 193 pages. 1976

Vol. 123: Multiple Criteria Decision Making. Kyoto 1975. Edited by M. Zeleny. XXVII, 345 pages. 1976.

Vol. 124: M. J. Todd. The Computation of Fixed Points and Applications. VII, 129 pages. 1976.

Vol. 125: Karl C. Mosler. Optimale Transportnetze. Zur Bestimmung ihres kostengünstigsten Standorts bei gegebener Nachfrage. VI, 142 Seiten. 1976.

Vol. 126: Energy, Regional Science and Public Policy. Energy and Environment I. Proceedings 1975. Edited by M. Chatterji and P. Van Rompuy. VIII, 316 pages. 1976.

Vol. 127: Environment, Regional Science and Interregional Modeling. Energy and Environment II. Proceedings 1975. Edited by M. Chatterji and P. Van Rompuy. IX, 211 pages. 1976.

Vol. 128: Integer Programming and Related Areas. A Classified Bibliography. Edited by C. Kastning. XII, 495 pages. 1976.

Vol. 129: H.-J. Lüthi, Komplementaritäts- und Fixpunktalgorithmen in der mathematischen Programmierung. Spieltheorie und Ökonomie. VII, 145 Seiten. 1976.

Vol. 130: Multiple Criteria Decision Making, Jouy-en-Josas, France. Proceedings 1975. Edited by H. Thiriez and S. Zionts. VI, 409 pages. 1976.

Vol. 131: Mathematical Systems Theory. Proceedings 1975. Edited by G. Marchesini and S. K. Mitter. X, 408 pages. 1976.

Vol. 132: U. H. Funke, Mathematical Models in Marketing. A Collection of Abstracts. XX, 514 pages. 1976.

Vol. 133: Warsaw Fall Seminars in Mathematical Economics 1975. Edited by M. W. Loś, J. Loś, and A. Wieczorek. V. 159 pages. 1976.

Vol. 134: Computing Methods in Applied Sciences and Engineering. Proceedings 1975. VIII, 390 pages. 1976.

Vol. 135: H. Haga, A Disequilibrium – Equilibrium Model with Money and Bonds. A Keynesian – Walrasian Synthesis. VI, 119 pages. 1976.

Vol. 136: E. Kofler und G. Menges, Entscheidungen bei unvollständiger Information. XII, 357 Seiten. 1976.

Vol. 137: R. Wets, Grundlagen Konvexer Optimierung. VI, 146 Seiten. 1976.

Vol. 138: K. Okuguchi, Expectations and Stability in Oligopoly Models. VI, 103 pages. 1976.

Vol. 139: Production Theory and Its Applications. Proceedings. Edited by H. Albach and G. Bergendahl. VIII, 193 pages. 1977.

Vol. 140: W. Eichhorn and J. Voeller, Theory of the Price Index. Fisher's Test Approach and Generalizations. VII, 95 pages. 1976.

Vol. 141: Mathematical Economics and Game Theory. Essays in Honor of Oskar Morgenstern. Edited by R. Henn and O. Moeschlin. XIV, 703 pages. 1977.

Vol. 142: J. S. Lane, On Optimal Population Paths. V, 123 pages. 1977.

Vol. 143: B. Näslund, An Analysis of Economic Size Distributions. XV, 100 pages. 1977.

Vol. 144: Convex Analysis and Its Applications. Proceedings 1976. Edited by A. Auslender. VI, 219 pages. 1977.

Vol. 145: J. Rosenmüller, Extreme Games and Their Solutions. IV, 126 pages. 1977.

Vol. 146: In Search of Economic Indicators. Edited by W. H. Strigel. XVI, 198 pages. 1977.

Vol. 147: Resource Allocation and Division of Space. Proceedings. Edited by T. Fujii and R. Sato. VIII, 184 pages. 1977.

Vol. 148: C. E. Mandl, Simulationstechnik und Simulationsmodelle in den Sozial- und Wirtschaftswissenschaften. IX, 173 Seiten. 1977.

Vol. 149: Stationäre und schrumpfende Bevölkerungen: Demographisches Null- und Negativwachstum in Österreich. Herausgegeben von G. Feichtinger. VI, 262 Seiten. 1977.

Vol. 150: Bauer et al., Supercritical Wing Sections III. VI, 179 pages. 1977.

Vol. 151: C. A. Schneeweiß, Inventory-Production Theory. VI, 116 pages. 1977.

Vol. 152: Kirsch et al., Notwendige Optimalitätsbedingungen und ihre Anwendung. VI, 157 Seiten. 1978.

Vol. 153: Kombinatorische Entscheidungsprobleme: Methoden und Anwendungen. Herausgegeben von T. M. Liebling und M. Rössler. VIII, 206 Seiten. 1978.

Vol. 154: Problems and Instruments of Business Cycle Analysis. Proceedings 1977. Edited by W. H. Strigel. VI, 442 pages. 1978.

Vol. 155: Multiple Criteria Problem Solving. Proceedings 1977. Edited by S. Zionts. VIII, 567 pages. 1978.

Vol. 156: B. Näslund and B. Sellstedt, Neo-Ricardian Theory. With Applications to Some Current Economic Problems. VI, 165 pages. 1978.

continuation on page 271

Lecture Notes
in Economics and
Mathematical Systems

Managing Editors: M. Beckmann and W. Krelle

229

Interactive Decision Analysis

Proceedings of an International Workshop on Interactive Decision Analysis and Interpretative Computer Intelligence Held at the International Institute for Applied Systems Analysis (IIASA), Laxenburg, Austria
September 20–23, 1983

Edited by M. Grauer and A. P. Wierzbicki

Springer-Verlag
Berlin Heidelberg New York Tokyo 1984

Managing Editors

Prof. Dr. M. Beckmann
Brown University
Providence, RI 02912, USA

Prof. Dr. W. Krelle
Institut für Gesellschafts- und Wirtschaftswissenschaften
der Universität Bonn
Adenauerallee 24–42, D-5300 Bonn, FRG

Editors

Dr. M. Grauer
International Institute for Applied Systems Analysis
Schlossplatz 1, A-2361 Laxenburg, Austria

and

Division of Mathematics and Cybernetics
Academy of Sciences of the GDR
Berlin, GDR

Prof. A. P. Wierzbicki
International Institute for Applied Systems Analysis
Schlossplatz 1, A-2361 Laxenburg, Austria

and

Institute of Automatic Control
Technical University of Warsaw
Warsaw, Poland

ISBN 3-540-13354-2 Springer-Verlag Berlin Heidelberg New York Tokyo
ISBN 0-387-13354-2 Springer-Verlag New York Heidelberg Berlin Tokyo

Printed in Germany

Printing and binding: Beltz Offsetdruck, Hemsbach/Bergstr.
2142/3140-543210

FOREWORD

During the week of September 20-23, 1983, an International Workshop on Interactive Decision Analysis and Interpretative Computer Intelligence was held at the International Institute for Applied Systems Analysis (IIASA) in Laxenburg, Austria. More than fifty scientists representing seventeen countries participated. The aim of the Workshop was to review existing approaches to problems involving multiple conflicting objectives, to look at methods and techniques for interactive decision analysis, and to demonstrate the use of existing interactive decision-support systems.

The Workshop was motivated, firstly, by the realization that the rapid development of computers, especially microcomputers, will greatly increase the scope and capabilities of computerized decision-support systems. It is important to explore the potential of these systems for use in handling the complex technological, environmental, economic and social problems that face the world today.

Research in decision-support systems also has another, less tangible but possibly more important, motivation. The development of efficient systems for decision support requires a thorough understanding of the differences between the decision-making processes in different nations and cultures. An understanding of the different rationales underlying decision making is not only necessary for the development of efficient decision-support systems, but is also an important factor in encouraging international understanding and cooperation.

IIASA is a unique forum for comparison and exchange of approaches developed in East and West and has built on this in its research on interactive decision analysis, having held several international conferences in this field. The early stages of this research were presented at an IIASA Workshop in 1975 and recorded in a book Conflicting Objectives in Decisions, edited by D.E. Bell, R.L. Keeney and H. Raiffa, and published by Wiley in 1977. More recently, a Task Force Meeting on multiobjective and stochastic optimization was held at IIASA at the end of 1981: a volume containing the Proceedings of this Task Force Meeting was published by IIASA under the title Multiobjective and Stochastic Optimization in 1982.

The Proceedings of the 1983 IIASA Workshop are divided into four main sections. The first section consists of an introductory lecture by *Wierzbicki*, in which he describes a unifying approach to the use of computers and computerized mathematical models for decision analysis and support. The paper presents a mathematical formalization of the interpretative aspect of computer intelligence and proposes an approach which integrates the major formal frameworks for rational decision making.

The second section, which is concerned with approaches and concepts in interactive decision analysis, begins with a paper by *Grauer, Lewandowski and Wierzbicki* reporting on the progress made in the development of the decision-support system DIDASS at IIASA. The mathematical background is outlined, methods of implementation and computational aspects are discussed and three applications are summarized. The next contribution, by *Carlsson*, looks at how conflicts (in a management context) can be handled with the help of models for fuzzy multiple-criteria optimization. He shows that the theory of fuzzy sets offers a few more degrees of freedom for handling conflicts than a traditional operational research model. *Forgó* then presents a game-theoretic approach for multicriteria decision making. In the next paper, *Sugihara and Ichikawa* analyze the decision-making process from the social sciences viewpoint, and show that, to adapt to the environment effectively and efficiently, the manager should make use of the systems approach and adopt what they call the "contingency view". *Zionts and Wallenius* give an overview of their work over the last ten years and present their methods for multiple-objective linear programming, for multiple-objective integer linear programming, for choosing among discrete alternatives in the multicriteria case and for handling multicriteria problems involving multiple decision makers. *Peschel and Breitenecker* then describe an interactive structure design principle and a related simulation technique, and in the last paper in this section *Mazurik* discusses how to organize interactive computer support for the construction of complex models.

The third section is devoted to methods and techniques for interactive decision analysis, and begins with two theoretical papers. *Serafini* presents duality results for multiobjective optimization, and shows how these ideas can be applied to discrete multiobjective problems by introducing the concept of dual relaxation and using it in a branch-and-bound-type technique. In the next contribution, *Vlach* shows that the technique developed by Levitin, Miljutin and Osmolovski can be applied to optimization problems with nonscalar-valued objective functions. The next two papers investigate the use of fuzzy set theory in interactive decision making. The paper by *Seo and Sakawa* is concerned with fuzzy assessment of multiattribute utility functions, while *Sakawa's* individual contribution deals with interactive fuzzy decision making in multiobjective nonlinear programming problems. Both papers present some numerical results obtained from computer runs. *Nakayama and Sawaragi* report on an interactive method for multiobjective programming called the satisficing trade-off method, and provide some examples of its use in practice. The paper by *Guddat and Wendler* describes a method, based on parametric optimization, for dealing with multicriteria optimization problems. The authors discuss certain special features of interactive algorithms for the linear and nonlinear cases. *Steuer's* paper is concerned with operating considerations pertaining to the interactive weighted Tchebycheff procedure. The strategy of the Tchebycheff approach is to sample a series of successively smaller subsets of the set of all nondominated criterion vectors--this paper gives the results of some computational experiments and describes the essential features of the method. The paper by *Bischoff* deals with extensions to existing reference point methods for multiple-objective decision making through the incorporation of an a posteriori trade-off analysis. In the next paper, *Korhonen and Laakso* propose an interactive method for solving multiple-criteria decision problems with convex constraints and a pseudoconcave and differentiable utility function. The last paper of the third section, which is by *Tarvainen*, investigates the implementation of the interactive surrogate worth trade-off method.

The fourth and final section of the Proceedings contains descriptions of a wide range of applications of interactive techniques, covering the fields of economics, public policy planning, energy policy evaluation, hydrology and industrial development. *Lootsma et al.* present their experiences with two pairwise-comparison methods in a multicriteria analysis of various energy technologies. This study was designed to assist the Energy Research Council of The Netherlands in deciding on their budget allocations. The paper by *Isermann* presents an interactive decision-support system for distributing cash dividends from a firm to the various partners according to their individual time preferences. Also from the field of finance, *Morse* reports on a multiobjective expert system for suppliers of out-of-the-money options. *Hafkamp and Nijkamp* present an integrated approach to regional economic-environmental-energy policy analysis, based on a triple-layer interactive model. A computerized interactive system which supports the making of collective decisions in a gaming framework is described by *Fortuna and Krus*; it is illustrated by application to a regional development model. The papers by *Szidarovszky* and *Kaden* deal with the application of multiobjective approaches to hydrology and mining. Decision support via simulation is the subject of the contribution by *Breitenecker and Schmid*; an application to a hydroenergetic system is described. The paper by *Lotov and Stolyarova* describes the use of the generalized reachable set method in forestry management problems. The last paper in the volume deals with an application from the chemical industry: *Górecki et al.* propose a multiobjective procedure for project formulation and discuss its use.

The Editors would like to thank IIASA for financing, organizing and running the Workshop and Helen Gasking for her hard work in preparing the Proceedings. We also wish to thank the authors for permission to publish their contributions in this volume.

February, 1984

M. Grauer
A. Wierzbicki

CONTENTS

I. INTRODUCTORY LECTURE

INTERACTIVE DECISION ANALYSIS AND INTERPRETATIVE COMPUTER INTELLIGENCE

A. Wierzbicki
International Institute for Applied Systems Analysis, Laxenburg, Austria

SUMMARY

This paper presents a unifying approach to the issue of using computers and computerized mathematical models for decision analysis and support. The interpretative aspect of computer intelligence is an essential part of this approach; this paper presents a mathematical formalization of this aspect. Another essential part of this approach is a proposal to integrate the three major formalized frameworks for rational decision making: utility theory (mostly normative), aspiration theory (mostly behavioral), and the (mostly hierarchical) theory of goal- and program-oriented management. These two elements lead to the formulation of principles for a broad class of decision support systems, which includes many existing systems but which also opens new possibilities. Two main cases of decision support are discussed: joint decision making (i.e., involving only one decision maker or several decision makers who have to reach a consensus) and independent decision making (assuming a game-like situation with several decision makers). These cases are illustrated by reference to the DIDASS system, its applications and extensions.

1. INTRODUCTION AND METHODOLOGICAL SURVEY

1.1. General Motivation

Over the last forty years, the development of computers has led to new opportunities in information processing, research and development, automatization and robotization of technological processes--the possibilities are endless. However, it will probably take hundreds of years to take full advantage of this new technology: several generations must assimilate the new computerized culture, learn to use and live with computers, adjust the social fabric to the requirements of the new computer era.

An essential goal for researchers preparing for this change is to devise new principles for the development of computer hardware and software. While hardware development is moving ahead rapidly (vis. the Japanese project on fifth-generation computers), software and, in particular, general principles for computer use have been lagging behind. Yet the future will depend just as much, if not more, on the uses to which computers are put as on technological hardware developments which we can visualize now.

One broad class of computer use is decision, policy and strategy analysis. Computerized mathematical models of various aspects of human activity have long been used for these purposes. However, the *principles* behind computerized decision analysis and support are by no means universally agreed upon, and there are many different schools of thought about how computers should be used. Some support the paradigm of predictive models, which give unique answers but with limited accuracy or validity; some weaken this paradigm by scenario analysis. Some believe in normative models that prescribe how things *should* happen (based on some theory), and reinforce this by exploiting the tools of mathematical optimization and game theory. Others criticize this approach for its lack of realism and put forward instead the idea of descriptive, behavioral modeling; this criticism is often directed without discrimination at both the normative methodological assumptions and the mathematical tools.. Yet others instinctively dislike any models that imply hierarchical organizations; some take hierarchy in organizations for granted and develop methods and tools for handling hierarchical models.

There are even various schools and approaches with regard to mathematical tools: some prefer static models, while others claim that without accounting for dynamic effects any decision analysis is doomed to failure; the different mathematical descriptions of dynamic processes (e.g., difference equations, ordinary or partial differential equations, equations with delay, differential inclusions, integral equations) all have their adherents. The proponents of linear versus nonlinear models, differentiability versus nondifferentiability, and various methods of handling uncertainty also create dissent. Some prefer to handle uncertainty using deterministic models with scenarios and interval analysis, some using statistical models, others broader probabilistic and stochastic approaches, others adaptive and learning procedures, while yet others argue for the use of fuzzy sets.*

With all these divisions, increasing numbers of mathematical modellers and systems analysts have come to the conclusion that mathematical models for decision or policy analysis must be built and used interactively, that is, involving the eventual users at all stages of the process. Again, there are different interpretations of what is meant by interaction. Some understand it to mean simply some way of improving communication between a user and a computerized model. Others stress the educational, learning and adaptive aspects of computerized simulation, experimenting with models, computerized simulated gaming, and procedures for organizing interaction between groups of experts, users, and decision makers. Others understand interaction as a tool in decision making, and combine multiobjective optimization with normative decision theory to construct an interactive decision support system. Others (including the author) try to broaden the principles of interaction while preserving some mathematical rigour and exploiting a wide range of existing mathematical tools.

Such a heterogeneity of approaches is not only an inevitable, but also a desirable consequence of the turbulent history of computer modeling. However, new directions can often be found by trying to bridge the gaps between existing approaches. This paper presents an attempt to bridge various gaps in this field, by proposing a unified approach to the interactive use of models in decision and policy analysis. To do this, we first

---

*I feel compelled to present my own position in this debate. I happen to believe that a diversity of mathematical tools is necessary, and we should develop all of them, not narrowly and arrogantly force any one particular class of tools to be used. However, the development of mathematical tools should be motivated by substantive and methodological issues. As to the latter, I would say that a purely normative approach is like searching for a lost ring only under the lamp, and a purely descriptive approach is like describing the lost ring in great detail instead of concentrating on searching for it; denying hierarchical aspects in human organizations is like saying that the ring should not be lost at all and then there would be no problem.

analyze the meaning of computer intelligence and try to define one particular aspect of it: interpretative intelligence. This characterizes the computer side of a man-computer interactive system. From the human side, we have to analyze the various types of human organizations, and several competing definitions of a rational decision. Integration of these frameworks leads to a broad principle for organizing man-computer interactions, provides a basis for many practical applications and introduces several new theoretical questions.

1.2. The Interpretative Aspect of Computer Intelligence

Different authors--see, for example, Hayes et al. (1982), Latombe (1978) and Nilsson (1980)--define computer intelligence in different ways. Some of these definitions deny that this concept can be formalized mathematically, while others stress only the mathematical aspects, such as the ability to prove theorems. There are also various schools of thought as to how certain aspects of computer intelligence should be formalized. For example, one of the most widely studied mathematical formalizations is related to the *ability to learn*. This is typically associated with the problem of pattern recognition, i.e., given a number of observations consisting of vectors of data which are each linked with binary outcomes or classifications, what binary outcome or classification should we assign to a new vector of data? This question has received much attention and many different answers--see, for example, Zhuravlev (1976, 1977).

However, one of the oldest interpretations of computer intelligence has not received so much attention. We instinctively understand what is meant by expecting a computer to interpret our commands intelligently--it is similar to expecting a secretary to respond intelligently to the directives of the boss. This question of intelligent interpretation is not simply concerned with quick recognition of a command (which may soon even be given to computers verbally): this is an elementary requirement. We tend to say that a software package is intelligent if it does not have to be guided by detailed commands at each step, or if, given a short command and a context, it provides the answers most appropriate to the context.

A mathematical formalization of this concept might be linked to the *selection of solutions for ill-defined mathematical problems* (Tikhonov and Arsenin, 1975). The context in which a command is given could be represented as a set of possible answers, described mathematically by various constraints--equations, inequalities, and logical relations. This set typically contains many answers; when a command is given in this context, it also provides additional data which guides the selection of an answer. Various selection principles are possible, going much further than the simplest requirement of obeying the command exactly. For example, the computer could construct a logical transformation of the command, or minimize a distance of the actual outcome from the desired outcome, or maximize a function that parametrically depends on the command. The last possibility is closely related to problems of interactive decision analysis and will be discussed here in more detail.

1.3. Major Frameworks for Rational Decision Making

Any formalized framework for rational decision making must assume that the problem has some basic mathematical structure. This structure typically comprises:

-- a space of decisions (alternatives, policy options, controls, etc.), here denoted by E_x

-- a constraint set $X_0 \subset E_x$ defining the admissible decisions*

-- a space of outcomes (attributes, objectives, performance indices, etc.), here denoted by E_y

-- an outcome mapping** $f : E_x \rightarrow E_y$, which also defines the set of attainable outcomes $Y_0 = f(X_0) \subset E_y$

-- two types of generalized inequalities or preorderings*** in the space E_y. The fact that we actually have two different preorderings of outcomes that jointly define the decision problem is essential and should be emphasized. These preorderings are:

1. A partial preordering $\leqslant^P$ that is usually implied by the decision problem and has some obvious interpretation (for example, increasing gains or profits, or decreasing outlay or costs are obvious objectives in certain contexts).

2. A complete preordering $\leqslant^C$ that is typically not given in an explicit mathematical form (if it were, the decision problem would be trivial)-- it should be in some form specified by the decision maker.

The main differences between the various formalized frameworks for rational decison making are concerned with the way in which the complete preordering $\leqslant^C$ is characterized and the various assumptions about its properties and interpretation.

The most strongly established framework is that of *value or utility maximization*. If the complete preordering were context-free, independent of other factors present in the decision problem, then (under quite general assumptions--see Debreu (1959)) it could be represented by a utility function**** $u : E_y \rightarrow \mathbb{R}^1$ such

---

*We often also consider an additional space of constraints E_v , a mapping $g : E_x \rightarrow E_v$ called a constraining mapping, a generalized inequality $\leqslant_{E_v}$ defining a partial preordering in E_v, and an element $\bar{v}$ in E_v . The set X_0 is then defined as $X_0 = \{x \in E_x : g(x) \leqslant_{E_v} \bar{v}\}$. However, in the context of our discussion this means only that the set X_0 might be given implicitly and may have rather a complicated structure.

**Sometimes this mapping is not strictly defined and there are dimensions of the space E_y which can be quantified only by expert opinion. This leads to *partially quantified decision problems*. However, the discussion here will be limited to completely quantified decision problems for which the mapping f is given.

***These are inequality relations $\leqslant$ between the elements of the space E_y such that $y' \leqslant y''$ and $y'' \leqslant y'$ do not necessarily imply $y' = y''$; in other words, there are classes of equivalent elements in E_y that might contain more than a singleton $\{y\}$. This can also be called quasi-ordering (Debreu, 1959). Such preordering is called *partial* if there can exist elements y', $y'' \in E_y$ such that neither $y' \leqslant y''$ nor $y'' \leqslant y'$ holds, and *complete* (or *total*) if either $y' \leqslant y''$ or $y'' \leqslant y'$ holds for all y'', $y' \in E_y$.

****More precisely, a value function; a utility function would then be the value function transformed by the attitude of the decision maker towards risk. However, we could in principle include randomness in the definition of the mapping f and expectation in the definition of the function u. Thus we need not concern ourselves with this distinction in our general discussion of the framework.

that $y' \preccurlyeq y'' \Leftrightarrow u(y') \leq u(y'')$. By maximizing $u(f(x))$ over $x \in X_0$, we can select the decision that is most preferable to the decision maker. The only difficulty lies in eliciting information from the decision maker in such a way that either the function u or its maximum can be identified. This problem is not trivial, since the function u is actually defined nonuniquely only up to any strictly monotonic transformation (this is the classic difference between cardinal and ordinal utility functions in economic theory) and because of the need to take into account both uncertainty and the decision maker's attitude towards it (Keeney and Raiffa, 1976).

The utility maximization framework is actually the basis of most of neoclassical economic theory, large parts of game theory, and various branches of decision theory. However, it has been severely criticized for its key assumption--that the preference relation $\preccurlyeq^C$ is independent of the context of the decision. Many experiments--see, e.g., Tversky (1972)--have shown that this assumption cannot be justified in practice. The classical way of defending the utility function framework is to argue that we could include the context simply by expanding the outcome space E_y and redefining the function u. However, this is a tautology: we can certainly rationalize any decision in this way, but we lose any predictive power if we allow the utility function to be changed arbitrarily. The essential question is *how to usefully characterize the possible (and experimentally observed) nonstationarity of utility functions induced by changing contexts in decision making.*

The second major framework for rational decision making is that of *satisficing*. In this case decisions are made by comparing outcomes to adaptively formed aspiration levels--see Simon (1969), March and Simon (1958), Selten (1972) and Tietz (1983). With a much stronger experimental and behavioral basis than the utility maximization framework, the satisficing framework has been extended to question the assumption that decision makers display maximizing behavior and thus the usefulness of more sophisticated mathematical formalization. The basis of this framework is simply a dynamic adaptive equation for the formation of aspiration levels, for example:

$$\bar{y}_{t+1} = \bar{y}_t + \alpha_t(y_t - \bar{y}_t) \tag{1}$$

where $\bar{y}_t \in E_y$ is the aspiration level, $y_t \in E_y$ is an observed (though not necessarily acceptable) outcome, and α_t is a coefficient. Then a decision $x_t \in X_0$ is satisficing if $\bar{y}_t \preccurlyeq^P f(x_t)$; clearly, there may be many such decisions or none. If there are no satisficing decisions, the aspiration levels are corrected according to (1), and the search for a satisficing decision is repeated. If one satisficing decision is found, the process is terminated.

The proponents of satisficing decision making have three main criticisms of the utility-maximizing approach:

A. It can be shown experimentally that people *do* form aspiration levels (sometimes several types of aspiration level for each outcome) and actually use them in practical decision making. The changing of aspirations may be seen as one of the main indications of the influence of context on the decision process.
B. It is not possible to find the absolute maximum of a utility function under practical conditions, when time, information and other resources are limited.
C. Uncertainty and lack of information mean that the accuracy of any optimization is questionable.

While the first of the above criticisms is clearly important, the other two are rather technical. Anybody familiar with computational optimization knows that there is no such thing as absolute optimization--the accuracy of the optimization is limited by time and other resources. There are also various ways of dealing with uncertainty. At one end of the spectrum we have probabilistic or stochastic models; at the other an admission that information is lacking and that there are numerous possible solutions. Of course, there are several approaches between these extremes. However, in each of these approaches we can use optimization techniques, not necessarily as a goal of human behavior (as some strong proponents of utility maximization seem to believe) but rather as tools for selecting a decision. Recent developments in computer technology have increased the time, information and other resources available for such computations substantially.

We shall therefore accept only point A of the criticism and investigate *quasi-satisficing behavior*, where decisions are guided by changes in aspiration levels, but where optimization may be used as a technical tool. Before we move on to a mathematical description of this type of behavior, however, we should first mention another major framework for rational decision making, developed in the Soviet Union.

This framework is called *program- and goal-oriented (management) action* and has been developed by Glushkov (1972), Pospelov and Irikov (1976) and others. In some senses, this framework takes aspiration levels (goals) and even trajectories (programs, aspiration levels developing over time) for granted, but does not allow them to adapt. Instead, this framework assumes that given goals or programs can always be attained if sufficient resources are available; the problem is how to select the smallest amount of resources necessary to attain given goals or programs. There are two possible mathematical representations of this problem.

One is to assume that the goals and programs define the outcome space E_y and that the problem is to modify* the constraint set X_0 in such a way that the goals and programs become attainable. However, in this type of formulation we encounter the problem of defining the minimal change in the set X_0. The second formulation seems to be more useful: goals and programs define only a subspace E_y' of the outcome space; those resources that can be varied define another subspace E_y'' of the outcome space, and $E_y = E_y' \times E_y''$. Thus, variable constraints are interpreted as outcomes**; we assume only that the outcomes are ordered hierarchically and that those outcomes in subspace E_y' are associated with more rigid aspirations than those in subspace E_y''. This is the essence of program- and goal-oriented action: depending on the social and cultural conditions, some aspirations are more rigid and hierarchically dominant than others.

In addition to these three major frameworks for rational decision making, there are several other schools of thought. For example, we could assume that a decision maker does not act according to any of the frameworks, but rather uses some *decision rules* that transform the available information into a decision. In fact, most ordinary, everyday decisions are made in this way. Such decision rules are rational abbreviations of longer decision processes

---

*For example, by changing the constraining value $\bar{v}$ in the constraint space E_v, see earlier footnote.

**This interpretation seems to be appropriate for all types of variable constraints; after all, what is a constraint that can be violated or shifted other than an additional dimension of the outcome space? In particular, it is applicable to all chance or probability constraints.

that have been proven to be successful in the past. The question is: assuming that standard decisions are made following certain decision rules, is it possible to achieve a synthesis of the three major formalized frameworks for rational decision making in non-standard situations?

This goal can be achieved in the following way. We accept that decisions are guided by adaptively formed aspiration levels and that these levels might, under certain conditions, be elicited from the decision maker. We use these aspiration levels $\bar{y}$ *as exogenous parameters for certain special (quasi) utility functions called achievement functions; these are of the form* $u(y)=s(y,\bar{y})$. *This provides an explicit and constructive means of expressing the dependence of the decision on the context and nonstationarity of the utility functions. However, we must pay for this: an examination of the properties of the achievement functions shows that they must necessarily be nondifferentiable at the points corresponding to aspiration levels.*

1.4. An Ideal Organization Analogy

The properties of achievement functions can be understood by analogy with an ideal organization, in which the boss defines the task and the aspiration levels, and a highly intelligent, dedicated staff try to perform the task to the best of their abilities. What properties should the utility function of the staff have in such an ideal organization? This analogy, investigated in Wierzbicki (1982), can be taken in a number of different ways. It can be used to describe the behavior of a decision maker who first forms aspiration levels (like the boss) and then searches for decisions that are guided by the aspiration levels (like the staff). It can be used to represent the behavior of an ideal organization, although the assumptions about staff behavior are probably unrealistic--except in one important case. If the staff is replaced by an "intelligent" computer and the boss by a computer user, we might realistically expect that the behavior of the staff will in some senses be ideal.

In this ideal case, we assume full agreement between the boss and the staff on goals and basic priorities (the outcome spaces E_y and the natural partial preorderings $\preccurlyeq^P$ of the boss and the staff concide). We assume that the staff is efficient (it actually maximizes its utility or achievement function, guided parametrically by the aspiration levels set by the boss). However, we must make one essential additional assumption: that *the staff takes the boss seriously*. This means that if the boss (either by experience or through pure luck) specifies aspiration levels that can only just be attained, the staff should not propose action leading to any other outcome. In other cases, i.e., if the aspiration levels are either too high or too low, the staff is allowed more freedom in selecting decisions, although they should be consistent with the agreed basic priorities (that is, with the natural partial preordering $\preccurlyeq^P$).

This additional assumption is actually very strong and implies that the utility or achievement function of the staff has certain non-classical properties--in particular, that it is nondifferentiable at points corresponding to aspiration levels. This is expressed more precisely in the next part of the paper. Figure 1 illustrates the situation graphically.

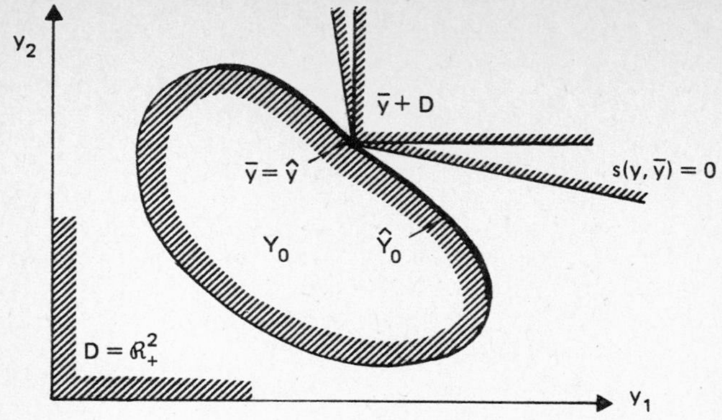

FIGURE 1 The consequences of taking the boss seriously. It is assumed that $E_y=\mathbb{R}^2$, $y' \leqslant^P y'' \Leftrightarrow y''-y' \in D=\mathbb{R}^2_+$, Y_0 is not necessarily convex, and $\hat{Y}_0$ denotes the set of nondominated elements of Y_0 in the sense of $\leqslant^P$. If the aspiration level set by the boss is nondominated ($\bar{y}=\hat{y} \in \hat{Y}_0$), the staff should not propose any other point $\hat{y}' \in \hat{Y}_0$; thus, the level set $\{y \in E_y : s(y,\bar{y}) \geq 0\}$ of their achievement function $s(y,\bar{y})$ should closely approximate the set $\bar{y}+D$, and the function $s(.,\bar{y})$ will be nondifferentiable at $y=\bar{y}$.

2. ASPIRATION LEVELS, ACHIEVEMENT FUNCTIONS, AND THEIR APPLICATIONS IN DECISION AND GAMING SUPPORT SYSTEMS

2.1. Achievement Functions

We assume here that E_y is a normed space and that the partial preordering relation $\leqslant$ in E_y is defined by a positive (closed, convex, proper) cone $D \subset E_y$:

$$y'' \leqslant y' \Leftrightarrow y'-y'' \in D. \tag{2}$$

We define several other relations in E_y:

$$y'' \lessdot y' \Leftrightarrow y' - y'' \in \tilde{D} = D \setminus (D \cap -D) \tag{3}$$

$$y'' \lessdot\lessdot y' \Leftrightarrow y' - y'' \in \mathring{D} = \text{int } D \tag{4}$$

$$y'' \leqslant_\varepsilon y' \Leftrightarrow y' - y'' \in D_\varepsilon = \{y \in E_y : \text{dist }(y,D) \leq \varepsilon \|y\|\} \tag{5}$$

$$y'' \lessdot_\varepsilon y' \Leftrightarrow y' - y'' \in \tilde{D}_\varepsilon = D_\varepsilon \setminus (D_\varepsilon \cap -D_\varepsilon) \tag{6}$$

$$y'' \lessdot\lessdot_\varepsilon y' \Leftrightarrow y' - y'' \in \mathring{D}_\varepsilon = \text{int } D_\varepsilon . \tag{7}$$

Given the set Y_0 of attainable outcomes in E_y, we define the set $\hat{Y}_0$ of D-maximal elements of Y_0, the set $\hat{Y}_0^0$ of weakly D-maximal elements, the set $\hat{Y}_0^{\varepsilon}$ of D_{ε}-maximal elements, and the set $\hat{Y}_0^{0\varepsilon}$ of weakly D_{ε}-maximal elements:

$$\hat{Y}_0 = \{y \in Y_0 : Y_0 \cap (y+\tilde{D}) = \emptyset\} \tag{8}$$

$$\hat{Y}_0^0 = \{y \in Y_0 : Y_0 \cap (y+\mathring{D}) = \emptyset\} \tag{9}$$

$$\hat{Y}_0^{\varepsilon} = \{y \in Y_0 : Y_0 \cap (y+\tilde{D}_{\varepsilon}) = \emptyset\} \tag{10}$$

$$\hat{Y}_{\varepsilon}^{0\varepsilon} = \{y \in Y_0 : Y_0 \cap (y+\mathring{D}_{\varepsilon}) = \emptyset\} . \tag{11}$$

The following inclusion holds:

$$\hat{Y}_0^{\varepsilon} \subset \hat{Y}_0^{0\varepsilon} \subset \hat{Y}_0 \subset \hat{Y}_0^0 . \tag{12}$$

A function $s : Y_0 \times E_y \to \mathbb{R}^1$ is called a strict achievement function if

$$\forall y', y'' \in Y_0 , \forall \bar{y} \in E_y , y'' \prec\!\prec y' \Rightarrow s(y'',\bar{y}) < s(y',\bar{y}) \tag{A1}$$

$$\forall y \in Y_0 , \forall \bar{y} \in E_y , s(y,y) = 0 \text{ and} \tag{B1}$$

$$\{y \in E_y : s(y,\bar{y}) \geq 0\} = S_{0\bar{y}} = \bar{y} + D .$$

A function $s : Y_0 \times E_y \to \mathbb{R}^1$ is called a strong achievement function if

$$\forall y', y'' \in Y_0 , \forall \bar{y} \in E_y , y'' \prec y' \Rightarrow s(y'',\bar{y}) < s(y',\bar{y}) \tag{A2}$$

$$\forall y \in Y_0 , \forall \bar{y} \in E_y , s(y,y) = 0 \text{ and, for some small } \varepsilon>0 , \tag{B2}$$

$$\bar{y} + D \subset \{y \in E_y : s(y,\bar{y}) \geq 0\} = S_{0\bar{y}} \subset \bar{y} + D_{\varepsilon} .$$

A differentiable function $s : Y_0 \times E_y \to \mathbb{R}^1$ is called a smooth achievement function if (A2) and (B2) hold with D_{ε} replaced by

$$D_{\varepsilon}^h = \{y \in E_y : \text{dist } (y,D) \leq \varepsilon . h(\|y\|)\} \tag{13}$$

where $h: \mathbb{R}_+^1 \to \mathbb{R}_+^1$ is a monotonic function with $\lim_{\tau \to 0} h(\tau) = 0$. Without this modification, achievement functions are nondifferentiable at $y=\bar{y}$. An ideal achievement function would combine properties (A2) and (B1); however, these properties are mutually inconsistent.

The properties of achievement functions are summarized by the following theorem (Wierzbicki, 1982):

THEOREM 1. If (A1), then $\operatorname{Arg\,max}_{y \in Y_0} s(y,\bar{y}) \subset \hat{Y}_0^0$. *If (A2), then*

$\underset{y \in Y_0}{Arg\ max}\ s(y,\bar{y}) \subset \hat{Y}_0$. *If (A1) and (B1) and if* $\bar{y} \in \hat{Y}_0^0$, *then* $\bar{y} \in \underset{y \in Y_0}{Arg\ max}\ s(y,\bar{y}) \subset \hat{Y}_0^0$ *and* $\underset{y \in Y_0}{max}\ s(y,\bar{y}) = 0$. *If (A2) and (B2) and if* $\bar{y} \in \hat{Y}_0^{\varepsilon}$, *then* $\bar{y} \in \underset{y \in Y_0}{Arg\ max}\ s(y,\bar{y}) \subset \hat{Y}_0$ *and* $\underset{y \in Y_0}{max}\ s(y,\bar{y}) = 0$.

Further properties of achievement functions are discussed in Wierzbicki (1977, 1980). Some examples of achievement functions are given below.

Example 1. Let $E_y = \mathbb{R}^n$, $D = \mathbb{R}^n_+$. Then $s_1(y,\bar{y}) = \min_{1 \le i \le n} (y_i - \bar{y}_i)$ is a strict achievement function and $s_2(y,\bar{y}) = s_1(y,\bar{y}) + \zeta \sum_{i=1}^{n} (y_i - \bar{y}_i)$ for some $\zeta > 0$ is a strong achievement function.

Example 2. Let $E_y = L^{\infty}([0;T]; \mathbb{R}^n)$, $D = \{y \in E_y : y(t) \in \mathbb{R}^n_+$ a.e.on $[0;T]\}$. Then $s_1(y,\bar{y}) = \operatorname{ess\,inf}_{t \in [0;T]} \min_{1 \le i \le n} (y_i(t) - \bar{y}_i(t))$ is a strict achievement function and $s_2(y,\bar{y}) = s_1(y,\bar{y}) + \zeta \int_0^T \sum_{i=1}^{n} (y_i(t) - \bar{y}_i(t))\, dt$ for some $\zeta > 0$ is a strong achievement function.

Example 3. Let E_y be a Hilbert space, D a closed convex cone in E_y (for example, $E_y = L^2([0;T]; \mathbb{R}^n)$ and $D = \{y \in E_y : y(t) \in \mathbb{R}^n_+$ a.e. on $[0;T]\}$), and let $y^* \in \overset{\circ}{D}{}^{*q} = \{y^* \in E_y^* = E_y : \langle y^*, y \rangle > 0\ \forall y \in D\}$. Then $s_1(y,\bar{y}) = \langle y^*, y-\bar{y} \rangle - \zeta \| (\bar{y}-y)_{\mathrm{Proj}\ D^*} \|$ is a strong achievement function and $s_2(y,\bar{y}) = \langle y^*, y-\bar{y} \rangle - \zeta \| (\bar{y}-y)_{\mathrm{Proj}\ D^*} \|^2$ is a smooth achievement function[†].

Example 4. Let $E_y = \mathbb{R}^n$, $D = \mathbb{R}^n_+$, and let $v : \mathbb{R}^n_+ \to \mathbb{R}^n_+$ be such that $y' \succ y'' \Rightarrow v(y') > v(y'')$ and $v(y) = 0\ \forall y \in \mathbb{R}^n_+ \setminus \overset{\circ}{\mathbb{R}}{}^n_+$. Then $s(y,\bar{y}) = v(y-\bar{y})$ for $y-\bar{y} \in \mathbb{R}^n_+$ and $s(y,\bar{y}) = -\zeta\, \mathrm{dist}\, (y-\bar{y}, D)$ for $y-\bar{y} \notin \mathbb{R}^n_+$ and some $\zeta > 0$ represents a strict achievement function.

Comments. The argument y in $s(y,\bar{y})$ is interpreted as the outcome of a decision and $\bar{y}$ as the corresponding aspiration level. Examples 2 and 3 show that we can also interprete $\bar{y}$ as an aspiration trajectory for a program of decisions which is useful in many applications. The second part of Theorem 1 implies that an achievement function can be interpreted as the utility function of an ideal staff "taking the boss seriously" as discussed in the preceding section.

---

† $(\cdot)_{\mathrm{Proj}\ D^*}$ denotes projection on the cone $D^* = \{y^* \in E_y^* = E_y : \langle y^*, y \rangle \ge 0\ \forall y \in D\}$. For properties of such projections see Moreau (1962), Wierzbicki and Kurcyusz (1977).

2.2. Applications of Decision Support Systems

Using the concepts of aspiration levels and achievement functions, we can propose principles for organizing user-computer interaction in a decision support system. These are outlined in Fig. 2.

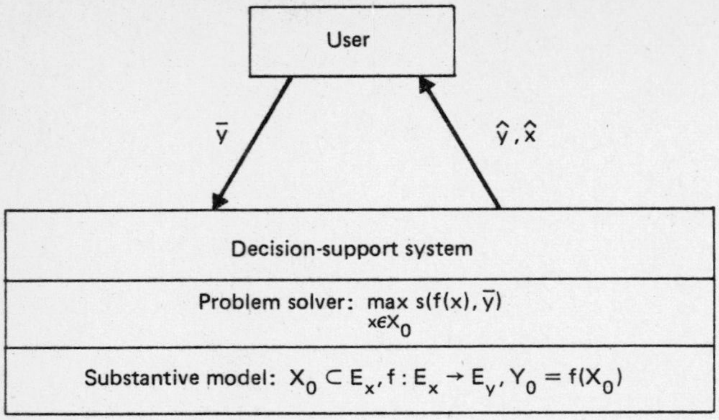

FIGURE 2 Principles for user-computer interaction in a decision support system (assuming interpretative computer intelligence).

A decision support system of this type generalizes many of the techniques of multiobjective optimization, such as goal programming (Ignizio, 1978), displaced ideal point (Zeleny, 1976) and many others. It also combines the properties of the three major analytical frameworks for rational decision making. It requires (i) that a *substantive model* of the problem to be analyzed should be constructed independently, (ii) that the user is familiar--though not necessarily in detail--with the model and can define the space E_y and the cone D for the variables of the model, and (iii) that an efficient and robust *problem solver*--an algorithm maximizing the (usually nondifferentiable) function $s(y,\bar{y})$--is included in the system. The system itself can then execute many commands: estimate the bounds of the Pareto set $\hat{Y}_0$; accept aspiration levels $\bar{y}$, check whether they are attainable, and respond with a Pareto-optimal $\hat{y} \in \hat{Y}_0$; scan the Pareto set around some $\hat{y}$ or $\bar{y}$. It can even help the user to select a sequence of $\bar{y}^{(k)}$ converging to some preferred $\hat{y}^{(\infty)}$.

These general principles, together with a solution algorithm for linear and dynamic linear programming problems, were used at IIASA to construct the decision support system DIDASS* (see, e.g., Kallio et al., 1980; Grauer and Lewandowski, 1982). This version of DIDASS has been applied to many problems --see, for example, Grauer et al. (1982a,b)--and has been made portable. It has now been transferred to over 40 research institutions throughout the world.

*Dynamic Interactive Decision Analysis and Support System.

DIDASS is now being extended to deal with nonlinear dynamic problems, stochastic problems and nondifferentiable problems. A new and distinct direction of research involves the use of aspiration levels and achievement functions to analyze multiactor decision situations.

2.3. Satisficing Selections of Game Equilibria and Gaming Support Systems

Although the concept of aspiration levels can also be applied to the problem of supporting consensus in decision making (Grauer et al., 1983), we shall concentrate here on applications related to the analysis of gaming results and general decision support in gaming (Wierzbicki, 1983b).

We consider here a simplified example of a game that has only historical significance, because most countries now refrain from fishing in each other's coastal waters. Two countries, $i=1,2$, fish in each other's, $\hat{i}=2,1$, coastal waters. Each country can decide how much to take from foreign waters (we denote this decision by x_1^i) and what restrictions to impose on foreign boats fishing in their waters (x_2^i); if the restrictions are disobeyed, both the offending country and the enforcing country incur additional costs. The payoff functions have the form:

$$q_i = f_i(x) = a_{i0}-a_{i1}x_1^{\hat{i}}+a_{i2}x_1^i-a_{i3}x_2^{\hat{i}}-a_{i4}(x_1^i+x_2^{\hat{i}}-\bar{x}^{\hat{i}})_+ -$$

$$-a_{i5}(x_1^{\hat{i}}+x_2^i-\bar{x}^i)_+ \tag{14}$$

where $(.)_+$ denotes taking the positive part, $a_{i0}-a_{i1}x_1^{\hat{i}}$ represents the net gain from the country's own waters (diminishing with increased fishing by outsiders, denoted by $x_1^{\hat{i}}$), $a_{i2}x_1^i-a_{i3}x_2^{\hat{i}}$ represents the net gain from fishing in foreign waters (diminishing with increased restrictions), the last but one term represents the penalties for disobeying the restrictions of other countries and the last term the cost of enforcing its own restrictions. All decision variables, $x = (x_1^1,x_2^1,x_1^2,x_2^2) \in \mathbb{R}^4$ are constrained by $0 \le x_j^i \le \tilde{x}_j^i$.

This example serves to illustrate the mathematical and computational difficulties involved in determining sets of noncooperative equilibria;* however, these difficulties can be overcome and the image of the game, together with the set of Nash equilibria N_q, is shown in Fig. 3 for $a_{i0}=2.4$, $a_{i1}=6$, $a_{i2}=1$, $a_{i3}=2$, $a_{i4}=a_{i5}=4$, $\tilde{x}_j^i=0.8$, $j,i=1,2$. The Nash equilibria in this case have a rather simple interpretation: they correspond to the situation in which each country strictly obeys the restrictions of others. The Nash outcomes of this game are not Pareto outcomes; Pareto outcomes correspond to dropping restrictions entirely, or, at the point P_0, to the complete cessation of fishing in foreign waters. It is interesting to note that the point P_0 has finally been reached through the historical

---

*This is equivalent to a min-max problem involving nondifferentiable functions that do not remain convex after the first maximization.

development of fishing practices.* However, in the course of this historical process there have also been cases in which the worst point SD has been reached. This point is attained when both countries decide to fish as much as possible in each other's waters and, at the same time, to impose and try to enforce extreme restrictions on anybody fishing in their own waters--a case of open fishing war. There are concepts in game theory that explain the development of this situation, albeit in a rather simplified fashion.

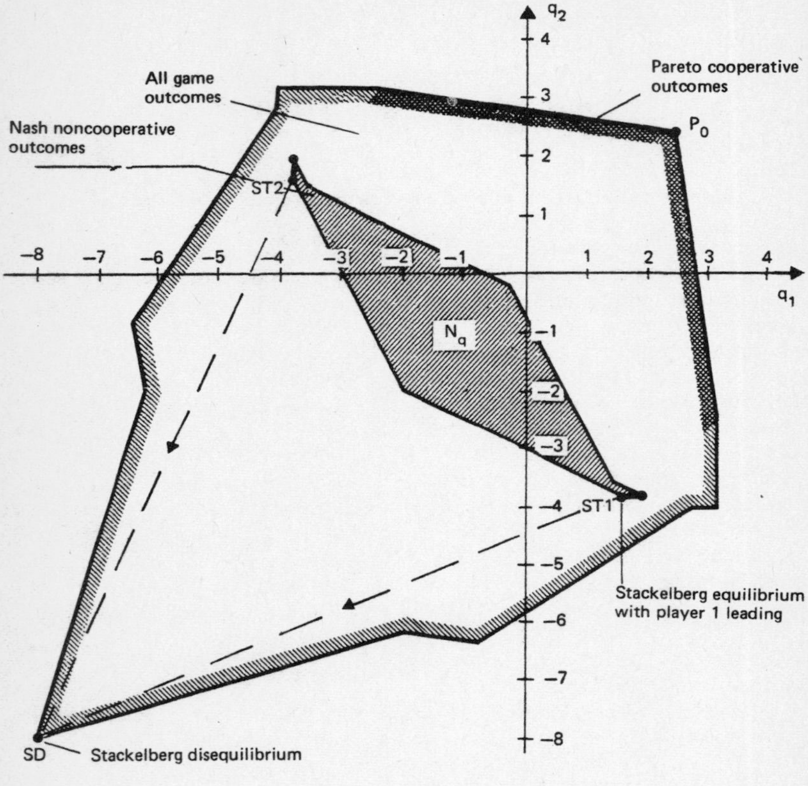

FIGURE 3 Image of the game:

$$q_1=f_1(x)=2.4-6x_1^2+x_1^1-2x_2^2-4[(x_1^1+x_2^2-1)_+ + (x_1^2+x_2^1-1)_+]$$

$$q_2=f_2(x)=2.4-6x_1^1+x_1^2-2x_2^1-4[(x_1^1+x_2^2-1)_+ + (x_1^2+x_2^1-1)_+]$$

$$x\in X = \{x\in\mathbb{R}^4 \ : \ 0\le x_j^i\le 0.8\} .$$

---

*The point P_0 is not a Nash equilibrium for the one-period game, but can be shown to be an evolutionary stable equilibrium for a repetitive game. Thus we might hope that all 'prisoner's dilemma', characterized by the difference of Nash and Pareto points, will finally be resolved in an evolutionary way (see also Hofstadter, 1983). In the case of the arms race, however, it is but small consolation for us to hope that other races in the universe might learn from our own evolutionary mistakes.

An old concept in game theory is that of a Stackelberg equilibrium (see, e.g., Aubin, 1979). Suppose one of the players has enough information to compute the responses of the other players (who wish to maximize their own payoffs) to any of his own decisions. If the responses are nonunique, he can assume, to be on the safe side, that only those that contribute least to his own payoff will be chosen. These response functions uniquely determine the dependence of his own payoff on his own decisions, taking into account the responses of others, and his own payoff can then be maximized. A player who makes his decisions in such a way is called the (Stackelberg) leader; if other players respond as predicted, they are called (Stackelberg) followers; the resulting outcome is called the Stackelberg equilibrium (this is one of the Nash equilibria, chosen through the (safe) maximization of the payoff of the leader). In the example considered here, if the first player wants to be the leader, he concludes that by sending the largest possible fleet to fish in his opponent's waters and by imposing the severest possible restrictions on intruders into his own waters, he might force the other player to "follow" him. Indeed, since both enforcing restrictions and violating them are very costly in this game, the second player might maximize his own short-term interests by imposing only the minimal restrictions compatible with the fleet of the leader (or even dropping restrictions altogether--but the leader cannot count on this) and sending only the smallest possible fleet to the leader's waters.

This interpretation shows, however, that the reasoning of the Stackelberg leader is completely unrealistic if no additional legal or institutional circumstances force the other player to become a follower. A sovereign country would not accept the follower's role and would denounce as hypocritical the explanations of the aspiring leader that the follower's role is logical from the point of view of economic payoffs. In the example considered here, the second player might well respond by repeating the actions of the first--this would result in a so-called Stackelberg disequilibrium (a situation in which both players try to become the leader) and corresponds to an open fishing war in our example.

Thus, the concepts of Stackelberg leadership and Stackelberg disequilibrium explain how open conflicts can occur--however, the explanation is not completely satisfactory since conflicts do not usually develop to this scale immediately. Historical evidence shows that if one country were to send its fishing fleet to another's waters, the other country would not necessarily reciprocate; in order to secure international support, the injured country would prefer to limit the fishing war to its own waters. We therefore need some additional concepts that could explain the processes of conflict escalation and de-escalation.

We apply here the concept of *quasi-satisficing behavior*: players maximize their objectives, but with a greater intensity below their aspiration levels than above them. Mathematically, such a distinction seems to have no sense: payoff maximization behavior is not changed by the intensity of maximization, and the set of Nash equilibria is not changed by assuming quasi-satisficing behavior. However, quasi-satisficing behavior might influence the way a player selects a Nash equilibrium: having attained his aspirations he might devote his remaining freedom of action to some other purpose, such as constructively preventing conflict escalation by letting other players maximize their objectives, or destructively hurting other players by trying to negatively affect their objectives.

In the previous example, the satisficing Nash equilibria for player 2, who has some aspiration level $\bar{q}_2$, are all of the Nash equilibria above and including the line $q_2=\bar{q}_2$ (see Fig. 4). Selection of the point SC_2 that satisfies $q_2=\bar{q}_2$ and is also good for the other player is a *constructive satisficing strategy*; selection of the point OD_2, which is the worst possible for the other player, is an *openly destructive strategy*,* selection of the point SD_2 that satisfies $q_2=\bar{q}_2$ but is the worst choice for the other player on this line is a *hidden destructive satisficing strategy*. The interpretation of the difference between constructive and hidden destructive satisficing strategies in the example considered is quite interesting. The parameters

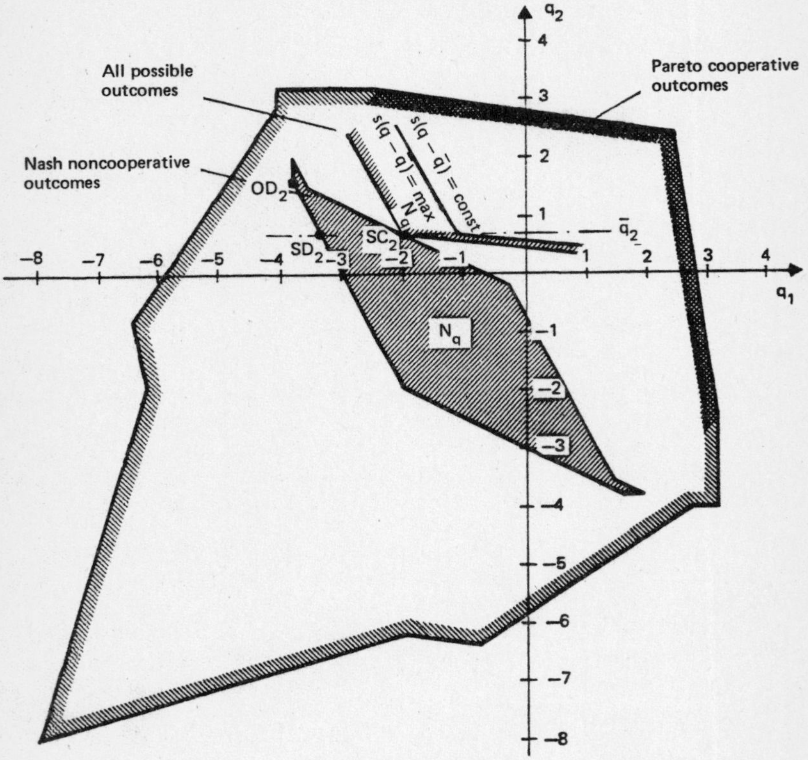

FIGURE 4 Satisficing game equilibria that could be selected by player 2: SC_2 represents a constructive satisficing move; SD_2 represents a hidden destructive satisficing move; OD_2 represents an openly destructive move. $s(q-\bar{q})$ represents a maximized function that helps to select a constructive satisficing strategy.

---

*In this case (although not necessarily in general), the openly destructive strategy OD_2 coincides with the Stackelberg maximizing strategy.

of the example are such that fish stocks are already heavily depleted and fishing in coastal waters hurts the host country more than it benefits the fishing country. A constructive satisficing strategy is then to decrease as much as possible your catch in the coastal waters of others (bearing in mind your economic aspirations), while imposing the strictest possible restrictions on outsiders fishing in your own waters. A hidden destructive strategy is to achieve the same economic aspiration level by fishing as much as possible in the coastal waters of others and imposing only such restrictions on foreigners fishing in your own waters as are necessary to attain your aspiration level. Each hidden destructive strategy can be 'rationalized' by invoking some seemingly plausible argument, for example, 'we believe in the freedom of fishing and restrict it only out of economic necessity'; nevertheless, it still remains destructive in the eyes of the other player.

A satisficing game equilibrium can be selected unilaterally when the aspiration levels of a particular player and the type of action to be taken (constructive, hidden destructive, etc.) are known; if the multiple objectives of the other side are to be taken into account, it is also necessary to have at least estimated aspiration levels for the other side. In fact, no matter whether you want to be constructive or destructive, you must have some idea of the aspirations of the other player--say, what economic and what ecological results would satisfy him; only when you assume (simplistically) that the other player has only a single objective can you disregard his aspirations. A satisficing game equilibrium for a given mathematical model of the game can also be computed by maximizing an achievement function over the set of Nash (or Pareto-Nash in the multiobjective case) game equilibria. In the simple example considered here, the constructive satisficing option for player 2 with aspiration level $\bar{q}_2$ can be computed by solving the following problem:

$$\underset{x\in N}{\text{maximize}} \; \frac{1}{\rho}\,(f_2(x)-\bar{q}_2)_+ - \rho(\bar{q}_2-f_2(x))_+ + f_1(x) \qquad (15)$$

where

$$N=\{x\in X:\ \min_{y\in X} \phi(x,y)=0\};\ \phi(x,y)=\sum_{i=1}^{2}(f_i(x^{\hat{i}},x^i)-f_i(x^{\hat{i}},y^i)) \qquad (16)$$

and $\rho>>1$ is a coefficient. If we denote $s(q-\bar{q})=\frac{1}{\rho}(q_2-\bar{q}_2)_+-\rho(\bar{q}_2-q_2)_++q_1$, then the equivalent problem $\max_{q\in N_q} s(q-\bar{q})$ can be interpreted in outcome space as shown in Fig. 4. We see that it is necessary to maximize a nondifferentiable function over a non-convex set.

The concept of satisficing selections can also be applied to the organization of decision support in gaming, or even support for negotiation and mediation (Wierzbicki, 1983a; Fortuna, 1984): decision support systems of this type are currently under development.

3. CONCLUSIONS

The concepts of aspiration levels, achievement functions and satisficing not only allow a synthesis of the three major frameworks for rational decision making, but also have further theoretical and practical applications. Theoretically, these concepts suggest a number of interesting mathematical questions. More pragmatically, they can be used to construct a variety of decision support systems with some aspects of interpretative computer intelligence.

REFERENCES

Aubin, J.-P. (1979). Mathematical Methods of Game and Economic Theory. North-Holland, Amsterdam.
Debreu, G. (1959). Theory of Value. Wiley, New York.
Fortuna, Z. (1984). A two-player multicriteria game with decision support, illustrated by an example based on a North-South trade model. Working Paper, International Institute for Applied Systems Analysis, Laxenburg, Austria (forthcoming).
Glushkov, V.M. (1972). Basic principles of automatization in organizational management systems. Upravlayuskchee Sistemy i Mashiny, 1 (in Russian).
Grauer, M. and Lewandowski, A. (1982). The reference point approach - methods of efficient implementation. WP-82-26. International Institute for Applied Systems Analysis, Laxenburg, Austria.
Grauer, M., Lewandowski, A., and Schrattenholzer, L. (1982a). Use of the reference level approach for the generation of efficient energy supply strategies. WP-82-19. International Institute for Applied Systems Analysis, Laxenburg, Austria.
Grauer, M., Lewandowski, A., and Wierzbicki, A.P. (1982b). Multiobjective and Stochastic Optimization. CP-82-S12. International Institute for Applied Systems Analysis, Laxenburg, Austria.
Grauer, M., Bischoff, E., and Wierzbicki, A.P. (1983). Mediation in long-term planning. In Proceedings of the SWIIS Conference, Laxenburg 1983, pp. 162-166.
Hayes, J.E., Michie, D., and Pao, Y.-H. (Eds.) (1982). Machine Intelligence 10. Ellis Horwood, Chichester, UK; Halsted Press, USA.
Hofstadter, D.R. (1983). Metamagical themes: computer tournaments of the prisoner's dilemma suggest how cooperation evolves. Scientific American, 248: 14-20.
Ignizio, J.P. (1978). Goal programming: a tool for multiobjective analysis. Journal of Operational Research, 29: 1109-1119.
Kallio, M., Lewandowski, A., and Orchard-Hays, W. (1980). An implementation of the reference point approach for multiobjective optimization. WP-80-35. International Institute for Applied Systems Analysis, Laxenburg, Austria.
Keeney, R.L. and Raiffa, H. (1976). Decisions with Multiple Objectives: Preferences and Value Trade-Offs. Wiley, New York.
Latombe, J.C. (Ed.) (1978). Artificial Intelligence and Pattern Recognition in Computer-Aided Design. North-Holland, Amsterdam.
March, J.G. and Simon, H.A. (1958). Organizations. Wiley, New York.
Moreau, J.J. (1962). Decomposition orthogonale d'un espace hilbertien selon deux cones mutuellement polaires. C.R. Acad. Sci. Paris, 225: 238-240.
Nilsson, N.J. (1980). Principles of Artificial Intelligence. Tioga Publishing Co., Palo Alto, California.
Pospelov, G.S. and Irikov, V.A. (1976). Program- and Goal-Oriented Planning and Management. Sovietskoe Radio, Moscow (in Russian).
Selten, R. (1972). The equity principle in economic behavior. In H.W. Gottinger and W. Leinfelder (Eds.), Decision Theory and Social Ethics. Dordrecht, pp. 289-301.
Simon, H.A. (1969). A behavioral model of rational choice. Quarterly Journal of Economics, 69: 99-118.

Tietz, R. (Ed.) (1983). Aspiration Levels in Bargaining and Economic Decision Making. Lecture Notes in Economics and Mathematical Systems, Springer Verlag.

Tikhonov, A.N. and Arsenin, W.J. (1975). Methods of Solving Ill-Posed Problems. Nauka, Moscow (in Russian).

Tversky, A. (1972). Elimination by aspects: a theory of choice. Psychological Review, 79: 281-299.

Wierzbicki, A.P. (1977). Basic properties of scalarizing functionals for multiobjective optimization. Mathematische Operations-Forschung und Statistik, Ser. Optimization, 8(1): 55-60.

Wierzbicki, A.P. (1980). Multiobjective trajectory optimization and model semiregularization. WP-80-181. International Institute for Applied Systems Analysis, Laxenburg, Austria.

Wierzbicki, A.P. (1982). A mathematical basis for satisficing decision making. Mathematical Modelling, 3: 391-405.

Wierzbicki, A.P. (1983a). A critical essay on the methodology of multiobjective analysis. Regional Science and Urban Economics, 13: 5-29.

Wierzbicki, A.P. (1983b). Negotiation and mediation in conflicts. I. The role of mathematical approaches and methods. In Proceedings of the SWIIS Conference, Laxenburg 1983, pp. 132-146.

Wierzbicki, A.P. and Kurcyusz, S. (1977). Projections on a cone, penalty functionals and duality theory for problems with inequality constraints in Hilbert space. SIAM Journal of Optimization and Control, 15: 25-26.

Zeleny, M. (1976). The theory of displaced ideal. In M. Zeleny (Ed.), Multiple Criteria Decision Making - Kyoto. Springer Verlag, Berlin.

Zhuravlev, Yu.I. (1976). Extremal algorithms in mathematical models for recognition and classification problems. Dokl. Akad. Nauk SSSR, 231(3): 532-535 (in Russian).

Zhuravlev, Yu.I. (1977). Algebras over sets of incorrect (heuristic) algorithms. Dokl. Akad. Nauk SSSR, 235(4): 761-763 (in Russian).

II. APPROACHES AND CONCEPTS IN INTERACTIVE DECISION ANALYSIS

DIDASS – THEORY, IMPLEMENTATION AND EXPERIENCES

M. Grauer[1], A. Lewandowski[2] and A. Wierzbicki[1]
[1] *International Institute for Applied Systems Analysis, Laxenburg, Austria*
[2] *Institute of Automatic Control, Technical University of Warsaw, Warsaw, Poland*

1. INTRODUCTION

The purpose of this paper is to report on the progress made in the System and Decision Sciences (SDS) research group at IIASA on the development of the decision support system DIDASS (Dynamic Interactive Decision Analysis and Support System). This system is based on methodology derived from the paradigm of satisficing decision making and the methodology of linear and nonlinear programming. The mathematical background to this approach (based on aspiration formation and the concept of scalarizing functions) is outlined in Section 2. Methods of implementation and computational aspects are discussed in Section 3. The fourth section summarizes three applications of DIDASS, and the paper ends with some conclusions.

2. THE ACHIEVEMENT SCALARIZING FUNCTION CONCEPT

In satisficing decision making it is assumed (March and Simon, 1958) that people set up aspiration levels for various outcomes of interest, modify them as they accumulate more information, and then make decisions that satisfy or come close to these aspiration levels. Many of the methods of multiobjective analysis, such as the displaced ideal point approach (Zeleny, 1976) and goal programming (Charnes and Cooper, 1977) have more or less consciously adopted this approach. A generalized method that combines the satisficing and aspiration level concepts with mathematical optimization was proposed by Wierzbicki (1980a,b). This approach concentrates on the construction of modified utility functions (called achievement functions) which express the utility or disutility of attaining or not attaining given aspiration levels. We will now give the problem description and show how the mathematical foundation of the method is derived.

Let $E_0 \subset E$ be the set of admissible decisions or alternatives to be evaluated. Let G be a (linear topological) space of objectives, performance indices, or outcomes. Let a mapping $Q : E_0 \to G$ be given, which defines numerically the consequences of each alternative. Let $Q_0 = Q(E_0)$ denote the set of attainable objectives. Let a natural inequality (a partial preordering) in G be given; to simplify the presentation, assume that the preordering is transitive and can be expressed by a *positive cone* (any closed, convex, proper cone) $D \subsetneq G$:

$$q_1, q_2 \in G,\ q_1 \le q_2 \Leftrightarrow q_2 - q_1 \in D\ . \tag{1}$$

A corresponding strong partial preordering is given by

$$q_1, q_2 \in G, \; q_1 < q_2 \Leftrightarrow q_2 - q_1 \in \tilde{D} \overset{\text{df}}{=} D \setminus (D \cap -D) \; . \tag{2}$$

If the cone D has a nonempty interior $\overset{\circ}{D}$, it is also possible to introduce a strict partial preordering:

$$q_1, q_2 \in G, \; q_1 \ll q_2 \Leftrightarrow q_2 - q_1 \in \overset{\circ}{D} \; . \tag{3}$$

Suppose that we maximize all objectives (gains, etc.). A generalized Pareto (nondominated) objective $\hat{q}$ is then a D-*maximal element* of Q_0:

$$\hat{q} \in Q_0 \text{ is D-maximal} \Leftrightarrow Q_0 \cap (\hat{q} + \tilde{D}) = \emptyset \; . \tag{4}$$

A slightly weaker definition, which includes a few points which are not nondominated, is that of *weak* D-maximal elements:

$$\hat{q} \in Q_0 \text{ is weakly D-maximal} \Leftrightarrow Q_0 \cap (\hat{q} + \overset{\circ}{D}) = \emptyset \; . \tag{5}$$

For a normed space G, we can also have a stronger definition (D_ε*-maximality*) which does not include all nondominated points:

$$\hat{q} \in Q_0 \text{ is } D_\varepsilon\text{-maximal} \Leftrightarrow Q_0 \cap (\hat{q} - \tilde{D}_\varepsilon) = \emptyset \; , \tag{6}$$

where D_ε is an ε-conical neighborhood of D:

$$D_\varepsilon \overset{\text{df}}{=} \{q \in G : \text{dist}(q,D) < \varepsilon \|q\|\} \; ; \; \tilde{D}_\varepsilon \overset{\text{df}}{=} D_\varepsilon \setminus (D_\varepsilon \cap -D_\varepsilon) \tag{7}$$

with

$$\text{dist}(q,D) = \inf_{\tilde{q} \in D} \|q - \tilde{q}\|$$

implied by the norm of the space G .

If the space G is normed, we can define an *achievement scalarizing function* (shortened to *achievement function*) $s : G \to R^1$, where s is assumed to satisfy either (8) and (10) below (the order representation case) or (9) and (11) below (the order approximation case). Thus, an achievement function should be

(a) *strictly order-preserving*: for all $\bar{q} \in G$, all $q_1, q_2 \in Q_0$:

$$q_1 \ll q_2 \Rightarrow s(q_1 - \bar{q}) < s(q_2 - \bar{q}) \; , \tag{8}$$

or, if possible, *strongly order-preserving*: for all $\bar{q} \in G$, all $q_1, q_2 \in Q_0$:

$$q_1 < q_2 \Rightarrow s(q_1 - \bar{q}) < s(q_2 - \bar{q}) \; , \tag{9}$$

where strong order preservation implies strict order preservation.

(b) *order-representing:*

$$S_0 \overset{\text{df}}{=} \{q \in G : s(q - \bar{q} \geq 0\} = \bar{q} + D \; ; \; s(0) = 0 \; , \tag{10}$$

or, at least, *order-approximating* for some small $\varepsilon > 0$,

$$\bar{q} + D \subset S_0 \overset{df}{=} \{q \in G : s(q - \bar{q}) \geq 0\} \subseteq \bar{q} + D_\varepsilon \ ; \ s(0) = 0 \ , \qquad (11)$$

where, clearly, order representation implies order approximation.

We see that the achievement function s is taken to be a function of the difference $q - \bar{q}$, where $q = Q(x)$, $x \in E_0$ is an attainable objective but $\bar{q} \in G$ is an *arbitrary* aspiration level, which is *not constrained* to Q_0, nor otherwise constrained. Moreover, an achievement function is usually constructed such that, if $\bar{q} \notin Q_0 - D$, then the maximization of $s(q - \bar{q})$ over $q \in Q_0$ represents the minimization of the distance between $\bar{q} + D$ and Q_0; if $\bar{q} \in Q_0 - D$, then the maximization of $s(q - \bar{q})$ represents the allocation of the surplus $q - \bar{q} \in D$. However, these comments are only descriptive and the axiomatic definition of an achievement function relies on requirements (a) and (b).

Using the above definition of an achievement scalarizing function we will now show how this approach can be implemented numerically on a computer.

3. METHODS OF IMPLEMENTATION AND COMPUTATIONAL ASPECTS

Our aim was to develop an interactive decision analysis package based on standard programming techniques, using the concept of an achievement function formulated above to support the solution of the multiple criteria problems that arise in practical situations. In particular, we attempted to use current mathematical programming techniques in the problem specification (standard MPS format for the LP part, and a suitably extended version of this to provide the additional information), in the storage of data (as packed data structures) and in the implementation of solution strategies (using efficient, modifiable and numerically stable implementations of linear and nonlinear solution programs, e.g., MINOS/AUGMENTED). Although the system was initially only suitable for linear and nonlinear multiple criteria problems, we have tried to design it to permit extensions and to make it portable to various computers with different operating systems. We have also tried to make it possible to use different solution programs.

We shall assume that the solution of the decision problem under consideration can be obtained by analyzing a general constrained multicriteria problem in the following standard form:

$$\max_{x_{nl}, x_l} \begin{bmatrix} f_1(x_{nl}) + c_1^T x_{nl} + d_1^T x_l = q_1 \\ f_2(x_{nl}) + c_2^T x_{nl} + d_2^T x_l = q_2 \\ \dots \quad \dots \quad \dots \\ f_p(x_{nl}) + c_p^T x_{nl} + d_p^T x_l = q_p \end{bmatrix} \qquad (12)$$

subject to:

$$g(x_{nl}) + A_1 x_l \leq b_1 \qquad (13)$$

$$A_2 x_{nl} + A_3 x_l \leq b_2 \qquad (14)$$

$$l \leq \begin{bmatrix} x_{nl} \\ x_l \end{bmatrix} \leq u \ , \qquad (15)$$

where $g(x_{nl}) = [g_1(x_{nl}), g_2(x_{nl}),\ldots,g_m(x_{nl})]^T$ is a vector of nonlinear constraints and $f_1(x_{nl}), f_2(x_{nl}),\ldots,f_p(x_{nl})$ in (12) represents the nonlinear parts of the performance criteria. The decision variables are divided into two subsets: a vector of "nonlinear" variables (x_{nl}) and a vector of "linear" variables (x_l). It is clear that when vectors f and g are nonexistent, formulation (12)-(15) is identical with the standard multicriteria linear programming problem. An overview of the various ways in which the reference point approach can be used in the linear case is given in Grauer and Lewandowski (1982), while the nonlinear case is described in Grauer (1983a).

The current computer implementation of the decision analysis and support system DIDASS is based on a two-stage model of the decision-making process. In the first stage--the exploratory stage--the user is informed about the range of his alternatives, thus giving him an overview of the problem. In the second stage--the search stage--the user works with the system in an interactive way to analyze the efficient alternatives $\{\hat{q}^k\}$ generated by DIDASS in response to his reference objectives $\{\bar{q}^k\}$. The initial information for the exploratory stage is provided by calculating the extreme points for each of the objectives in (12) separately. A matrix D_S which yields information on the range of numerical values of each objective is then constructed. We shall call this the *decision support matrix*.

$$D_S = \begin{bmatrix} q_1^* & q_2^1 \cdots q_i^1 \cdots q_p^1 \\ q_1^2 & q_2^* \cdots q_i^2 \cdots q_p^2 \\ \cdot & \cdot \quad \cdot \quad \cdot \\ \cdot & \cdot \quad \cdot \quad \cdot \\ \cdot & \cdot \quad \cdot \quad \cdot \\ q_1^j & q_2^j \cdots q_i^j \cdots q_p^j \\ \cdot & \cdot \quad \cdot \quad \cdot \\ \cdot & \cdot \quad \cdot \quad \cdot \\ \cdot & \cdot \quad \cdot \quad \cdot \\ q_1^p & q_2^p \cdots q_i^p \cdots q_p^* \end{bmatrix} . \qquad (16)$$

Row j corresponds to the solution vector x^j which maximizes objective q_j. The vector with elements $q_j^j = q_j^*$, i.e., the diagonal of D_S, represents the *utopia (ideal) point*. This point is not normally attainable (if it were, it would be the solution of the proposed decision problem), but it is presented to the user as an upper guideline to the sequence $\{\bar{q}^k\}$ of reference objectives. Let us consider column i of the matrix D_S. The maximum value in the column is q_i^*. Let q_i^n be the minimum value, where

$$\min_{1\le j\le p} \left\{ q_i^j \right\} = q_i^n \; .$$

We shall call this the *nadir* value. The vector with elements $q_1^n, q_2^n, \ldots, q_p^n$ represents the *nadir point*, and may be seen as a lower guideline to the values of the user's objectives.

In the linear case we use the following scalarizing function s(w), where minimization results in a linear programming formulation:

$$s(w) = -\min \left\{ \rho \min_i w_i \; ; \; \sum_{i=1}^{p} w_i \right\} - \varepsilon w \; . \tag{17}$$

Here $w_i \equiv (q_i - \bar{q}_i)/\gamma_i$, ρ is an arbitrary coefficient which is greater than or equal to p, γ_i is a scaling factor, and $\varepsilon = (\varepsilon_1, \varepsilon_2, \ldots, \varepsilon_p)$ is a non-negative vector of parameters.

In the nonlinear version of the package the following achievement scalarizing function is used:

$$s(w) = -\frac{1}{\rho} \ln \left[\frac{1}{p} \sum_{i=1}^{p} (w_i)^{\rho} \right] \; , \tag{18}$$

where $w_i = \gamma_i[(\tilde{q}_i - q_i)/(\tilde{q}_i - \bar{q}_i)]$, $\tilde{q}_i$ is an upper limit to the sequence of reference points, $\rho \ge 2$ is again an arbitrary coefficient greater than or equal to p, and γ_i acts here as a weighting factor. This achievement scalarizing function meets the following requirements:

-- It yields scaling factors which make additional scaling of objectives unnecessary.
-- It is a smoothly differentiable function that approximates the nonsmooth function $s = \max_i w_i$.
-- It is strongly order-preserving and weakly order-approximating.

The resulting single-criterion programming problems are solved using the solution package MINOS (Murtagh and Saunders, 1980).

The general structure of the DIDASS system is given in Fig.1. More details concerning the package can be found in Grauer (1983b).

4. APPLICATIONS

We consider here applications of DIDASS for two prototype decision situations: (i) the centralized single-actor situation (Sections 4.1, 4.2) and (ii) the centralized multiple-actor situation (Section 4.3).

4.1. Generation of Efficient Energy Supply Strategies

When analyzing the future development of an energy system it is necessary (i) to consider more than one objective and (ii) to study the time dependence of these objectives and thus the interplay between monetary

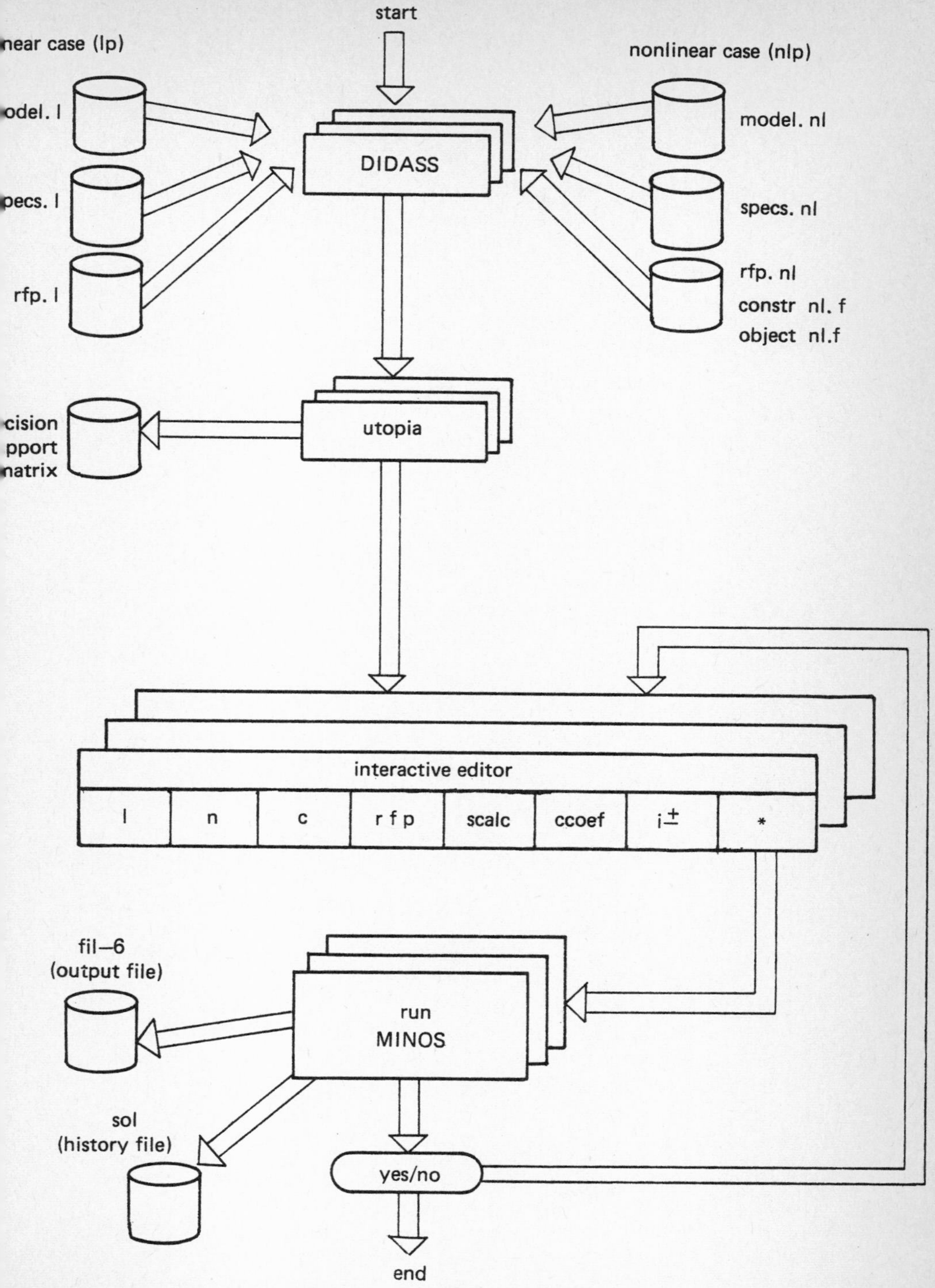

FIGURE 1 Structure of the DIDASS system.

outcomes and other factors (such as import dependence, the need to develop infrastructure, etc.) over time. In order to take these two factors into account we used the idea of reference objectives (Wierzbicki, 1980b) within the achievement function concept. To do this we have to construct an achievement functional with $G = L^2[0,T]$ and $D = \{q \in L^2[0;T] : q(t) \geq 0 \text{ on } [0;T]\}$:

$$s(q - \bar{q}) = \int_0^T \left\{ [q(t) - \bar{q}(t)]^2 - s[\bar{q}(t) - q(t)]_+^2 \right\} dt \,, \qquad (19)$$

where $\bar{q}(t)$ is the vector of reference objectives and T the planning horizon.

The use of DIDASS with an achievement function of type (19) is illustrated in Fig. 2. In this case we assume a single decision maker (minister) who might wish to minimize the use of imported oil and indigenous coal in energy production to save them as feedstocks for other industries, while also minimizing investment in the energy sector (Grauer et al., 1982). Since the energy supply model used in this study was of the linear programming type, we could use the achievement function (17) and the linear multiple-criteria part of the DIDASS package.

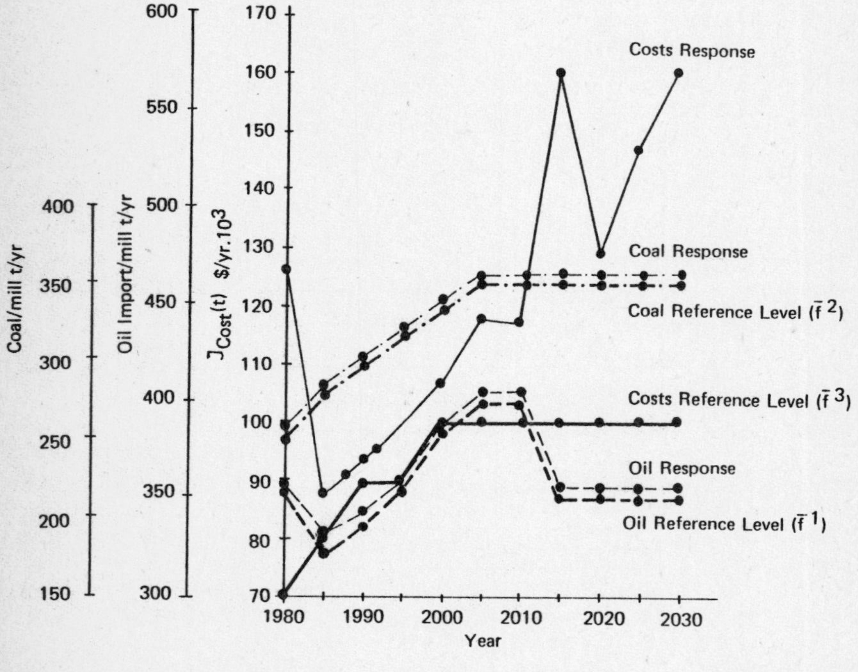

FIGURE 2 Reference trajectories (objectives) for imported oil supply, indigenous coal supply, and cost (Grauer et al., 1982).

4.2. Macroeconomic Planning under Conflicting Objectives

By its very nature, economic planning must involve the consideration of multiple criteria. Planners usually either employ alternative objective functions combined with parametrically varying constraints to determine several efficient variants of the plan, or they construct a social welfare function (a type of utility function) which somehow includes all of the objectives. However, we believe that an interactive decision support system provides a better means of communication between planners and modelers and a better way of analyzing efficient alternatives than the traditional methods outlined above. We therefore decided to carry out an experiment, using DIDASS to analyze 1976 data on the Hungarian economy (Grauer and Zalai, 1982) in conjunction with a multisectoral nonlinear programming model. This model is highly aggregated to simplify the analysis, containing only three sectors, which correspond roughly to the usual primary, secondary and tertiary sectors. Table 1 gives some indication of the results that can be obtained using this type of approach. It shows the decision support matrix (16); the last line gives a compromise solution for the situation considered by the planner, assuming that he wishes to maximize foreign trade, average consumption and investment.

TABLE 1 Decision support matrix and compromise solution (values given in millions of forints).

	Average consumption Obj(1)	Foreign trade deficit Obj(2)	Investment Obj(3)
Obj(1) → max	11 730.4	-22 822.1	172 404.4
Obj(2) → max	0.1	14 998.8	157 911.4
Obj(3) → max	0.1	-22 822.1	207 157.6
Compromise solution	1 486.8	- 1 019.3	159 632.3

As the results of the study proved to be useful, the approach was utilized to examine more disaggregated macroeconomic models.

4.3. Mediation in Long-Term Planning

This example is concerned with multiple decision makers with multiple criteria. It is possible to structure this decision problem as a negotiation process with a mediator, where the role of the mediator is to attempt to assist the parties involved through an analysis of the underlying conflict (sometimes known as conflict mediation). We therefore studied the use of a decision support system (DIDASS) as an aid in mediation.

The study was based on a macroeconomic planning model developed at IIASA. Built as part of an investigation of different options for the long-term development of the Austrian energy system, the model portrays the interrelationships between the consumption sphere, the energy production sector and the rest of the economy. It was designed as a means of examining the implications of different planning scenarios and as a vehicle for comparing different views about the possible development of the energy system. The approach considered here goes beyond a mere comparison of opinions in that it attempts to provide support for a process of concession-making which progresses from an initial situation of diverging views ("incompatible aspirations") to a consensus acceptable to all of the parties involved ("compatible aspirations").

Details of this approach and some results are given in Wierzbicki (1983) and Grauer et al. (1983).

5. CONCLUSIONS

The interactive decision analysis and support system currently being developed at IIASA has been shown to be of use in analyzing conflicts and assisting in decision-making situations. However, much still remains to be done, in terms of both algorithmic development and theoretical advances. Our experience has shown that it is possible to combine methodological reflection on the practical requirements of decision making with developments in game theory, hierarchical optimization, interactive programming and multicriteria analysis.

REFERENCES

Charnes, A. and Cooper, W.W. (1977). Goal programming and multiple objective optimization. European Journal of Operational Research, 1:39-59.

Grauer, M. and Lewandowski, A. (1982). The reference point approach - methods of efficient implementation. WP-82-26. International Institute for Applied Systems Analysis, Laxenburg, Austria.

Grauer, M. and Zalai, E. (1982). A reference point approach for nonlinear macroeconomic multiobjective models. WP-82-134. International Institute for Applied Systems Analysis, Laxenburg, Austria.

Grauer, M., Lewandowski, A., and Schrattenholzer, L. (1982). Use of the reference level approach for the generation of efficient energy supply strategies. WP-82-19. International Institute for Applied Systems Analysis, Laxenburg, Austria.

Grauer, M. (1983a). Reference point optimization - the nonlinear case. In P. Hansen (Ed.), Essays and Surveys on Multiple Criteria Decision Making. Springer Verlag, New York.

Grauer, M. (1983b). A dynamic interactive decision analysis and support system (DIDASS) - user's guide. WP-83-60. International Institute for Applied Systems Analysis, Laxenburg, Austria.

Grauer, M., Bischoff, E., and Wierzbicki, A. (1983). Mediation in long-term planning. In Proceedings of the SWIIS Conference, Laxenburg 1983, pp. 162-166.

March, J.G. and Simon, H.A. (1958). Organizations. John Wiley, New York.

Murtagh, B.A. and Saunders, M.A. (1980). MINOS/Augmented. Technical Report SOL-80-14, Systems Optimization Laboratory, Stanford University.

Wierzbicki, A.P. (1980a). A mathematical method for satisficing decision making. WP-80-30. International Institute for Applied Systems Analysis, Laxenburg, Austria.

Wierzbicki, A.P. (1980b). Multiobjective trajectory optimization and model semiregularization. WP-80-181. International Institute for Applied Systems Analysis, Laxenburg, Austria.

Wierzbicki, A.P. (1983). Negotiation and mediation in conflicts. I: The role of mathematical approaches and methods. In Proceedings of the SWIIS Conference, Laxenburg 1983, pp. 132-146.

Zeleny, M. (1976). The theory of displaced ideal. In M. Zeleny (Ed.), Multiple Criteria Decision Making - Kyoto. Springer Verlag, Berlin.

HANDLING CONFLICTS IN FUZZY MULTIPLE-CRITERIA OPTIMIZATION

Christer Carlsson
Department of Business Administration, Åbo Academy, Åbo, Finland

1. INTRODUCTION

Multiple criteria optimization is more and more accepted as the standard basis for problem solving tools and decision aids, as single criteria modelling in many cases has been proved to be a special case of some class of multiple criteria models. Multiple criteria imply multiple objectives, which in turn imply conflicts among the objectives - it is almost an axiom that there should be conflicts if we have many objectives. But conflicts are - or can be made - an asset in a management context: (i) conflicts can be dissolved by generating new alternatives or an ideal alternative; (ii) conflicts can be resolved through constructive compromises by reformulating or creating alternatives; (ii) conflicts can be solved by allowing a single objective to dominate temporarily, and (iv) conflicts can be neglected, contained, controlled and denied by various forms of power play.

In this paper the various ways of handling conflicts are studied with the help of models for fuzzy multiple criteria optimization. It is shown that the theory of fuzzy sets offers a few more degrees of freedom for handling conflicts than a traditional OR-model; the model is demonstrated with a fairly simple numerical example, which was run with the interactive IFPS/Optimum on a Prime computer.

2. FUZZY MULTIPLE CRITERIA OPTIMIZATION

The field of multiple criteria decision making is one of considerable growth and development, and is one of the fields of research in management science which show considerable potential for producing essential research results over the next few years. The growth of the field has given rise to a corresponding growth in the number of concepts used to describe phenomena in terms of multiple criteria. In order to avoid some of the confusion of terminology we will stick to one set of concepts, and apply those introduced by Zeleny (1982). Thus **multiple criteria** will be taken to include **multiple attributes**, **multiple objectives** and **multiple goals**. The differences between these concepts may be outlined as follows: **attributes** are descriptors of an objective reality; **objectives** represent directions of improvement or preference in attributes; **goals** are a decision maker's needs and desires, defined in terms of attributes or objectives; **criteria** are measures, rules and standards which are relevant for a decision maker.

In the following we will study situations in which we have multiple conflicting objectives, and find out how such situations could be dealt with. As conflicts traditionally have been handled by loosening up deadlocked positions, it may be worthwhile to try loose and flexible methods for handling conflicts in multiple criteria. The theory of fuzzy sets proposes to give the conceptual and theoretical framework for handling complexity, imprecision and vagueness (cf Bellman and Zadeh (1970)), and should thus be useful also as a basis for developing loose and flexible methods.

2.1. Conflicts among interdependent objectives

Let $A = \{a_1, a_2, \ldots, a_n\}$ represent a set of alternatives a decision maker has found to be relevant in some problem situation at a chosen point of time t. The alternatives are established through appropriate sets of attributes, which the decision maker has found to be adequate for describing the alternatives. Let G be a **fuzzy objective**, which is represented by a fuzzy subset of A,

$$G = \{(a_i, \mu_G(a_i))\}, \forall i \in [1,n], \text{ and} \tag{1a}$$

$$a_i \in A \text{ and } \mu_G : A \longrightarrow [0,1]$$

The function μ_G, the membership function, defines a subjective ordering on the set of decision alternatives, which is intended to show to what degree an alternative represents an attainment of G. The membership function is thus thought to cover all the relevant attribute dimensions, but it would be more realistic to have one membership function for each attribute dimension; for k dimensions we will then have,

$$G^{(j)} = \{(a_i^{(j)}, \mu_G^{(j)}(a_i^{(j)}))\} \quad \forall i, j \in [1,n] \text{ and } [1,k] \tag{1b}$$

It is also possible that several alternatives **together** represent an attainment of G; for three alternatives we have,

$$G = \{(a_{i1}, a_{i2}, a_{i3}; \mu_G(a_{i1}, a_{i2}, a_{i3}))\}, \forall i \in [1,n] \tag{1c}$$

so that combining (1 b) and (1 c) we get,

$$\mathbf{G} = \{(a_{im}^{(j)}, \boldsymbol{\mu}_G(a_{im}^{(j)}))\} \quad \forall i, j, m \in [1,n] \text{ and } [1,k] \tag{1d}$$

where $\boldsymbol{\mu}_G$ is a family of membership functions, which give a fairly rich representation of combinations of alternatives and their attributes.

If we then have multiple objectives, $\mathbf{G} = \{G_1, G_2, \ldots, G_p\}$, each of which is defined as in (1 d), the corresponding families of membership functions $\boldsymbol{\mu}_\mathbf{G}$ would show for each alternative a_i, and even for each attribute dimension of each alternative, $a_i^{(j)}$, to which degree it represents an attainment of each one of the objectives. Let us for a moment consider $\boldsymbol{\mu}_\mathbf{G}$ as existing and well-defined.

In order to deal with the problem situation at hand the decision maker should find an alternative which represents an attainment of all the objectives of G. This will be achieved by combining membership functions,

$$\mu_D = \bigwedge_r \mu_{G_r} \text{ , where } r \in [1,p] \quad (2)$$

where the conjunction is interpreted as,

$$\mu_D (a_i) = \min [\mu_{G_r}] \text{ , } \forall r \in [1,p] \text{ , } \forall a_i \in A, \quad (3)$$

and "the best" alternative is found through,

$$\mu_D (\overset{*}{a}) = \max \mu_D (a_i) \text{ , } \forall i \in [1,n] \quad (4)$$

which is a traditional minmax-approach.

The operations defined in (2)-(4) are possible with existing and well-defined μ_G. Zeleny (1983) points out that a μ_G normally is not well-defined, and exists only as a subjective construct which is bound to vary between problem situations, alternatives and goals. Furthermore "... membership functions ... should not be **functions** at all ... multiple membership values are being assigned by humans to identical levels of variables". In this statement Zeleny touches the core of an unsolved problem in the theory of fuzzy sets. So let us stay with the original assumption on an existing and well-defined μ_G for one more moment.

In case of conflicts within the **G**, $\mu_D(a_i) \simeq 0$ in (3). Let us simplify matters a bit in order to discuss the case of conflicting objectives: (i) we will not consider multiple dimensions or multiple attributes; (ii) we will create a space in which evaluation and comparison of conflicting objectives could be carried out: let A be a universe and f an ordinary function from A to another universe B; now it can be shown that f could be defined for a fuzzy domain - and given a fuzzy range as well - iff,

$$\mu_{H_k} (f(a_i)) \geq \mu_{G_r} (a_i) \text{ , } \forall a_i \in A \quad (5)$$

where G_r is a fuzzy subset of A, and H_k correspondingly of B. (cf Dubois and Prade (1980)).

With two **conflicting** objectives G_r, G_s ($\in$ **G**) an alternative a_i will have membership values $\mu_{G_r} (a_i) \approx 0$ and $\mu_{G_s} (a_i) \approx 1$; with an appropriate function f it should be possible to find a $f(a_i)$ for which $\mu_{H_r} (f(a_i))$ is "not too close to 0", and $\mu_{H_s} (f(a_i))$ is "not too close to 1", i.e. a point of compromise like "rather low on H_r and rather high on H_s", $(\mu_{H_r} \wedge \mu_{H_s})(f(a_i))$.

The universe B is just for illustrative purposes, the mapping could be into A; but it demonstrates the use of fuzzy sets as a means for **resolving** conflicts among multiple objectives.

The "most satisfactory" alternative $\overset{*}{a}$ for resolving conflicts among multiple objectives is given by,

$$\overset{*}{a} = \max\, [\mu_{H_1} \wedge \mu_{H_2} \wedge \; \ldots \wedge \mu_{H_p}],\ \forall a_i \in A \tag{6}$$

which only outlines the principle: the min-operator gives a rather poor performance for conflicting goals, and should be modified. According to (5) it is possible to establish ranking relations $\forall a_i \in A$ relative to each one of H_1 - H_p; let the corresponding fuzzy subset be A_1 - A_p. Then we have for every subset A_v, starting with the element $a_i^{(v)}$ of the highest rank,

$$\mu_w^{(v)}\,(a_i) : a_i^{(v)} \longrightarrow [0,1],\ \forall\, w \in [1,p],\ \text{but } v \neq w, \tag{7}$$

which is a subjective assessment of how satisfactory the alternative is in relation to each one of the w objectives other than v, taking into account the conflicts with v. The membership values in (7) will be systematic - when taken $\forall i$ and $\forall v$ - but subjective evaluations by the decision maker of all alternatives relative to all the objectives.

The next step is to find out how the alternatives perform in terms of an overall attainment of the objectives. This could be done as follows,

(i) consider an $a_i^{(v)}$

(ii) compute $\alpha_i^{(v)} = 1 - (\wedge\, \mu_w^{(v)}\,(a_i)),\ \forall w \in [1,p],\ \text{but } v \neq w$ (8)

(iii) use $\mu_w^{\alpha}\,(f(a_i))$ as an assessment of how satisfactory the alternative a_i is.

Some numerical experiments with this method are reported in Carlsson (1982), and the method seems to work. It does demonstrate that conflicts in multiple objectives could be resolved through the use of the theory of fuzzy sets - with the reservation that we develop some appropriate way for constructing membership functions.

2.2. Fuzzy multiple objective programming

Let us now describe the set A of decision alternatives with the element of a decision space X defined by,

$$X = \{\, x \in \mathbf{R}^n \mid f(x) \geq 0 \,\} \tag{9}$$

where $f(x) = (f_1(x), f_2(x), \ldots, f_m(x))$ are m criteria functions. Consider $X \subset \mathbf{R}^n$ and a criteria space $Y = h[\mathbf{X}]$, where $y \subset \mathbf{R}^1$; for any point $y \in Y$, let $D(y)$ be a fuzzy set in $\mathbf{R}^1$, with membership function μ_D, such that $\mu_D(d)$, where $d = g(y', y)$, is the grade of membership for y' to be dominated by y ($\mu_D\,(0) = 1$ for all $y \in Y$). The family $\{D(y) \mid y \in Y\}$ is called the **fuzzy domination structure** in Y; it is convenient to decompose $D(y)$ into its constituent level sets and to assume, without much loss of generality, that $D(y)$ is a fuzzy convex cone Λ.

If now sup $\mu_D(d)$, for $y \in Y$, and $y' \neq y$, is taken to be the degree to which y' is dominated by y, and $\mu_N(y') = 1 - \sup \mu_D(d)$ the membership function defining the set N of nondominated alternatives in Y, then the level sets of D (y) are defined as $\Lambda\alpha = \{d \in \mathbf{R}^1 | \mu_\Lambda(d) \geq \alpha\}$. The levels α may be chosen subjectively, and the structure is given by the grade of membership of dominance. If all the $\Lambda\alpha$, $\forall\alpha$, are convex cones, the fuzzy set Λ is also a convex cone (a fuzzy set Λ in $\mathbf{R}^1$ is a convex cone iff $\mu_\Lambda(d) = \mu_\Lambda(\gamma \cdot d)$, $\gamma > 0$, $\forall d \neq 0$, $d \in \mathbf{R}^1$ and $\mu_\Lambda(d) = 1$ for $d = 0$).

With these concepts, and as $X = h^{-1}(y)$, it is possible to trace the fuzzy set $N[X|\Lambda]$ of nondominated decision alternatives, which will have a fuzzy domination structure in the form of a fuzzy convex cone, and each alternative associated with a grade of membership representing its relative degree of dominance. As the domination structure is based on the m criteria functions, this is, in principle, an elegant and efficient way of representing multiple criteria.

The constructs used here are developed as if the membership functions exist as objective and well-defined descriptors, which describe and represent overall relative dominances for the alternatives in relation to the m criteria functions. As this is not an easy task to achieve the implicit assumption is rather simplifying, and clearly indicates that some work should be done to penetrate the problems of fuzzy, relative dominance.

If we stick to the implicit assumption, however, much can be done. Takeda and Nishida (1980) show that the fuzzy set N of nondominated decision alternatives can be "squeezed" between two fuzzy sets, the inner and outer approximates; in Carlsson (1982) it is shown that this "squeezing" can be carried on to produce a fuzzy set of nondominated decision alternatives, which is approximated by a fuzzy Pareto-optimal set and a fuzzy set based on optimal trade-offs between the criteria. These results can be applied as a basis for forming fuzzy constraints in a fuzzy multiobjective linear programming model.

Consider the following multiobjective programming problem,

$$\max\,[C(x)\,|\,\Lambda] = \max\,[C_1(x), C_2(x), \ldots, C_m(x)] \tag{10}$$
$$\text{s.t. } Ax \simeq b$$
$$x \geq 0, \text{ and } x \in X$$

where ($\simeq$) denotes a fuzzy constraint, i.e. there are membership functions,

$$\mu_{b_i} = \begin{cases} 1 & \text{if } (Ax)_i \leq b_i \\ 1 - \dfrac{(Ax)_i - b_i}{\delta_i} & \text{if } b_i < (Ax)_i \leq b_i + \delta_i \\ 0 & \text{if } (Ax)_i > b_i + \delta_i \end{cases} \tag{11}$$

which show that the constraints are not absolute; $(Ax)_i$ refers to the i th row of the matrix of constraints.

Let $\mu_b = \mu_{b1} \wedge \mu_{b2} \wedge \ldots \wedge \mu_{bk}$ be the fuzzy feasible region, and let μ_P, μ_O and μ_N be further fuzzy constraints, which are scalar-valued representations and approximations of the above-mentioned fuzzy cone-dominance structures; μ_P represents the fuzzy set of Pareto-optimal alternatives, and $\mu_P \wedge \mu_b$ would be the feasible Pareto-optimal decision alternatives; μ_O would be the fuzzy set of alternatives which give optimal trade-offs between the criteria, and $\mu_O \wedge \mu_b$ the fuzzy set of optimal compromises; μ_N represents the fuzzy set of nondominated alternatives relative to the m criteria, and $\mu_N \wedge \mu_b$ the fuzzy set of feasible, nondominated decision alternatives. In this way we could then use the multiobjective programming formulation to "browse" through fuzzy sets of decision alternatives and sort them out in various fashions, according to Pareto-optimality, optimal trade-offs or nondominance.

If we have conflicting objectives fuzzy constraints give a decisive advantage - we do not end up with infeasibilities as in standard linear programming formulations. We will see that illustrated in the next section, but before that we need one more approximation as there is no software available which could handle (10) and the various combinations of membership functions.

As shown by Wiedey and Zimmermann (1978) the model in (10)-(11) could be rewritten in the following form;

$$\begin{aligned} &\max \ \lambda \\ &\text{s.t. } \lambda \delta_i + (A'x)_i \leq b'_i + \delta_i \\ &\qquad x \geq 0 \end{aligned} \tag{12}$$

where i denotes the i th row of the system of equations; A' is the matrix A combined with the criteria functions C(X). This is a standard LP-form; we will make use of (12) in the following section.

3. A NUMERICAL EXAMPLE

Consider the following plywood production planning problem: we want a production plan for 5 consecutive periods which attains the following objectives and constraints:

There are 7 standard forms of plywood which according to forecasted demand will be produced as follows in the five periods,

PLW1 = 1544, * 1.07, * 1.01, * 1.12, * 0.75

PLW2 = 654, * 1.05, * 1.10, * 1.07, * 1.03

PLW3 = 1580, * 0.85, * 0.93, * 1.25, * 1.13

PLW4 = 825, * 0.85, * 0.75, * 0.90, * 1.10

PLW5 = 576, * 1.10, * 1.12, * 1.15, * 1.20

PLW6 = 286, * 1.12, * 1.30, * 1.50, * 0.90

PLW7 = 138, * 1.04, * 1.04, * 1.04, * 1.04

for which the following capacities are needed in four production lines,

PROD1 = .022 PLW1 + .030 PLW2 + .028 PLW4 + .015 PLW5 + .045 PLW7 - OUT1 ≤ 90, 40, 95, 90, 90

PROD2 = .039 PLW1 + .041 PLW3 + .043 PLW4 + .045 PLW6 + .052 PLW7 - OUT2 ≤ 180, 170, 200, 195, 195

PROD3 = .041 PLW1 + .044 PLW2 + .037 PLW3 + .042 PLW5 + .062 PLW7 - OUT3 ≤ 185, 185, 215, 215, 220

PROD4 = .062 PLW1 + .059 PLW3 + .070 PLW4 + .082 PLW6 + .095 PLW7 - OUT4 ≤ 282, 270, 315, 305, 305

but for which we have the following restriction on overtime:

OVERUSE = OUT1 + OUT2 + 2OUT3 + 3OUT4 ≤ 30, 30, 5,5,5 (13)

Production costs are given by,

$$TCOST = C11 * PLW1 + C12 * PLW2 + C13 * PLW3 + C14 * PLW4 + C15 * PLW5 + C16 * PLW6 + C17 * PLW7 \quad (14)$$

where C11 = 25.2, * 1.10/period   C15 = 32.3, * 1.12

C12 = 41.2, * 1.07   C16 = 58.3, * 1.07

C13 = 31.3, * 1.09   C17 =118.3, * 1.04

C14 = 75.4, * 1.02

i.e. the costs are expected to rise with the indicated percentages/periods.

The standard forms are cut into special dimensions for which the managerial incomes are known, and for which the demand is known:

[0,50] PLW1 : 4PLW11 (74,8), 2PLW12 (71.7), 2PLW13 (73.3)
$2200 \leq PLW1x \leq 6990$

[0,200] PLW2 : 2PLW21 (58.8), 2PLW22 (57.9), 6PLW23 (56.2), 4PLW24 (60.2)
$1280 \leq PLW2x \leq 4760$

[0,400] PLW3 : 4PLW31 (68.7), 2PLW32 (70.2)
$2860 \leq PLW3x \leq 9150$

[0,150] PLW4 : 2PLW41 (24.6), 2PLW42 (26.2)
$1200 \leq PLW4x \leq 1660$

[0,100] PLW5 : 2PLW51 (67.7), 4PLW52 (65.2), 2PLW53 (68.8)
$1320 \leq PLW5x \leq 4460$

[0,125] PLW6 : 2PLW61 (41.7), 6PLW62 (42.5)
$560 \leq PLW6x \leq 3350$

[0,20] PLW7 : 1PLW71 (-18.3)
$130 \leq PLW7x \leq 165$

The numbers in brackets show the minimum and maximun limits of the buffer stores needed of the standard forms each period.

The total marginal income from the special dimensions is given by,

$$MARGINAL = \sum_{i,j} M_{ij} PLW_{ij} \geq 1\,000\,000,\ 1\,200\,000,\ 1\,200\,000,\ 1\,450\,000,\ 2\,000\,000 \quad (15)$$

and should reach at least the indicated levels for the periods 1-5. Cutting the standard forms will produce trimming losses,

PLW1 : 4PLW11 (0.0), 2PLW12 (0.15), 2PLW13 (0.05)
$\leq$ 1520, 1550, 1770, 1380, 1300

PLW2 : 2PLW21 (0.40), 2PLW22 (0.125), 6PLW23 (0.05), 4PLW24 (0.10)
$\leq$ 650, 720, 770, 800, 800,

PLW3 : 4PLW31 (0.0), 2PLW32 (0.0)
$\leq$ 1550, 1550, 1800, 2400, 2600

PLW4 : 2PLW41 (0.05), 2PLW42 (0.05)

$\leq$ 800, 700, 700, 620, 800

PLW5 : 2PLW51 (0.0), 4PLW52 (0.0), 2PLW53 (0.064)

$\leq$ 560, 650, 840, 1000, 1200

PLW6 : 2PLW61 (0.064), 6PLW62 (0.064)

$\leq$ 280, 380, 550, 520, 520

PLW7 : 1PLW71 (0.005)

$\leq$ 138, 140, 160, 160, 170

which are collected in the following expression

$$\text{TRIMLOSS} = \sum_{i,j} E_{ij}\, \text{PLW}_{ij} \leq 1000 \qquad (16)$$

The task to be carried out is to find a production programme which is feasible in relation to all the constraints and represents an attainment of the conflicting objectives (13)-(16). For that purpose we used the model in (12), in which the λ's represent "overall buffers" against the conflicts in the objectives; from the solution below we can see that some of the conflicts remain, because $\lambda = 1$ would mean "no conflict" and $\lambda = 0$ "full conflict" which simultaneously means "no feasible solution".

	1	2	3	4	5
OVERUSE	30	30	2.559	.4278	4.405

	1	2	3	4	5
TCOST	230000	239000	290000	315000	355000

	1	2	3	4	5
MARGINAL	999999	1200000	1200000	1450000	2000000

	1	2	3	4	5
TRIMLOSS	359.9	734.1	1000	961.0	719.7

	1	2	3	4	5
SLAMBDA	.0589	.2023	.3398	.4063	.5601

	1	2	3	4	5
PLW1	1544	1559	1747	1310	1127
PLW2	654	719.4	769.8	792.9	753.2
PLW3	1580	1469	1837	2076	2283
PLW4	825	618.8	556.9	612.6	735.1
PLW5	576	645.1	741.9	890.3	1113
PLW6	286	371.8	557.7	501.9	401.5
PLW7	138	143.5	149.3	155.2	161.4

	1	2	3	4	5
PROD1	90	89.35	94.95	90	90
PROD2	180	170	200	193.2	195
PROD3	183.3	185	213.9	212.4	220
PROD4	274.0	262.3	315	302.5	304.3

	1	2	3	4	5
STORE1	25.41	38.30	50	0	50
STORE2	61.30	62.70	194.4	200	160.4
STORE3	135.7	59.93	250.5	217.7	400
STORE4	150	150	108.2	101.5	38.09
STORE5	16.47	12.74	95.73	85.94	0
STORE6	6.353	99.01	125	117.5	0
STORE7	8.118	11.92	20	20	20

	1	2	3	4	5
DEMAND1	6080	4243	3476	2723	4321
DEMAND2	3554	4311	1280	1576	4760
DEMAND3	2893	6200	6603	8442	8424
DEMAND4	1351	1240	1200	1240	1600
DEMAND5	1320	1320	1320	1801	2400
DEMAND6	560	560	3189	3053	3114
DEMAND7	130	140	141.5	155.4	161.7

	1	2	3	4	5
BOARD1	1544	1585	1785	1360	1127
BOARD2	654	780.7	832.5	987.2	953.2
BOARD3	1580	1605	1897	2326	2501
BOARD4	825	768.8	706.9	720.8	836.6
BOARD5	576	661.6	754.6	986.0	1199
BOARD6	286	378.2	656.7	626.9	519.1
BOARD7	138	151.6	161.2	175.2	181.4

	1	2	3	4	5
TRIM1	1520	1550	1738	1362	1080
TRIM2	593.5	720	640	788.2	794.9
TRIM3	1446	1550	1651	2111	2106
TRIM4	675.6	620.2	600	620	800
TRIM5	560	650	660	900.6	1200
TRIM6	280	280	532.5	509.8	520
TRIM7	130	140	141.5	155.4	161.7

	1	2	3	4	5
LOSS1	0	293.5	480.0	408.5	0
LOSS2	177.7	215.6	128	157.6	238
LOSS3	0	0	0	0	0
LOSS4	69.18	63.51	61.44	63.49	81.92
LOSS5	58.88	81.92	84.48	115.3	153.6
LOSS6	35.84	35.84	204.1	195.4	199.3
LOSS7	.6500	.7000	.7073	.7768	.8087

	1	2	3	4	5
PLW11	6080	2286	0	0	4321
PLW12	0	1957	3062	2723	0
PLW13	0	0	414.1	0	0
PLW21	0	0	0	0	0
PLW22	0	0	0	0	0
PLW23	3554	4311	0	0	4760
PLW24	0	0	1280	1576	0
PLW31	0	6200	6603	8442	8424
PLW32	2893	0	0	0	0
PLW41	1351	1240	1200	1240	0
PLW42	0	0	0	0	1600
PLW51	0	0	0	0	0
PLW52	400	40	0	0	0
PLW53	920	1280	1320	1801	2400
PLW61	560	560	0	0	0
PLW62	0	0	3189	3053	3114
PLW71	130	140	141.5	155.4	161.7

4. IN CONCLUSION

We have studied the problem of conflicts in multiple criteria and discussed two methods, both based on the theory of fuzzy sets, for handling that problem. We found (i) that the methods represent feasible ways of handling the conflicts, and (ii) that the constructs with fuzzy sets offer a few more degrees of freedom for handling conflicts than a traditional OR-model. The second method was illustrated with a numerical example.

5. REFERENCES

Bellman, R.E. and Zadeh, L.A. (1970). Decision-making in a fuzzy environment, Management Sci. (1970) 141-164

Carlsson, C. (1982). Tackling an MCDM-problem with the help of some results from fuzzy set theory, EJOR 3 (1982) 270-281.

Dubois, D. and Prade, H. (1980). Fuzzy sets and systems: theory and applications, Academic Press, New York.

Takeda, E. and Nishida, T. (1980). Multiple criteria decision problems with fuzzy domination structures, Fuzzy Sets Systems, 3 (1980) 123-136.

Wiedey, G. and Zimmermann, H-J. (1978). Media selection and fuzzy linear programming, J. Operational Res. Soc. 29 (1978) 1071-1084.

Zeleny, M. (1982). Multiple criteria decision making, McGraw-Hill, New York.

Zeleny, M. (1983). Qualitative versus quantitative modelling in decision making, HSM 4 (1983) 39-42.

A GAME-THEORETIC APPROACH FOR MULTICRITERIA DECISION MAKING

Ferenc Forgó
Karl Marx University of Economics, Budapest, Hungary

We address the following decision problem. We have to choose the "best" out of the alternatives $A_1, A_2, \ldots, A_r$ each of which is characterized numerically according to m criteria i.e. we have r m-vectors $\underline{\underline{a}}_1, \underline{\underline{a}}_2, \ldots, \underline{\underline{a}}_r$ associated with the alternatives. We assume that larger values represent better ones for all criteria and only Pareto-optimal alternatives are considered.

Our approach for treating this problem can briefly be outlined in the following manner. We set up requirements which seem intuitively rational and which must be met by a "solution". The system of requirements should preferably be strict enough to single out a unique solution. Good examples of this approach can be found in the theory of cooperative games: the SHAPLEY-value (Shapley 1953, Szép-Forgó 1974) for games given in characteristic function form and NASH's solution (Nash 1950, Szép-Forgó 1974) for games without side-payment. NASH's solution, originally developed for two-person games, has been generalized for n-person games by SZIDAROVSZKY (Szidarovszky 1978). In this paper we formulate our decision problem as a cooperative game without side-payment and investigate some features of SZIDAROVSZKY's solution.

As a first step we enlarge the set of feasible alternatives i.e. the set of feasible outcomes will be the polytope P spanned by the vectors $\underline{\underline{a}}_1, \underline{\underline{a}}_2, \ldots, \underline{\underline{a}}_r$. Then we assign to each criterion a "player" whose aim is to choose an alternative giving as large a numberical value as it is possible as to the criterion represented by that particular player. Formally, the strategy set of each player is the finite set $S = \{A_1, A_2, \ldots, A_r\}$ and the pay-off function f_i of player i is defined as

$$f_i(A_{j1}, A_{j2}, \ldots, A_{jr}) = \begin{cases} a_{ij} & \text{if } j_1 = j_2 = \ldots = j_r = j \\ -\alpha_i & \text{otherwise} \end{cases} \quad ,(i=1,\ldots,m)$$

where α_i is a suitable /generally large/ positive number $(i=1,\ldots,m)$.

In other words, this means that if all players choose the same alternative, say A_j, then they get the corresponding entries of $\underline{\underline{a}}_j$ as pay-offs. But if at least one of them "deviates", then the pay-off for everybody gets very "bad", there is a penalty α_i imposed on every player i, (i=1,...,m) for lack of consensus.

For the game $G = \{S, S, \ldots, S; f_1, f_2, \ldots, f_r\}$ thus defined we look for a cooperative "solution".

For two-person games NASH (Nash 1950) proposed a solution concept which has been generalized by HARSANYI (Harsanyi 1977) and SZIDAROVSZKY (Szidarovszky 1978) for n-person games. Because of its axiomatic development and convincing interpretability we apply SZIDAROVSZKY's solution.

We assume that a point $\underline{\underline{f}}^{*} \in R^m$ is given, which we call the status quo point and which is interpreted as follows: In case the players cannot come to an agreement they get the components of $\underline{\underline{f}}^{*}$ as pay-offs.

Let $L \subset R^m$ be a closed, bounded, convex set (the set of feasible outcomes), $\underline{\underline{f}}^{*} \in R^m$ a vector (the status quo point), for which $\underline{\underline{f}} > \underline{\underline{f}}^{*}$ for some $f \in L$. Let $\underline{\underline{\Psi}}$ be a function assigning to any pair $(L, \underline{\underline{f}}^{*})$ an m-vector (the "best compromise") which satisfies the following axioms:

1. $\underline{\underline{\Psi}}(L, \underline{\underline{f}}^{*}) \in L$ (feasibility).

2. $\underline{\underline{\Psi}}(L, \underline{\underline{f}}^{*}) \geq \underline{\underline{f}}^{*}$ (rationality).

3. Relations $\underline{\underline{f}} \in L$ and $\underline{\underline{f}} \geq \underline{\underline{\Psi}}(L, \underline{\underline{f}}^{*})$ imply $\underline{\underline{f}} = \underline{\underline{\Psi}}(L, \underline{\underline{f}}^{*})$ (Pareto-optimality).

4. If $L_1 \subseteq L$ and $\underline{\underline{\Psi}}(L, \underline{\underline{f}}^{*}) \in L_1$, then $\underline{\underline{\Psi}}(L, \underline{\underline{f}}^{*}) = \underline{\underline{\Psi}}(L_1, \underline{\underline{f}}^{*})$ (independence of unfavourable alternatives).

5. Let $\mu_k > 0$, β_k, $(k = 1, \ldots, m)$ be arbitrary real numbers and

$$\underline{\underline{f}}^{*\prime} = (\mu_1 f_1^{*} + \beta_1, \ldots, \mu_m f_m^{*} + \beta_m) \ ,$$

$$L' = \{(\mu_1 \ell_1 + \beta_1, \ldots, \mu_m \ell_m + \beta_m) \,|\, (\ell_1, \ldots, \ell_m) \in L\} \ .$$

If $\underline{\underline{\Psi}}(L, \underline{\underline{f}}^{*}) = (\Psi_1, \ldots, \Psi_m)$, then $\underline{\underline{\Psi}}(L, f^{*}) = (\mu_1 \Psi_1 + \beta_1, \ldots$ $\ldots, \mu_m \Psi_m + \beta_m)$ /independence of monotone increasing linear transformations/.

6. Suppose that $f_i^{*} = f_j^{*}$ for some indices i,j. If the relation $\underline{\underline{f}} = (f_1, \ldots, f_m) \in L$ implies the relation $\underline{\underline{\varphi}} = (\varphi_1, \ldots$ $\ldots, \varphi_m) \in L$, $(\varphi_k = f_k,\ k \neq i,\ k \neq j,\ \varphi_i = f_j,\ \varphi_j = f_i)$, then $\Psi_i = \Psi_j$ must hold /symmetry/.

SZIDAROVSZKY (Szidarovszky 1978) proved the following theorem: *Theorem 1.* There is a unique function $\underline{\underline{\Psi}}$ satisfying axioms 1-6.

The proof of this theorem also provides a method for finding the best compromise. It is the unique solution of the programming problem

$$\prod_{k=1}^{m} (x_k - f_k^*) \to \max$$
$$\underline{\underline{x}} = (x_1, \ldots, x_m) \in L \qquad (1)$$
$$\underline{\underline{x}} \geq \underline{\underline{f}}^*$$

Since the components of the status quo point $\underline{\underline{f}}^*$ have been interpreted as the consequences (penalties) of disagreement it is only natural to choose $\underline{\underline{f}}^* = -(\alpha_1, \ldots, \alpha_m)$.

Let $\underline{\underline{\alpha}} = (\alpha_1, \ldots, \alpha_m)$ satisfy $\underline{\underline{x}} > -\underline{\underline{\alpha}}$ for any $\underline{\underline{x}} \in P$ i.e. any (mixed) decision is better than the disagreement. We can now rewrite (1) as

$$F(\alpha): \quad \prod_{k=1}^{m} (x_k + \alpha_k) \to \max$$
$$\underline{\underline{x}} = \underline{\underline{A}}\, \underline{\underline{\lambda}} \qquad (2)$$
$$\underline{\underline{\lambda}} \geq \underline{\underline{O}}$$
$$\underline{\underline{1}}\, \underline{\underline{\lambda}} = 1 ,$$

where $\underline{\underline{A}} = (\underline{\underline{a}}_1, \ldots, \underline{\underline{a}}_r)$.

It is worth noting that the controversal issue of assigning "weights" to the criteria has not emerged explicitly in our game theoretical setting. It seems to us, however, that without incorporating parameters providing explicit or implicit information about the relative "importance" of criteria we cannot come to a meaningful solution. Unlike "traditional" methods using weights of criteria our approach heavily relies on the reasonable choice of the penalty vector $\underline{\underline{\alpha}}$. The relative importance of the criteria comes into effect through the choice of the vector $\underline{\underline{\alpha}}$.

We now mention a few possibilities for choosing $\underline{\underline{\alpha}}$ which seem to be "rational". Of course, in concrete decision situations it must be thoroughly thought over which one (or possibly something else) should be applied.

1. Let us suppose that we would like to improve a "situation" characterized by a positive vector $\underline{\underline{a}}_o$ and to this end we have r alternatives to choose from. These are also given by vectors $\underline{\underline{a}}_1, \ldots, \underline{\underline{a}}_r$ of the same dimension as $\underline{\underline{a}}_o$. We assume furthermore that the situation can really be improved i.e. there is a convex linear combination $\hat{\underline{\underline{a}}}$ of $\underline{\underline{a}}_1, \ldots, \underline{\underline{a}}_r$ to satisfy $\underline{\underline{a}}_o < \hat{\underline{\underline{a}}}$. Then we set $\underline{\underline{\alpha}} = \underline{\underline{a}}_o$ which can be interpreted in a straightforward way: if no decision has been made because of disagreement among players (criteria), then the situation will not be any better, it still remains to be characterized by $\underline{\underline{a}}_o$.

2. If we cannot choose from among the alternatives, then a random mechanism will do so according to a probability distribution $\underline{\underline{p}}$ which is known or can be estimated. If $\underline{\underline{A}}\, \underline{\underline{p}} > \underline{\underline{O}}$ and there is an $\hat{\underline{\underline{a}}} \in P$ to satisfy $\underline{\underline{A}}\, \underline{\underline{p}} < \hat{\underline{\underline{a}}}$, then the choice $\underline{\underline{\alpha}} = \underline{\underline{A}}\, \underline{\underline{p}}$ is possible.

3. Let $\underline{\underline{A}} > \underline{\underline{O}}$ and $\alpha_i = \min a_{ij}$, $(i = 1,\ldots,m)$. The vector $\underline{\underline{\alpha}} = (\alpha_1,\ldots,\alpha_m)$ thus defined will be considered the penalty vector. The rational behind this choice is the following. If we do not know anything about the consequences of the failure to reach a consensus, then each "player" (criterion) must even consider the worst case. Thus going as far as possible from an "ideally bad point" which may never realize but its components express real dangers might be desirable.

4. Finally we consider the case when lack of consensus is absolutly out of question, some choice among alternatives should be made and disagreement is to be treated only formally as a mathematical device. In other terms this means that we are looking for a solution (if there exists any) which can be obtained if the "penalty" tends to infinity. In particular, we assume that

$$\underline{\underline{\alpha}} = \alpha\ \underline{\underline{r}}$$

where $\underline{\underline{r}}$ is a positive vector representing the relative share of the players from the penalty and α measures its magnitude. We will investigate what happens if α tends to infinity.

Denote $\underline{\underline{x}}(\alpha)$ the (unique) optimal solution of (2) if $\underline{\underline{\alpha}} = \alpha\ \underline{\underline{r}}$ and take a sequence of real numbers $\alpha_1, \alpha_2, \ldots$ tending to infinity. Then the elements of the sequence $\{\underline{\underline{x}}(\alpha_k)\}$ (the solutions of the programming problem $F(\alpha)$) are uniquely determined and the sequence has at least one cluster point since P is closed and bounded. However, it is far from being trivial that it has only one cluster point. This conceptual difficulty is resolved by the following theorem.

Theorem 2. If $\lim_{k\to\infty} \alpha_k = \infty$, then the sequence $\{\underline{\underline{x}}(\alpha_k)\}$ has exactly one cluster point.

Proof. The objective function of $F(\alpha)$ is a polynomial of order m of the positive parameter α. Let this polynomial be

$$s(\underline{\underline{x}}, \alpha) = h_m(\underline{\underline{x}})\ \alpha_m + h_{m-1}(\underline{\underline{x}})\ \alpha^{m-1} + \ldots + h_1(\underline{\underline{x}})\ \alpha + h_o(\underline{\underline{x}}).$$

We know that for any fixed positive α $s(\underline{\underline{x}}, \alpha)$ is quasiconcave on the positive orthant R^+ . Let $K \subset R^+$ be an arbitrary convex set. Let j be the largest index for which $h_j(\underline{\underline{x}})$ is not constant on K. We claim that $h_j(\underline{\underline{x}})$ is quasiconcave on K. Suppose on the contrary that there exist $\underline{\underline{x}}_1, \underline{\underline{x}}_2, \in K$ and λ $(0 < \lambda < 1)$ such that

$$h_j(\lambda\ \underline{\underline{x}}_1 + (1 - \lambda)\ \underline{\underline{x}}_2) < \min\{h_j(\underline{\underline{x}}_1), h_j(\underline{\underline{x}}_2)\}.$$

This means that for sufficiently large α

$$s(\lambda\ \underline{\underline{x}}_1 + (1 - \lambda)\underline{\underline{x}}_2, \alpha) < \min\{s(\underline{\underline{x}}_1, \alpha), s(\underline{\underline{x}}_2, \alpha)\}$$

contradicting to the fact that $s(\underline{\underline{x}}, \alpha)$ is quasiconcave on R^+.

Let $P^m = P$ and P^k be the set of optimal solutions to the following programming problem.

$$h_k(\underline{\underline{x}}) \to \max$$
$$\underline{\underline{x}} \in P^{k+1} \tag{3}$$

for k = m-1,...,1,0. Obviously

$$P^m \supseteq P^{m-1} \supseteq \dots \supseteq P^1 \supseteq P^o$$

and problem (3) is solvable for any k since P is closed and bounded and h_k is continuous (k = 0,...,m) being a polynomial. The set P^m is convex and $h_j(\underline{\underline{x}})$ ($j \geq k+1$) is constant on P^{k+1}, therefore $h_k(\underline{\underline{x}})$ is quasiconcave on P^{k+1}. This implies that P^k is convex for any k, as well.
P^o consists of a single point since the last problem is

$$h_o(\underline{\underline{x}}) \equiv x_1 \cdot x_2 \cdot \dots \cdot x_m \to \max$$
$$\underline{\underline{x}} \in P^1 \tag{4}$$

which is equivalent to

$$\log x_1 + \log x_2 + \dots + \log x_m \to \max$$
$$\underline{\underline{x}} \in P^1$$

which has a strictly concave objective function.

We assert that the only element of P_o, say $\underline{\underline{x}}_o$, is the unique cluster point of the sequence $\{\underline{\underline{x}}(\underline{\underline{\alpha}}_k)\}$. Assume on the contrary that there is a cluster point $\underline{\underline{x}}_1$ of $\{\underline{\underline{x}}(\alpha_k)\}$ for which $\underline{\underline{x}}_1 \neq \underline{\underline{x}}_o$. It suffices to show that $s(\underline{\underline{x}}_o, \alpha) = s(\underline{\underline{x}}_1, \alpha)$ which is impossible since P^o has only one element.

Suppose that $s(\underline{\underline{x}}_o, \alpha) \neq s(\underline{\underline{x}}_1, \alpha)$ and j is the largest index for which $h_j(\underline{\underline{x}}_o) > h_j(\underline{\underline{x}}_1)$. Then, there exists an α_o such that for any $\alpha \geq \alpha_o$ we have $s(\underline{\underline{x}}_o, \alpha) > s(\underline{\underline{x}}_1, \alpha)$. Since $\underline{\underline{x}}_1$ is a cluster point, therefore in any ε-neighbourhood $K_1(\underline{\underline{x}}_1, \varepsilon)$ there are infinitely many points $\underline{\underline{x}}(\alpha_k)$. The radius ε can be chosen so small that $h_j(\underline{\underline{x}}_o) > h_j(\underline{\underline{x}}(\alpha_k))$ and $s(\underline{\underline{x}}_o, \alpha_o) > s(\underline{\underline{x}}(\alpha_k), \alpha_o)$ hold for any $\underline{\underline{x}}(\alpha_k) \in K(\underline{\underline{x}}_1, \varepsilon)$. This implies that $s(\underline{\underline{x}}_o, \alpha) > s(\underline{\underline{x}}(\alpha_k), \alpha_o)$ holds for any $\alpha \geq \alpha_o$ and $\underline{\underline{x}}(\alpha_k) \in K(\underline{\underline{x}}_1, \varepsilon)$. For sufficiently large k we have $\alpha_k \geq \alpha_o$ and hence $s(\underline{\underline{x}}_o, \alpha_k) > s(x(\alpha_k), \alpha_k)$ which contradicts to the assumption that $\underline{\underline{x}}(\alpha_k)$ is an optimal solution of $F(\alpha_k)$.

From the proof it turns out that to determine the unique cluster point we have to solve at most m programming problems having quasiconcave objective functions. Since $h_{m-1}(\underline{\underline{x}}) \equiv \sum_{i=1}^{m} (\prod_{j \neq i} r_j) x_i$ is linear, therefore the first problem to be solved

$$h_{m-1}(\underline{\underline{x}}) \to \max$$
$$\underline{\underline{x}} \in P$$

is a linear programming problem which generally (except in the case of dual-degeneration) has a unique solution. This solution is a vertex of P i.e. it is an original ("pure") alternative.

The proportion vector $\underline{\underline{r}}$ has a crucial role in this model. We may choose $\underline{\underline{r}}$ to represent the magnitude of the numerical values characterizing the criteria. The simplest idea is to set

$$r_i = \frac{1}{r} \sum_{j=1}^{r} a_{ij} \quad (i = 1,\ldots,m)$$

i.e. the penalties tend to infinity proportionally to the average values.

It is worth noting that uniqueness of the optimal solution to (2) does not imply the uniqueness of $\underline{\underline{\lambda}}$.

REFERENCES

Forgó, F. (1981). Multicriteria decision making: a game theoretic approach (Hungarian) SZIGMA XIV(2):29-38.

Harsanyi, J.C. (1977). Rational behaviour and bargaining equilibrium in games and social situations. Cambridge Univ. Press, Cambridge.

Krekó, B. (1966). Optimization. Közgazdasági és Jogi Kiadó, Budapest, (Hungarian).

Martos, B. (1976). Nonlinear programming theory and methods. Akadémiai Kiadó, Budapest.

Nash, J. (1950). The bargaining problem. Econometrica, 18(1): 155-162.

Philip, J. (1972). Algorithms for the vector maximization problem. Mathematical Programming 2(2):2o7-2o9.

Roy, B. (1971). Problems and methods with multiple objective functions. Mathematical Programming. 1(2):239-266.

Shapley, L.S. (1953). A value for n-person games. In Contributions to the Theory of Games II. Annals of Math. Studies, 28, Princeton N.J. Princeton University Press.

Szép, J. and Forgó, F. (1974). Introduction to the theory of games. Közgazdasági és Jogi Kiadó, Budapest, (Hungarian).

Szidarovszky, F. (1978). A generalization of NASH's solution of cooperative games. (Hungarian),SZIGMA, IX.(1-2):69-74.

Zeleny, M. (1976). Linear multiobjective programming. Lecture Notes in Economics and Mathematical Systems 95. Springer.

THE SYSTEMS APPROACH AND CONTINGENCY VIEW IN MANAGERIAL BEHAVIOR AND MANAGEMENT ORGANIZATION

Nobuo Sugihara and Mitsugu Ichikawa
Faculty of Business Administration, Kyoto Sangyo University, Kyoto, Japan

1. INTRODUCTION

Business management has played an important part in industrial society. Most social interactions are mediated by business. There are, however, diverse interest groups that take part in social interaction, each having its own goals and purposes. The managers should reconcile conflicts among interest groups to be able to carry out their policies and operating plans which are contingent to the situation. The managers with bounded rationality[2] cannot reach the best policy, but they are making up better policies enough to satisfy the expectation of them. In those processes, to adapt to the environment effectively and efficiently, they should take advantage of systems approach and contingency view[3] as managing tools. Here, we will inquire into these problems from the standpoint of methodology.

2. MANAGERIAL ABILITY TO RECONCILE CONFLICTS AMONG GROUPS

Management science, so far, set a single objective to solve a problem, and analyzed it by using mathematical procedures. Sciences, in future, must tackle with a difficult problem in which managers should integrate various

---

[1]This paper mainly depends upon an unpublished paper of Prof. N. Sugihara, a representative of our study group which researches fundamental features of human behavior from the methodological viewpoint of social science.

[2]The premise of the theory of Simon (1957) is "Administrative Man". Administrative Man has only limited rationality. As he does not have enough intelligence and information to reach the best result, he cannot but satisfy with some level of aspiration. The analysis on the managers with limited rationality is treated more detail in his book (1957) and his joint work with March (1958).

[3]Contingency theory means an adaptive theory to environment. Recently, contingency theory is developed in each theoretical field of management, and is treated as the adaptive process of business management. Kast and Rosenzweig (1979) think business management from the viewpoint of systems theory and contingency theory. They say that systems approach is effective for organizational behavior, and contingency view is for the necessary prediction and control.

conflicting objectives and solve them simultaneously. In dealing with many variables, a systems approach as a frame of reference or way of thinking becomes important for managerial decision-making. The claims of interest groups to management plans must be concidered in a complex decision-making problem, thus introducing many factors that cannot be transacted by a single objective computation.

The problem, here, is how to evaluate systematically the merits of various actions or alternatives. On this point, Easton (1973) explains the amalgamation procedure of valuation. Amalgamation procedures are treated mathematically in the study of operations research as the problem of weighting of objectives. The following equation represents the procedures[4];

$$O_1V_{i1} + O_2V_{i2} + \cdots + O_nV_{in} = \sum_{j=1}^{n} O_jV_{ij}$$

In this equation, O_j represents the jth element of alternative's valuation score-set, and V_{ij} represents the weights allocated to the jth element ith alternative.

This procedure, however, produces difficult problems that can be answered only by applying subjective judgement. Namely, such weighting is influence and decided by the amount of pressure applied by each group. Thus, the calculation rules of amalgamation are accompanied by the preference attitudes of managers which are built up in their weighting process. In short, the problem of weighting should start from the subjective attitude of individual human being.

The competence of the manager to evaluate, judge and decide the optimum alternative rests on both innate and acquired talent. As a human being, the manager senses, perceives and recognizes with his brain. According to the latest researches in cerebral physiology, the cerebrum consists of two hemispheres, the left one govering computational operations and the right one, judgemental operations. Thinking operations function for understanding and explaining. In other words, the right brain accepts the stimuli of information in analogue form and the left brain in digital form. Quality and quantity, pattern and numeric; these features of the aspects of the cerebral hemispheres have to be synthesized in unity. This unification integrates human actions to adapt to environment and allows systematic behavior.

3. A STUDY IN FORMALIZING MANAGERIAL COMPETENCE: FOUR PROBLEMS IN DEVELOPMENT OF BEHAVIORAL TALENT IN MANAGERS

In a complex decision, the manager will be most effective if he makes use of the standardized procedure and routine work for problem-solving. The standardized procedure provides a foundation on which the manager exercises

---

[4]These procedures are described in detail by Churchman, Ackoff and Arnoff (1957). The problem of how to derive a measure of value of a social group from its indivisual manager's value is an amalgamation problem, for which extensive argument is given by Arrow (1951).

his subjective judgement. In such problem situations, inquiries into the competence of the manager, above all his decision-making ability, should cover a broad spectrum: (a) matters dealing with multiple interests and other influences that contribute to the complexity of managerial decisions, (b) the stage in the decision process beginning with perception of a need for action and ending with the presentation of multi-attributes alternative solutions to the decision problem, (c) the treatment of multi-valued alternatives in preparation for rannking them in order of attractiveness or classifying them into merit categories, (d) specific techniques for merit-ordering of multi-valued alternatives for finding the best or for placing them into merit categories, (e) a wraping- up and synthesis.

Relating to these inquiries, we should ask what constitutes the competence of the manager to handle the problem-solving and decision-making, that is, to compute and judge the situational conditions. The question can be presented in four forms: (a) explication of the decision process, (b) individual differences in decisions, (c) computerization of the decision process, and (d) simulation of the individual decision process. Four questions of Easton asked whether the decision-making of human being could be left in a computer's hands[5].

The answers of these questions are conditionally "yes" for one aspect, and "no" for another. Because, it is very difficult for computer to understand the subjective feeling or a sense of values of human beings. The manager will be more effective if he can make the most of the various human factors inside and outside the organization. This is the advantage of socio- psychological approaches. Both the objective and subjective attitudes of the manager interact to bring managerial decision-making to completion. In short, management needs to make complex decisions involving multiple objectives, which have both computational and judgemental aspect of human behavior. Both aspects are mediated by the subjective decision attitudes or modes which are formed systematically in the learning process. Integrating function of system works in the stage of the formation of attitudes.

4. QUANTITATIVE MEASUREMENT OF PSYCHOLOGICAL ELEMENTS

Since it is troublesome to manage problems simultaneously, a single objective is set in analyzing a problem and seeking a practical result. It can provide a mathematically expressed result. This decision manner, however,

---

[5]Easton's four questions are as follows; 1) Is it possible to derive a decision procedure where despite the need for judgement, the procedure can be fully explicated and each step made defensible? 2) Why is it that men of good will, presented with identical alternatives and who agree on the essential facts in a problematic situation, still arrive at quite different choices of alternatives? 3) Is it possible to break down a class of multiple-objectives decision problems so that it can be programmed on a digital computer and therefore so routinized that complex decisions can be made by computers? 4) Can the decision processes of a particularly skilled administrator be simulated and reproduced so that he can delegate many of his complex decisions to subordinates with reasonable assurance that their decisions would not differ materially from those he would have made under similar circumstances?

gives only a "semi optimum" solution, which is of no use in the real world of management. Dissatisfied interest groups will apply pressure to constrain the actions of management. The task of satisfying these frastrations and getting the "total optimum" requires decisions which satisfy multiple objectives simultaneously, and which also arbitraite between them by trade-off. The decision-maker should enlarge the constraint concern in all directions, including social, moral, political and the living environment, so that he can reduce pressures on management. And he should develop a flexible and responsive attitude to adapt to a contingency, disciplining himself in the accumulation of experience acquired in the trial and error process.

Indeed the objective analysis looks like objective, but it is no more than a subjective judgement in which we think from the mathematical viewpoint In fact, a sense of values enters in most mathematical analysis. In a complex decision, the manager must leave the enchantment and be involved in the troublesome problems of the real world, broadening his range of view. Similarly, the manager should relate to real life's affaires with the attitude of behavior that is called "Alltaglichkeit", mundane life. In this situation, such attitudes as "muddling through" complex situation should be a better way of managing. That is, management cannot take a clear-cut attitude. The manager cannot draw a picture of business from the beginning, but he should make a picture contingently.

5. SOME FEATURES OF THE SYSTEMS APPROACH AND SYSTEMS CONCEPTS—— A TAXONOMY OF SYSTEMS

The systems approach has been broadly used in various areas where human actions are conducted on a large scale. The concepts used in the systems approach, however, are not always defined clearly and used appropriately. We turn now to some meanings of systems approach and a taxonomy of systems.

The systems concepts pertinent to this paper are as follows: (a) a frame or structure for use in a comparative analysis of management, (b) a function for integrating interactions among people in a cooperative relationship, and (c) a model that can be operated as a business game and a simulation, synthesized from structure and function.

The systems concept (c), that is, the synthetic viewpoint, emphasizes the aspect of the system as a going concern that is changing in a continuous adaptive process. It views the system not as a fixed mechanism, but as a pattern of adaptation to the supra-system, namely, the environment. It examines, moreover, the interrelated continuity of succesive patterns of adaptive behavior that are, at the same time, interconnected interactions between its parts.

6. SOME METHODOLOGICAL INSTRUMENTS FOR GRASPING THE BEHAVIORAL ASPECT OF HUMAN ORGANIZATION

The meaning of the systems concept of a mechanism that synthesizes both rational and irrational factors is too difficult to interpret monistically; rather, a pluralistic understanding and explanation are needed. Moreover, a dynamic approach to the system can grasp uncertain and contingent system behaviors. In view of the theoretical character of the methodology, it is probably better to use the system as something to be operated in business games or simulations.

The various tools of business education have been used in training effective decision attitudes and teaching business policy through role-playi and case methods. Together with these, the business games are the most effec tive tool. Every participant in the business games will acquire certain attitude that they can make better decisions by playing repeatedly. They cooperate with their team-mates in choosing among alternative decision items, such as products, sales volume, price, inventory and advertisement. A coalition of team members with different attitudes should be instituted in bargaining processes among members. This coalition itself tends to have its own attitude toward decisions.

Likert (1961) classifies the attitude situations of the system into four: (a) exploitive authoritative, (b) benevolent authoritative, (c) consultative, and (d) participative. These are his "System Four". He views the systems concept as the base of comparative analysis, which relies upon the interaction and influence system. For systems concept, he seems to use an eclectic analysis.

We have developed the three types of systems concepts so that eclectic usage of these concepts make it possible to explain and predict through understanding by experience. That is to say, the functioning process of thinking consists of such elements as experience, comparison, understanding, computation, judgement and so on. However, their order in the thinking process is not clearly defined. Rather, the purpose of eclectic use of the systems concept is explanation and prediction of human behavior, in the same way as the study of behavioral science.

7. SUBJECTIVE ATTITUDES REGULATING THE FUNCTIONS AND STRUCTURE OF THE MANAGEMENT SYSTEM

Managerial behavior is one form of human behavior in industrial society. To explain and predict managerial behavior, many variables in the complex organizational context must be incorporated into the system. These variables contain such human factors as aspiration, sentiment and value. This class of intermediate variables, which significantly influence such end results as production, sales, profits, and net earnings to sales, is neglected in the present measurements made by management. They also reflect the current conditions of the internal state of management. It consists of such variables as loyalty, skill, motivation, capacity for effective interaction, communication and decision-making.

The failure to measure the impact of human factors relates to the problems with which we are confronted in our study of managerial behavior in industrial society. These are problems of measuring imponderable human factors in computable terms. Easton and Likert tried to solve these problems. Other authers of management theory, especially organization theory, like Luthans and Miles, analyze the internal state of management system in the same way.

As a human behavior is a many-sided and complex process, we need cooperation of many disciplines to understand human behavior. For making use of human resource which recently becomes one of tasks of management, it is necessary to predict and control the organizational behavior. Thus, Luthans (1977) shows an eclectic model of cognitive approach and behavioral approach, as a model of organizational behavior. According to Luthans, cognitive approach gives some intelligence for understanding of organizational behavior, and behavioral approach, for prediction and control of it.

On the other hand, Miles (1975) presents the model which shows manager's theories as a factor influencing the choice of integrative mechanism. In Figure 1, he explains that in addition to organization variables and people variables, manager's theories which concern traditional, human relations, and human resources viewpoint or attitudes are needed. These attitudes grow up in the processes of decision-making, and are built in the system. The processes which make up the attitudes have the psychological features of

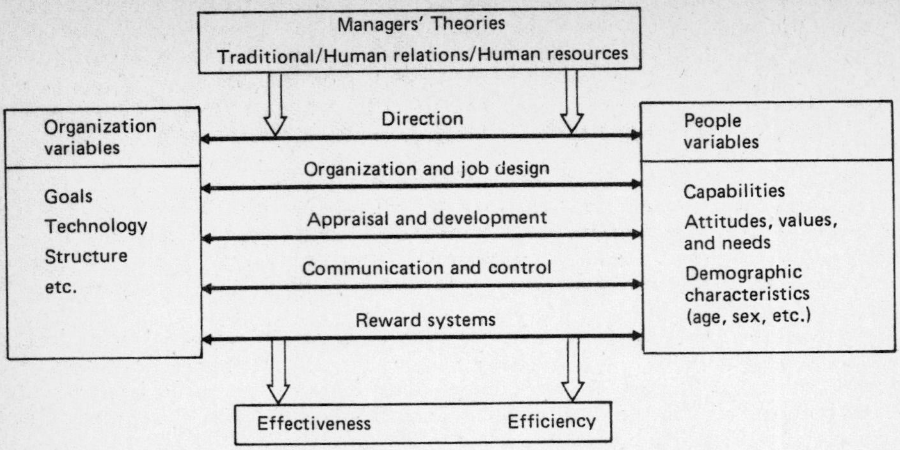

FIGURE 1 Managers' theories as a factor influencing choice of integrative mechanisms.

stimulus-reaction, senses, perception, and recognition. The experience of behavior becomes memories, memories form consciousness, and consciousness is realized as attitude. Attitude is unique to each person and classified as category of character.

A taxonomy of attitudes of styles of managerial decision-making and the management system. As Weber (1956) understood, the idealized religious origin of capitalism, that the Protestant ethic was contingent or relevant to the capitalistic spirit, so Otsuka (1981) insists that there are human subjectively categorized forms of behavior behind or underlying social actions and the social system, and emphasizes the need for the study of human subjective factors in social science research.

Miles's theories of managers and Likert's characteristics of management system are the results of crystallization of managerial attitudes. The problem of how crystallization occurs is made by research into managerial practices in various types of management systems. As the result of research efforts, it follows that various forms of managerial behavior can be classified into categories of management philosophy or managers' theories. These categories are gathered up into the vocabulary of concepts, Weber's "Kasuistik". This vocabulary of concepts to be applied as criteria in comparative analysis is necessary for investigation from all angles of the manner of action of managers and management systems.

8. THE SUBJECTIVE DIMENSION OF ACCOUNTING MEASUREMENT OF SYSTEMS PERFORMANCE

The functions relating to management of the end results of management performance are important for all kinds of interest groups. The accounting system takes charge of the execution of these functions, employing a system of double-entry bookkeeping. Above all, it undertakes to report impartially enough information to satisfy all interest groups.

The financial accounting measures money, and the end results are summarized in report form. Its purpose is to report impartially, therefore, its measurement should be objective for calculation of performance. Managerial accounting, on the other hand, has different characteristics. While it also use the data of double-entry bookkeeping in common with financial accounting, its usage differs in many respects.

Briefly, managerial accounting is more subjective than financial accounting. In managerial accounting, the data derived from the subjectively processed bookkeeping record should be linked to physical or real terms. Interpretation and conjugation of data are needed for managerial accounting. The pragmatic tool for this data application is the systems approach with the above mentioned meanings.

The function of systematizing the data from double-entry bookkeeping, through subjective attitudes of the system composed of human behavior, is to apply the data to the needs of managerial control. Ultimately, one more direction is to be added to double-entry bookkeeping. It is, so to speak, three dimensional accounting thought, and might be called "tripple bookkeeping" to bring out its distinctive feature[6].

We will use attitude conjugation as the subjective factor and system mechanism described here. Human resources accounting is a system for calculation the performance and cost of human factors. It is the one of the behavioral aspects of the accounting system that transforms the data derived from double-entry bookkeeping by applying the third dimension to interpretation of management behavior.

REFERENCES

Arrow,K. J. (1951). Social Choice and Individual Values. Wiley, New York.

Chiba, J. (1980). The Fundamental Structure of Accounting. Moriyama Shoten, Tokyo.

Chiba, J. (1981). The Fundamental Structure of Modern Corporate Accounting (2): The Accounting Institution of Joint-Stock Company and the Idea of Trust Law in England. Economy and Economics, No. 46, Tokyo Municipal University.

Churchman, C. W., Ackoff, R. L., and Arnoff, E. L. (1957). Introduction to Operations Research. Wiley, New York.

Easton, A. (1973). Complex Managerial decisions Involving Multiple Objectives. Wiley, New York.

Kast, F. E. and Rosenzweig, J. E. (1979). Organization and Management: A Systems and Contingency Approach. McGraw-Hill, New York.

Likert, R. (1961). New Patterns of Management. McGraw-Hill, New York.

Luthans, F. (1977). Organizational Behavior. McGraw-Hill, New York.

March, J. G. and Simon, H. A. (1958). Organization. Wiley, New York.

Miles, R. E. (1975). Theories of Management. McGraw-Hill, New York.

Otsuka, H. (1981). The Human Being in Social Science. Iwanami Shoten, Tokyo.

Simon, H. A. (1957). Administrative Behavior: A Study of Decision-Making Process in Administrative Organization. Mcmillan, New York.

Sugihara, N. (1981). The Conceptual Models of the Subjective Behavior of Managers. Sangyo Daigaku Ronshu. Kyoto Sangyo University, Kyoto.

Takamatsu, M. (1980). The Data-base Orientation in Vatter's Fund Theory. Rissho Management Review, No. 22. Rissho University, Tokyo.

Weber, M. (1956). Soziologie, Weltgeschichtliche Analysen, Politik. herausgegeben von J. Winckelmann. Alfred Kroner, Stuttgart.

[6]The choice of the third dimension differs with every researcher who introduce such an approach into the accounting system. For example, see Takamatsu (1980) and Chiba (1980, 1981).

RECENT DEVELOPMENTS IN OUR APPROACH TO MULTIPLE-CRITERIA DECISION MAKING

Stanley Zionts[1] and Jyrki Wallenius[2]
[1] *State University of New York at Buffalo, USA*
[2] *University of Jyväskylä, Jyväskylä, Finland*

1. INTRODUCTION

Approximately ten years ago we began a study of multiple criteria decision making at the European Institute for Advanced Studies in Management in Brussels. The project started as a way of finding a multiple objective linear programming method that would work better than those tested by Wallenius (1975). We did a substantial amount of work on the problem and came up with such a method (Zionts and Wallenius, 1976). Wallenius' (1975) thesis, one of the first outputs of that project, comprises a rather significant piece of research in the multiple criteria area. Since that time our work has continued. We have worked together on a great deal of it; some of it has involved students and other faculty colleagues. In presenting this update, we make every effort to accurately attribute (and reference) each piece of research to the appropriate person(s). Though we have tried not to omit any references or acknowledgments, or both, we apologize in advance for any inadvertant omissions.

2. THE BACKGROUND OF OUR APPROACHES

Our methods all involve the use of pairwise comparisons by a decision maker who chooses between selected pairs of alternatives. His choices reveal a preference to which we locally fit a linear function. The use of a linear function is not meant to imply that the decision maker's underlying utility function (if one exists) is linear. In many (perhaps most) cases it is not. Further since our linear function is not unique and we may find different functions for different problems with the same decision maker (even if he is acting in a consistent manner with a well-behaved utility function), we downplay the importance of the function we identify. Rather than use this function as a utility function, we use it to identify good (and hopefully optimal) alternatives, and present these to the decision maker in helping him to make a decision. Our approach is in contrast to the utility assessment models which assess the utility function directly by an interview process, come up with a utility function, and then rank order the alternatives for further consideration by the decision maker. The latter methods, developed and maintained by Keeney, Raiffa among others (see for example, Keeney and Raiffa, 1976), come up with a utility function that could conceivably be transferred from one decision situation to another. Though our function could be transferred from one decision situation to another, that is not our intention; we have no evidence to suggest that such a procedure is worthwhile for our methodological framework.

Our work has three major branches:

1. A multiobjective linear programming method that assumes an underlying unknown pseudoconcave utility function;
2. A multiobjective integer linear programming method that assumes an underlying linear utility function;
3. A multiobjective method for choosing among discrete alternatives. Here we assume an underlying quasiconcave utility function;

plus a smaller fourth branch -- a multi-person, multiobjective method for handling problems of type 1 and type 3.

In this section we have introduced and overviewed what we present in this paper. In section three we briefly review our original method. Then in the following section we overview recent results in the branches of our research. This includes both the theory we have developed and what practical experience we have had to date. We then draw conclusions.

3. REVIEW OF OUR MULTIPLE OBJECTIVE LINEAR PROGRAMMING MODEL

Our method (Zionts and Wallenius (1976)) for multiple objective linear programming uses weights. A numerical weight (arbitrary though generally chosen equal) is chosen for each objective. Then each objective is multiplied by its weight, and all of the weighted objectives are then summed. The resulting composite objective is a proxy for a utility function. (The manager need not be aware of the combination process.) Using the composite objective, we solve the corresponding linear programming problem. The solution to that problem, an efficient or nondominated solution, is presented to the decision maker in terms of the levels of each objective achieved. Then the decision maker is offered some trades (leading to adjacent efficient solutions) from that solution, again only in terms of the marginal changes to the objectives. The trades take the form, "Are you willing to reduce objective 1 by so much in return for an increase in objective 2 by a certain amount, an increase in objective 3 by a certain amount, and so on?" The decision maker is asked to respond either yes, no, or "I don't know" to the proposed trade. The method then develops a new set of weights consistent with the responses obtained, and a corresponding new solution. The process is then repeated until a presumably "best" solution is found.

The above version of the method is valid for underlying linear utility functions. However, the method is extended to allow for the maximization of a general but unspecified psuedo concave function of objectives. The changes to the method from that described above are modest. First, where possible the trades are presented in terms of scenarios, e.g., "Which do you prefer, alternative A or alternative B?" Second, each new nondominated extreme point solution to the problem is compared with the old, and either the new solution, or one preferred to the old one is used for the next iteration. Finally, the procedure terminates with a neighborhood that contains the optimal solution. Experience with the method has been good. With as many as seven objectives on moderate-sized linear programming problems (about 300 constraints) the maximum number of solutions is about ten, and the maximum number of questions is under 100.

4. RECENT WORK ON OUR METHODS

In this section we consider the methods in the order outlined in Section 1. We do this in a series of subsections, one for each method.

4.1 The Multiple Objective Linear Programming Method

Our earliest computer codes incorporated only the linear version of our method. To implement the concave and then the pseudoconcave extensions of the method we made several changes to the method. First we partitioned the questions to be asked of the decision maker into six groups. The first three groups consist of questions that are efficient with respect to old responses; the second three groups consist of questions that are efficient, but not with respect to old responses. Within each set of three groups we have a partition of efficient questions. The first group of efficient questions are those that lead to distinctly different solution vectors of objective functions. Those questions are asked as scenarios, i.e., "Which do you prefer, solution A or solution B?" Operationally, distinctly different solutions are not well defined. We define the term in a working context to mean some specified minimum difference in at least one criterion. The second group of efficient questions include those that lead to solutions that are not distinctly different. We present those questions as tradeoffs: "If you are at solution A, would you like to decrease the first objective by so much, in return for increasing the second objective by so much, etc.?" The third group of efficient questions are those corresponding to distinctly different solutions that were not preferred to the reference solution by the decision maker. These are presented to the decision maker a second time, but as tradeoffs. The decision maker proceeds through the sequence of questions. Whenever a group of questions is completed and the decision maker has liked a tradeoff or an alternative, a new set of weights (consistent with responses) is generated and the corresponding solution that maximizes the weighted objective function is found. The procedure continues from that solution. If the decision maker does not prefer any alternative to the reference solutions (and does not like any tradeoff), then the reference solution is optimal. If the decision maker liked one or more tradeoffs, <u>and</u> if an extreme point solution preferred to the reference solution cannot be found, we know that there are solutions preferred to the reference solution. To find them we cannot restrict ourselves to corner point solutions, and some other procedure must be used. This presentation is of necessity brief; some steps have been simplified for exposition. For more details on these changes see Zionts and Wallenius (1983).

An extension of the method for multiobjective linear programming, Deshpande (1981) has developed a search procedure for finding optimal solutions when the procedure terminates at an extreme point solution that is not optimal. In some work currently underway at SUNYAB, Steven Breslawski, a Ph.D. student, and Zionts are investigating how close the best extreme point found by the method is to the true optimal solution for a class (or several classes) of assumed nonlinear utility functions. Our contention is that the solutions are generally close. Of course, we have to define close in an operational manner. If the solutions do not turn out to be close, then we will begin with Deshpande's proposal and make it into (or evolve it into) an effective approach. Some tests have involved the change in order of questions, and the use of middle most weights, as well as the maintaining of an incumbent or best-known solution. The results of these tests are still preliminary, though positive. Other tests currently planned explore the results of our procedure as a function of decision maker errors in responses. The idea is that a decision maker can only approximately express his preferences (or have them assessed). In expressing his preferences he may make errors. We want to see how robust our procedure is in the face of such errors. We are also exploring other refinements to our method, such as what use if any to make of "I don't know" responses of the decision maker, the use of strength of preference (Malakooti (1982, 1983) and others) in answering questions, and the use of dominance cones to eliminate solutions.

As far as the application of our method is concerned, we have programmed the method and have used it in several different forms. We and various organizations have prepared and adapted programs to solve different problems. Our most current program is one on the CDC-174 Cyber that uses Marsten's XMP (1979) package for the linear programming routines. We are using this code for our tests. We hope to prepare a user-oriented version of it in due time.

Many practical problems have been solved with variations of the method. They include problems in both profit and not-for-profit organizations, and problems in various areas such as financial and strategic planning. The problems solved have had as many as seven objectives and several hundred constraints. See Wallenius and Zionts (1976), Wallenius, Wallenius and Vartia (1978), and Wallenius and Deshpande (1978) for more information on some of these applications.

The computational requirements for this method involve solving one linear programming solution plus some additional work for each setting or revision of weights. The maximum number of settings or revisions of weights has always been less than ten in our applications. The total number of questions asked of the decision maker has always been less than 100, and generally less than 50. We believe that fewer questions are required.

4.2 The Multiple Objective Integer Linear Programming Method

Shortly after we published our initial paper (Zionts and Wallenius, 1976), an extension of our procedure was proposed for solving multiple criteria integer programming problems (Zionts, 1977). Bernardo Villareal, a Ph.D. student in Industrial Engineering, SUNYAB, followed upon this in a thesis under Mark Karwan, a professor in the Industrial Engineering Department and Zionts. The thesis (Villareal, 1979) developed several methods, including an improved version of what Zionts had proposed. In extensive testing, Villareal had found that, although the methods had done well for small problems, the method did not appear to have promise for problems of any reasonable size. See also Villareal, Karwan, and Zionts (1979). The procedure uses a branch-and-bound approach after first solving the corresponding noninteger linear programming problem. The procedure is like the standard branch-and-bound method, except that it uses some special approximations in the branch-and-bound process.

As a result of that thesis, Karwan, Zionts, and Villareal (1983) made several substantial improvements to the earlier work.

1. Eliminating response constraints on weights that have become redundant.
2. Finding a "most consistent" or "middle most" set of weights

rather than any set of consistent weights given constraints on the weights.

3. Finding a heuristic starting solution.

We shall now consider these ideas in detail.

4.2.1 Eliminating Redundant Constraints

Constraints on weights are generated by decision-maker responses and are used for:

a) determining which tradeoff questions are efficient;
b) determining a feasible set of weights;
c) determining whether a decision-maker's response to a choice between two solutions can be inferred from previous responses.

Because the set of constraints on the weights grows with the number of responses and because the feasible region shrinks, we believed that a number of constraints become redundant. Although it is not possible to predict what fraction (or number) of constraints are redundant in general, we know for certain that with two objectives, there could be at most two nonredundant constraints. Accordingly, we altered our computer program so that after each set of constraints was added to the set of constraints on weights, we used the Zionts-Wallenius (1982) method for identifying redundant constraints to eliminate whichever constraint or constraints had become redundant.

4.2.2 Finding a Most-Consistent Set of Weights

In our multicriteria integer programming procedure we need to find a new set of feasible weights whenever the decision maker likes an efficient tradeoff offered by the procedure. Previously, we found an arbitrary solution to the set of inequalities on the weights using the dual simplex method. The resulting set of weights, an extreme point of the feasible region of the weight-space to be sure, was generally quite close to the previous set of weights. As a result, the new solution or node in the branch and bound procedure was "close" in terms of objective function values to the old one. It was proposed to change the procedure to find a most-consistent or middle-most set of weights by maximizing the minimum slack of the constraints on the weights. The questions generated are thereby intended to decrease the set of feasible weights as quickly as possible.

The results of these simple changes were very good. We ran two sample sets of 0 - 1 multicriteria linear programming problems. The times to solve problems having two objectives, four constraints, and twenty variables decreased from 57.7 seconds to 10.8 seconds of CPU time; similarly, the times to solve a problem having three objectives, four constraints, and ten variables decreased from 23.7 seconds to 8.6 seconds (of CPU time). A further improvement was to use various heuristics to identify a good initial integer solution. The empirical results of these improvements were to <u>further reduce</u> CPU times by an additional factor of three. We also examined such questions as the relation between computation time and various problem parameters and the effect on problem solution times of the initial set of weights. With relatively minor changes in our approach, we have brought our approach to the threshold of computational feasibility.

Karwan and Zionts are currently working with another Ph.D. student in Industrial Engineering at SUNYAB, R. Ramesh, on a related topic. Ramesh is exploring various options as to when the weights on objective functions should be revised. He is also using dominance cones (to be discussed) to eliminate solutions.

4.3 A Multicriteria Method for Choosing Among Discrete Alternatives

About the time that we published our first article on the Multiple Objective Linear Programming problem, a colleague not at all familiar with multiple criteria models said he didn't understand why the linear programming approach could not be used to solve the discrete alternative problems -- for example, the choice of a house by a prospective buyer. This comment lead to the publication (Zionts, 1981), which presented a model for choosing among discrete alternatives. Some early applications were made to about four or five different decision problems, each involving a decision maker in a choice situation. All involved a very small number of alternatives (less than fifteen), so the value of the method was not clear, although in each case the method seemed to do well. Zahid Khairullah (1981) in his doctoral thesis did some exhaustive test comparisons of this and other methods.

In a sequel paper (Korhonen, Wallenius, and Zionts, 1981) we provided several improvements over the previous method. First, we weakened the assumption of the underlying utility function to be quasiconcave and increasing. Second, we use a convex cone based on decision-maker choices to eliminate some of the alternatives. Simply put, (for two-point cones) if alternative A is preferred to alternative B, then any solution lying in or dominated by the half-line that begins at B collinear with the line may be eliminated.

In a newly completed dissertation at SUNYAB, Koksalan (1983), has extended some of the concepts of the earlier approaches, including the cones, the choice of alternatives, and so on. He has been working with randomly generated problems to evaluate the different methods. Koksalan has also worked with ordinal as well as cardinal criteria, both together as well as separately.

Koksalan has some remarkable results, one of which is that for the size of problems he tested (up to five objectives and 150 alternatives), the method generally finds the solution that it finds (usually but not always the most preferred solution) in fewer than twenty questions. He has also come up with some interesting results for ordinal criteria, and cardinal criteria treated as ordinal.

4.4 A Multiple Decision Maker, Multicriteria Model

The fourth problem in the area on which we have worked is a multiple criteria problem in which there are two or more decision makers. This problem is extremely difficult compared to the earlier problems considered because of the lack of problem resolution if the different members of the group cannot reach an agreement. Our approach (Korhonen, Wallenius, Zionts, 1980) considers both the multiobjective linear programming problem as well as the multiobjective discrete alternative problem. Both are based on our earlier methods. The procedures work similarly. First each member of the group uses the method by himself to identify his most preferred solution. Then a bargaining procedure based on the above methods is used to try to achieve agreement among group members. The procedure has been used in several situations with students at Purdue University and at the University of Jyvaskyla, Finland. See Moskowitz, Wallenius, Korhonen, and Zionts (1981). The situation involved a labor-management negotiation problem where students representing labor and students representing management had to come up with a mutually satisfactory labor contract. We experimented in this study to find out whether our structured approach based on the discrete alternative method seemed to be better than an unstructured form of bargaining. In every instance each group used both forms of bargaining. In the first set of experiments (at Purdue), the structured approach seemed to do slightly better than the unstructured approach, although the results were not significantly different. Further, there seemed to be a learning effect; that is, whichever method was used second was usually preferred. An improved set of instructions for the methods were used for the second study at the University of Jyvaskyla, Finland. The results were a bit more conclusive. There the structured approach was found superior to the unstructured approach. More work will be undertaken in the multiple decision maker model; we believe that problem to be extremely important.

5. CONCLUSION

In this paper we have briefly summarized our recent progress in our multiple criteria decision making project. Work is continuing along all directions: a linear programming method; an integer programming method; a discrete alternative method; and a multiple decision maker method. Even though we have worked on this project for several years, we continue to be excited and challenged by the problems that remain. The problems provide us with a challenge that helps us overcome it. On reviewing what work we have done in the field, we cannot help but say (immodestly) that we have not done badly in our research. However, as always, even greater challenges remain ahead.

REFERENCES

Deshpande, D. (1980). Investigations in Multiple Objective Linear Programming-Theory and an Application," Unpublished Doctoral Dissertation, School of Management, State University of New York at Buffalo.

Karwan, M. H., Zionts, S., Villareal, B. (1982). "An Improved Interactive Multicriteria Integer Programming Algorithm," Working Paper No. 530, School of Management, State University of New York at Buffalo.

Keeney, R. L. and Raiffa, H. (1976). Decisions with Multiple Objectives: Preferences and Value Tradeoffs, John Wiley and Sons, New York.

Khairullah, Z. (1981). "A Study of Algorithms for Multicriteria Decision Making," Unpublished Doctoral Dissertation, State University of New York at Buffalo.

Koksalan, M. M. (1983). "Multiple Criteria Decision Making with Discrete Alternatives," Unpublished Doctoral Dissertation, Department of Industrial Engineering, State University of New York at Buffalo.

Korhonen, P., Wallenius, J., and Zionts, S. (1979). "Some Thoughts on Solving the Multiple Decision Maker/Multiple Criteria Decision Problem and an Approach," Working Paper No. 414, School of Management, State University of New York at Buffalo.

Korhonen, P., Wallenius, J. and Zionts, S. (1981). "Solving the Discrete Multiple Criteria Problem using Convex Cones", Working Paper No. 498, School of Management, State University of New York at Buffalo. Forthcoming in Management Science.

Malakooti, B. (1982). "An Interactive Paired-Comparison Method for Multiple Criteria Decision Making and Optimization," Unpublished Doctoral Dissertation, School of Industrial Engineering, Purdue University, W. Lafayette.

Malakooti, B. (1983). "Assessment Through Strength of Preference," Working Paper 120-83, Department of Systems Engineering, Case Western Reserve University, Cleveland.

Marsten, R. E. (1979). "XMP: A Structured Library of Subroutines for Experimental Mathematical Programming," Technical Report No. 351, Management Information Systems, University of Arizona, Tucson.

Moskowitz, H., Wallenius, J., Korhonen, P. and Zionts, S. (1981). "A Man-Machine Interactive Approach to Collective Bargaining," Working Paper No. 521, School of Management, State University of New York at Buffalo.

Villareal, B. (1979). Multicriteria Integer Linear Programming, Doctoral Dissertation, Department of Industrial Engineering, State University of New York at Buffalo.

Villareal, B., Karwan, M. H., and Zionts, S. (1979). "An Interactive Branch and Bound Procedure for Multicriterion Integer Linear Programming," in Fandel, G. and T. Gal (eds.), Multiple Criteria Decision Making: Theory and Application Proceedings, 1979, Number 177, Lecture Notes in Economics and Mathematical Systems, Springer-Verlag, Berlin, 1980, pp. 448-467.

Wallenius, J. (1975). Interactive Multiple Criteria Decision Methods: An Investigation and an Approach, Ph.D. Dissertation, The Helsinki School of Economics, Helsinki.

Wallenius, J. (1975). "Comparative Evaluation of Some Interactive Approaches to Multicriterion Optimization," Management Science, 21, pp. 1387-1396.

Wallenius, H., Wallenius, J., and Vartia, P. (1978). "An Approach to Solving Multiple Criteria Macroeconomic Policy Problems and an Application, Management Science, 24, pp. 1021-1030.

Wallenius, J. and Zionts, S. (1976). "Some Tests of an Interactive Programming Method for Multicriterion Optimization and an Attempt at Implementation," in H. Thiriez and S. Zionts (eds.), Multiple Criteria Decision Making, Jouy-en-Josas, France, 1975, Springer-Verlag, Berlin, pp. 319-330.

Zionts, S. (1977). "Integer Linear Programming with Multiple Objectives," Annals of Discrete Mathematics, Vol. 1, 1977, pp. 551-562.

Zionts, S. (1981). "A Multiple Criteria Method for Choosing Among Discrete Alternatives," European Journal of Operations Research, Vol. 7, No. 2, June, 1981, pp. 143-147.

Zionts, S. and Deshpande, D. (1977). "A Time Sharing Computer Programming Application of a Multiple Criteria Decision Method to Energy Planning -- A Progress Report," in S. Zionts (ed.), Multiple Criteria Problem Solving, Proceedings, Buffalo, NY, Springer-Verlag, Berlin, 1978, pp. 549-560.

Zionts, S. and Wallenius, J. (1976). "An Interactive Programming Method for Solving Multiple Criteria Problem," Management Science, 1976, Vol. 22, No. 6, pp. 652-663.

Zionts, S. and Wallenius, J. (1980). "Identifying Efficient Vectors: Some Theory and Computational Results," Operations Research, Vol. 28, No. 3, Part 2, 1980, pp. 788-793.

Zionts, S. and Wallenius, J. (1982). "Identifying Redundant Constraints and Extraneous Variables in Linear Programming," Chapter 3 in Karwan, M., Lotfi, V., Telgen, J., and Zionts, S., Redundancy in Mathematical Programming, Springer-Verlag, Heidelberg.

Zionts, S and Wallenius, J. (1983). "An Interactive Multiple Objective Linear Programming Method for a Class of Underlying Nonlinear Utility Functions," Management Science, Vol. 29, No. 5, 1983, pp. 519-529.

INTERACTIVE STRUCTURE DESIGN AND SIMULATION OF NONLINEAR SYSTEMS FROM A MULTIOBJECTIVE VIEWPOINT USING THE LOTKA–VOLTERRA APPROACH

M. Peschel[1] and F. Breitenecker[2]

[1] *Division of Mathematics and Cybernetics, Academy of Sciences of the GDR, Berlin, GDR*

[2] *Institute of Applied Mathematics, Technical University of Vienna, Vienna, Austria*

1 INTRODUCTION

Peschel and Mende (1981a,1981b,1982,1983) propose an interactive structure design principle which allows to represent an arbitrary system of (nonlinear) differential equations by a system of Lotka-Volterra equations.
The structure design principle which is based on an ecological background offers a large degree of freedom so that one may choose between different representations in Volterra-form, depending on the aims of the problem. Choosing a suitable representation is consequently a problem of multiobjective decision making.
Using instead of the continuous logarithmic differential operator the discrete approximation of this operator for the structure design yields to an approximation for the system behaviour by local models consisting of chains of product-systems based on a reference point in the state space (Breitenecker, Mende and Peschel,1983; Peschel, Mende and Grauer, 1983). Choosing a suitable number of reference points in order to get a sufficient approximation of any point again is a problem of multiobjective decision making.
The Lotka-Volterra systems can be imbedded into the class of multinomial systems of differential equations (Peschel and Mende, 1982; Peschel, Mende and Grauer, 1982). Regular transformations within these multinomial systems generate equivalence classes with specific properties. Choosing a suitable equivalence class again is a problem of multiobjective decision making.
A further problem of multiobjective decision making is linked with the qualitative analysis of Lotka-Volterra systems: Peschel, Mende and Grauer (1983) make use of shift-cones to construct local Ljapunov functions for qualitative analysis; choosing a suitable base in the shift-cone is again a problem for multiobjective decision making.
The outlined "fundamental" problems of multiobjective decision making within the structure design principle are presented in section 2.
Section 3 deals with interactive decision making using the structure design principle as simulation tool. Before going into details first implementations of Volterra- and product-macros replacing all other nonlinear macros within simulation languages are discussed (Peschel, Breitenecker and Mende, 1983). After showing the advantage of the simulation of nonlinear systems in Volterra-form using the macros (Peschel, Breitenecker and Mende, 1983; Peschel, Breitenecker, Grauer and Mende, 1983) the first problem of interactive decision making is discussed in approximating a biological curve by a finite sum of hyperlogistic growth models. Simulating an unstable linear system in Volterra-form (Breitenecker, 1983a) requires the cancellation of suitable unstable equations by multiobjective decision. To complete, an interactive

simulation package based on high-level simulation software is presented (Breitenecker, 1983b) , where Volterra systems are simulated and analysed autc matically: interactive decision supported by automatized decision on Volterra systems allows to analyse and simulate the system in consideration.

2 MULTIOBJECTIVE ASPECTS OF THE STRUCTURE DESIGN PRINCIPLE

2.1 Structure Design

In our world we meet dynamic processes, interactions and competition on all le vels. Growth and structure-building are the impressing phenomena of evolution in biology, ecology, energy consumption, etc. One approach for the simulation of these phenomena is based on decomposition of the system to be studied into subsystems and on the simulations of the subsystems, which are linked in orde to simulate the total system behaviour. As the number of unknown parameters increases with the number of subsystems this approach soon results in too complex high-dimensional problems. Another approach is based on the assumptio that the system develops as a whole. Consequently the interrelation between subsystems has to fulfill a certain uniform evolution law for the entire syst This approach drastically reduces the dimension of the model to be formulated but the appropriate evolution law is much more difficult to find.
In their works Peschel and Mende ((1981a,1981b,1982,1983)) start with the sec approach. Observing a growth process one usually meets a s-formed state transition, the so-called "evolon" (fig.1). This curve starts with an extensi phase well represented by an autocatalytic growth law $dx/dt = kx^p$ and approaches a saturation limit B with an intensive phase well represented by $dx/dt = k(B-x)^q$. Combining the two phases and generalizing results in the generalized hyperlogistic growth law

$$dx/dt = kx^p(B-x^r)^q \tag{1}$$

which models a large class of "evolons".
Causal reasons for this growth law can be found in chains of rate-coupled exponentially growing systems (first approach)

$$dx_i^N/dt = k_i x_i^N x_{i+1}^N, \quad i=0,..,N \tag{2}$$

where i and N are indices of hierarchical level and chain length. Basic rate-coupled chains are the exponential tower

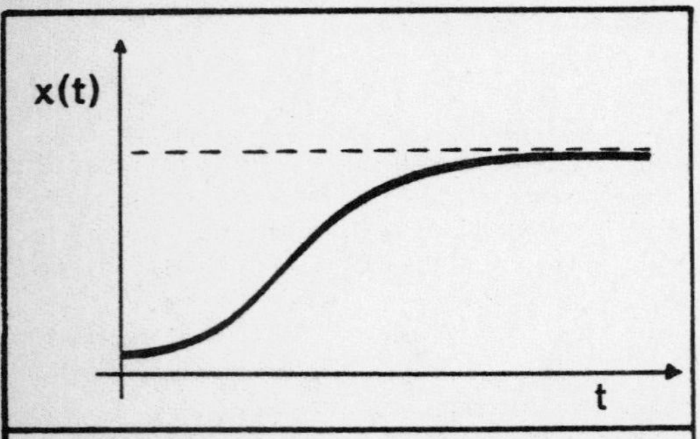

Fig.1: Evolon

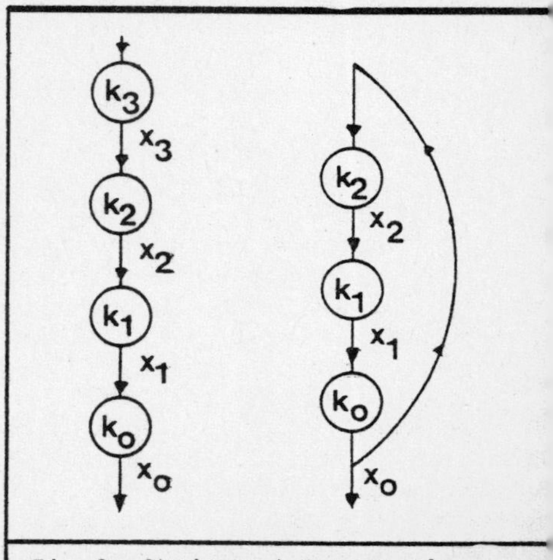

Fig.2: Chain and Hypercycle

and the hypercycle (fig. 2), which has been extensively studied by Eigen and Schuster (1979) as concept for describing biological and physical growth processes.
Mende and Peschel (1977) found out, that under weak assumption the infinite exponential tower (2) converges to the solution of $dx/dt = kx^p$ with N to infinity. It is to be noted, that the logarithmic differential operator $F = d\ln/dt$ generates these exponential towers and hypercycles where the coefficients k are related to the initial values of the levels; if all states x are normalized with $x_i(0)=1$.

$$Fx_i = k_i x_{i+1} \qquad k_i = Fx_i\Big|_{t=0} = F^{i+1} x_0\Big|_{t=0} \tag{3}$$

The saturation process $dx/dt = (B-x)^q$ also can be approximated by an infinite chain, so that consequently it can be shown, that the generalized hyperlogistic growth law (1) can be represented by an infinite chain (2). Considering the growth law (1) and the representation as infinite chain (which is not unique) the question arises whether the process can be represented also by a finite structure consisting of coupled finite exponential towers and hypercycles. Following Peschel and Mende (1981 a,1981 b, 1982,1983) and Peschel, Mende, Grauer (and Breitenecker) (1983, 1983) and Peschel, Breitenecker and Mende (1983) such finite structures exist and can be constructed, if in generating a chain (2) the operator F is used more flexibly.
Instead of applying F consecutively onto each new right- hand side of (2), the following rules allow to generate a finite structure:

1) F is applied to any intermediate state x_i: $Fx_i = A_i$

   The result A_i is not introduced as a new state as in the case of an exponential chain; it is an arithmetic expression buildt up from states already known, states unknown up to this stage of the design process and nonlinear transformations of states of both types.
2) The known states are identified and linked by a feedback with their previous appearance only unknown signals and nonlinear expressions of known und unknown signals are treated as new states.
3) The structure design process comes to an end if all arithmetic expressions in the last stage of the process contain only known signals.

Consequently the system (2) becomes more complex. But using this structure designing process it is possible to represent an (system of) arbitrary function x(t) (obeying e.g. a highly nonlinear differential equation) as (system of) Lotka- Volterra equations (Lotka, 1920; Volterra, 1931):

$$Fx_i = \sum_{j=0}^{n} G_{ij} x_j, \qquad x(t) = x_o(t) \tag{4}$$

Representing e.g. the generalized hyperlogistic growth (1) as Volterra system results in

$$Fx_o = kb^q x_1, \quad Fx_1 = \bar{p}kb^q x_1 - rqkb^{\bar{q}} x_2, \quad Fx_2 = (\bar{p}+r)kb^q - r\bar{q}kb^{\bar{q}} x_2 \tag{5}$$

with $b=B-1$, $\bar{p}=p-1$, $\bar{q}=q-1$. Figure 3 shows this structure: obviously the second- order predator- prey model for x_1, x_2 "drives" the process x(t).
The Volterra- structure (5) can be used without modification for simulation. But in other examples the structure design may produce singularities in the new state variables, because $Fx_i = d\ln x_i/dt = \dot{x}_i/x_i$ becomes singular if x_i has a zero within the time interval in consideration (in case of ecological

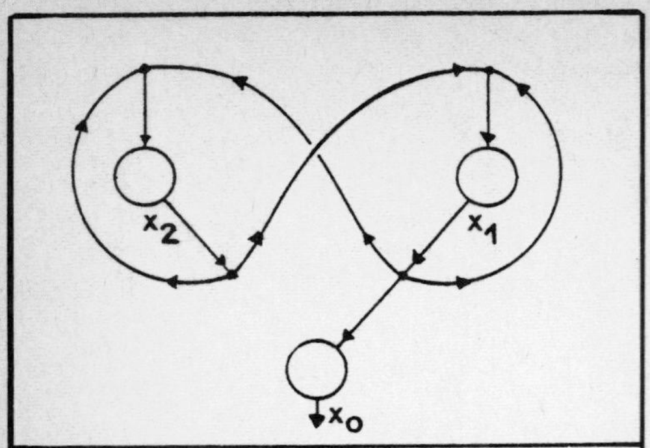

Fig.3: Volterra structure of of hyperlogistic growth

processes that usually cannot happen). Sometimes this disadvantages can be overcome by transformation of the basi state $x(t)$, if some information about the process is available.
In general singularities can be prohibited by preserving linear transformations $\bar{x}_i = x_i + r_i$ (r_i regularisation parameters) for each new state. If this requirement is met at all stages of the structure design process always ultimatively a unified Volterra representation can be obtained. There the dimension of the non-regularized representation (4) is increased because int mediate states $r_i/\bar{x}_i$ are generated. But usually one needs a regularisation only for certain states. Consequently there exist usually many Volterra representations with different dimension f a (system of) differential equation because of the ambiguity introduced by the intermediate states.
The procedure which transforms a given (system of) differential equation int Volterra representation can be formalized in Backus notation (Peschel and Mende, 1983) so that a compiler or interpreter for this transformation can b designed.
Because of the outlined ambiguity the (automatized) structure design has to be performed in an interactive mode by choosing suitable intermediate states in order to prohibit singularities.
The outlined decision whether an intermediate state should be constructed has the character of multiobjective decision making where two different goals exist. First of all, the number of states should be as small as possible; that is the case if no regularisation is done. On the other hand side the procedure should prohibit all possible singularities; that is the case if each state is regularized. Let now be

Q1...number of basic states in $Fx_i = \sum G_{ij} x_j$, $j=0,..,m$ (regularized in parts, m>n)

Q2...number of "parasitic" poles (singularities) generated by zeros of states and of derivatives of states

The goal is now to find a suitable equilibrium between the two numbers, whi is a problem of multiobjective decision: both numbers should be as small as possible, but reduction of the states (decreasing Q1) results in additional singularities (increasing Q2); on the other hand side singularities can be prohibited (decreasing Q2) by introducing intermediate states (increasing Q1

2.2 Equivalence transformation of Lotka- Volterra equations

As outlined before there exist different Volterra representations for a process because of intermediate states. These representations are in some se equivalent because they all represent the trajectories of the same system, although they have different dimensions. Consequently (usual) transformatio are not sufficient, because they transform only special representations and not the Volterra equations themselves.
Peschel and Mende (1982) propose another transformation which is based on imbedding the Volterra representation (4) into the broader class of multinominal differential equations

$$Fx_j = \sum_J A_{iJ} \prod_r x_r^{a_{Jr}} \qquad (6)$$

To avoid complex numbers one assumes that all states are not negative. The driving force of the multinomial differential equation is appearently a superposition of terms consisting of "power-products" of the states.
A linear regular affine transformation on the space spanned by $\ln x_i$

$$x_i = \prod z_r^{t_{ir}}, \qquad T = (t_{ij}) \text{ regular}$$

defines a homogeneous term- consistent coordinate transformation resulting

$$Fz_i = \sum_{j,J} t_{ij}^{-1} A_{jJ} \prod_r z_r^{\sum a_{js} t_{sr}} \qquad Fz = T^{-1} A \prod z^{aT} \qquad (7)$$

where the second term expresses the transformation symbolically in a short form. The form of the multinominal equation (6) remains unchanged under these transformations. Due to (7) matrix pairs ($T^{-1}A$, aT) now define a class of multinomial differential equations, where T can to be choosen arbitrarely (but regular). Consequently these transformations can be used to derive suitable normal forms for multinomial differential equations an also, indirectly, for Volterra representations: every multinomial differential equation can immediately be transformed into a Volterra representation after renaming each different term (as single state).
Using now the matrix T as "resource" one tries to find suitable normal forms, e.g. normal forms which simplify a given representation.
Obviously one may persue simplification in a number of different ways, so that a multiobjective decision problem arises
Rewriting the equivalences classes by $(((f^1, A_{.J})), ((a_{J.}, e_j)))$, e_j, $j=1,..n$ being a base in $\mathbb{R}^n$ and f^i being the corresponding dual base, different goals of simplification can be formulated as follows ($a_{J.}$, $A_{.J}$,... denotes rows or columns of a and A):

Q1.. Number of variables in terms
Matrix a should have as many zero elements as possible to minimize the number of times variables occur in the terms, that means that many $(a_{J.}, e_j) = 0$.

Q2.. Number of terms
Matrix A should have as many zero elements as possible to minimize the number of terms occuring in the driving forces, that means that many $(f^i, A_{.J}) = 0$.

Q3.. Dimension- first integrals
Matrix A should have as many zero rows as possible, because every zero row means that the corresponding transformed state is a first integral of the motion in term form, so that the dimension is reduced.
Formally that means that many $(f^i, A_{.J}) = 0$ for all J.

Q4.. Dimension- elimination of states
Matrix a should have as many zero columns as possible, because every zero column represents a state which can be eliminated, so that the dimension is reduced. Formally that means that many $(a_{J.}, e_j) = 0$ for all J.

To combine these various types of simplification is really a multiobjective decision problem because one is interested pursuing several of these goals Q1, Q2, Q3, Q4 simultaneously, where only one regular matrix T can be used as control resource. Methods to solve this multiobjective decision problem are e.g. vector optimization (the goals are non-cooperative) or hierarchical optimization (Peschel, Mende and Grauer ,1983).

2.3 Qualitative analysis of Volterra- Lotka equations

Rewriting the Lotka- Volterra equations (4) in the form

$$Fx = \sum x_j G_{.j}, \quad G_{.j} \text{..j-th column of } G, \; x_i > 0 \tag{8}$$

a qualitative analysis can be done by defining the sets

$$H = \left\{ \sum c_j G_{.j} \mid c_j > 0, \sum c_j = 1 \right\} \quad , \quad K = \left\{ ch \mid h \in H, c > 0 \right\} \tag{9}$$

where H is the convex hull of columns of $G_{.j}$ and K is the convex cone spanned by H (Peschel, Mende and Grauer ,1983b).
If now the zero vector is element of H, then there exists a positive stationary solution of (8) with vanishing small forces driving the growth rate. On the other hand side if there exists a stationary solution of (8) with the outlined properties then the zero vector belongs to H. Consequently, if and only if det G = 0 then there exists a stationary solution with the outlined properties.
If the zero vector does not belong to H, then H and the zero vector span the cone K. Integrating (8) formally from the reference point $z(t_o)$ results

$$z(t) = z(t_o) + \sum \left(\int_{t_o}^{t} x_j(u)du \right) G_{.j} \, , \quad z_i = \ln x_i \tag{10}$$

Consequently - because the zero vector does not belong to H - there holds

$$z(t) \in z(t_o) + K \quad \text{for } t>t_o, \qquad z(t) \in z(t_o) - K \quad \text{for } t<t_o$$

These formulas construct the so-called "shift-cones" and have the following meaning: for $t>t_o$ and any reference point $z(t_o)$ the velocity vector dz/dt of any trajectory is directed into the cone $z(t_o)+K$, in case of $t<t_o$ into $z(t_o)-K$ (fig. 4) - (the shift cones constructed there are very similar to the so called "light- cones" in the theory of special relativity). In particular, the existence of such a shift cone for the transformed Volterra system (10) means that there exists no cyclical motion (limit cycles, spirals or combinations).
Now one has some degree of freedom in constructing the definition of H and K in (9) and by using a suitable Volterra-representation (8). That again is a multi-objective decision problem which should result in the following: if the Volterra system has a shift cone and if the shift cone can be choosen as substitute of the Pareto cone then the Volterra system shows always an efficiency-oriented behaviour .

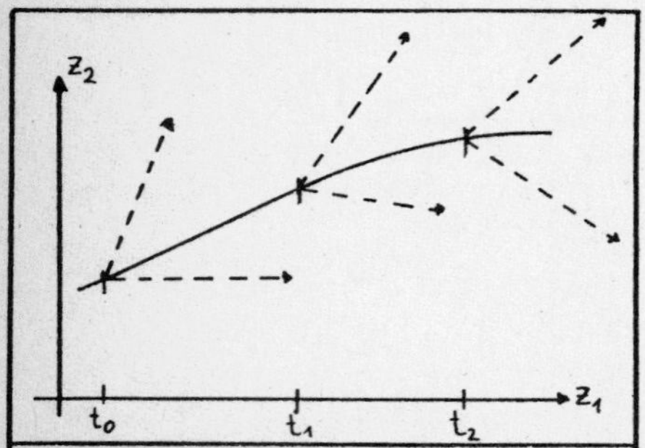

Fig.4: Shift-cones

2.4 Lokal approximation of functions by chains

Generalizing the chain construction (2) by means of an arbitrary differentiable and monotonic function f(u) results in a general differential operator F with

$$Fx_i = df(x_i)/dt = f^{-1}(f(k_i) + f(x_{i+1}), \quad f(x_i(t_o)) = 0 \tag{11}$$

Discretising (11) in a general way (substituting the differential quotient in (11) by a difference quotient with weighting function g(u)) yields to

$$(f(x_i(t)) - f(x_i(t_o))) \;/\; (g(t) - g(t_o)) = f^{-1}(f(k_i) + f(x_{i+1})),$$

$$i = 1,2... \tag{12}$$

For $f(u)=g(u)=u$ the formula (12) is equivalent to a Taylor series expansion, in case of $f(u)=g(u)=\ln(u)$ with expansion up to order N (12) becomes the following local approximation of order N for x(t) (Peschel, Mende and Grauer, 1983; Breitenecker, Mende and Peschel, 1983):

$$(\ln x_i(t)/(x_i(t_o)) \;/\; \ln(t/t_o), \quad i=0,..,N$$

The outlined approximation can e.g. be used for the approximation of functions in the following way:- (i) spline- like methods by a sequence of local models, - (ii) approximation by linear superposition.
As example fig. 5 shows a first- order spline- like approximation of a curve using the local model $x = x(t_o)(t/t_o)^a$. As to be seen, this approximation works better than approximation by tangents (in t^+), in e.g. t^- it works worse- this disadvantage disappears by using more than one reference point choosing e.g. t^- as second reference point, etc. (corresponding to (i)). Figure 6 shows the same approximation with a changed reference point $x = (B-x(t_o))((u-t)/(u-t_o))^a$ corresponding to (ii).
In order to improve the approximation either the order of the approximation can be increased or the number of local models (=reference points) can be increased. Consequently one has to deal with a multiobjective decision problem:

Q1.. number of local models
Q2.. order of approximation (second and higher derivatives)

Q1 and Q2 should be as small as possible for obtaining a suitable approximation. The goals are non- cooperative because decreasing the order of approximation results in a larger number of local models if the quality of approximation should remain unchanged. It should be noted that the multiobjective aspect especially of Q1 is linked with the aspiration level methods for the description of the efficient set (Wierzbicki, 1979).

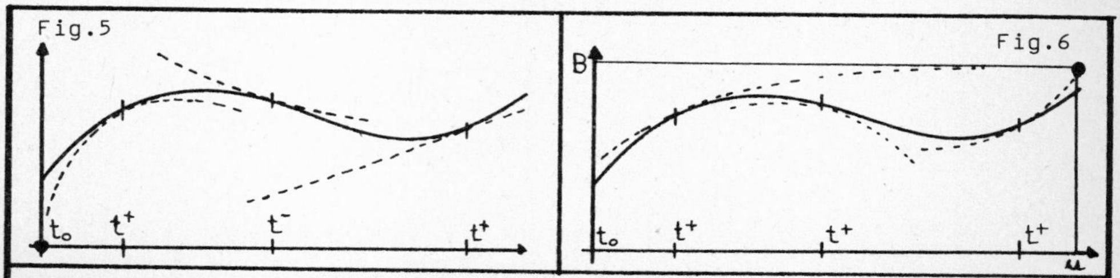

Lokal Volterra Approximation

3 ASPECTS OF INTERACTIVE AND MULTIOBJECTIVE DECISION MAKING IN SIMULATION WITH VOLTERRA REPRESENTATIONS

3.1 Implementation of Volterra representation for Simulation

The outlined representation of an arbitrary (system of) differential equation as Lotka- Volterra system is an appropriate tool for computer simulation: the operator inverse to $F = d\ln/dt$, the so- called exponential integrator, as basic macro is able to replace all other nonlinear elements of the system description.

Using e.g. a block- oriented simulation language this basic macro can be implemented easily by a combination of summing, multiplying and integrating (fig.7). The structure diagrams (fig.2, fig.3, fig.9, fig.13) can be interpreted as generalized block diagrams where each node represents an exponential integrator.

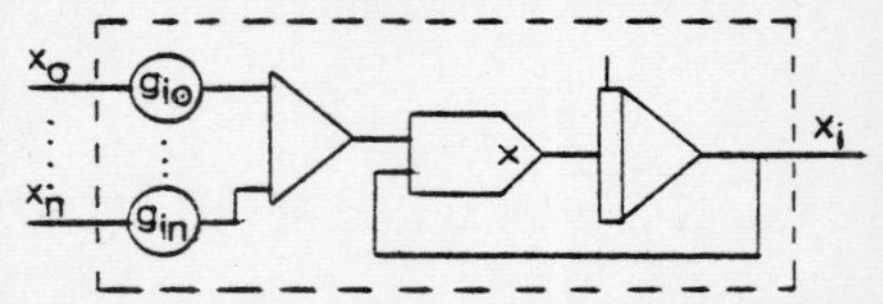

Fig.7: Exponential Integrator

As first example a projection of world energy consumption and world population up to the year 2000 is considered. Kriegel, Mende and Peschel (1983) found out that these processes can be described by specializing the hyperlogistic growth (1) by r=1 and p=q. The model is based on data 1900-1980; the saturation limit B can be expressed in terms of parameter p and of the value x_M of the state at the time t_M of maximal growth rate, which is probably already behind us. Figure 8 shows the (projection of) world primary energy consumption for three different time instants of maximal growth rate. Using the Volterra representation (5) for simulation no troubles caused by singularities arise because all states are positive; that means tha for the multiobjective decision of 2.1 there holds Q1=3 and Q2=0; concerning the multiobjective decision problem of 2.2 also representation (5) is the best one.

As outlined before the growth $x(t)=x_o$ is "driven" by the states x_1, x_2 which interact as predator and prey; it can be shown that this predator- prey syste is structurally stable if both autocatalytic coefficients are unequal to zero in the considered case must hold only $k \neq 0$ or $B \neq 1$ or $p=q \neq 1$ in order to make the system structurally stable. It is to be noted that digital simulation usually solves structurally unstable systems as well as stable one, while analog or hybrid computation gets into troubles in simulating structurally un stable systems because the analog model in form of electronic circuits is a physical model of the process- and structurally unstable models are usually useless models for any process (Breitenecker and Kleinert, 1983).

Fig.8: World primary energy consumption
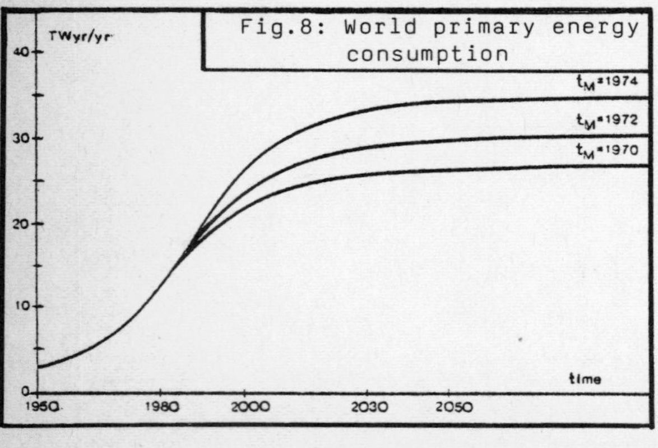

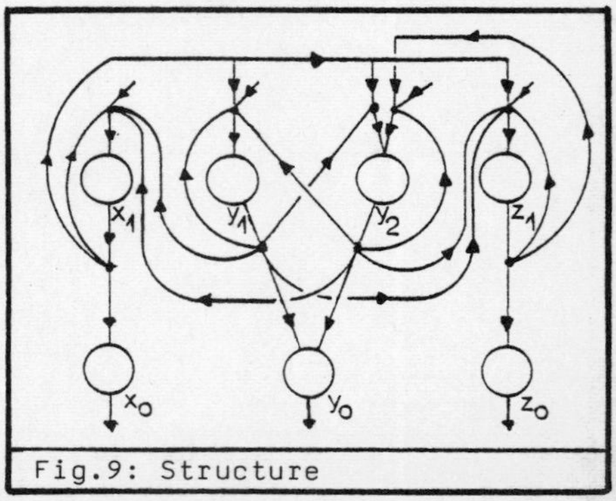

Fig.9: Structure

An interesting example is the Volterra- representation for the Lorentz attractor

$$\dot{x} = -10x + 10y, \quad \dot{y} = -y + ax - xz, \quad \dot{z} = -8z/3 + xy \tag{13}$$

resulting in a Volterra- system of order 7 ($x_o=x$, $y_o=y$, $z_o=z$, $a=28$):

$$Fx_o=-10+10x_1, \quad Fx_1=9-10x_1+ay_1-y_2, \quad x_1=x_o/y_o=1/y_1, \quad y_2=x_o z_o/y_o$$
$$Fy_o=-1+ay_1-y_2, \quad Fy_1=-9+10x_1-ay_1+y_2, \quad Fy_2=-35/3+10x_1-ay_1+y_2+z_1$$
$$Fz_o=-8/3+z_1, \quad Fz_1=-25/3+10x_1+ay_1-y_2-z_1, \quad z_1=x_o y_o/z_o \tag{14}$$

Figure 9 shows the structure diagram. Starting a simulation in (x,y,z) = (1,1,1) x(t) and y(t) change the sign in [0.45, 0.55] so that x_1,y_1 and y_2 have poles(fig.10) which can be prohibited by intermediate states. Consequently for the multiobjective decision problem of 2.1 there holds Q1=7, Q2=3 before and Q1=10, Q2=0 after the solution of the problem. Simulating without regularisation shows, that in [0.5, 4] starting with (-2.7, -8.4, 28.8) at t=0.5 (corresponding to (1,1,1) at t=0) the Volterra-representation (14) works better than direct solution of (13); the reason for that seems to be that the additional states "stabilize" the oscillation (fig. 11); in [0, 0.4] x_o and y_o of (14) are damped too much because y_1 and y_2 become very large (fig. 12).
To complete, the structure generating principle (section 2.1) also is able to represent certain integro-differential equations as Volterra systems: for instance, systems of a Volterra integro-differential equations modelling problems from virology with a certain intoxication time can be represented and simulated as system of Volterra equations (Peschel, Breitenecker and Mende, 1983).
Sometimes it is also useful to transform a system of linear differential equations $\dot{x} = Ax$, $x \in \mathbb{R}^n$ into Volterra- representation resulting in

$$Fu_i = \sum a_{ij}u_{ij}, \quad Fu_{ij} = \sum (a_{jk}u_{kj} - a_{ik}u_{ki}), \quad x_i = u_i \tag{15}$$

The system (15) is of dimension $n+n^2$; but due to numerical reasons $(n^2-n)/2$ equations for u_{ij} have to be cancelled ($Fu_{ij}=-Fu_{ji}$) in order to get a (locally Ljapunov-) stable Volterra system (Breitenecker, 1983 a); choosing

Fig.12

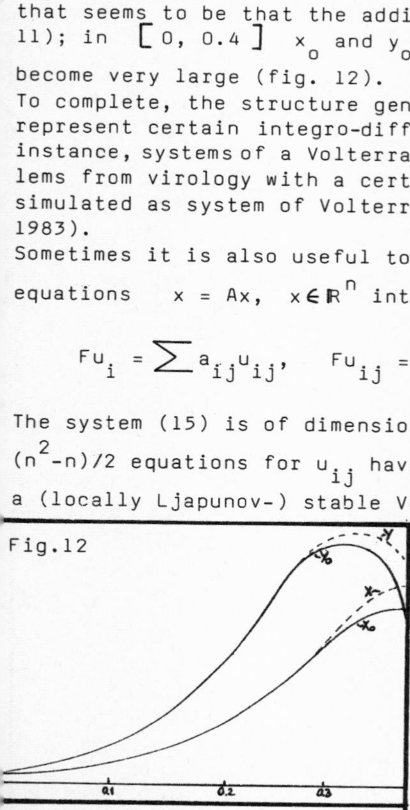

Solutions of Lorentz attractor

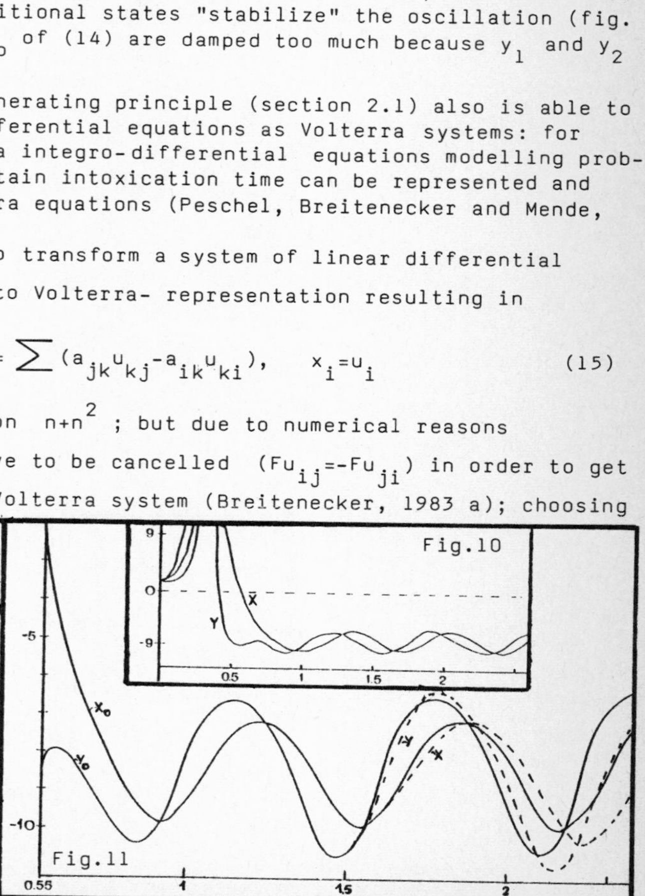

Fig.11

suitable states to be cancelled again is a problem of multiobjective decision: the modified Volterra system (reciprocical states occur explicitely! has to be stable- the dimension has to be reduced- the modified system shoul remain simple). Equ.(15) is similar to an imbedding method (Breitenecker,198

3.2 Dynamic approximation of (biological) curves using special Volterra systems

It is well known that (biological) curves $y(t)$ can be approximated by a sum $\bar{y}(t)$ of exponential functions (Braess, 1967; Braess 1970):

$$\bar{y}(t) = \sum_{j=1}^{m} a_i x_i(t), \quad x_i(t) = e^{k_i t} \quad (\dot{x}_i = k_i x_i) \tag{16}$$

There usually m=4 is sufficient to approximate y(t) with suitable accuracy (characterized by eight parameters).
Now it is to be noted that the exponential function is the simpliest form of the generalized hyperlogistic growth law (1) with p=1, r=0 or p=1, q=0. Assuming that the exponential integration (section 3.1, figure 7) is a basic arithmetic operation (e.g. in case of analog computing) the question arises whether the approximation can be improved by using more general functions- described by (1) instead of the exponential functions- or whether the qualit of approximation remains unchanged by using less but more general functions instead of exponential functions. There exist three stages of generalisatior of the exponential growth:

$$\dot{x}_i = k_i x_i^{p_i} \rightarrow Fx_{io} = k_i x_{i1}, \; Fx_{i1} = k_i x_{i1} \tag{17}$$

$$\dot{x}_i = k_i (B - x_i^{r_i})^{q_i} \rightarrow Fx_{io} = k_i x_{i1}, \; Fx_{i1} = k_{i1} x_{i2} - k_{i2} x_{i1}, \; Fx_{i2} = k_{i2} x_{i1} - k_{i1} x_{i2} \tag{18}$$

$$\dot{x}_i = k_i x_i^{p_i} (B - x_i^{r_i})^{q_i} \rightarrow Fx_{io} = h_i x_{i1}, \; Fx_{i1} = h_{i1} x_{i2} - h_{i2} x_{i1}, \; Fx_{i2} = h_{i2} x_{i1} - h_{i1} x_{i2} \tag{19}$$

where (18) and (19) are structure- equivalent (fig. 3, equations (5)), with three or resp. four parameters instead of one in the case of an exponential function. But already the simpliest generalisation (17) with a simple Volterra structure (fig. 13) and with two instead of one characterizing para meter may improve the approximation: figure 14 shows the approximation of a biological curve modelling the glucose production rate of an isolated rat liver (simulated with glucogan) using a sum of two exponential functions ($\hat{y}(t)$, m=2) and using a sum of functions of form (17) ($\bar{y}(t)$, m=2).

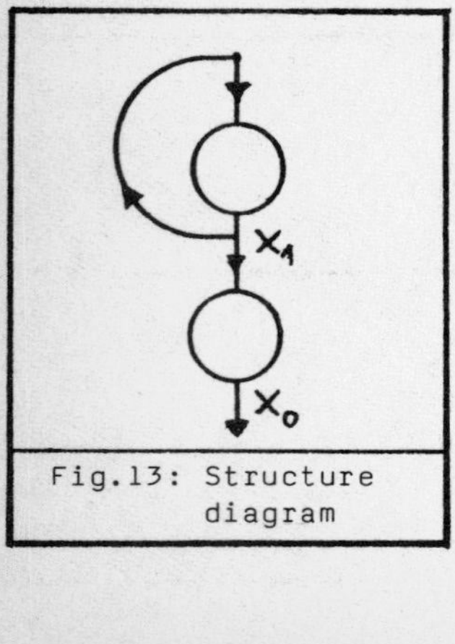

Fig.13: Structure diagram

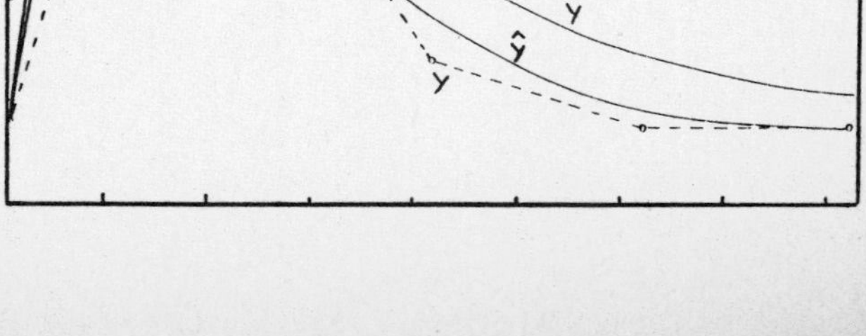

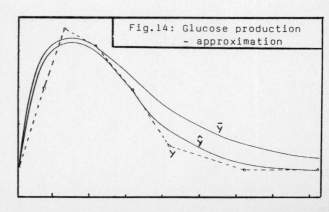

Fig.14: Glucose production - approximation

Again one deals with an interactive multiobjective decision problem:

Q1.. the approximation has to be as accurate as possible
Q2.. the number of terms in the sum has to be as small as possible
Q3.. the approximating functions x_i have to be as "suitable" as possible

It is to be noted that the goals Q1 and Q2 are non-cooperative while Q3 itself depends on the properties of the curve to be approximated.

3.3 Interactive decision analysis of Volterra systems

The representation of a (system of) differential equation as a Volterra system is also an appropriate tool for analysing the properties of the solution by analysing the solution of the corresponding Volterra system. This analyse can be done by using well known results on Volterra equations.
This analyse and the simulation of Volterra systems was implemented as interactive simulation package within the hybrid simulation language HYBSYS (Kleinert,Berger,Stallbaumer and Wittek,1982; Solar,Berger and Blauensteiner,1982). This interactive simulation package (Breitenecker,1983b) was implemented in the so-called supermacro-technique (Breitenecker,1983d) where a general macro initialises and performs special investigations on the model.
Analysing and simulating a Volterra system (representation) starts with the automatic generation of the differential equations depending on the input of the dimension. In the moment a "Volterra-precompiler" is in stage of designing which transforms an arbitrary equation into Volterra representation (interactively taking into account the outlined multiobjective decision problems) so that one may start with the input of the equation to be analysed.
The simulation of the system and the documentation of the results are then performed by standard features of HYBSYS. Additional features allow to analyse the properties of the system and to perform interactive decision analysis: the main cases of interest are the questions of stability, limit cycles, equilibrium solutions, boundedness, sensivity of parameters,etc.
First of all the programm checks whether the system is a conservative one (G skew-symmetric) or whether some extended assumptions are fulfilled.
In an interactive way the user may proceed with the following actions:

(i) simulation of the trajectories with (graphic) documentation
(ii) variation of parameters and initial values with (graphic) documentation
(iii) calculation of equilibrium population
(iv) local stability analysis by linearisation around the equilibrium or initial population
(v) global stability analysis by special investigations on the system
(vi) global stability analysis by a graph-theoretic method
(vii) stability analysis by stochastic methods

The actions (i) and (ii) are performed by standard features of HYBSYS while actions (iii)-(vii) are additional features which were programmed in overlay -technique and can be performed by simple command words. Action (iii), the calculation of stationary solutions,requires the simple solution of a linear system. The local stability analysis (action (iv)) is the usual local eigenvalue analysis in the neighbourhood of a special point: after linearisation around this point the eigenvalues and eigenvectors are calculated.
But it is clear that global stability analysis is far more relevant. This question is tried to be answered by actions (v)-(vii). Action (v) performs special investigations on the system depending on the dimension: in case of dimension n=2 the question is answered completely by using the Poincare-Bendixson theory (Braun,1978); the stability of the three-species case is analysed by consideration of 34 cases depending on the sign and relative values of the coefficients in G (Krikorian,1979) so that the system can also be classified (food chains, loops, two predators acting for one prey and one predator acting for two preys); in case of n>3 also a significant body of results for

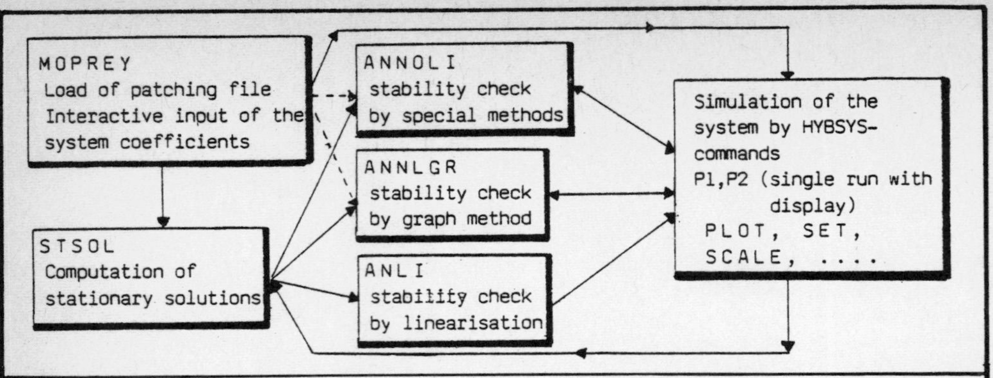

Fig.15: Structure of the simulation package

generalized conservative systems (Takeuchi,Adachi and Tojumaru,1978; Yorke and Anderson, 1973) is used for the stability analysis. Action (vi) makes use of a graph-theoretic method (Redheffer and Zhiming,1980): the coefficients of G build up a graph with opened or closed loops where each node represents one of the populations and is specially marked depending on the sign of the autocatalytic coefficient; a fundamental principle establishes rules to reduce the number of special critical nodes depending on the connections. Action (vii) is a stochastic analysis for a population where one of the coefficients of G or a initial value is disturbed with small values obeying a certain statistical distribution; as result the medium value curve for the population is displayed and the standard deviation is listed.

Figure 15 summarises the features of this interactive simulation package: the different actions are connected by arrows showing the possible seriell and parallel analysis and simulation of the system.

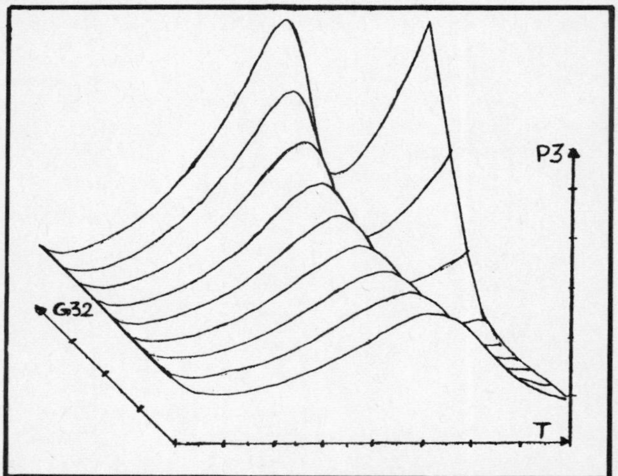

Fig.16: HYBSYS - documentation of simulation

Usually the user starts with the macro MOPREY which generates the model equations depending on the input (dimension). Then he may proceed either with simulation of the system (actions (i),(ii)) or with analysis of the system activating the macros STSOL (action (iii)), ANLI (action (iv)), ANNOLI (action (v)), ANNLGR (action (vi)) and ANSTOC (action (viii)).

It is to be noted that simulation can be performed and documentated very comfortably using standard HYBSYS features. For instance, the simple command " PLOT P3 OVER T AND G32=1,2,0.1 " performs ten simulation runs where the parameter G32 of G varies from 1 up to 2 in steps of 0.1 and displays the result as threedimensional plot for population P3 (fig.16).

REFERENCES

Braess, D. (1967). Approximation by exponential sums. Computing 2: 309-321.

Braess, D. (1970). On the structure of the signs in an exponential sum. Journal of Approximation Theory 3: 101-113.

Braun, M. (1978). Differential Equations and Their Applications. Springer, New York.

Breitenecker, F. (1982). On the solution of the linear-quadratic optimal control problem. Messen-Steuern-Regeln (msr), 25(9): 485-489 (in German).

Breitenecker, F. (1983a). Solution of the linear-quadratic optimal control problem using Volterra- and Riccati- techniques. Messen-Steuern-Regeln (msr), to appear (in German).

Breitenecker, F. (1983b). Simulation package for predator-prey systems. Proc. Int.Conf. Simulation of Systems '83, Prague, July 1983, 3/13:213.

Breitenecker, F. (1983c). On the solution of the linear-quadratic optimal control problem by extended invariant imbedding. Optimal Control-Application & Methods (OACM), 4(2): 129-138.

Breitenecker, F. (1983d). The concept of supermacros in today's and future simulation languages. Mathematics and Computers in Simulation,XXV:279-289.

Breitenecker,F., Mende,W. and Peschel,M. (1983). The Riccati representation as tool for generating local models for regulator plants. Messen- Steuern-Regeln (msr), 26(6): 344-345 (in German).

Breitenecker,F. and Kleinert,W. (1983). Does hybrid simulation more than solving the system governing differential equations. Proc. Int. Conf. Simulation of Systems '83, Prague, July 83.

Eigen,M. and Schuster,P. (1979). The Hypercycle, Springer, Berlin.

Kleinert,W., Berger,F., Stallbaumer,H. and Wittek,E. (1982). The hybrid timesharing system MACHYS at the Technical University Vienna. Informatik-Fachbericht 56, Springer, Berlin: 234 - 241.

Kriegel,U., Mende, W. and Peschel,M. (1983). An evolutionary analysis of world energy consumption and population. IIASA Collaborative Paper CP-83-34. International Institute for Applied System Analysis, Laxenburg, Austria.

Krikorian,N. (1979). The Volterra model for three species predator- prey systems: boundedness and stability. J. Math., Biology, 7: 117 -132.

Lotka,A.J. (1925). Elements of physical biology. William and Wilkins Comp., Baltimore.

Mende,W. and Peschel,M. (1981 a). Structure design of nonstationary and nonlinear systems. Messen- Steuern- Regeln (msr), 24 (10): 581-583 (in German).

Peschel,M. and Mende,W. (1981 b). Problems in mathematical modelling of evolutionary processes. Messen-Steuern-Regeln (msr), 12 (in German).

Peschel,M. and Mende,W. (1977). Problems of fuzzy modelling, control and forecasting of time- series and some aspects of evolution. Proc. IFAC-Symposium on Control Mechanism in Bio- and Ecosystems, Leipzig, 1977.

Peschel,M. and Mende,W. (1982). Volterra models of nonlinear and nonstationary systems and corresponding equivalent transformations. Messen-Steuern-Regeln (msr),25 (2): 102 - 104 (in German).

Peschel,M. and Mende,W. (1983). Do we live in a Volterra- world?- An ecological approach to applied system analysis. Akademie- Verlag, Berlin (in German).

Peschel,M., Breitenecker,F. and Mende,W. (1983). On a new concept for the simulation of dynamic systems. Proc. First European Simulation Congress, Aachen, September 1983, Informatik- Fachbericht 71, Springer, Berlin:91-98.

Peschel,M., Mende,W. and Grauer,M. (1982). An ecological approach to system analysis based on Volterra equations. IIASA Collaborative Paper CP-82-20 . International Institute for Applied System Analysis, Laxenburg, Austria.

Peschel,M., Mende,W. and Grauer,M. (1983). Qualitative analysis of nonlinear systems by the Lotka- Volterra approach. IIASA Collaborative Paper CP-83, to appear. International Institute for Applied System Analysis, Laxenburg, Austria.

Peschel,M., Breitenecker,F., Grauer,M. and Mende,W. (1983). System analysis based on Volterra equarions. Proc. IFAC-Int. Workshop on Supplemental Ways Improving International Stability (SWIIS 1983),Sept.'83, to appear.

Redheffer,R. and Zhiming,Z. (1980). Global asymptotic stability for a class of many- variable Volterra predator- prey systems.
Solar,D., Berger,F. and Blauensteiner,A. (1982). HYBSYS- an interactive simulation software for a hybrid multiple- user system. Informatik- Fachbericht 56, Springer, Berlin: 257-265.
Takeuchi,Y., Adachi,N. and Tojumaru,H. (1978). Global stability of ecosystems of the generalized Volterra type. Mathematical Biosciences, 42: 119-138.
Volterra,V. (1931). Lecons sur la theorie mathematique de la lutte pour la vie. Gauthier- Villars, Paris.
Wierzbicki,A.P. (1979). The use of reference objectives in multiobjective optimisation- theoretical implications and practical experience. IIASA Working Paper. International Institute for Applied System Analysis, Laxenburg, Austria.
Yorke,J.A. and Anderson,W.N. (1973). Predator- prey patterns. Proc. Nat. Acad. Sci. 70: 2069 - 2071.

HIERARCHICAL MODEL-ORIENTED SYSTEM ORGANIZATION

V. Mazurik
Computing Center of the USSR Academy of Sciences, Moscow, USSR

1. INTRODUCTION

The problems arising in such areas as agriculture, climate, and energy development are becoming increasingly complex. It is now impossible to model these problems adequately without using a set of mathematical models. For example, it is necessary to analyze both linear and nonlinear model variants, make iterative corrections, and investigate both static and dynamic aspects.

The use of complex models generally results in a nonlinear growth in the complexity of the analysis. It becomes impossible to carry out this analysis for any length of time without letting the user exert some influence on the model. In this paper we shall consider how to organize software support for complex modeling in order to construct a really useful instrument for interactive analysis.

2. SEMANTIC COMPLETENESS

The more complex is the model to be investigated, the more important it becomes to ensure that the subject areas, concepts and operations available in the interactive dialogue are appropriate to the needs and expectations of the user. This would make the non-formal interactive control of the model by the user really effective.

The set of notions constituting the model, and their representations, are very often artificial due to the attempt to save computer memory. The new hardware now available simplifies the problem to some extent, but another problem arises. We are used to fitting the structure of the model to the needs of calculation procedures. This was reasonable enough in the days of batch processing, when we had enough time to "decode" the results from their procedure-oriented form to a form more suitable for analysis. The advent of interactive modeling has entirely changed the situation, emphasising the need for procedures for model-based interactive decision making. However, the problem cannot be reduced simply to the choice of representations: it is also necessary to provide semantic completeness.

If, for example, the user wishes to extend his optimization model by including the dual vector, simply adding an array of given dimension to the model does not solve the problem. To extend the model properly it is necessary to include a description of dual space itself and the relations connecting it with initial space, etc.

Another example is provided by the system which is intelligent enough to calculate the matrix of second derivatives of a given function, but does not understand what is meant by the distance between two points in, say, euclidian space. This may seem rather strange to the user.

Systems lacking semantic completeness are not convenient to use. This comes across clearly in some comments made by users concerning such systems:
"The system language is too poor and does not adequately reflect my image of the model".
"The dialogue is not flexible enough, that's why it is not effective".
"If this system can.... then why can't it....?"
"Why can't this system understand such simple things as....?"
"I can't rely on the results obtained with the help of this system".

It is impossible to provide semantic completeness in problem-oriented systems, because it is difficult or impossible to restrict and formally describe the semantic area important to the user. However, it does seem possible to overcome these problems in model-oriented systems based on a formal mathematical model or a set of interconnected models.

3. MULTILEVEL ORGANIZATION

Let us now consider the technological and structural aspect of system organization in complex modeling. The usual software base for such a system is provided by packages of numerical methods. However, the problem of complex modeling cannot be solved simply by extending the list of software that can be run on a given computer. In this case, due to the qualitatively different level of complexity, there is no analogy with service program libraries, where simple extension provides the user with new computing resources. A package is a set of numerical methods connected with a certain mathematical model, which is represented in a strictly defined form. The use of the package implies that a problem area is being mapped onto the structure, and this can be rather a complicated procedure. Complex modeling makes the task even more difficult by necessitating input-output coordination of the different models. Thus, there is an evident need to develop a general approach based on the properties common to models in a given class.

The problem is to formulate a procedure which would allow effective development of unified model-oriented software based on the semantic scope of a given class of mathematical models. We suggest the following procedure, which is based on multilevel software development. First a strict analysis of the semantic scope of the mathematical models in a given class is carried out. This defines a set of notions and relations common to all the models in the class. These fundamental notions are then implemented, creating a basic software level. A second level, which includes each model in a given class together with their specific properties and input-output relationships, is then implemented. Note that this implementation is based on high-level mathematical notions, which simplifies the work and makes the system more "intelligent".

We shall now demonstrate this procedure for the class of optimization models which includes unconstrained optimization, nonlinear programming, optimal control, solution of nonlinear equations, and global optimization.

The semantic scope of the basic software required by this class of models is actually quite general and could be used for a wide variety of operations research models.

4. BASIC SOFTWARE LEVEL

We may treat the basic level as a virtual computer which differs from ordinary computers in its level of 'mathematical education'.

The memory cells of this computer contain such mathematical notions as vector spaces and subspaces, coordinate systems, mapping from space to space (in particular, functions), derivatives at a given point, and so on. The computer can be instructed to create spaces, to evaluate mappings, to transfer to indicated subspaces, to change the coordinate system in order to correct the properties of the functions under investigation, to create complex functions by superposition, etc.

This basic software level is based on a small number of mathematical notions, which are listed below.

Vector spaces. Vector spaces are represented in terms of cartesian products. The simplest vector spaces are real fields and Galois fields, and they provide the basis for the arithmetic and logical operations of the virtual computer. An N-dimensional vector space on the field P is represented by the n-th cartesian product of the field P .

Mappings. A mapping is a means of specifying the relations between vector spaces and their cartesian products. Mappings may be defined in two different forms: functional and algorithmic. The functional definition is given in a language which at its most complex approaches the traditional algebraic notation. The algorithmic form is based on the notions of memory assignment, and includes structured selection and iteration routines typical of programming languages such as FORTRAN and PASCAL.

Functions are one of the most important types of mapping. It is possible to define a new function either by the means mentioned above, or by superposition. Analysis of the local (differential) and global properties of functions is actually the main purpose of the virtual computer in question. In particular, the virtual computer automatically provides a special mapping which maps any point of vector space to the gradient vector of a given function at this point. Thus, the notion of a derivative is included in the semantics at this level.

Linear mapping. Another important case of mapping is the linear mapping, which is recognized as being of particular interest. Mappings of this type are the basis for efficient implementation of a great number of transformations designed to correct function properties. These include the reduction of dimension by fixing coordinates, transfer to subspaces with 'fast gradients' and 'slow gradients' for a given function, and so on.

Vectors, areas. The elements of vector spaces are the vectors and areas within these spaces. On creating a vector space it is possible to explicitly define a set of points (vectors) and areas within it. These areas are treated by Boolean algebra 2^V for the given vector space V . The fundamental terms in the algebraic representation are function names for the functions defined in vector space V . These functions are treated as characteristic functions of the areas.

The introduction of areas into the semantic scope of the virtual computer makes it possible to treat the problem under consideration in terms of "geometric images". For example, in a nonlinear programming model each restriction represents some area and their intersection forms the permissible area for optimization. This area is represented in the virtual computer by an expression in Boolean algebra which has the form of a combination of function names, each name corresponding to a single restriction. The computer uses these areas to calculate the inclusion predicate for a given point, or to find a point which satisfies such a predicate (i.e., it minimizes the penalty incurred by violation of restrictions).

The newly created objects in the virtual computer strictly correspond to their mathematical semantic description. For example, on creating a new object of the vector-space type, the computer automatically creates the mappings which define vector addition, subtraction and multiplication of a vector by a scalar. These operations define the vector space as a mathematical notion. The user thus creates a vector space of a given dimension by one simple phrase, the rest of the work being carried out by the virtual computer. The particular calculation algorithms are induced by corresponding operations in the field over which the vector space is defined.

There is one additional virtual computer level, which contains more specific objects. This level includes, for example, the notion of euclidian vector space. While creating an object of this type, the computer sets up the "euclidian" operations of scalar product, norm and distance calculation in addition to the ordinary vector space operations.

Thus, we have outlined the basic level properties which allow for the creation, modification and elimination of vector spaces, mappings and their elements in accordance with the mathematical semantics of these objects. In other words, the virtual computer implements the semantic area of linear algebra to an extent sufficient to provide a basis for the second, model-oriented software level.

5. MODEL-ORIENTED SOFTWARE LEVEL

This level contains interconnected optimization models of the type mentioned above. One of the main characteristics of this level is the introduction of new notions which are specific to particular models and therefore were not included at the basic level (e.g., dual variables for nonlinear programming problems, control vectors for optimal control problems). This level also includes packages of numerical methods, one for each of the optimization models considered at this level. The availability of numerical packages creates its own specific semantics, including, for example, the possibility of changing methods during problem solution, the notion of a list of parameters for each method, and the notion of the solution trajectory.

The hierarchical structure of this level is defined first of all by the properties of the numerical methods required for each optimization model. For example, nonlinear programming methods are often based on the reduction of the initial problem to a specific unconstrained minimization problem. The inner problem is sometimes solved in dual space rather than in the primal space. Optimal control methods can create a subordinate nonlinear programming problem performing time discretization, etc.

It is often important that there should be interaction with the solution process on each of these hierarchical levels. In this case the semantic scope on each level of the hierarchy should no longer be determined solely by the method, but should be suitable for use in an interactive dialogue. It is essential that the semantics of initial and subordinate tasks be highly interconnected.

For the optimization models mentioned above the mapping of these higher-level notions onto the virtual computer basic-level notions is relatively simple and consists, in general, of labelling the basic notions. For example, to define a nonlinear programming problem it is necessary to specify the function to be minimized in a given vector space and to give two additional sets of functions which define inequality and equality constraints. Note that this latter definition creates a specific 'geometrical' image of the constraints - they become areas with all the associated semantic consequences.

Of course, the use of the basic level to implement the model-oriented level automatically makes all the facilities of this basic level available for treating optimization models. Thus, when solving, say, an optimal control problem, the virtual computer understands both specific directives such as "evaluate the initial value of the control vector", and more general ones such as "change the coordinate system", or "estimate the value of the function at a given point".

This provides an extremly flexible means of modifying the task at hand. For example, it is possible to use a linear mapping to fix a certain number of coordinates and thus to decrease the dimension of the problem. It is important to note that the virtual computer is designed in such a way that all task functions are automatically projected onto the appropriate subspace. This operation corresponds exactly to the semantics implied by using the notion of fixed coordinates.

Another example: for unconstrained optimization problems it is possible to create two subspaces, which correspond to subsets containing a certain range of gradient components for a given function, and to choose the most suitable optimization method in each subspace.

The virtual computer levels described above form an efficient instrument for the further implementation of problem-oriented systems in different applied areas. A two-level virtual computer structure capable of treating the optimization models discussed above has already been implemented on a PDP 11/35 computer. It is planned to develop the suggested approach by incorporating multicriteria and decision-making models into the semantics of the virtual computer in the future.

III. METHODS AND TECHNIQUES FOR INTERACTIVE DECISION ANALYSIS

DUAL RELAXATION AND BRANCH-AND-BOUND TECHNIQUES FOR MULTIOBJECTIVE OPTIMIZATION

Paolo Serafini
Institute of Mathematics, Informatics and Systems Theory,
University of Udine, Udine, Italy

1. INTRODUCTION

This paper is concerned with duality results for multi objective (m.o.) optimization problems. The core of the paper is a duality theorem derived by usual separation techniques. This theorem generalizes known results in view of the applications to m.o. problems, which are presented in Section 3.

Actually Sections 2 and 3 constitute an attempt toward building a duality theory for multi objective optimization problems, in the same spirit of the known duality theory for scalar constrained optimization problems. As the latter is a powerful theory, it is expected that a duality theory for m.o. problems would also yield useful results.

Indeed the second aim of this paper is to present in Section 4 an application of these ideas to discrete (or in general non convex) m.o. problems by introducing the concept of dual relaxation for m.o. problems and using it for a technique of a branch and bound type. Due to the nature of m.o. problems several incumbents and bounds are present at the same time and interaction with the decision maker is needed in order to find optima.

2. A GENERAL DUALITY THEOREM

We shall first consider a generalization of the following well known duality result :

$$\inf_{y \in K} \|y\| = \max_{\|\pi\| \leq 1} -h(\pi)$$

where K is a convex set in a real normed space Y, $0 \notin K$, π is an element of the dual space Y^* and $h(\pi)$ is the support functional of K, i.e.

$$h(\pi) = \sup_{y \in K} \pi y$$

(see Luenberger (1969) p. 136).

The generalization consists in replacing the norm with a convex functional ρ (not necessarily finite) defined on K , with the property that

$\rho(\alpha y) = \alpha\rho(y) > 0$ for $\alpha>0$ $y \in K$. To this purpose let us define

$$\rho^*(\pi) = \sup_{y\in K} |\pi y|/\rho(y)$$

$$K^- = \{ \pi : \pi y \leq 0 \ \ \forall\, y\in K \}$$

Then we have :

Theorem 1

Suppose $v = \inf_{y\in K} \rho(y) < \infty$ and $\rho^*(\pi)=0$ iff $\pi=0$. Then

$$\inf_{y\in K} \rho(y) = \max_{\rho^*(\pi)\leq 1} -h(\pi) = -h(\pi_o)$$

and $\pi_o \in K^-$.

Proof

Let $C = \{ y\in Y : \alpha y\in K$ for some $\alpha \geq 0 \}$. We may extend ρ to C by virtue of its property and define $C_\varepsilon = \{ y\in C : \rho(y) \leq \varepsilon \}$. We shall first prove $v\geq -h(\pi)$. It suffices to consider $h(\pi)<0$. In this case $\pi\in K^-$ and the hyperplane $H_\pi = \{ y : \pi y = h(\pi)\}$ separates strictly the origin and K. Now, for each π, let $\bar{\varepsilon}$ be the largest number such that H_π separates C_ε and K for every $0\leq\varepsilon\leq\bar{\varepsilon}$. Since $\alpha\rho(y)=\rho(\alpha y)$ and $v<\infty$ we must have

$$h(\pi) = \inf_{y\in C_{\bar{\varepsilon}}} \pi y$$

Obviously $\bar{\varepsilon}\leq v$. Now, if $\rho^*(\pi)\leq 1$, we have

$$-h(\pi) = -\inf_{y\in C_{\bar{\varepsilon}}} \pi y = \sup_{y\in C_{\bar{\varepsilon}}} -\pi y = \sup_{y\in C_{\bar{\varepsilon}}} |\pi y| = \bar{\varepsilon} \sup_{y\in C} |\pi y|/\rho(y) = \bar{\varepsilon} \sup_{y\in K} |\pi y|/\rho(y)$$

$$= \bar{\varepsilon}\, \rho^*(\pi) \leq \bar{\varepsilon} \leq v \ .$$

Moreover C_v and K are convex sets and K does not contain interior points of C_v . Therefore there exists a separating hyperplane H_{π_o} (take w.l.o.g. $\rho^*(\pi_o)=1$), i.e.

$$\pi_o y_1 \geq h(\pi_o) \geq \pi_o y_2 \quad \forall\ y_1\in C_v \ ,\forall\ y_2\in K$$

Obviously $\pi_o \in K^-$. Since $h(\pi_o) \leq \inf_{y\in C_v} \pi_o y = -v$, we get $-h(\pi_o) = v$ □

The motivation for Theorem 1 lies in the fact that for some problems a concept much weaker than a norm is available, as it will be shown in the next section.

3. APPLICATIONS TO MATHEMATICAL PROGRAMMING

In this Section we are concerned with the following m.o. mathematical programming problem, with objective function $f : \Omega \to Y$ and partial order $\geq$ in Y defined by a closed convex cone Λ :

Problem M

optimize (with respect to Λ) $f(x)$
s.t. $x \in \Omega$ □

We recall that an optimum is any point x such that $f(x') - f(x) \notin \Lambda \setminus \{0\}$ for all x' in Ω. We shall use the term optimum also for the image f(x) of an optimum x.

Let us define $K = f(\Omega) - \Lambda - \{p\}$, where p is any element of Y such that $0 \notin K$. It is known that K is convex if f is concave. We shall assume in this section that K is convex. It is not difficult to show :

$$K^{-} = [f(\Omega) - \{p\}]^{-} \cap (-\Lambda)^{-}$$

The key in the application of Theorem 1 is the choice of ρ. It makes sense to let ρ reflect the partial order so that minimizing ρ corresponds to finding optima. Therefore we choose :

$$\rho(y) = \min \{ \delta : y + \delta q \in \Lambda \} \qquad (\rho(y)=\infty \text{ if there exists no such } \delta$$

where q is a parameter. It is not difficult to derive :

$$\rho^{*}(\pi) = \pi q \qquad \text{if} \quad \pi \in K^{-}$$

Hence

$$\inf_{y \in K} \rho(y) = \max_{\pi q \leq 1} -h(\pi) \tag{1}$$

The left-hand-side of (1) is a scalarization of Problem M studied in detail by Pascoletti and Serafini (1984). It can be proven that for each optimum y of Problem M there exist q and p such that y minimizes $\rho(y)$ and that for every q and p the minimizing subset of $\rho(y)$ contains, if not empty, at least one optimum for Problem M. Hence if the minimum of $\rho(y)$ is strict, it is an optimum for Problem M. The cases when the minimum of $\rho(y)$ is not strict can be viewed as exceptional and actually they affect only marginally the results of this paper. Hence we assume with little loss of generality that the minimum of $\rho(y)$ is strict.

We may therefore consider the l.h.s. of (1) as a primal scalarization and, as it is obvious from our derivation, the r.h.s. as a dual scalarization.

It is immediate to verify from the definitions of ρ and K and the optimality of y_o that, if $\inf \rho(y) = \rho(y_o)$, one has $y_o = -\rho(y_o)q$. Hence by (1)

$$y_o = h(\pi_o)\, q \tag{2}$$

In other words we may find optima by solving the dual problem. We shall exploit this result later. Now let us make the following comments:

If K is strictly convex we have (by separation property)

$$y_o = h(\pi_o)\, q = \pi_o y_o q$$

and it is more convenient to compute y_o directly from $h(\pi_o)$ rather than from (2). But, if K is just convex, the set

$$Y_o = \{ y : \pi_o y = h(\pi_o) \} \tag{3}$$

(which consists of optima) may have more than one element and in this case we have

$$Y_o = h(\pi_o)\, Q_{\pi_o} \tag{4}$$

with $Q_{\pi_o} = \{q : \max\limits_{\pi q \leq 1} -\mathbf{h}(\pi) = -h(\pi_o)\}$

Computation of Y_o is more convenient through (4) rather than (3) and this is especially true for linear programs.

The above results can be further specialized giving also an insight into the role played by the objectives and the explicit constraints of a mathematical programming problem.

Thus, let $f : \Omega \to Y_f$ be the objective function, $g : \Omega \to Y_g$ the constraint function, $\Lambda_f \subset Y_f$, $\Lambda_g \subset Y_g$ closed convex cones, and consider the following problem:

Problem CM

$$\begin{aligned} &\text{optimize (with respect to } \Lambda_f) && f(x) \\ &\qquad\qquad \text{s.t.} && g(x) \in \Lambda_g \\ &&& x \in \Omega \end{aligned}$$

□

(note that $\Lambda_g = R^s_+$ and $\Lambda_g = \{0\}$ correspond to usual inequality and equality constraints respectively)

Let $Y = Y_f \oplus Y_g$

$\Lambda = \Lambda_f \oplus \Lambda_g$

$K = \binom{f}{g}(\Omega) - \{\binom{p}{0}\} - \Lambda$

$q = \binom{q_f}{q_g}$ with $q_g = 0$

$\rho(y) = \min \{ \delta : y + \delta q \in \Lambda \}$

It can be shown again that strict minima of $\rho(y)$ are optima for Problem CM for any choice of q_f. Putting $\pi = (\pi_f, \pi_g)$ and applying Theorem 1 we get :

$$\inf_{y \in K} \rho(y) = \max_{\pi q \leq 1} -h(\pi) = \max_{\pi_f q_f \leq 1} -h(\pi_f, \pi_g) \tag{5}$$

Let us comment the above result :

a) if $Y_f = R$ (single objective) (5) can be rewritten, after some manipulations :

$$\sup_{\substack{x:\\ g(x)\in\Lambda_g\\ x\in\Omega}} f(x) = \min_{\substack{\pi:\\ 0\leq\pi_f\leq 1\\ \pi_g\in-\Lambda_g^-}} \left[\sup_{x\in\Omega} [\, \pi_f f(x) + \pi_g g(x) \,] \right]$$

which is the classical strong duality property of convex constrained scalar problems (note that if one drops the assumption on ρ^* in Theorem 1,the resul holds with inf instead of min; this accounts for constraint qualification);

b) a closer glance at (5) shows that objectives and constraints differ in the values of the components of q only, that is one has $q_i\neq 0$ for objectives and $q_i=0$ for constraints. In other words constraints are the limiting case of objectives and the duality result (5) unifies them into a single concept;

c) the role played by the functional ρ resembles the one of a penalty function. In fact $q_g=0$ implies $\rho(x)=\infty$ for $g(x) \notin \Lambda_g$.

4. NON CONVEX PROBLEMS

If K is not convex, the previous results apply to the convex hull [K] of K. So we have (both for Problem M and Problem CM) :

$$\inf_{y\in[K]} \rho(y) = \max_{\pi q\leq 1} -h(\pi) = d$$

$$v = \inf_{y\in K} \rho(y) \geq \max_{\pi q\leq 1} -h(\pi) = d$$

and (v-d) is the duality gap (for the particular choice of q).

We shall call the family of problems (parametrized by q)

Problem D(q)

$$\begin{array}{ll} \max & -h(\pi) \\ \text{s.t.} & \pi q\leq 1 \end{array}$$ □

the dual relaxation of Problem CM (or of Problem M), in the sense that, fc any optimal y in K there exists an optimal $\hat{y}$ in [K] given by

$$\hat{y} = d\, y \qquad \text{with} \qquad d = \max_{-\pi y\leq 1} -h(\pi)$$

More generally points of the form

$$\hat{y} = -\, d\, q = h(\pi_o)\, q$$

with d optimal value of D(q) can be called bounds for Problem CM, because they are not dominated by points in K.

The possibility of finding bounds suggests to implement a branch and bound procedure, modified in an appropriate way in order to handle the multi objective case.

The main difference consists in the presence at the same time of several incumbents and several bounds. It is assumed that the reader is acquainted with branch and bound techniques (just to quote one reference see Shapiro (1979)). In order to describe the procedure it is convenient to define the following operations on subsets $A,B \subset Y$:

$$A \dot{\cup} B = \{ y \in A \cup B : \nexists x \in A \cup B \ , x - y \in \Lambda \setminus \{0\} \}$$

$$A \dot{\sim} B = \{ y \in A : \nexists x \in A \cup B \ , x - y \in \Lambda \setminus \{0\} \}$$

Moreover let

K_k be a subset of K ($K_o=K$)

$[K_k]$ be the convex hull of K_k

Z_k be the optima in K_k

$\hat{Z}_k$ be the optima in $[K_k]$

then

$W_k = Z_k \cap \hat{Z}_k$ are the incumbents for K_k

$B_k = \hat{Z}_k \setminus W_k$ are the bounds for K_k

We shall first define an "abstract" branch and bound procedure as a general model for particular implementations.

<u>Abstract branch and bound</u>

```
     k:= 0
     h:= 0
(*)  compute  W_k, B_k
     W := W U̇ W_k
     for j:= k to h do  B_j := B_j ~̇ W
     if  B_k = Ø  then  K_k is fathomed
           else partition K_k=K_h+1 U K_h+2 U...U K_h+n
                 for j:= h+1 to h+n do  B_j:= B_k
                 h := h+n
                 k := k+1
     if ( B_j= Ø  for any  k≤j≤h ) then Stop
           else    while  B_k= Ø  do  k:=k+1
                   goto (*)
```

□

This procedure will stop in a finite number of steps if K is discrete, eventually producing $W=Z$. If K has infinite cardinality, W will approximate Z as k tends to infinity.

However an actual implementation requires W_k, B_k to be replaced by finite subsets $\bar{W}_k \subset W_k$, $\bar{B}_k \subset B_k$. Besides, as the computation goes on, a direct comparison of W and $\bar{B}_k$ could suggest not to further partition K_k , when $\bar{B}_k$ bounds "not interesting" optima. In this case $\bar{B}_k$ could be dropped. We call this operation "forced" fathoming.

By taking into account the above remarks we have :

Branch and bound for multi objective problems

k:= 0
h:= 0
(*) compute $\bar{W}_k$, $\bar{B}_k$
$W := W \dot{\cup} \bar{W}_k$
for j:= k to h do $\bar{B}_j := \bar{B}_j \dot{\sim} W$
if K_j has to be forcedly fathomed set $\bar{B}_j := \emptyset$
if $\bar{B}_k \neq \emptyset$ then partition $K_k = K_{h+1} \cup K_{h+2} \cup \ldots \cup K_{h+n}$
for j:= h+1 to h+n do $\bar{B}_j := \bar{B}_k$
h := h+n
k := k+1
if ($\bar{B}_j = \emptyset$ for any $k \leq j \leq h$) then Stop
else while $\bar{B}_k = \emptyset$ do k:=k+1
goto (*)

□

It is clear that even the above procedure is a general model. A real program requires many non trivial technical details to be worked out. This is matter of current research.

It is worth to point out that this procedure works interactively. The interaction comes in for the computation of $\bar{W}_k$ and $\bar{B}_k$ and for the forced fathoming.

REFERENCES

Luenberger, D.G. (1969). Optimization by Vector Space Methods. Wiley, New York.
Pascoletti, A. and Serafini, P. (1984). Scalarizing Vector Optimization Problems. Journal of Optimization Theory and Applications, 42 (4).
Shapiro, J.F. (1979). Mathematical Programming, Structures and Algorithms. Wiley, New York.

LEVITIN–MILJUTIN–OSMOLOVSKII CONDITIONS FOR LOCAL PARETO OPTIMALITY

Milan Vlach
Department of Operations Research and Computer Science, Charles University, Prague, Czechoslovakia

The purpose of this talk is to show that the technique developed by Levitin, Miljutin and Osmolovskii (1974, 1978) can easily be applied to optimization problems with nonscalar valued objective functions.

1. PRELIMINARIES

Let $f = \{f_i\}_{i=1}^{p}$ be a finite family of real valued functions on a topological space X. Let us define the sets B_x, B'_x and B''_x as follows:

$$B_x = \{y \in X \mid f(y) \leq f(x),\ f(y) \neq f(x)\},$$

$$B'_x = \{y \in X \mid f(y) \leq f(x),\ y \neq x\},$$

$$B''_x = \{y \in X \mid f(y) < f(x)\}.$$

Given f and a set $S \subset X$, a point $x \in X$ is called a local Pareto minimum point for (f,X) if $x \in S$ and there is a neighbourhood N_x of x such that

$$N_x \cap S \cap B_x = \emptyset. \tag{1}$$

If B_x is replaced in (1) by B'_x, then x is called a strict local Pareto minimum point for (f,S). If B_x is replaced by B''_x, then x is called a local weak Pareto minimum point for (f,S).

From now on we shall assume that X is a Banach space and S is the set of all solutions to the system

$$g(x) \leq 0,$$

$$h(x) = 0,$$

where $g = \{g_j\}_{j=1}^{q}$ is a finite family of real valued functions on X and h is a mapping of X into a Banach space Y. Let x be a point in X and let us define $f^x = \{f_i^x\}$ by

$$f_i^x(y) = f_i(y) - f_i(x), \quad i=1,2,\dots,p.$$

Let γ be a nonnegative real valued function on X continuous at 0 and such that $\gamma(0) = 0$. It is not difficult to verify that:

a) If x is a local weak Pareto minimum point for (f,S), then there are no $\varepsilon > 0$ and no sequence $\{y_n\}$ of points in X such that $y_n \to 0$ and for all n

$$f_i^x(x + y_n) + \varepsilon\gamma(y_n) < 0, \quad i=1,2,\dots,p$$

$$g_j(x + y_n) + \varepsilon\gamma(y_n) < 0, \quad j=1,2,\dots,q$$

$$h(x + y_n) = 0.$$

b) If $x \in S$ and if there is $\varepsilon > 0$ such that there is no sequence $\{y_n\}$ of nonzero points in X such that $y_n \to 0$ and for all n

$$f_i^x(x + y_n) - \varepsilon\gamma(y_n) \leq 0, \quad i=1,2,\dots,p$$

$$g_j(x + y_n) - \varepsilon\gamma(y_n) \leq 0, \quad j=1,2,\dots,q$$

$$h(x + y_n) = 0,$$

then x is a strict local Pareto minimum point for (f,S).

We recall some notions of convex analysis that will be employed in the next sections. Let F be a continuous convex function on X, let x^* be a continuous linear function on X and let $N(x^*,F)$ denote the negative of th conjugate function of F, that is

$$N(x^*,F) = \inf_{x \in X} \{F(x) - x^*(x)\}.$$

Let ∂F denote the set $\{x^* \in X^* \mid N(x^*,F) > -\infty\}$ and let η be a nonnegative number. We shall need the following set and function:

$$\partial_\eta F = \{x^* \in X^* \mid N(x^*,F) \geq F(0) - \eta\},$$

$$F^\eta = \max_{x^* \in \partial_\eta F} \{N(x^*,F) + x^*(x)\}.$$

2. LEVITIN-MILJUTIN-OSMOLOVSKII APPROXIMATIONS

The main technical tools we shall need are the approximations introduced by Levitin, Miljutin and Osmolovskii (1974, 1978). See also Ioffe (1979).

We shall say that a real valued function f on a Banach space X satisfies Levitin-Miljutin-Osmolovskii condition at $x \in X$ if there are a neighbourhood N_0 of zero and a real valued function F^x on $X \times X$ such that

(i) for every $y \in N_O$ the function $F^x(y,\cdot)$ is convex and continuous on X;

(ii) there is $M > 0$ such that $|F^x(y,z)| \leq M$ for all $y,z \in N_O$;

(iii) for every $y \in N_O$ and every $z \in X$

a) $f(x + y) = F^x(y,0)$

b) $f(x + y + z) \leq F^x(y,z) + r(y,z)\|z\|$

where $r(y,z) \to 0$ whenever $(y,z) \to 0$.

Every F^x with these properties is called an LMO-approximation of f at x.

A mapping $H^x: X \times X \to Y$ is called an LMO-linear approximation of $h: X \to Y$ at x if

(i) $H^x(y,\alpha u + \beta v) = \alpha H^x(y,u) + \beta H^x(y,v)$
for all $y,u,v \in X$ and all $\alpha,\beta \in R$, $\alpha + \beta = 1$;

(ii) H^x is bounded in a neighbourhood of 0 in $X \times X$;

(iii) for every $y,z \in X$

$h(x + y + z) = H^x(y,z) + r(y,z)\|z\|$

where $r(y,z) \to 0$ whenever $(y,z) \to 0$.

<u>Example</u>: If f is continuously F-differentiable at x, then

$$F^x(y,z) = f(x + y) + f'(x + y)z$$

and

$$F^x(y,z) = f(x + y) + f'(x)z$$

are LMO-approximations of f at x. If f is Lipschitz in a neighbourhood of x and L is a sufficiently large positive number, then

$$F^x(y,z) = f(x + y) + L\|z\|$$

is an LMO-approximation of f at x. If $h: X \to Y$ is continuously F-differentiable at x, then

$$H^x(y,z) = h(x + y) + h'(x)z \tag{2}$$

is an LMO-linear approximation of h at x. For more sophisticated examples of LMO-approximations see Levitin et al.(1974, 1978) and Ioffe (1979).

We shall say that an LMO-linear approximation H^x of h at x satisfies Ljusternik condition if it has form (2) and $h'(x)X = Y$.

Let $(B,\leq)$ be a nonempty set directed in the sense that $\leq$ is a partial order on B such that for every $\beta_1, \beta_2 \in B$ there is β_3 such that $\beta_3 \leq \beta_1$ and $\beta_3 \leq \beta_2$. A family $\{F^x\}_{\beta \in B}$ of LMO-approximations of f at x is said to be a net of LMO-approximations of f at x if there is a neighbourhood N_O such that

$$\beta_1 \leq \beta_2,\ y \in N_O,\ z \in X \Rightarrow F^x_{\beta_1}(y,z) \leq F^x_{\beta_2}(y,z).$$

3. OPTIMALITY CONDITIONS. CASE $\gamma = 0$

From now on we shall consider a problem (f,S) and a point x satisfying the following conditions:

(i) all functions f_i^x, g_j are continuous and satisfy LMO-condition at x;

(ii) the mapping h has an LMO-linear approximation at x;

(iii) $g(x) = 0$, $h(x) = 0$.

The following theorems follow from the results of Levitin, Miljutin and Osmolovskii (1978).

Theorem 1

If (a) x is a local weak Pareto minimum point for (f,S);

(b) $\{F_i^x\}_{\beta \in B}$ $i=1,2,\ldots,p$

$\{G_j^x\}_{\beta \in B}$ $j=1,2,\ldots,q$

are nets of LMO-approximations of f_i^x and g_j at x;

(c) H^x is an LMO-linear approximation of h at x satisfying Ljusternik-condition;

then for every $\beta \in B$ and every $\eta > 0$ there is $\rho > 0$ such that the following system has no solution in X x X:

$$\|y\| < \rho,\ \|z\| < \rho,\ H^x(y,z) = 0,$$

$$F^{x\eta}_{i\beta}(y,z) + \eta\|z\| < 0, \quad i=1,2,\ldots,p$$

$$G^{x\eta}_{j\beta}(y,z) + \eta\|z\| < 0, \quad j=1,2,\ldots,q.$$

To dualize these necessary conditions we consider the space Z of all $\lambda = (\alpha,\beta,u,v,w)$ where $\alpha \in R^p$, $\beta \in R^q$, $u \in (X^*)^p$, $v \in (X^*)^q$ and $w \in Y$. The set $\{\lambda \in Z \mid \alpha \geq 0,\ \beta \geq 0\}$ will be denoted by Z^+. Given $y \in X$, $\eta > 0$, nets $\{F^x_{i\beta}\}$, $\{G^x_{j\beta}\}$ and H^x satisfying Ljusternik condition, the set $\Lambda^\beta_\eta(y)$ is defined as the set of all $\lambda \in Z^+$ such that

$$u_i \in \partial_\eta F^x_{i\beta}(y,\cdot), \quad i=1,2,\ldots,p$$

$$v_j \in \partial_\eta G^x_{j\beta}(y,\circ), \quad j=1,2,\dots,q$$

$$\Sigma\alpha_i + \Sigma\beta_j + \|w\| = 1,$$

$$\|\Sigma\alpha_i u_i + \Sigma\beta_j v_j + wh'(x)\| \leq \eta.$$

We shall also define the following functions:

$$\varphi(y,\lambda,\beta) = \Sigma\alpha_i N(u_i,F^x_{i\beta}(y,\cdot)) + \Sigma\beta_j N(v_j,G^x_{j\beta}(y,\cdot) + w(h(x+y)),$$

$$\phi^\beta_\eta(y) = \sup_{\lambda\in\Lambda^\beta_\eta(y)} \varphi(y,\lambda,\beta).$$

Theorem 2

If (a), (b) and (c) of the previous theorem hold, then for every $\beta \in B$ and $\eta > 0$ there is a neighbourhood N_0 of zero such that

$$\phi^\beta_\eta(y) \geq 0 \quad \text{for all } y \in N_0.$$

Theorem 3

If (b) and (c) of theorem 1 hold, then x is a strict local Pareto minimum point for (f,S) if and only if for every $\beta \in B$, $\eta > 0$ and every sequence $\{y_n\}$ of nonzero points converging to zero there is n_0 such that

$$\phi^\beta_\eta(y_n) > 0 \quad \text{for all } n > n_0.$$

4. HIGHER-ORDER OPTIMALITY CONDITIONS

In addition to the previous assumptions on γ we shall assume that γ is Lipschitz in a neighbourhood of zero and such that $\gamma(y) > 0$ whenever $y \neq 0$.

Theorem 4

If (a), (b) and (c) of theorem 1 hold, then for every $\beta \in B$ and $\eta > 0$

$$\inf \varliminf_{n\to\infty} \frac{\phi^\beta_\eta(y_n)}{\gamma(y_n)} \geq 0 \tag{3}$$

where infimum is taken over all sequences $\{y_n\}$ of nonzero elements converging to zero.

Theorem 5

If (b) and (c) of theorem 1 hold and if for every $\beta \in B$ and $\eta > 0$ the inequality (3) is strict, then x is a strict local Pareto minimum point for (f,S).

References

Ioffe, A.D. (1979). Necessary and sufficient conditions for a local minimum, 2: Conditions of Levitin-Miljutin-Osmolovskii type. SIAM J. Control and Optimization, Vol 17: 251-265

Levitin, E.S., Miljutin, A.A., and Osmolovskii, N.P. (1974). On conditions for a local minimum in a problem with constraints. Mathematical Economic and Functional Analysis, Mitjagin, ed., Nauka, Moscow: 139-202 (In Russi

Levitin, E.S., Miljutin, A.A., and Osmolovskii, N.P. (1978). Higher order con ditions for a local minimum in problems with constraints. Uspechi Matemat. Nauk XXXIII, 6(204): 85-148 (In Russian).

FUZZY ASSESSMENT OF MULTIATTRIBUTE UTILITY FUNCTIONS

Fumiko Seo[1] and Masatoshi Sakawa[2]
[1] *Kyoto Institute of Economic Research, Kyoto University, Kyoto, Japan*
[2] *Department of Systems Engineering, Kobe University, Kobe, Japan*

1. INTRODUCTION

This paper is concerned with deriving fuzzy multiattribute utility functions (FMUF) based on extensions of the fuzzy set theory. The general procedure of assessing the MUF is composed of three steps; (i) evaluating unidimensional (single-attribute) utility functions (UNIF), (ii) assessing the scaling constants k_i, K on them and (iii) obtaining representation forms of the MUFs. The step (i) corresponds to the lowest-level system's decomposition in which preferential and utility independence among the attributes are assumed. In the step (ii), system's coordination is executed from the societal point of view and value trade-off experiments among the attributes are performed. The step (iii) is simply concerned with formal representation and calculation of numerical (viz. cardinal) MUFs. This method has shown to be particularly useful for manipulating noncommensurateness and conflict of the multidimensional objective systems. The main limitation of this method is to neglect multiple agent problems. The evaluation is exclusively based on individual preferences of the single decision maker. The method ultimately have some individual assert a set of preference as "socially" desirable. Collective choice or group decision problems are not taken into considerations.

This paper intends to fuzzify the value assessment in the step (ii), the coordination process, by including the social choice problems. In the step (ii), fuzzification can be performed twofold: before and after the value trade-off experiments among attributes. First before the experiments, objects (attributes) should be compared with each other and a preference ordering should be found. In this process, a fuzzy preference ordering due to diversified evaluations can be explicitly considered and defuzzified. With this device, a non-fuzzy social preference ordering can be derived. Then according to the derived preference ordering, the value trade-off experiments can be executed consistently to find the indifferent point x_{sx} in the following.

$$u(x_{i1}, x_{s0}) = u(x_{i0}, x_{sx}) \tag{1}$$

From the representation theorem [Keeney and Raiffa 1976] and (1),

$$k_i = k_s u_s(x_{sx}) \quad \text{or} \quad k_i/k_s = u_s(x_{sx}),\ i = 1,\dots,m,\ i \neq s. \tag{2}$$

Second, after the value trade-off experiments, a numerical value of the scaling constant k_s for the utility function u_s of the most preferable attribute x_s should be assessed. In this process, a specific chance lotte technique is used, and the probability can be assessed as a fuzzy number. Finally, using the algebraic operations on the fuzzy numbers, the FMUF can b derived and calculated.

In the following sections, basic concepts for fuzzy preference relation [Zadeh 1971] are reviewed and discussed in relation to a general procedure for evaluating the FMUF (Section II). Then operations on fuzzy numbers are discussed for obtainning numerical values of parameters (scaling constants) of the FMUFs (Section III). Finally a brief summary of the method is provid and some illustrations to evaluate the FMUF are presented with a computer assistance (Section IV and Appendix).

2. FUZZY PREFERENCE RELATIONS AND FUZZY ORDERING

A fuzzy binary relation R is defined with a fuzzy set of ordered pair of objects (attributes) in a set A. Thus the fuzzy (preference) relation R ($\succ$ or $\sim$) is a fuzzy subset of $X \times Y$ characterized by a membership function μ_R which associates with each pair (x, y), $x \in X$, $y \in Y$, its "grade of membership" $\mu_R(x, y)$ in R. We can simply assume that the numbe of $\mu_R(x, y)$ takes a range of interval [0, 1]; which represents the strength of a preference relation between x and y.

Properties of the fuzzy preference relation are defined with the member ship function $\mu_R(x, y)$ for all $x \in X$ and $y \in Y$ in dom R as follows.

(i) connectivity: $x \neq y \Rightarrow \mu_R(x, y) > 0$ or $\mu_R(y, x) > 0.$ (3)

(ii) reflexivity: $\mu_R(x, x) = 1.$ (4)

(iii) symmetry: $\mu_R(x, y) = \mu_R(y, x).$ (5)

(iv) transitivity: $R \supset R \circ R.$ (6)

where $\circ$ denotes a twofold composition. In alternative expression,

$$\mu_R(x, z) \geq \bigvee_y (\mu_R(x, y) \wedge \mu_R(y, z)) \quad (7)$$

(v) antisymmetry: $\mu_R(x, y) > 0$ and $\mu_R(y, x) > 0 \Rightarrow x = y$. (8)

Using those properties of the fuzzy preference relations, classes of th fuzzy preference ordering are defined as follows:

(a) fuzzy preordering (or fuzzy quasi-ordering): reflexive and transitive.
(b) fuzzy partial ordering: reflexive, transitive and anti-symmetric.
(c) fuzzy linear ordering: connective, transitive and antisymmetric.
(d) fuzzy weak ordering (complete ordering or total ordering): connective and transitive.

The fuzzy preference ordering can be used in any permutation operation on the objects for social choice. In other words, social preference pattern can be generated by a permutation mapping $\psi : A \rightarrow A$. This permutation operation can be used for constructing a non-fuzzy social preference orderin among attributes.

First a hierarchical structure of the fuzzy preference ordering can be considered in resolution of the fuzzy binary relation R into a union of several non-fuzzy sets. For a number α in [0, 1], an α-level set R_α of a fuzzy relation R is defined by

$$R_\alpha = \{(x, y) \mid \mu_R(x, y) \geq \alpha\} \tag{9}$$

The R_α is a non-fuzzy set in $X \times Y$ and those sets form a nested sequence of non-fuzzy relations with $\alpha_i \geq \alpha_j \Rightarrow R_{\alpha_i} \subset R_{\alpha_j}$.

The α is interpreted as an agreement level in social choice. The proposition is stated with this decomposition device.

Proposition 1 [Zadeh]

Any fuzzy relation in $X \times Y$ admits of the resolution

$$R = \sum_\alpha \alpha R_\alpha, \quad 0 < \alpha \leq 1 \tag{10}$$

where $\sum_\alpha$ stands for the union $\bigcup_\alpha$ and αR_α denotes a subnormal non-fuzzy set defined by

$$\mu_{\alpha R_\alpha}(x, y) = \alpha \mu_{R_\alpha}(x, y) \tag{11}$$

or equivalently

$$\mu_{\alpha R_\alpha}(x, y) = \begin{cases} \alpha & \text{for } (x, y) \in R_\alpha \\ 0 & \text{otherwise} \end{cases} \tag{12}$$

For the resolution of a fuzzy preference relation to subnormal non-fuzzy subsets, a relation matrix for μ_R can be constructed. For instance, consider an objects (attributes) set $X = (x_1, x_2, x_3, x_4) \subseteq A$, and assume a simple majority rule for n voters [Blin and Whinston 1974]. Let $O = \{O_{ij}\}$ denote a fuzzy set of preference ordering between x_i and x_j, and $N(O)$ is a number of a score (vote). The majority rule can be represented as

$$\mu_R(x_i, x_j) = \frac{1}{n} N(O), \quad n = 20 \text{ (number of voters).} \tag{13}$$

Assume that the following score sheet has obtained in collective choice:

$$\begin{aligned}
&O_1 = (x_1, x_2, x_3, x_4),\ N(O_1) = 4; \quad O_6 = (x_3, x_1, x_4, x_2),\ N(O_6) = 1 \\
&O_2 = (x_1, x_2, x_4, x_3),\ N(O_2) = 2; \quad O_7 = (x_1, x_3, x_2, x_4),\ N(O_7) = 3 \\
&O_3 = (x_2, x_1, x_3, x_4),\ N(O_3) = 2; \quad O_8 = (x_4, x_1, x_2, x_3),\ N(O_8) = 2 \\
&O_4 = (x_2, x_1, x_4, x_3),\ N(O_4) = 1; \quad O_9 = (x_4, x_1, x_3, x_2),\ N(O_9) = 1 \\
&O_5 = (x_3, x_1, x_2, x_4),\ N(O_5) = 2; \quad O_{10} = (x_2, x_4, x_3, x_1),\ N(O_{10}) = 2
\end{aligned} \tag{14}$$

The problem is to find a non-fuzzy social preference ordering from the fuzzy set $O = \{O_{ij}\}$ obtained as a result of the collective choice. The collective choice (14) will derive a relation matrix for the fuzzy social preference relation on $X_i \times X_j$, $i \neq j$, $i,j = 1,\ldots,4$, as follows.

$$\mu_R = \begin{matrix} & 1 & 2 & 3 & 4 \\ 1 & 0 & .75 & .75 & .7 \\ 2 & .25 & 0 & .65 & .8 \\ 3 & .25 & .35 & 0 & .6 \\ 4 & .25 & .2 & .4 & 0 \end{matrix} \tag{15}$$

It is shown that the relation matrix (15) represents the connectivity but intransitivity has occured in triples (x_1, x_2, x_4), (x_4, x_1, x_2) and (x_4, x_3, x_2). It means that the fuzzy preference ordering includes some contradiction. For ensuring the transitivity, the strength (viz. characteristic values) of the binary relations (x_i, x_4) and (x_4, x_2) in (15) must be reexamined and the relation matrix should be interactively revised to obtain

$$\mu_R' = \begin{bmatrix} 0 & .75 & .75 & .75 \\ .25 & 0 & .65 & .8 \\ .25 & .35 & 0 & .6 \\ .25 & .35 & .4 & 0 \end{bmatrix} \tag{16}$$

Now it is found that the μ_R' ensures the transitivity and represents the weak ordering (complete or total ordering). If the revised values are acceptable to the assessors, a non-fuzzy relation matrix representing a social preference ordering has been obtained. In other words, by decomposing a fuzzy set of social preference orderings (14) into an union of its α-level sets, we can derive a non-fuzzy set characterized with the weak ordering as follows.

$$\begin{aligned} R_{\alpha=.8} &= (x_2, x_4) \\ R_{\alpha=.7} &= R_{\alpha=.8} \cup ((x_1, x_2), (x_1, x_3), (x_1, x_4)) \\ R_{\alpha=.6} &= R_{\alpha=.7} \cup ((x_2, x_3), (x_3, x_4)) \\ R_{\alpha=.4} &= R_{\alpha=.6} \cup (x_4, x_3) \\ R_{\alpha=.3} &= R_{\alpha=.4} \cup (x_3, x_2) \\ R_{\alpha=.2} &= R_{\alpha=.3} \cup ((x_2, x_1), (x_3, x_1), (x_4, x_1), (x_4, x_2)) \end{aligned} \tag{17}$$

If the relation matrix is a partially ordered set, an extension of the Szpilrajn theorem [Baer and Østerby 1969] guarantees the existence of a mapping σ of the fuzzy partially ordered set X^P onto a fuzzy linear-order set X^L [Zadeh 1971].

Now we can construct the most agreeable preference ordering for the objects (attributes) set $X = (x_1, x_2, x_3, x_4) \subset A$. For this purpose, classes of the weak (total) ordering set (16) are defined corresponding to the α-level decompositions (17):

$$\left.\begin{aligned} C_1 &= (x_2, x_4) && \ldots \text{ level } .8 \\ C_2 &= ((x_1, x_2), (x_1, x_3), (x_1, x_4)) && \ldots \text{ level } .7 \end{aligned}\right\} \tag{18}$$

$C_3 = ((x_2, x_3), (x_3, x_4))$ ... level .6

Taking the intersection, we can find a single ordering

$$C_1 \cap C_2 \cap C_3 = (x_1, x_2, x_3, x_4) \tag{19}$$

or in another expression

$$x_1 \succ x_2 \succ x_3 \succ x_4 , \tag{20}$$

which can be called the weak ordered non-fuzzy solution to our problem in the level 0.6. Or preferably, using the membership function $\mu_{C_1 \cap C_2 \cap C_3}(x, y) = .6$, we can say about (20) "the degree or strength of agreement is 0.6.".

With this device, the range and degree of disagreement which is included in the first phase of the step (ii) also can be ascertained. For instance, counter-ordering classes can be obtained from the α-level set (17):

$$\left.\begin{array}{ll} C_1' = (x_4, x_3) & \text{... level .4} \\ C_2' = (x_3, x_2) & \text{... level .3} \\ C_3' = ((X_2, x_1), (x_3, x_1), (x_4, x_1), (x_4, x_2)) & \text{... level .2} \end{array}\right\} \tag{21}$$

Taking the intersection,

$$C_1' \cap C_2' \cap C_3' = (x_4, x_3, x_2, x_1). \tag{22}$$

Then we can say about the social preference ordering (20) "it is disagreeable in level 0.4" or preferably, using the membership function $\mu_{C_1' \cap C_2' \cap C_3'}(x_i, x_j) = 0.25$, "the degree or strength of disagreement is .25".

After constructing the best-compromized social preference ordering (20) with the above reservations, the value trade-off experiments between each pair of attributes can be executed and relative ratios of the scaling constants are obtained.

3. OPERATIONS FOR ASSESSING THE FUZZY SCALING CONSTANTS AND DERIVING FMUF

Now the second phase of the fuzzification process in the step (ii) should be examined. After obtaining the relative values k_i/k_s of the scaling constants in (2), a numerical value of k_s for the utility function $u_s(x_s)$ of the most preferable attribute should be determined. For that purpose, an indifference experiment on m objects (attributes) can be executed answering the following question:

<u>Question</u> Let consider a lottery which will take alternatively with a probability p_s the best values x_{i1} for all the attributes i, i = 1,..., m, or with a probability $1 - p_s$ the worst values x_{i0}, i = 1,...,m, for all the ones. On the other hand, let consider a certain consequence in which the most preferable attribute takes its best value x_{s1} and the other ones take

their worst values $\{x_{\bar{s}0}\}$, $\bar{s} = 1, \ldots, s-1, s+1, \ldots, m$. Then what is the numerical value of the probability p_s with which the lottery and the certai consequence will become indifferent?

The fuzzification device here is to take the probability p_s as a fuzzy number $\tilde{p}_s = (\bar{p}_s, \beta, \gamma)$, where $\bar{p}_s$ denotes a mean value of $\tilde{p}_s$ and β and γ denote respectively the left and right-side spreads from $\bar{p}_s$. The parameters β, γ and $\bar{p}_s$ can be obtained as minimum, maximum and medium evaluations of the probability p_s in the collective choice or the group decision making. Then the scaling constant k_s can be assessed by

$$\tilde{p}_s = \tilde{k}_s = (\bar{k}_s, \beta, \gamma). \tag{23}$$

We can take the L-R type of fuzzy numbers and perform the algebraic operations on them [Dubois and Prade 1978]. The corresponding utility value u_s in (2) can be also reexamined as a fuzzy number $\tilde{u}_s = (\bar{u}_s, \delta, \eta)$, where the parameters δ, η and $\bar{u}_s$ are obtained respectively as minimum, maximum and medium values of reevaluations in the group decision making. With those fuzzy numbers $\tilde{k}_s$ and $\tilde{u}_s$, all the fuzzy scaling constants $\tilde{k}_i$, $i = 1, \ldots, i \neq s$, in (2) can be obtained.

The fuzzification of the scaling constants will have some effects on choosing the representation forms (multiplicative or additive) of the MUFs. Thus the following check should be performed.

$$\begin{aligned}
&\text{(a)} \quad \text{if} \quad \sum_{i=1}^{m} \tilde{k}_i > 1, \qquad \text{then} \quad -1 < K < 0 \text{ (multiplicative)} \\
&\text{(b)} \quad \text{if} \quad \sum_{i=1}^{m} \tilde{k}_i < 1, \qquad \text{then} \quad K > 0 \text{ (multiplicative)} \\
&\text{(c)} \quad \text{if} \quad \sum_{i=1}^{m} \tilde{k}_i = 1, \qquad \text{then} \quad K = 0 \text{ (additive)}
\end{aligned} \tag{24}$$

Because the scaling constant k_i is a fuzzy number, the assertion (> and <) for that is still fuzzy. Thus it should be asked that what the truth value of the assertion " $\sum_{i=1}^{m} \tilde{k}_i$ is greater (or smaller) than 1" is. The separation theorem of two fuzzy sets [Zadeh 1965, Dubois and Prade 1980] is applied to the comparison of the fuzzy numbers $\sum_{i}^{m} \tilde{k}_i$ and $\tilde{1} = (1, 0, 0)$. The separation theorem asserts that when M is the maximal grade of the intersection of two bounded convex fuzzy sets, the degree of separation D of those sets is obtained by $D = 1 - M$. For making an answer to the questic we can choose a threshold level θ. If $M > \theta$ then it is called that $\sum_{i=1}^{m} \tilde{k}_i = \tilde{1}$ in level θ. The FMUF can be represented in the following forms.

additive

$$\tilde{U}(x_1,\ldots, x_m) = \sum_{i=1}^{m} \tilde{k}_i \tilde{u}_i(x_i) \tag{25}$$

multiplicative

$$1 + K\tilde{U}(x_1,\ldots, x_m)= \sum_{i=1}^{m} (K\tilde{k}_i \tilde{u}_i(x_i) + 1), \tag{26}$$

The values of FMUF are calculated for alternative policies in which different numerical values of attributes x_i, $i = 1,\ldots,m$, are assigned. The values of the single-attribute utility function $u_i(x_i)$, $i = 1,\ldots,m$, $i \neq s$, can be assessed as the fuzzy number $\tilde{u}_i = (\bar{u}_i, 0, 0)$ or $\tilde{u}_i = (\bar{u}_i, \xi, \nu)$ where $\bar{u}_i$, ξ and ν are also determined from the reevaluation by the collective decision making. Based on the assessment of FMUF for the alternative policies A, B, C, D, a preference relation is found. For instance,

$$\tilde{U}(C) > \tilde{U}(B) > \tilde{U}(A) > \tilde{U}(D) \quad \Leftrightarrow \quad C \succ B \succ A \succ D \tag{27}$$

Because the comparison (27) on the fuzzy number $\tilde{U}$ is still fuzzy, the previous procedure for ascertaining if $\tilde{U}(C)$ is truly larger than $\tilde{U}(B)$, etc. should be applied here again. Thus the priority of the best prefered policy C can be confirmed with the threshold level θ.

4. CONCLUDING REMARKS

The fuzzification of the multiattribute utility analysis can be considered with its social-choice extensions. Evaluations for the fuzzy preference ordering and the fuzzy number operations can be executed meaningfully in the context of collective decision making. Although many steps of those evaluations still depend on subjective man-to-man experiments, computer programs are available in some aspects for interactive repetitions of assessment and calculations. ICOPSS/F has been newly developed for the fuzzy number operations in the process of deriving the FMUF based on ICOPSS/I [Sakawa and Seo 1981]. FKSET command assigns the fuzzy scaling constants and determines the K. FEVAL command assesses the FMUF and GRAPHF command displays graphically the FMUF values for the best two alternatives as the fuzzy numbers; which would largely facilitate the fuzzy comparison and evaluations. Some illustrations of the computer program ICOPSS/F for the interactive fuzzy decision making are provided in Appendix.

REFERENCE

Baer, R.M. and Østerby, O. (1969). Algorithms over partially ordered sets, BIT, 9:97-118.

Blin, J.M. and Whinston, A.B. (1974). Fuzzy sets and social choice. Journal of Cybernetics, 3(4):28-36.

Blin, J.M. (1974). Fuzzy relations in group decision theory. Journal of Cybernetics, 4(2):17-22.

Dubois, D. and Prade, H. (1978). Operations on fuzzy numbers. International Journal of Systems Science, 9(6):613-626.

Dubois, D. and Prade, H. (1980). Systems of linear fuzzy constraints.

Fuzzy Sets and Systems, 3:37-48.
Keeney, R.L. and Raiffa, H. (1976). Decisions with Multiple Objectives, Preferences and Value Tradeoffs. John Wiley, New York.
Sakawa, M. and Seo, F. (1982). Integrated methodology for computer-aided decision analysis. in T. Robert, F. de P. Hanika and R. Tomlinson (Ed. Progress in Cybernetics and Systems Research. 10:333-341.
Zadeh, L.A. (1965). Fuzzy sets. Information and Control, 8:338-353.
Zadeh, L.A. (1971). Similarity relations and fuzzy orderings. Information Sciences, 3:177-200.

APPENDIX Demonstrations of ICOPSS/F

Illustration 1.

```
COMMAND:
=FKSET
INPUT MNAME:
=KIPAFWT
INPUT FUZZY P SUCH THAT
  LOTTERY --- ALL ARE BEST WITH PROBABILITY FUZZY P
          !- ALL ARE WORST WITH PROBABILITY FUZZY 1-P
AND
  CERTAINTY CONSEQUENCE --- KIPAFWTN IS BEST
                         !- THE OTHERS ARE WORST
ARE INDIFFERENT (MEAN,SPREAD) :
=0.90 0.005
```

Illustration 2.

```
COMMAND:
=GRAPHF
INPUT TWO ALT NAMES :
=ALT1 ALT3
  1.00+---------O---------X---------!---------!---------+
      !                                                 !
      !                                                 !
      !        O  O     X  X                            !
      !                                                 !
      !                                                 !
      !      O     O   X     X                          !
      !                                                 !
      !                                                 !
      !     O        #        X                         !
  0.50-                                                 -
      !   O         X O         X                       !
      !                                                 !
      !                                                 !
      !  O        X     O        X                      !
      !                                                 !
      !                                                 !
      !O         X       O         X                    !
      !                                                 !
      !                                                 !
  0.  O---------X---------!O--------X---------!---------+
   7.3018    7.5018    7.7018    7.9018    8.1018    8.3018
      (10E-1)
```

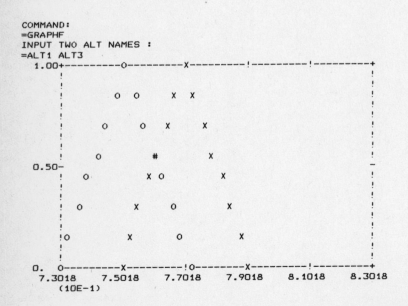

INTERACTIVE FUZZY DECISION MAKING FOR MULTIOBJECTIVE NONLINEAR PROGRAMMING PROBLEMS

Masatoshi Sakawa
Department of Systems Engineering, Kobe University, Kobe, Japan

1. INTRODUCTION

An application of fuzzy approach to multiobjective linear programming (MOLP) problems was first presented by Zimmermann (1978) and further studied by Leberling (1981) and Hannan (1981). Following the maximizing decision proposed by Bellman and Zadeh (1970) together with linear, hyperbolic or piecewise linear membership functions, they proved that there exists an equivalent linear programming problem.

However, suppose that the interaction with the decision maker (DM) establishes that the first membership function should be linear, the second hyperbolic, the third piecewise linear and so forth. In such a situation, the resulting problem becomes a nonlinear programming problem and cannot be solved by a linear programming technique.

In order to overcome such difficulties, Sakawa (1983) has proposed a new method by combined use of bisection method and linear programming method together with five types of membership functions; linear, exponential, hyperbolic , hyperbolic inverse and piecewise linear functions. This method was further extended for solving multiobjective linear fractional programming (MOLFP) problems (Sakawa and Yumine 1983).

In this paper, assuming that the DM has fuzzy goals for each of the objective functions in multiobjective nonlinear programming (MONLP) problems, the fuzzy goals of the DM are quantified using the same kind of membership functions. Then by selecting one of the three possible fuzzy decisions, the compromise solution of the DM can be derived from among fuzzy or nonfuzzy Pareto optimal solutions, where fuzzy Pareto optimal solutions are introduced to deal with the fuzzy goal like "z should be in the vicinity of C". On the basis of the proposed method, a time-sharing computer program is written in FORTRAN and an illustrative numerical example is demonstrated together with the computer outputs.

2. INTERACTIVE FUZZY DECISION MAKING

In general, the multiobjective nonlinear programming (MONLP) problem is represented as

$$\left.\begin{aligned} &\min \; f(x) \triangleq (f_1(x), f_2(x), \ldots, f_k(x))^T \\ &\text{subject to} \quad x \in X \subseteq E^n \end{aligned}\right\} \quad (1)$$

where $f_1, \ldots, f_k$ are k distinct objective functions of the decision vector x and X is the feasible set of constrained decisions. Here, it is assumed that all f_i, $i=1,\ldots,n$ are convex and differentiable and constraint set X is convex and compact.

Fundamental to the MONLP is the Pareto optimal concept, also known as a noninferior solution. Usually, Pareto optimal solutions consist of an infinite number of points, and some kinds of subjective judgement should be added to the quantitative analyses by the DM. The DM must select his compromise solution from among Pareto optimal solutions.

In order to determine the compromise solution of the DM, there are three major approaches:

(1) goal programming (e.g. Charnes and Cooper (1977)).

(2) interactive approach (e.g. Geoffrion et al. (1972), Haimes et al. (1975), Zionts and Wallenius (1976), Wierzbicki (1979), Sakawa (1982)).

(3) fuzzy approach (e.g. Zimmermann (1978), Hannan (1981), Sakawa (1983)).

Each of these approaches has its own advantages and disadvantages relative to the other approaches.

In this paper, considering that the DM may have fuzzy goals for each of the objective functions, we adopt the fuzzy approach. In a minimization problem, a fuzzy goal stated by the DM may be to achieve "substantially less" than A. This type of statement can be quantified by eliciting a corresponding membership function.

In order to elicit a membership function $\mu_{f_i}(x)$ from the DM for each of the objective functions $f_i(x)$, we first calculate the individual minimum f_i^{min} and maximum f_i^{max} of each objective function $f_i(x)$ under given constraints. By taking account of the calculated individual minimum and maximum of each objective function, the DM must select his membership function in a subjective manner from among the following five types of functions; linear, exponential, hyperbolic, hyperbolic inverse and piecewise linear functions. Then the parameter values are determined through the interaction with the DM. Here, except for TYPE 3, it is assumed that $\mu_{f_i}(x) = 0$ if $f_i(x) \geqq f_i^0$ and $\mu_{f_i}(x) = 1$ if $f_i(x) \leqq f_i^1$, where f_i^0 is a worst acceptable level for $f_i(x)$ and f_i^1 is a totally desirable level for $f_i(x)$.

(1) Linear membership function (TYPE 1)

$$\mu_{f_i}(x) = [f_i(x) - f_i^0]/[f_i^1 - f_i^0]. \tag{2}$$

The linear membership function can be determined by asking the DM to specify the two points f_i^0 and f_i^1 within f_i^{max} and f_i^{min}.

(2) Exponential membership function (TYPE 2)

$$\mu_{f_i}(x) = a_i[1 - \exp\{- b_i(f_i(x) - f_i^0)/(f_i^1 - f_i^0)\}] \tag{3}$$

where $a_i > 1$, $b_i > 0$ or $a_i < 0$, $b_i < 0$.

The exponential membership function can be determined by asking the DM to specify the three points f_i^0, $f_i^{0.5}$ and f_i^1 within f_i^{max} and f_i^{min}, where f_i^a represents the value of $f_i(x)$ such that the degree of membership function $\mu_{f_i}(x)$ is a.

(3) Hyperbolic membership function (TYPE 3)

$$\mu_{f_i}(x) = (1/2) \tanh ((f_i(x) - b_i)\alpha_i) + (1/2). \qquad (4)$$

The hyperbolic membership function can be determined by asking the DM to specify the two points $f_i^{0.25}$ and $f_i^{0.5}$ within f_i^{max} and f_i^{min}.

(4) Hyperbolic inverse membership function (TYPE 4)

$$\mu_{f_i}(x) = a_i \tanh^{-1}((f_i(x) - b_i)\alpha_i) + (1/2). \qquad (5)$$

The hyperbolic inverse membership function can be determined by asking the DM to specify the three points f_i^0, $f_i^{0.25}$ and $f_i^{0.5}$ within f_i^{max} and f_i^{min}.

(5) Piecewise linear membership function (TYPE 5)

$$\mu_{f_i}(x) = \sum_{j=1}^{N_i} \alpha_{ij} |f_i(x) - g_{ij}| + \beta_i f_i(x) + \gamma_i. \qquad (6)$$

Here, it is assumed that $\mu_{f_i}(x) = t_{ir} f_i(x) + s_{ir}$ for each segment $g_{ir-1} \leqq f_i(x) \leqq g_{ir}$. The piecewise linear membership function can be determined by asking the DM to specify the degree of membership in each of several values of objective functions within f_i^{max} and f_i^{min}.

After determining the membership functions for each of the objective functions, the DM must select one of the following three possible fuzzy decisions:

(1) a fuzzy decision given by:

$$\min_{1 \leqq i \leqq k} (\mu_{f_i}(x), \mu_{f_2}(x), \ldots, \mu_{f_k}(x)). \qquad (7)$$

(2) a convex-fuzzy decision given by:

$$\sum_{i=1}^{k} \alpha_i \mu_{f_i}(x) \qquad \sum_{i=1}^{k} \alpha_i = 1, \quad \alpha_i \geqq 0. \qquad (8)$$

(3) a product-fuzzy decision given by :

$$\prod_{i=1}^{k} \mu_{f_i}(x). \qquad (9)$$

In every case, following the maximizing decision which maximizes one of the three fuzzy decisions, the compromise solution of the DM can be derived.

If the DM selects a fuzzy decision, the resulting problem to be solved is equivalent to solving the following problem:

$$\max_{x \in X} \lambda \quad \text{subject to} \quad \lambda \leqq \mu_{f_i}(x),\ i = 1,\ldots,k \tag{10}$$

If the DM selects a convex-fuzzy decision, the problem to be solved is:

$$\max_{x \in X} \sum_{i=1}^{k} \alpha_i \mu_{f_i}(x) \tag{11}$$

If the DM selects a product-fuzzy decision, the problem to be solved becomes:

$$\max_{x \in X} \prod_{i=1}^{k} \mu_{f_i}(x) \tag{12}$$

The relationships between the optimal solutions of the above three types of problems and the Pareto optimal concept of the MONLP can be characterized by the following theorem.

<u>Theorem 1</u>

(1) If x^* is a unique optimal solution to (10), then x^* is a Pareto optimal solution to the MONLP.

(2) If x^* is an optimal solution to (11) with $0 < \mu_{f_i}(x^*) < 1$ holding for all i, then x^* is a Pareto optimal solution to the MONLP.

(3) If x^* is an optimal solution to (12) with $0 < \mu_{f_i}(x^*) < 1$ holding for all i, then x^* is a Pareto optimal solution to the MONLP.

If x^* is an optimal solution to (10), (11), or (12), and if none of the sufficiency conditions for Pareto optimality in Theorem 1 are satisfied, then we can test the Pareto optimality for x^* by solving the following problem:

$$\left.\begin{aligned} &\max_{x \in X} \sum_{i=1}^{k} \varepsilon_i \\ &\text{subject to } f_i(x) + \varepsilon_i = f_i(x^*),\quad \varepsilon_i \geqq 0 \quad (i = 1,\ldots,k). \end{aligned}\right\} \tag{13}$$

Let $\bar{x}$ be an optimal solution to (13). If all $\varepsilon_i = 0$, then x^* is a Pareto optimal solution. If at least one $\varepsilon_i > 0$, we adopt the solution $\bar{x}$ as the compromise solution of the DM, because it can easily be shown that $\bar{x}$ is a Pareto optimal solution.

So far we have considered a minimization problem and consequently assumed that the DM has a fuzzy goal such as "$f_i(x)$ should be substantially less than a_i". In the followings, we further consider a more general case where the DM has two types of fuzzy goals, namely fuzzy goals expressed in words such as "$f_i(x)$ should be in the vicinity of b_i" (fuzzy equal) as well as "$f_i(x)$ should be substantially less than a_i" (fuzzy min) are assumed.

Therefore, the problem to be solved is:

$$\left.\begin{array}{ll} \text{fuzzy min} \quad f_i(x) \quad (i \in I) & \\ & I \cup \bar{I} = \{1, 2, \ldots, k\} \\ \text{fuzzy equal} \; f_i(x) \quad (i \in \bar{I}) & \\ \text{subject to} \qquad x \in X. & \end{array}\right\} \quad (14)$$

In order to elicit a membership function from the DM for a fuzzy goal like "$f_i(x)$ should be in the vicinity of b_i", it is obvious that we can use different functions to the left and right sides of b_i. In this case, the DM can select his left and right functions from among the same kind of membership functions described previously (excluding TYPE 3).

After determining the membership functions for two types of fuzzy goals, the compromise solution of the DM can be derived by solving one of the three types of problems (10), (11) and (12) according to the DM's decision.

Now, we introduce the concept of fuzzy Pareto optimal solutions which is defined in terms of membership functions instead of objective functions.

Definition 1 (A Fuzzy Pareto Optimal Solution)

A decision $\hat{x}$ is said to be a fuzzy Pareto optimal solution to (14), if and only if there does not exist another $x \in X$ so that $\mu_{f_i}(x) \geq \mu_{f_i}(\hat{x})$, $i = 1,\ldots,k$, with strict inequality holding for at least one i.

Note that the set of Pareto optimal solutions is a subset of the set of fuzzy Pareto optimal solutions.

Using the concept of fuzzy Pareto optimality, the following fuzzy version of Theorem 1 can be obtained under slightly different conditions.

Theorem 2

(1) If x^* is a unique optimal solution to (10), then x^* is a fuzzy Pareto optimal solution to (14).

(2) If x^* is an optimal solution to (11), then x^* is a fuzzy Pareto optimal solution to (14).

(3) If x^* is an optimal solution to (12) with $\mu_{f_i}(x^*) \neq 0$ holding for all i, then x^* is a fuzzy Pareto optimal solution to (14).

Similar to the minimization case, a numerical test of fuzzy Pareto optimality for x^* can be preformed by solving the following problem:

$$\left.\begin{array}{ll} \max\limits_{x \in X} \; \sum\limits_{i=1}^{k} \varepsilon_i & \\ \text{subject to} \quad \mu_{f_i}(x) - \varepsilon_i = \mu_{f_i}(x^*), \quad \varepsilon_i \geq 0 \quad (i = 1,\ldots,k). & \end{array}\right\} \quad (15)$$

Let $\bar{x}$ be an optimal solution to (15). If all $\varepsilon_i = 0$, then x^* is a fuzzy Pareto optimal solution. If at least one $\varepsilon_i > 0$, we adopt the solution $\bar{x}$ as the compromise solution of the DM, because fuzzy Pareto optimality of $\bar{x}$ can be establised.

3. AN INTERACTIVE COMPUTER PROGRAM AND AN ILLUSTRATIVE EXAMPLE

Fuzzy decision making processes for multiobjective nonlinear programming problems include eliciting a membership function from the DM for each of the objective functions. Thus, mitigation and speed-up of computation works are indispensable to this approach, and interactive utilization of computer facilities is highly recommended. Based on the method described above, we have developed a new interactive computer program. Our new package includes graphical representations by which the DM can figure the shapes of his membership functions, and he can find incorrect assessments or inconsistent evaluations promptly, revise them immediately and proceed to the next stage more easily.

Our program is composed of one main program and several subroutines. The main program calls in and runs the subprograms with commands indicated by the user (DM). Here we give a brief explanation of the commands prepared in our program.

(1) MINMAX: Displays the calculated individual minimum and maximum of each of the objective functions under the given constraints.

(2) MF: Elicits a membership function from the DM for each of the objective functions.

(3) GRAPH: Depicts graphically the shape of the membership function for each of the objective function.

(4) GO: Selects one of the three fuzzy decisions and derives the compromise solution of the DM by solving the corresponding maximization problem.

(5) STOP: Exits from the program.

Consider the following multiobjective decision making problem.

fuzzy equal $f_1(x) = x_1^2 + x_2^2$

fuzzy min $f_2(x) = (x_2 - 10)^2 + (x_2 - 10)^2$

fuzzy min $f_3(x) = (x_1 - 10)^2 + x_2^2$

fuzzy min $f_4(x) = (x_1 + 10)^2 + (x_2 + 20)^2$

fuzzy min $f_5(x) = (x_1 - 20)^2 + (x_2 + 10)^2$

subject to $x \in X = \{(x_1, x_2) | 0 \leqq x_i \leqq 10, \quad i = 1, 2\}$.

In applying our computer program to this problem, suppose that interaction with the hypothetical DM establishes the following membership functions and corresponding assessment values for the five objective functions.

f_1: left: linear, $(f_1^0, f_1^1) = (10, 50)$.
right: exponential, $(f_1^0, f_1^{0.5}, f_1^1) = (195, 160, 50)$.

f_2: linear, $(f_2^0, f_2^1) = (130, 10)$.

f_3: hyperbolic, $(f_3^{0.25}, f_3^{0.5}) = (130, 100)$.

f_4: hyperbolic inverse, $(f_4^0, f_4^{0.25}, f_4^{0.5}) = (1200, 1100, 900)$.

f_5: exponential, $(f_5^0, f_5^{0.5}, f_5^1) = (750, 600, 220)$.

In Appendix, the interaction processes using the GO command are shown, where a fuzzy decision is selected by the DM and the corresponding maximization problem is solved for his membership functions. Then by performing the fuzzy Pareto optimality test the fuzzy Pareto optimal solution is obtained as a compromise solution of the DM.

4. CONCLUSION

In this paper, by selecting one of the three fuzzy decisions together with the five types of membership functions, we have proposed an interactive method in order to deal with the fuzzy goals of the DM in multiobjective nonlinear programming problems. By performing a fuzzy or nonfuzzy Pareto optimality test, fuzzy or nonfuzzy Pareto optimality of the compromise solution of the DM is also guaranteed in our method, where fuzzy Pareto optimal solutions are introduced to deal with the fuzzy goal like "should be in the vicinity of ...". Based on the proposed method, the time-sharing computer program has been written to facilitate the interactive processes.

An illustrative numerical example demonstrated the feasibility and efficiency of both the proposed technique and its interactive computer program under the hypothetical DM. However, applications to real-world problems must be carried out in cooperation with a person actually involved in decision making. From such experiences the proposed technique and its computer program must be revised.

ACKNOWLEDGEMENTS

The author is indebted to Professor Yoshikazu Sawaragi of Kyoto Sangyo University for his constant encouragement. The author also wishes to thank his students T. Yumine and Y. Nango for their cooperation in this study.

REFERENCES

Bellman, R.E. and Zedah, L.A. (1970). Decision making in a fuzzy environment. Management Sci., 17(4), 141-164.

Charnes, A. and Cooper W.W. (1977). Goal programming and multiple objective optimizations. European J. Operational Res., 1(1), 39-54.

Geoffrion, A.M., Dyer, J.S. and Feinberg, A. (1972). An interactive approach for multi-criteria optimization, with an application to the operation of an academic department. Management Sci., 19(4), 357-368.

Haimes, Y.Y., Hall, W.A. and Freedman, H.T. (1975). Multiobjective Optimization in Water Resources Systems: The Surrogate Worth Trade-off Method. Elsevier, New York.

Hannan, E.L. (1981). Linear programming with multiple fuzzy goals, Fuzzy Sets and Systems, 6(3), 235-248.

Leberling, H. (1981). On finding compromise solution in multicriteria problems using the fuzzy min-operator. Fuzzy Sets and Systems, 6(2), 105-118.

Sakawa, M. (1982). Interactive multiobjective decision making by the sequential proxy optimization technique: SPOT. European J. Operational Res., 9(4), 386-396.

Sakawa, M. (1983). Interactive computer programs for fuzzy linear programming with multiple objectives. Int. J. Man-Machine Studies, 18(5), 489-503.

Sakawa, M. and Yumine, T. (1983). Interactive fuzzy decisionmaking for multiobjective linear fractional programming problems. Systems and Control, 27(2), 138-146 (in Japanese: revised version is to appear in

Large Scale Systems).
Wierzbicki, A.P. (1979). A methodological guide to multiobjective optimization. Working Paper WP-70-122, International Institute for Applied Systems Analysis, Laxenburg, Austria.
Zimmermann, H.J. (1978). Fuzzy programming and linear programming with several objective functions. Fuzzy Set and Systems, 1(1), 45-55.
Zionts, S. and Wallenius, J. (1976). An interactive programming method for solving the multiple criteria problem. Management Sci., 22(6), 652-663.

APPENDIX

INTERACTIVE FUZZY DECISION MAKING PROCESSES

```
COMMAND:
=GO
SELECT YOUR DECISION:
  (1) A FUZZY DECISION
  (2) A CONVEX-FUZZY DECISION
  (3) A PRODUCT-FUZZY DECISION
=1


( KUHN-TUCKER CONDITIONS SATISFIED )

                    MAXIMIZE THE MINIMUM MEMBERSHIP
 ----------------------------------------------------------------------
   X( 1)= 0.5781828056D+01          X( 2)= 0.3673624325D+01
 ----------------------------------------------------------------------
           I OBJECTIVE FUNCTION I              MEMBERSHIP
 ----------+--------------------+--------------------------------------
   F( 1)   I   0.4692505135D+02  I             0.9231262836D+00
   F( 2)   I   0.5781600373D+02  I             0.6015333022D+00
   F( 3)   I   0.3128849023D+02  I             0.9252727426D+00
   F( 4)   I   0.8095065855D+03  I             0.6015333022D+00
   F( 5)   I   0.3891244156D+03  I             0.8602914496D+00
 ----------------------------------------------------------------------
                                   MINIMUM= 0.6015333022D+00


( KUHN-TUCKER CONDITIONS SATISFIED )

                      FUZZY PARETO OPTIMALITY TEST
 ----------------------------------------------------------------------
   X( 1)= 0.5782640165D+01          X( 2)= 0.3673082918D+01
 EPS( 1)= 0.1353516330D-03        EPS( 2)= 0.
 EPS( 3)= 0.2741271073D-04        EPS( 4)= 0.
 EPS( 5)= 0.4235596267D-04
 ----------------------------------------------------------------------
           I  FUZZY PARETO OPTIMUM  I        MEMBERSHIP
 ----------+-----------------------+-----------------------------------
   F( 1)   I    0.4693046541D+02    I    0.9232616352D+00
   F( 2)   I    0.5781600373D+02    I    0.6015333022D+00
   F( 3)   I    0.3127766210D+02    I    0.9253001553D+00
   F( 4)   I    0.8095065855D+03    I    0.6015333022D+00
   F( 5)   I    0.3890865172D+03    I    0.8603338056D+00
```

SATISFICING TRADE-OFF METHOD FOR MULTIOBJECTIVE PROGRAMMING

Hirotaka Nakayama[1] and Yoshikazu Sawaragi[2]
[1] *Department of Applied Mathematics, Konan University, Kobe, Japan*
[2] *The Japan Institute of Systems Research, Kyoto, Japan*

1. Introduction

In recent years, many kinds of interactive optimization methods have been developed for solving multiobjective programming problems. Such interactive programming methods have also a role of the interface between men and computers. In developing them, therefore, it is important to make the best use of the strong points of ability of men and computers. However, it seems that many of existing interactive optimization methods require too high degree of judgment to decision makers, and too large number of auxiliary optimizations to be applied to practical problem.

For example, in structural design problems, function forms of several criteria can not be obtained explicitly, but their values are usually obtained by complex structure analysis. Therefore, much computation cost is usually required for each auxiliary scalar optimization. In design of camera lens, the number of criteria is over one hundred, and in addition their values can be evaluated by simulation of ray trace. For these problems, many of existing interactive optimization methods become invalid.

On the basis of the above consideration, we shall suggest in this paper a new type of interactive method for multiobjective programming called the satisficing trade-off method.

2. Satisficing trade-off method

As long as we take an approach of optimization, we can not help requiring decision makers such high degree of judgment as marginal rate of substitution or ordering among a set of alternatives. Therefore, we shall take another approach for interactive programming methods in order to decrease the load of decision makers. H. Simon asserted that human behavior is not always based on optimization but in many cases on satisficing due to limitation of ability of human judgment and available information [9]. Let X be a set of alternatives, and let each alternative $x \varepsilon X$ be evaluated by criteria $f=(f_1,\ldots,f_r)$ for which higher level is more desirable. Then satisficing is to find a satisfactory solutions x in the sense that the inequality

$$f(x) \geq \bar{f} \qquad (2.1)$$

holds, where $\bar{f}$ is the aspiration level of the decision maker. However, it seems more natural to consider that even among satisfactory solutions, the betters are better than just satisfactory solutions. Accordingly, we shall find a solution among satisfactory solutions as better as possible.

Definition 2.1 Let $\bar{f}$ be an aspiration level of the decision maker. Then an alternative $\tilde{x}$ is said to be a satisfactory Pareto solution if

$$f(x) \not> f(\tilde{x}) \qquad \text{for all } x \in X$$

and

$$f(\tilde{x}) \geqq \bar{f}.$$

In general, satisfactory Pareto solutions constitute a subset of X. However, we can narrow down the set of satisfactory Pareto solution set and obtain a solution close to the optimal one by increasing the aspiration level, if necessary. On the other hand, even if there does not exist any satisfactory Pareto solution for the initial aspiration level, we can attain one by relaxing the aspiration level. On the basis of the above consideration, the author have proposed a method called the satisficing trade-off method which finds a reasonable satisfactory Pareto solution by an appropriate adjustment of the aspiration level [5]. Its algorithm is summarized as follows:

Step-1 (setting the ideal point) The ideal point $f^*=(f_1^*,\dots,f_r^*)$ is set, where f_i^* is large enough, for example, $f_i^*=\text{Max}\ \{f_i(x)\mid x\in X\}$. This value is fixed throughout the following process.

Step-2 (setting the aspiration level) The aspiration level $\bar{f}_i^k$ of each objective function f_i at the k-th iteration as asked to the decision maker. Here $\bar{f}_i^k$ should be set as $\bar{f}_i^k < f_i^*$. Set k=1.

Step-3 (weighting and finding a Pareto solution by the Min-Max method) Set

$$w_i^k = \frac{1}{f_i^* - \bar{f}_i^k}, \tag{2.2}$$

and solve the Min-Max problem

$$\underset{x\in X}{\text{Min}}\ \underset{1\leqq i\leqq r}{\text{Max}}\ w_i^k|f_i^* - f_i(x)| \tag{2.3}$$

or equivalently

$$\underset{x,z}{\text{Min}}\ z$$

$$\text{subject to}\qquad w_i^k(f_i^* - f_i(x)) \leqq z, \quad i=1,\dots,r \tag{2.4}$$

$$x\in X$$

Let x^k be a solution of (2.4).

Step-4 (trade-off) Based on the value of $f(x^k)$, the decision maker classifies the criteria into three groups, namely,

(i) the class of criteria which he wants to improve more,

(ii) the class of criteria which he may agree to relaxing,
(iii) the class of criteria which he accept as they are.

The index set of each class is represented by I_I^k, I_R^k, I_A^k, respectively. If $I_I^k=\emptyset$, then stop the procedure. Otherwise, the decision maker is asked his new acceptable level of criteria $\tilde{f}_i^k$ for the class of I_I^k and I_R^k For $i\varepsilon I_A^k$, set $\tilde{f}_i^k=f_i(x^k)$.

<u>Step-5</u> (feasibility check) Let λ_i (i=1,...,r) be the optimal Lagrange multipliers to the problem (2.4). If for a small nonnegative ε

$$\sum_{i=1}^{r}\lambda_i w_i^k(\tilde{f}_i^k - f_i(x^k)) \leqq \varepsilon, \tag{2.5}$$

then set the new aspiration level $\bar{f}_i^{k+1}$ as $\tilde{f}_i^k$ and return to the step 3.

Otherwise, $\tilde{f}_i^k$ might be infeasible in the sense of linear approximation as will be explained later. Then, by taking the degree of difficulty for solving the Min-Max problem into account, we choose either to trade-off again or to return to the step 3 by setting $\bar{f}_i^{k+1}=\tilde{f}_i^k$. In case of trading off again, the acceptable level of criteria for I_I^k and/or I_R^k should be reset lower than before, and go back to the beginning of the step 5.

Now we shall give two theorems providing basis to the above algorithm in the following.

Theorem 2.1 Suppose that for any $x\varepsilon X$

$$f_i^* \geqq f_i(x), \qquad i=1,...,r. \tag{2.6}$$

If we set for a given aspiration level $\bar{f}$

$$w_i = \frac{1}{f_i^* - \bar{f}_i}, \qquad i=1,...,r \tag{2.7}$$

then the solution $\tilde{x}$ to

$$\min_{x\varepsilon X}\ \max_{1\leqq i\leqq r}\ w_i|f_i^* - f_i(x)| \tag{2.8}$$

is a satisfactory Pareto solution in case of $\bar{f}$ being feasible, while it is assured to be a Pareto solution even in case of $\bar{f}$ being infeasible.

<u>Proof</u> See [5].

Theorem 2.2 Let $(\tilde{x},\tilde{z})$ be a solution to

$$\min_{x,z}\ z$$

$$\text{subject to}\quad w_i(f_i^* - f_i(x)) \leqq z, \qquad i=1,...,r \tag{2.9}$$

$$x\varepsilon X$$

which is equivalent to the Min-Max problem (2.8), and let $\tilde{\lambda}=(\tilde{\lambda}_1,...,\tilde{\lambda}_r)$ be the optimal Lagrange multipliers. If $\tilde{x}$ is of the interior to the set and each f_i has appropriate smoothness, then we have

$$\sum_{i=1}^{r} \tilde{\lambda}_i = 1, \qquad \tilde{\lambda}_i \geqq 0, \qquad i=1,\dots,r \tag{2.10}$$

$$\sum_{i=1}^{r} \tilde{\lambda}_i w_i \nabla f_i(\tilde{x}) = 0. \tag{2.11}$$

Moreover, if the problem (2.9) is convex, namely, if each f_i is concave and the set X is convex, then for any $x \varepsilon X$

$$\sum_{i=1}^{r} \tilde{\lambda}_i w_i (f_i^*(x) - f_i(\tilde{x})) \leqq 0. \tag{2.12}$$

Proof See [5].

We shall list outstanding features of the satisficing trade-off method in the following:

1) We do not need to pay much attention to setting the ideal point f^*. It suffices to set f^* sufficiently large enough to cover all or almost of all Pareto solutions as candidates for a decision solution in the following process. In case of Max $\{f_i(x) \mid x \varepsilon X\}$ being finite, for example, set f_i^*=Max $\{f_i(x) \mid x \varepsilon X\}$. Otherwise, set f_i^* to be sufficiently large.

2) The weights w_i $(i=1,\dots,r)$ are automatically set by the ideal point f^* and the aspiration level $\bar{f}$. For the weight with (2.2), the value of $w_i(f_i^* - f_i(x))$ can be considered to present the normalized degree of non-attainability of $f_i(x)$ to the ideal point f_i^*. This enables us to need not to pay an extra attention to the difference among the dimension and the numerical order of criteria.

3) By solving the Min-Max problem with the above weight, we can get a satisfactory Pareto solution in case of the aspiration level $\bar{f}$ being feasible, and just a Pareto solution even in case of $\bar{f}$ being infeasible. Interpreting this intuitively, in case of $\bar{f}$ being feasible the obtained satisfactory Pareto solution is the one which improves each criterion as much as possible equally in some sense, and in case of $\bar{f}$ being infeasible we get a Pareto solution nearest to the ideal point which share an equal normalized sacrifice for each criterion. This practical meaning encourages the decision maker to accept easily the obtained solution.

4) At the stage of trade-off, the new aspiration level is set in such a way that

$$\bar{f}_i^{k+1} > f_i(x^k) \qquad \text{for any} \quad i \varepsilon I_I^k,$$

$$\bar{f}_i^{k+1} < f_i(x^k) \qquad \text{for any} \quad l \varepsilon I_R^k,$$

In this event, if $\bar{f}^{k+1}$ is feasible, then in view of Theorem 2.1 we have

$$f_i(x^{k+1}) > f_i(x^k) \qquad \text{for any } i \in I_I^k.$$

In other words, the solution to the Min-Max problem with $w_j^{k+1}=1/(f_j^* - \bar{f}_j^{k+1})$ assures the improvement of criteria f_i for any $i \in I_I^k$. In setting the new aspiration level, therefore, it is desirable to pay attention such that it becomes feasible.

5) In order that the new aspiration level $\bar{f}^{k+1}$ may be feasible, the criteria f_i $(i \in I_R^k)$ should be relaxed sufficiently enough to compensate for the improvement of $f_i(x^k)$ $(i \in I_I^k)$. To make this trade-off successful without solving a new Min-Max problem, we had better make use of sensitivity analysis on the basis of Theorem 2.2. Since we know already x^k is a Pareto solution, the feasibility of x^{k+1} can be checked by (2.5). Here ε is introduced to make (2.5) available for nonconvex cases where (2.12) does not necessarily hold. Moreover, observe in view of (2.11) that

$$\alpha_i = \lambda_i w_i, \qquad i=1,\dots,r \tag{2.13}$$

represents the sensitivity which reflects the mutual effect of change of each criterion restricted to the Pareto surface. Based on this information of sensitivity, the decision maker can easily judge how much the criteria f_i for $i \in I_I^k$ should be improved and how much the criteria f_i for $i \in I_R^k$ should be relaxed. In particular, since a little relaxation of f_j with j such that $\lambda_j=0$ can not compensate the improvement of f_i $(i \in I_i^k)$ under the condition that $\bar{f}^{k+1}$ should be on the Pareto surface, we have to relax at least one f_j for j such that $\lambda_j \neq 0$.

Remark 2.1 The stated feasibility check is just for the purpose of decreasing the number of solving Min-Max problems, and is not necessarily performed strictly. In some cases, several trials for trade-off can not succeed in holding (2.5) and the decision maker would tend to be tired of trading off again and again. In this circumstance, we had better go to solving Min-Max problem immediately even if (2.5) does not hold. However, in cases where it is necessary a lot of effort to solve Min-Max problems, a few retrials of trade-off could not be helped.

Remark 2.2 One may notice that the satisficing trade-off method is along a similar line as STEM ([1]) and interactive satisficing method based on scalarizing functions ([11]). In STEM, however, the aspiration level is not treated explicitly, and at phase of trade-off the decision maker is asked just to relax some of criteria. In practical situations, however, we encounter many cases where decision maker want to improve acutely some of criteria. The Min-Max problem, which plays an important role in the satisficing trade-off method, is a special type of scalarizing functions by Wierzbicki [11]. As was stated above, it has a useful practical implications and good features for interaction. Without going so far as to modify it in a complex form, therefore, the Min-Max problem sufficiently fits our purpose. These points enable the satisficing trade-off method simple and easy to treat.

3. Illustrative examples

In order to show the effectiveness of the satisficing trade-off method, we consider a hypothetical water quality control problem which was previously solved by the interactive relaxation method [9]. A river basin in the middle-western part of Japan is modeled: there are three branches necessary. Each of other two branches in the upper reach have its own treatment-plant which is supported by a local government in the upper reach. Another local government around the lower reach takes care of a treatment-plant in the lower reach. Under this situation, we have three objectives to be minimized:

1) treatment cost in the upper reach

$$f_1(x) = 287.58 + 2295.59(x_1 - 0.45)^2 + 404.46(x_2 - 0.45)^2 \quad (10^4\text{yen/day})$$

2) treatment cost in the lower reach

$$f_2(x) = 1050.73 + 10035.34(x_3 - 0.45)^2 \quad (10^4\text{yen/day})$$

3) BOD concentration at the inflow point into the sea

$$f_3(x) = 36.03 - (8.05x^1 + 1.04x_2 + 24.00x_3) \quad (\text{ppm})$$

Here x_1, x_2 denote the percent treatment to be used at the two treatment plants in the upper reach, and x_3 denote the one in the lower reach. Our constraints are as follows:

$$0.45 \leqq x_1, x_2, x_3 \leqq 1.0$$

It is natural to consider that the two local governments are both decision makers in this problem who share the cost for maintaining clear water. However, suppose here that we have a central authority who is responsible for the final decision.

One of results of our experiment is as follows: The ideal point is set as $(f_1^*, f_2^*, f_3^*) = (0.0, 0.0, 0.0)$. The initial aspiration level was given by $(\bar{f}_1^1, \bar{f}_2^1, \bar{f}_3^1) = (700.0, 3000.0, 5.0)$. By solving the Min-Max problem we have the following Pareto solution.

```
******** PARETO SOLUTION BY MIN-MAX METHOD ( 1) ********

        F( 1)= 0.78906D+03         ASPF( 1)= 0.70000D+03
        F( 2)= 0.33817D+04         ASPF( 2)= 0.30000D+04
        F( 3)= 0.56361D+01         ASPF( 3)= 0.50000D+01

   DO YOU COMPPOMISE WITH EACH F(I) ? (Y/N)? N
```

Observing this result, one may see that the initial aspiration level took too much for granted. Since this result is not satisfactory, however, the central authority classifies the criteria into three groups.

```
******** CLASSIFICATION OF CRITERIA ********

   PLEASE CLASSIFY THE CRITERIA INTO THREE GROUPS (I,R,A):

        I: IF YOU WANT TO IMPROVE F(I)
        R: IF YOU MAY RELAX F(I)
        A: IF YOU ACCEPT F(I), AS IT IS

   F( 1) ?
        = R

   F( 2) ?
        = R
```

```
F( 3) ?
        = I


 ******** CONFIRMATION ********

     LEVEL WHICH YOU WANT TO IMPROVE
       F( 3)= 0.56361D+01

     LEVEL WHICH YOU MAY RELAX
       F( 1)= 0.78906D+03
       F( 2)= 0.33817D+04

     LEVEL WHICH YOU ACCEPT, AS IT IS
       NONE

DO YOU WANT TO CHANGE YOUR JUDGE? (Y/N)? N
```

The central authority wanted to make BOD concentration to be less than 5.0 by all means, and to this end he agreed to relax the cost of two local governments. Now the central authority answers the quantity how much he wants to improve or how much he may relax by taking sensitivity of each criterion into account.

```
 ******** TRADE OFF ********

      ----- PLEASE IMPROVE -----

      F( 3)= 0.56361D+01          SENSITIVITY( 3)= 0.65829D-01
  NEW ASPF= ? 0.5D1


      ----- PLEASE RELAX -----

      F( 1)= 0.78906D+03          SENSITIVITY( 1)= 0.25838D-03
  NEW ASPF= ? 0.8D3

      F( 2)= 0.33817D+04          SENSITIVITY( 2)= 0.16333D-03
  NEW ASPF= ? 0.35D4
```

Although the improvement of f_3, 5.64–5.00=0.64, looks to be small at a glance, we can see in view of the sensitivity of f_i that ordinary sacrifice of f_1 and f_2 could not compensate for it. According to the feasibility check based on Theorem 2.2, in order to compensate for the improvement of f_3 we have to take f_1 and f_2 in such a way that

$$0.258\times10^{-3}\times\Delta f_1 + 0.163\times10^{-3}\times\Delta f_2 \geq 0.658\times10^{-1}\times(5.64 - 5.00)$$

Otherwise, it can not be expected to realize a Pareto solution which attains f_3=5.00. Therefore, by taking several circumstances into account, the new aspiration level of f_1 was relaxed to 800.0 (increasing by about 1.4%) and the one of f_2 to 3500.0 (increasing by about 3.5%).

The feasibility check is made for the answered level of criteria.

```
******** FEASIBILITY CHECK ********

  NOT FEASIBLE --- AS LINEAR APPROXIMATION

WHICH DO YOU WANT TO GO TO 1, OR 0 ?

    0:  MIN-MAX PROBLEM
    1:  TRADE-OFF AGAIN
```

```
? 1

------- INPUT AGAIN -------
```

Since the new aspiration level of each criterion is not feasible in the sense of linear approximation, we asked the central authority to trade-off again. Here the effort of the local government at the upper reach was admitted to be reasonable, and therefore the central authority requested the one at the lower reach further sacrifice

```
******** TRADE OFF ********

      ----- PLEASE IMPROVE -----

      F( 3)= 0.56361D+01        SENSITIVITY( 3)= 0.65829D-01
   NEW ASPF= ? 0.5D1

      ----- PLEASE RELAX -----

      F( 1)= 0.78906D+03        SENSITIVITY( 1)= 0.25838D-03
   NEW ASPF= ? 0.8D3

      F( 2)= 0.33817D+04        SENSITIVITY( 2)= 0.16333D-03
   NEW ASPF= ? 0.37D4


******** FEASIBILITY CHECK ********

      FEASIBLE --- AS LINEAR APPROXIMATION
```

The revised trade-off is now feasible in the sense of linear approximation, and therefore we solved Min-Max problem with the weight w_i based on the new aspiration level.

```
******** PARETO SOLUTION BY MIN-MAX METHOD ( 2) ********

       F( 1)= 0.79183D+03        ASPF( 1)= 0.80000D+03
       F( 2)= 0.36622D+04        ASPF( 2)= 0.37000D+04
       F( 3)= 0.49489D+01        ASPF( 3)= 0.50000D+01

  DO YOU COMPPOMISE WITH EACH F(I) ? (Y/N)? Y
 END OF GO,SEVERITY CODE=00
```

The obtained result was compromised by all local governments, and hence the iteration was stopped here. Note that if one of local governments could not agree with this result, the other local government was forced to bear a bigger cost or f_3 was to be sacrificed. The final compromise was made by considering this matter quite enough.

Throughout the experiments, we can observe several nice features of the satisficing trade-of method:

1) The judgment required to decision makers is only their aspiration levels. This is much easier than marginal rate of substitution and ranking vectors.

2) Decision makers can trade-off among <u>all</u> objectives at the same time. Therefore, they can easily adust the total balance among objectives.

3) Decision makers can easily accept the obtained solution because the auxiliary Min-Max problem gives it a practical meaning: if the aspiration level is feasible, the solution is in a situation desirable as much as possible, while it is nearest in a sense of <u>equality</u> to the aspiration level in case of the aspiration level being infeasible.

4) The number of auxiliary scalar optimization to be solved is quite few. This encourages us to apply the method to practical problems with a large number of objectives.

4. Concluding remarks

In this paper, we showed the effectiveness of the satisficing trade-off method for multi-objective programming along a hypothetical example of water quality management problem. the method is very easy and simple to carry out in comparison to many existing methods. On this point, it is competitive with the reference point method proposed by Wierzbicki [11]. However, the satisficing trade-off method has a merit that it provides a practical meaning of equality to the solution by using Min-Max problems as an auxiliary scalar optimization. The effectiveness of the method has been also confirmed by other applications to, for example, a system reliability problem and a bridge design problem [6],[8].

Even in cases with multiple decision makers, it can be applied similarly. In fact, recall that we have two local governments as decision makers in the hypothetical problem in the previous section. In our experiments, however, we considered the central authority as a single final decision maker. On the other hand, the role of the central authority can be weakened more. For example, we can consider the central authority just as a mediator between two local governments. Then, in our method the supply of a Pareto solution by solving Min-Max problem is considered to be the role of the mediator. Like this, the satisficing trade-off method can be expected to be applied to wide range practical problems.

Incidentally, the tandem quasi-Newton method for nonlinear optimization, which was developed by one of the authors and others [7], was used for solving auxiliary Min-Max problems.

Acknowledgment

We would like to express sincere gratitude to Prof. K. Inoue, Kyoto University, and Mr. M. Sano, Japan Telephone and Telegram Public Corporation, for their help in developing the computer programm of the satisficing trade-off method.

REFERENCES

[1] Benayoun, R., J. de Montgofier, J. Tergny and O. Larishev, Linear Programming with Multiple Objective Functions: Step Method (STEM), Mathematical Programming, Vol. 1, pp. 365-375, 1971

[2] Geoffrion, A. M., J. S. Dyer and A. Feinberg, An Interactive Approach for Multi-criterion Optimization with an Application to the Operation of Academic Department, Management Science, Vol. 19, pp. 357-368, 1972

[3] Haimes, Y. Y., W. A. Hall and H. T. Friedmann, Multiobjective Optimization in Water Resource Systems, The Surrogate Worth Trade-off Method, Elsevier Scientific, 1975

[4] Kobayashi, S. and A. Ichikawa, An Interactive Algorithm for Multiple Criteria Problems Pairwise Comparison of Optimal Solutions, in T.

Myoken (ed.) Optimal Control Systems, Decision Structures, and Economic Applications, Bunshindo, Tokyo, pp. 203-210, 1978

[5] Nakayama, H., Proposal of Satisficing Trade-off Method for Multi-objective Programming, submitted for publication. (in Japanese)

[6] Nakayama, H. and K. Furukawa, Satisficing Trade-off Method applied to Structural Design Problems in Civil Engineering, 9-th Systems Symposium, Tokyo, 1983 (in Japanese)

[7] Nakayama, H., M. Orimo and K. Inoue, Proposal of Tandem Quasi-Newton Method for Nonlinear Optimization, to appear in JAACE, Vol. 27, No. 12, 1983, (in Japanese)

[8] Nakayama, H., M. Sano and K. Inoue, System Reliabilitiy Design by Use of Satisficing Trade-off Method, submitted for publication

[9] Nakayama, H., T. Tanino and Y. Sawaragi, An Interactive Optimization Method in Multicriteria Decision Making, IEEE Trans. Systems, Man and Cybernetics, Vol. SMC-10, pp. 163-169, 1980

[10] Simon, H., Models of Man: Social and Rational, John Wiley, 1957

[11] Wierzbicki, A. P., A Mathematical Basis for Satisficing Decision Making, in J. Morse (ed.), Organizations: Multiple Agents with Multiple Criteria, Springer, 1981

ON DIALOGUE ALGORITHMS FOR LINEAR AND NONLINEAR VECTOR OPTIMIZATION FROM THE POINT OF VIEW OF PARAMETRIC OPTIMIZATION

Jürgen Guddat and Klaus Wendler
Department of Mathematics, Humboldt University, Berlin, GDR

1. INTRODUCTION

In treating vector optimization problems, dialogue methods play an ever increasing role (see e.g. R. Dupré et al /2/, A. Wierzbicki /11/, A. Lewandowski et al /8/, S. Zionts et al /13/).

Our research group at the Humboldt-University Berlin has done research work in parametric optimization (see for instance /9/ and /1/) for many years.

For this reason we consider vector optimization from the point of view of parametric optimization.

Moreover, we ask ourselves what we can do for the vector optimization with our knowledge and experience in parametric optimization.

We consider the following vector optimization problem

$$\text{(VOP)} \quad \max \left\{ (z_1(x), \dots, z_l(x)) \mid x \in M \right\},$$

where $M \subseteq R^n$ and $z_j : R^n \longrightarrow R$ $(j = 1, \dots, l)$ are given functions. The corresponding parametric optimization problem then reads

$$P(\lambda) : \max \left\{ \sum_{j=1}^{l} \lambda_j z_j(x) \mid x \in M \right\}, \ \lambda \in \Lambda$$

where

$$\Lambda = \left\{ \lambda \in R^l \mid \lambda_j \geq 0, \ j = 1, \dots, l, \ \sum_{j=1}^{l} \lambda_j = 1 \right\}.$$

We denote by $\psi_{opt}(\lambda)$ the set of all global maximizers and by $\psi_{loc}(\lambda)$ the set of all local maximizers.

It results from the well-known relation between vector optimization and parametric optimization that all points of the set

$$\bigcup_{\lambda \in \Lambda} \psi_{opt}(\lambda) \quad \text{resp.} \quad \bigcup_{\lambda \in \Lambda} \psi_{loc}(\lambda)$$

are interesting for decision making.

In our opinion, a dialogue method should satisfy at least the following demands:

1) An efficient algorithm to compute points of

$$\bigcup_{\lambda\in\Lambda} \Psi_{opt}(\lambda) \text{ resp. } \bigcup_{\lambda\in\Lambda} \Psi_{loc}(\lambda)$$

should be available.

2) Dialogue control should be easy and clear and performed approximately as follows:

(i) Computation of a point $x^k \in \bigcup_{\lambda\in\Lambda} \Psi_{opt}(\lambda)$ $(x^k \in \bigcup_{\lambda\in\Lambda} \Psi_{loc}(\lambda))$

(ii) Estimation of the point x^k basing on certain additional information like
a) values for the individual objective functions at x^k,
b) derivations from the values

$$\bar{\bar{z}}_j = \max \left\{ z_j(x)/x \in M \right\} , \quad j = 1, \ldots, l$$

(and possibly also

$$\bar{\bar{z}}_j = \min \left\{ z_j(x)/x \in M \right\} , \quad j = 1, \ldots, l),$$

we assume that these problems are solvable,

c) dual information etc.

(iii) Computation of a point $x^{k+1} \in \bigcup_{\lambda\in\Lambda} \Psi_{opt}(\lambda)(x^{k+1} \in \bigcup_{\lambda\in\Lambda} \Psi_{loc}(\lambda$
by taking into account

a) the pieces of information (ii) a),b),c) concerning x^k, and such points x^{k-1}, x^{k-2}, ... which where possibly computed already before,

b) the preference ideas of the decision maker.

We want to try to find an answer to the following two questions.

1. Are there efficient algorithms to compute points of

$$\bigcup_{\lambda\in\Lambda} \Psi_{opt}(\lambda) \quad \left(\bigcup_{\lambda\in\Lambda} \Psi_{loc}(\lambda)\right) ?$$

2. How can we organize a dialogue in the sense described above?

Our experience shows that already in the linear case the solution of the multi-parametric optimization problem $P(\lambda)$ demands considerable computational expense, hence we take another way.

In our approach to the computation of points of

$$\bigcup_{\lambda\in\Lambda} \Psi_{opt}(\lambda) \quad \left(\bigcup_{\lambda\in\Lambda} \Psi_{loc}(\lambda)\right)$$

we use algorithms basing on parametric optimization, where, contrary to M. Zelemy /12/ and other authors, we "solve" a series of one-parametric optimization problems.

For fixed λ^0, $\lambda^1 \in \Lambda$, $\lambda^0 \neq \lambda^1$ we consider the one-parametric optimization problem along the connecting line between λ^0 and λ^1

$$P(t, \lambda^o, \lambda^1) : \max \left\{ \sum_{j=1}^{l} (\lambda^o_j + t(\lambda^1_j - \lambda^o_j)) z_j(x) / x \in M \right\}, t \in [0,1] \quad .$$

In the linear case, there exist efficient solution methods (see e.g. F. Nožička et al /9/, Bank et al /1/, C. van de Panne /10/). Then we obtain a point of

$$\Psi_{opt}(\lambda), \quad \lambda \in \Lambda$$

after each simplex step. In the nonlinear case, we can apply methods for the pointwise approximation of continous selection functions from the point-to-set mapping $\Psi_{loc} : t \longrightarrow \Psi_{loc}(t)$ of the one-parametric optimization problem $P(t, \lambda^o, \lambda^1)$ which have the advantage that locally convergent algorithms with a least superlinear rate of convergence can be used here (see e.g. J. Guddat et al /6/, H. Gfrerer et al /7/). In this way we provide a positive answer to the first question.

To give an answer to the second question, we consider the problem $P(t, \lambda^o, \lambda^1)$. Here we have first of all the parameter vectors λ^o and λ^1 for the control of the dialogue.

Basing on this, a dialogue algorithm, which we want to denote by A1 here, is proposed. As this algorithm has the disadvantage that only the improvement of one objective function value can be guaranteed and, in the linear case, only efficient extremal points are computed. We introduce a dialogue method eliminating these disadvantages in chapter 3.

2. THE ALGORITHM A1

We assume that $P(\lambda)$ is solvable for all $\lambda \in \Lambda$ (that means there exists a global resp. local maximizer):

Step 1:

Solve the l optimization problems

$$\max \{ z_j(x) \; / \; x \in M \} \; ,$$

and let x^j be a solution,

$$\bar{z}_j = z_j(x^j) \qquad (j = 1, \ldots, l).$$

Step 2:

Input of a start-wight-vector $\lambda^o \in \Lambda$ for the objective functions, $i = 0$.

Solve $P(\lambda^o)$. Let $x^{1,o}$ be a solution of $P(\lambda^o)$.

Step 3:

$i = i + 1, \; x^{i,o} = x^{1,o}$.

Step 4:

Input of a goal-weight-vector $\lambda^1 \in \Lambda$ for the objective functions, $k = 0$, $t_o = 0$, $\lambda^{i,o} = \lambda^o$.

Step 5: (for linear vector optimization problems)

Determine an upper bound t_{k+1} for the parameter t such that the linear parametric optimization problem $P(t, \lambda^o, \lambda^1)$ has the solution $x^{i,k}$ for $t_k \leq t \leq t_{k+1}$ (by using a modified simplex method (see for instance /9/)).
Compute $\lambda^{i,k+1} = \lambda^o + t_{k+1} (\lambda^1 - \lambda^o)$, $z^{i,k} = (z_1(x^{i,k}), \ldots, z_l(x^{i,k}))$.

Step 5: (for nonlinear vector optimization problems)

Determine t_{k+1} and compute an approximation $x^{i,k+1}$ of $x(t_{k+1})$ as a solution of $P(t_k, \lambda^o, \lambda^1)$ by using the imbedding algorithm proposed in /6/ and /7/.

Compute $\lambda^{i,k+1} = \lambda^o + t_{k+1} (\lambda^1 - \lambda^o)$,

$$z^{i,k+1} = (z_1(x^{i,k+1}), \ldots, z_l(x^{i,k+1})).$$

Step 6:

Evaluate the solution $x^{i,k}$ (linear case) and $x^{i,k+1}$ (non-linear case), respectively, by the decision maker. Decision about the print and storage of the solution.
Decision about the continuation of the dialogue:

(i) further increase of the parameter t $\longrightarrow$ step 7,

(ii) choice of a new goal-weight-vector λ^1 $\longrightarrow$ step 3,

(iii) continuation of the dialogue with an already determined and stored solution as a start solution $\longrightarrow$ step 8,

(iv) choice of a new goal- and start-weight vector $\longrightarrow$ step 2,

(v) finishing the dialogue $\longrightarrow$ step 9.

Step 7:

$k = k+1$, if $t_k \geq 1 \longrightarrow$ step 3.

If $t_k < 1$, then a) in the nonlinear case $\longrightarrow$ step 5,

b) in the linear case, by carrying out a simplex step, let $x^{i,k}$ be the solution $\longrightarrow$ step 5.

Step 8:

Read in an already calculated and stored solution $x^{p',k'}$ from the

working memory (inclusively the weight vector $\lambda^{p',k'}$),

$i = i + 1$, $x^{i,0} = x^{p',k'}$, $\lambda^0 = \lambda^{p',k'} \longrightarrow$ step 4.

Step 9:

End of the dialogue

The dialogue is essentially controlled by selecting λ^0 and λ^1 on the basis of the deviations of the objective function values of the computed points from already determined bounds $\bar{z}_j (j = 1, \ldots, l)$,

$$\bar{z}_j = \max \left\{ z_j(x)/x \in M \right\} \quad (j = 1, \ldots, l).$$

For the evaluation of the solution $x^{i,k}$, the decision maker gets for instance the following information:

$\bar{z}$	$z(x^{i,k})$	%	$\lambda^{i,k}$	$\lambda^{i,k+1}$
$\bar{z}_1$	$z_1(x^{i,k})$	$100\ z_1(x^{i,k})/\bar{z}_1$	$\lambda_1^{i,k}$	$\lambda_1^{i,k+1}$
$\bar{z}_l$	$z_l(x^{i,k})$	$100\ z_l(x^{i,k})/\bar{z}_l$	$\lambda_l^{i,k}$	$\lambda_l^{i,k+1}$
			t_k	t_{k+1}

By a particular determination of λ^1 the improvement of exactly one objective function value can also be guaranteed. For detailed explanations the reader is referred to the work mentioned above. Telescreen-pictures are contained for the linear case in J. Guddat et al /4/. The algorithm was implemented for the linear case.

3. ON THE ALGORITHM A2

In order to eliminate the disadvantages mentioned in the introduction, we consider a known efficient point x^*, which was computed with the algorithm A1 for instance. By $K \subset \{1, \ldots, l\}$ we denote the index set of those objective functions whose value is to be increased. Further, let $\bar{K} = \{1, \ldots, l\} \setminus K$.

Analogous to the proceeding described above we formulate the following parametric optimization problem

$$P(x^*, \underset{(\bar{K})}{\lambda} \underset{(K)}{\mu}) : \max \left\{ \sum_{j \in \bar{K}} \underset{(\bar{K})}{\lambda}_j z_j(x)/x \in M(x^*, \underset{(K)}{\mu}) \right\},$$

$$\underset{(\bar{K})}{\lambda} \in \underset{(\bar{K})}{\Lambda}, \quad \underset{(K)}{\mu} \in \underset{(K)}{M}(x^*),$$

where

$$M(x^*, \underset{(K)}{\mu}) = \{x \in M / \ z_j(x) \geq z_j(x^*) + \underset{(K)}{\mu}_j, \ j \in K\},$$

$$\underset{(\bar{K})}{\Lambda} = \{\underset{(\bar{K})}{\lambda} \ / \ \underset{(\bar{K})}{\lambda}_j \geq 0, \ j \in \bar{K}, \ \sum_{j \in \bar{K}} \underset{(\bar{K})}{\lambda}_j = 1\}$$

$$\underset{(K)}{\mathcal{M}}(x^*) = \{\underset{(K)}{\mu} \ / \ 0 < \underset{(K)}{\mu}_j \leq \bar{z}_j - z_j(x^*), \ j \in K\} .$$

If we choose $\underset{(\bar{K})}{\lambda^0}, \underset{(\bar{K})}{\lambda^1} \in \underset{(\bar{K})}{\Lambda}, \underset{(K)}{\mu^0} \in \underset{(K)}{\mathcal{M}}(x^*)$ fixed, we can again investigate a one-parametric optimization problem, namely

$$P(x^*, \underset{(\bar{K})}{\lambda^0}, \underset{(\bar{K})}{\lambda^1}, \underset{(K)}{\mu^0}, t) : \max \{\sum_{j \in \bar{K}} (\underset{(\bar{K})}{\lambda^0_j} + t(\underset{(\bar{K})}{\lambda^1_j} - \underset{(\bar{K})}{\lambda^0_j}))z_j(x) /$$

$$x \in M(x^*, \underset{(K)}{\mu^0}, t)\}, \ t \in [0, 1],$$

where

$$M(x^*, \underset{(K)}{\mu^0}, t) = \{x \in M / z_j(x) \geq z_j(x^*) + t \underset{(K)}{\mu^0_j}, \ j \in K\} .$$

In this case the dialogue is mainly controlled by the choice of the vectors $\underset{(\bar{K})}{\lambda^0}$, $\underset{(\bar{K})}{\lambda^1}$ $\underset{(K)}{\mu^0}$ and the index set K.

Figure 1 illustrates the set $M(x^*, \underset{(K)}{\mu^0}, t)$ geometrically for an example with 4 objective functions $z_1, \ldots, z_4$ and the set $K = \{3, 4\}$.

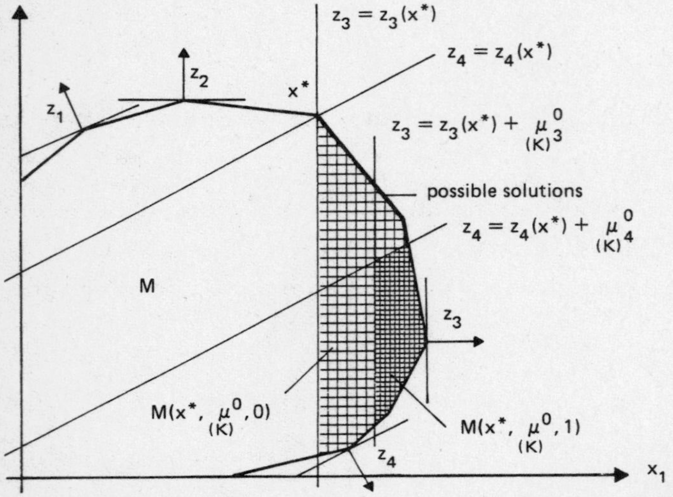

FIGURE 1 Geometrical example

Basing on this, we give an algorithm A2 eliminating the disadvantages of the algorithm A1 metioned at the end of section 1.

Algorithm A2:

Step 1:
.
.
.
Step 5: } see A1

Step 6: See A1, and we add a possibility (vi) for the decision maker:
.
.
.
(vi) improvement of several objective functions (let x^* be computed by A1) $\longrightarrow$ step 9

Step 7:
.
.
.
Step 8: } see A1

Step 9: Input of the index set K,

input of the vector $\mu^o_{(K)} \in \mathcal{M}_{(K)}(x^*)$.

Step 10: Input of the weight vector $\lambda^o_{(\bar{K})} \in \Lambda_{(\bar{K})}$ p = 0 .

Solve $P(x^*, \lambda^o_{(\bar{K})}, 0)$. Let $y^{1,o}$ be a solution of $P(x^*, \lambda^o_{(\bar{K})}, 0)$.

Step 11: Input of the weight vector $\lambda^1_{(\bar{K})} \in \Lambda_{(\bar{K})}$, $p = p+1$, $y^{p,o} = y^{1,o}$, $q = 0$, $t_o = 0$.

Step 12: (for linear vector optimization problems)
Determine an upper bound t_{p+1} for the parameter t such that the linear parametric optimization problem

$P(x^*, \lambda^o_{(\bar{K})}, \lambda^1_{(\bar{K})}, \mu^o_{(K)}, t)$

has the solution $y^{p,q}(t)$ for $t_p \leq t \leq t_{p+1}$ (with the same basis as $y^{p,q}(t_p)$, $y^{p,q}(0) = y^{p,q}$)
by using a modified simplex method.

Compute $z^{p,q}(t) = (z_1(y^{p,q}(t)), \ldots, z_l(y^{p,q}(t)))$.

Step 12: (for nonlinear vector optimization problems)
anologue to step 5 for nonlinear vector optimization problems

Step 13: If $t_{p+1} > 0 \longrightarrow$ step 14.

If $t_{p+1} = 0$ decision about the continuation of the dialogue

(i) choice of another index set K and choice of another vector $\mu^{o}_{(K)} \in \mathcal{M}_{(K)}(x^{*}) \longrightarrow$ step 9,

(ii) possibilities (ii) - (iv) of step 5,

(iii) finishing the dialogue $\longrightarrow$ step 16.

Step 14: Evaluation of the solutions $y^{p,q}(t)$, $t_p \leq t \leq t_{p+1}$ by the dicision maker. Decision about the print and storage of special solutions $y^{p,q}(t)$ for fixed parameter values t (only in the linear case).
Decision about the continuation of the dialogue:

(i) further increase of the parameter t (if $t < 1$) $\longrightarrow$ step 15,

(ii) choice of other vectors $\lambda^{1}_{(\bar{K})} \in \Lambda_{(\bar{K})} \longrightarrow$ step 11,

(iii) choice of other vectors $\lambda^{o}_{(\bar{K})}, \lambda^{1}_{(\bar{K})} \in \Lambda_{(\bar{K})} \longrightarrow$ step 10,

(iv) choice of another index set K and another vector $\mu^{o}_{(K)} \in \mathcal{M}_{(K)}(x^{*}) \longrightarrow$ step 9,

(v) possibilities (ii) - (iv) of step 5,

(vi) finishing the dialogue $\longrightarrow$ step 16.

Step 15: $q = q + 1$,
carry out a simplex step, let $y^{p,q}(t)$ be the solution (only in the linear case) $\longrightarrow$ step 12.

Step 16: End of the dialogue.

REFERENCES

/1/ Bank, B., Guddat, J., Klatte, D., Kummer, B., Tammer, K., Nonlinear parametric optimization, Akademie-Verlag Berlin 1982

/2/ Dupré, R., Huckert, K., Jahn, J.. Lösung linearer Vektoroptimierungsprobleme durch das STEM-Verfahren. In H. Späth, Ausgewählte Operations Research Software in Fortran, Oldenbourg Verlag München, Wien, 1979

/3/ Guddat, J., Wendler, K.. O primenenyi parametriceskovo progammirovanija v vektornoi optimisazii - ob odnom dialogovom algoritme dlja resenija linejnych i nelinejnych sadac vektornoi optimisazii. To appear in Institut Report of Inst. Math. Mech. of Ac. of Science USSR, Swerdlowsk

/4/ Guddat, J., Wendler, K., Wernsdorf, R.. Über die Lösung von Vektor-optimierungsproblemen mit Hilfe der parametrischen Optimierung. In Seminarbericht Nr. 37 der Sektion Mathematik der Humboldt-Universität Berlin

/5/ Guddat, J., Wendler, K.. Über zwei Dialogverfahren zur Vektoroptimierung basierend auf der parametrischen Optimierung. To appear in Seminarbericht Nr. 50 der Sektion Mathematik der Humboldt-Universität Berlin

/6/ Guddat, J., Wacker, Hj., Zulehner, W.. On imbedding and parametric optimization - a concept of a globally convergent algorithm for nonlinear optimization. Institutsbericht Nr. 200, Math. Inst. Universität Linz. To appear in : Math. Programming Study

/7/ Gfrerer, H., Guddat, J., Wacker, Hj.. A globally convergent algorithm based on imbedding and parametric optimization. Computing 30, 225-252 (1983)

8/ Lewandowski, A., Grauer, M.. The reference point optimization approach - methods of efficient implementation in multiobjective and stochastic optimization. Proceedings of an IIASA Task Force Meeting Nov. 30 - Dec. 4, 1981, 353-376

/9/ Nožička, F., Guddat, J., Hollatz, H., Bank, B.. Theorie der linearen parametrischen Optimierung. Akademie-Verlag Berlin 1974

10/ van de Panne, C.. Methods for linear and quadratic programming. North Holland, Amsterdam-Oxford 1975

11/ Wierzbicki, A.. The use of reference objectives in multiobjective optimization - Theoretical implications and practical experience. IIASA-Working Paper 79-66

12/ Zeleny, M.. Linear multiobjective Programming, Lecture Notes 95, Springer-Verlag, Berlin, Heidelberg, New York 1974

13/ Zionts, S., Wallenius, J.. An interactive programming method for solving the multiple criteria problem. Man. Science, 22(1976),6, 652-663

OPERATING CONSIDERATIONS PERTAINING TO THE INTERACTIVE WEIGHTED TCHEBYCHEFF PROCEDURE

Ralph E. Steuer
College of Business Administration, University of Georgia, Athens, Georgia, USA

1. INTRODUCTION

The interactive weighted Tchebycheff method for solving the multiple objective program

$$\begin{array}{ll} \max & \{f_1(x) = z_1\} \\ \max & \{f_2(x) = z_2\} \\ & \vdots \\ \max & \{f_k(x) = z_k\} \\ \text{s.t.} & x \in S \end{array}$$

is described in [11] and [12]. A multiple objective linear programming application of the weighted Tchebycheff procedure is given in [10]. Multiple objective integer and multiple objective nonlinear programming applications are also possible with the Tchebycheff approach.

The strategy of the Tchebycheff approach is to sample a series of successively smaller subsets of the set of all nondominated criterion vectors. The name "Tchebycheff" is used in the title of the approach because variations of the Tchebycheff (L_∞) metric are used to conduct the sampling. The procedure concludes when a criterion vector has been identified that is close enough to being optimal for the decision maker to be willing to terminate the decision process.

The effectiveness of the Tchebycheff method is derived from its endeavor to sample the subsets of nondominated criterion vectors in a maximally dispersed fashion. By maximally dispersed we mean that the criterion vectors comprising the sample are as far apart as possible from one another in the subset in question. In this way, such samples can be expected to provide better coverings of the nondominated subsets than random samples.

In the next section is summarized the weighted Tchebycheff procedure followed in Sections 3 to 9 by a discussion of some of the finer points pertaining to the effective operation of the method.

2. WEIGHTED TCHEBYCHEFF ALGORITHM

In negotiation with the decision-maker, let p be the number of criterion vectors presented to the decision-maker at each iteration and t be the intended number of iterations the procedure is to run. The analyst then selects a value for w which is the final iteration λ-vector interval width (of the $[\ell_i^{(t)}, \mu_i^{(t)}]$). This is done so that a $\overline{\Lambda}$-reduction factor r, the factor that controls the convergence of the algorithm, can be computed. It is recommended that all four quantities be set in accordance with the guideline relationships

$$p \gtrapprox k$$

$$t \approx k$$

$$1/(2k) \lessapprox w \lessapprox 3/(2k)$$

$$\sqrt[k]{1/p} \lessapprox r \lessapprox \sqrt[t-1]{w}$$

where ≈ means approximately and k is the number of objectives. Then from [12] we have the weighted Tchebycheff algorithm.

Step 1: Solve for the ideal criterion vector $z^{**} \in R^k$ where

$$z_i^{**} = \max \{f_i(x) \mid x \in S\} + \varepsilon_i$$

in which it suffices for the ε_i to be moderately small positive scalars.

Step 2: Normalize (rescale) the objective functions.

Step 3: Let h = 1. Let $[\ell_i^{(1)}, \mu_i^{(1)}] = [0, 1]$ for all i.

Step 4: Let h = h + 1. Form

$$\overline{\Lambda}^{(h)} = \{\lambda \in R^k \mid \lambda_i \in [\ell_i^{(h)}, \mu_i^{(h)}], \sum_{i=1}^{k} \lambda_i = 1\}$$

Step 5: Randomly generate 50 x k weighting vectors from $\overline{\Lambda}^{(h)}$.

Step 6: Filter the 50 x k weighting vectors to obtain the 2 x k most different.

Step 7: Using the 2k weighting vector representatives of $\overline{\Lambda}^{(h)}$, solve the 2k associated augmented (or lexicographic) weighted Tchebycheff programs

$$\min \quad \{\alpha + \rho \sum_{i=1}^{k} (z_i^{**} - z_i)\}$$

or

$$\text{lexmin} \{\alpha, \sum_{i=1}^{k} (z_i^{**} - z_i)\}$$

$$\text{s.t.} \quad \alpha \geqq \lambda_i (z_i^{**} - z_i) \qquad 1 \leqq i \leqq k$$

$$w_i = z_i^{**} - z_i \qquad 1 \leqq i \leqq k$$

$$f_i(x) = z_i \qquad 1 \leqq i \leqq k$$

$x \in S$

where ρ is a sufficiently small positive scalar.

Step 8: Filter the criterion vectors resulting from Step 7 to obtain the p most different. Then present the p nondominated criterion vectors to the decision-maker.

Step 9: From the sample of p nondominated criterion vectors, the decision-maker selects his most preferred designating it $z^{(h)}$.

Step 10: If the decision-maker wishes to stop iterating prematurely, go to Step 15. Otherwise, go to Step 11.

Step 11: Let $\lambda^{(h)}$ be the λ-vector whose components are given by

$$\lambda_i^{(h)} = \begin{cases} \dfrac{1}{|z_i^{**} - z_i^{(h)}|}\left[\displaystyle\sum_{i=1}^{k} \dfrac{1}{|z_i^{**} - z_i^{(h)}|}\right]^{-1} & \ldots \text{ if } z_i^{(h)} \neq z_i^{**} \text{ for all } i \\ 1 \ldots\ldots\ldots\ldots & \text{if } z_i^{(h)} = z_i^{**} \\ 0 \ldots\ldots\ldots\ldots & \text{if } z_i^{(h)} \neq z_i^{**} \text{ but} \\ & \exists j \in z_j^{(h)} = z_j^{**} \end{cases}$$

Step 12: Let $\lambda^{(h)}$ be the weighting vector computed in Step 11. Form

$$\bar{\Lambda}^{(h+1)} = \{\lambda \in R^k \mid \lambda_i \in [\ell_i^{(h+1)}, \mu_i^{(h+1)}], \sum_{i=1}^{k} \lambda_i = 1\}$$

where

$$[\ell_i^{(h+1)}, \mu_i^{(h+1)}] = \begin{cases} [0, r^h] \ldots\ldots\ldots & \text{if } \lambda_i^{(h)} - \frac{r^h}{2} \leqq 0 \\ [1-r^h, 1] \ldots\ldots\ldots & \text{if } \lambda_i^{(h)} + \frac{r^h}{2} \geqq 1 \\ [\lambda_i^{(h)} - \frac{r^h}{2}, \lambda_i^{(h)} + \frac{r^h}{2}] & \text{. otherwise} \end{cases}$$

in which r^h is r raised to the hth power.

Step 13: If $h < t$, go to Step 4. If $h \geq t$, go to Step 14.

Step 14: If the decision-maker wishes to keep iterating, go to Step 4. Otherwise, go to Step 15.

Step 15: With $x^{(h)}$ an inverse image of $z^{(h)}$, stop with $(z^{(h)}, x^{(h)})$ as the final solution.

In Step 5 we generate the weighting vectors using the LAMBDA code from the ADBASE [9] package. To obtain the most different representatives in Steps 6 and 8 we use the FILTER code from the same package. If the problem to be solved is a multiple objective linear or integer program, we can use MPSX-MIP [4] for the repetitive optimizations of Step 7. If the problem to be solved is a multiple objective linear or nonlinear program we can use MINOS [7 and 8]. The advantage of MPSX-MIP and MINOS is that subsequent optimizations in a sequence of similar problems can be commenced from a "flying start" using information from the previous optimal solution.

To understand some of the finer points of the Tchebycheff algorithm, we now discuss the following topics:

(a) criterion value ranges over the efficient set
(b) early fixation on a candidate solution
(c) number of solutions presented at each iteration

(d) scaling the objectives
(e) most preferred criterion vector as filtering seed point
(f) insertion of criterion value lower bounds
(g) ε_i values in integer and nonlinear cases

3. CRITERION VALUE RANGES OVER THE EFFICIENT SET

Prior to the commencement of any interactive procedure (such as [1, 2, 3, 12 and 14]) it is advisable to schedule some sort of problem "warm-up" stage for the decision-maker. One goal of the warm-up stage is to adapt the decision-maker's (perhaps overoptimistic) aspirations to the confines of his feasible region. One thing that can be done in this regard is to display the different criterion value ranges over the efficient set in bar chart fashion as follows.

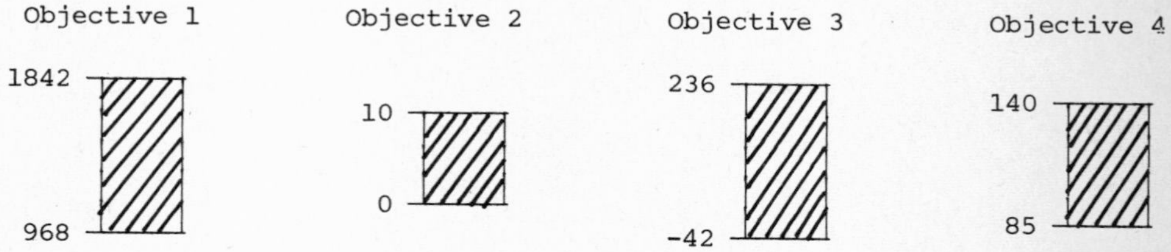

The difficulty with the bar charts, however, is in obtaining the minimum criterion values over the efficient set. Methods such as computing minimum criterion values from payoff tables as in STEM [2] can result in values that substantially overestimate the minimums. The challenge is to find a method that will yield a global minimum over the efficient set, not a local minimum. Currently no such method, apart from computing all efficient extreme points in the linear case, exists in the literature, but one is being worked on in [5].

4. EARLY FIXATION ON A CANDIDATE SOLUTION

Step 10 of the Tchebycheff algorithm provides for an early exit. Step 14 allows the decision-maker to override the originally intended number of iterations and continue iterating as long as he wishes. The early exit has been provided because the author has noticed in the behavior of some users a tendency to fixate on one of the early candidate solutions presented to him. It is as if the decision-maker decides he likes one of the solutions and then adapts his utility function to it. Then he spends the rest of his iterations trying to see whether or not minor improvements can be made upon the criterion vector. It almost seems to this author that a decision-maker is more likely to select a given criterion vector as his final solution if he sees it early rather than discovers it late. On large problems requiring six or eight iterations, a decision-maker exhibiting such behavior may very well ask, to the consternation of the analyst, for an early exit claiming that he has already seen what he wanted to see. This type of behavior is not seen with all users, but it happens often enough to warrant comment.

5. NUMBER OF SOLUTIONS PRESENTED AT EACH ITERATION

In Miller [6] we have the article about the number "seven, plus or minus two." This article is well-known in the multiple objective literature. Its influence is that it has caused many people to feel that multiple criterion problems should not be modeled with more than about seven objectives. Also, a decision-maker should not be presented with more than about seven solutions at a time. Otherwise, the limits to his information processing abilities might be surpassed and he would suffer from "information overload." This may be true for some decision-makers, but it is not true for all. Some decision-makers, people who are familiar with the concept of nondominance and know what they are looking for, can process up to 20 criterion vectors in one sitting. This author has found that the objectives and the number of solutions that can be presented at one time does not so much depend on the number seven, plus or minus two. Rather it depends more upon the problem and type of decision-maker with which one is working. This is encouraging because the larger the number of solutions that can be presented to the decision-maker at each iteration, the faster algorithms such as the Tchebycheff method can converge.

6. SCALING THE OBJECTIVES

In most iterative procedures, the Tchebycheff method included, it is advisable to scale the objective functions. One way to do this is to multiply the ith objective by

$$\pi_i = \frac{1}{R_i}\left[\sum_{j=1}^{k} \frac{1}{R_j}\right]^{-1}$$

where R_i is the range of the ith criterion value over the efficient set and then add an appropriate constant

$$K_i$$

to the objective function. The π_i weights equalize the criterion value ranges of the objectives over the efficient set and the constants K_i equalize the midpoints of the scaled ranges. Since the scaling need not be perfect to achieve good numerical results, we may wish to use the powers of 10 closest to the π_i as scaling factors. In this way, we only move the decimal point in the objective function coefficients--we do not change any of the significant digits. The π_i weights are considered to be better than scaling factors derived from the family of L_p-norms. With normalization scaling factors there is no assurance that the criterion values or their ranges will be brought into the same order of magnitude, particularly when there are both positive and negative coefficients in the objective functions.

7. MOST PREFERRED CRITERION VECTOR AS FILTERING SEED POINT

Consider any iteration other than the first. If we filter in Step 8 the criterion vectors produced in Step 7 without regard to the decision-maker's most recent criterion vector selection, one of the criterion vectors presented in Step 9 may be similar to this criterion vector. To prevent this (in the interest of extracting the most out of each Tchebycheff iteration), we should use the most recent criterion vector selection as the filtering seed point (see [13]) in Step 8. Then as the decision-maker examines the p new criterion vectors versus his most recent selection, he is assured that none of the p+1 vectors is unnecessarily similar to any of the others. In this way, given that we can only present p criterion vectors at a time, we are presenting the maximum amount of information possible per iteration.

8. INSERTION OF CRITERION VALUE LOWER BOUNDS

In the process of examining solutions iteration to iteration, the decision-maker may conclude that values below certain levels for some of the criteria would never be acceptable under any circumstances. In such cases it would behoove procedures such as the Tchebycheff method to add lower bounding constraints on the criterion values of the pertinent objectives before proceeding with subsequent iterations. Of course, it would make no sense to add lower bounding constraints with RHS's less than the minimum criterion values over the efficient set. By giving the decision-maker the option to configure any scheme of lower bounds on his criterion values, the efficient set is reduced and convergence of the algorithm only can, if anything, be favorably affected.

9. ε_i VALUES IN INTEGER AND NONLINEAR CASES

In Step 1 of the algorithm it suffices for the ε_i to be moderately small positive scalars. The idea of such ε_i is to make each $z_i^{**} > \max \{f_i(x) | x \in S\}$. In the linear case there is no problem, but in integer and nonlinear cases, we may have to work with approximations of the $\max \{f_i(x) | x \in S\}$ because of CPU time or infinite convergence difficulties. However, if we are able to obtain upper bounds on the maximal criterion values as in branch and bound integer programming, we can set the ε_i to values greater than the difference between the current criterion values and the upper bounds thus assuring that $z_i^{**} > \max \{f_i(x) | x \in S\}$.

REFERENCES

[1] Anderson, M. D., R. G. March and J. M. Mulvey. (1981). "Solving Multi-Objective Problems via Unstructured and Interactive Dialogue," Research Report No. EES-81-8, Department of Civil Engineering, Princeton University, Princeton, New Jersey.

[2] Benayoun, R., J. de Montgolfier, J. Tergny and O. Laritchev. (1971). "Linear Programming with Multiple Objective Functions: Step Method (STEM)," Mathematical Programming, Vol. 1, No. 3, pp. 366-375.

[3] Geoffrion, A. M., J. S. Dyer and A. Feinberg. (1972). "An Interactive Approach for Multicriterion Optimization, with an Application to the Operation of an Academic Department," Management Science, Vol. 19, No. 4, pp. 357-368.

[4] IBM Document No. GH19-1091-1. (1979). "IBM Mathematical Programming System Extended/370: Primer," IBM Corporation, Data Processing Division, White Plains, New York.

[5] Isermann, H. and R. E. Steuer. (1984). "Payoff Tables and Minimum Criterion Values Over the Efficient Set," in preparation.

[6] Miller, G. (1956). "The Magical Number Seven Plus or Minus Two: Some Limits on Our Capacity for Processing Information," Psychological Review, Vol. 63, No. 2, pp. 81-97.

[7] Murtagh, B. A. and M. A. Saunders. (1980). "MINOS/AUGMENTED User's Manual," Report SOL 80-14, Department of Operations Research, Stanford University, Stanford, California.

[8] Preckel, P. V. (1980). "Modules for Use with MINOS/AUGMENTED in Solving Sequences of Mathematical Programs," Report SOL 80-15, Department of Operations Research, Stanford University, Stanford, California.

[9] Steuer, R. E. (1983). "Operating Manual for the ADBASE Multiple Objective Linear Programming Package," College of Business Administration, University of Georgia, Athens, Georgia.

[10] Steuer, R. E. (1983). "Multiple Criterion Function Goal Programming Applied to Managerial Compensation Planning," Computers and Operations Research, forthcoming.

[11] Steuer, R. E. (1982). "On Sampling the Efficient Set Using Weighted Tchebycheff Metrics," in Grauer, M., A. Lewandowski and A. P. Wierzbicki (eds.), Multiobjective and Stochastic Optimization, IIASA, Laxenburg, Austria.

[12] Steuer, R. E. and E.-U. Choo. (1983). "An Interactive Weighted Tchebycheff Procedure for Multiple Objective Programming," Mathematical Programming, forthcoming.

[13] Steuer, R. E. and F. W. Harris. (1980). "Intra-Set Point Generation and Filtering in Decision and Criterion Space," Computers and Operations Research, Vol. 7, Nos. 1-2, pp. 41-53.

[14] Zionts, S. and J. Wallenius. (1983). "An Interactive Multiple Objective Linear Programming Method for a Class of Underlying Nonlinear Utility Functions," Management Science, Vol. 29, No. 5, pp. 519-529.

A POSTERIORI TRADE-OFF ANALYSIS IN REFERENCE POINT APPROACHES

Eberhard E. Bischoff
International Institute for Applied Systems Analysis, Laxenburg, Austria and Department of Management Science and Statistics, University College of Swansea, Swansea, UK

1. INTRODUCTION

This paper is concerned with extensions to existing reference point methods for multiple objective decision making (MODM) through the incorporation of an a-posteriori trade-off analysis, i.e. an examination of the trade-offs between objectives which are implied by a given, tentative solution to the problem under consideration. The term reference point method is used in this context to include both conventional goal programming approaches, where the reference point represents the decision maker's actual aspiration levels (cf. Lee 1972; Ignizio 1976), and the more recent interactive procedures where the reference point is used as a primarily technical means of exploring the feasible region (Wierzbicki 1979a, 1979b; Lewandowski and Grauer 1982).

The principal motivation for the paper derives from the observation that there is a strong tendency in the literature to treat weighting and reference point methodologies as mutually exclusive and basically incompatible. The choice between the two types of approach is usually made on the basis of qualitative considerations in which the analyst's subjective preferences often play a not insubstantial role. The aim here is to show how by integrating the concept of weighting the objectives with that of setting aspiration levels this problematic choice can be avoided. Moreover, such an integrated approach, in allowing different rationales to be applied simultaneously, has considerable advantages over the use of either methodology separately.

While the conceptual issues raised are of relevance to both linear and nonlinear MODM problems, the chief concern here is with the linear case. More precisely, it is assumed that the problem to be solved has the form

$$\begin{aligned} &\max \quad c_1^t x \\ &\cdots \\ &\max \quad c_r^t x \\ \\ &\text{s.t.} \quad A x \leqq b \end{aligned} \tag{1}$$

where x represents the n-vector of decision variables, $c_1, c_2, \ldots, c_r$ are n-vectors, A is an m x n matrix, and b an m-vector.

The remainder of this paper is divided into four sections. The next section takes a critical look at the way in which reference point methods are used in practice and identifies the benefits to be gained from supplementing current procedures by a trade-off analysis. The following section describes in detail the approach suggested. This is illustrated in the fourth section by a numerical example. The fifth and final part summarizes the main points raised.

2. CURRENT PRACTICE

The usual reference point approaches require the decision maker to express his preferences with respect to the objectives involved through two sets of parameters:

(i) aspiration levels representing desirable values for the objectives; and

(ii) weighting factors indicating the relative degree of importance accorded to the attainment of the aspiration levels set.

In goal programming approaches both cardinal and ordinal ('pre-emptive') weighting systems may be employed. Denoting cardinal weighting factors by w_i ($w_i \geq 0$), $i = 1,\dots,r$, and using the symbols P_j, $j = 1,\dots,k$, to denote pre-emptive weights (with the property that $P_j \ggg P_{j+1}$, i.e. that $P_j a > P_{j+1} b$ for any two positive numbers a and b) the model used can be expressed in general form as follows:

$$\min \quad P_1 \left[\sum_{i \in C_1} (w_i d_i)^p \right]^{1/p} + \dots + P_k \left[\sum_{i \in C_k} (w_i d_i)^p \right]^{1/p}$$

$$\text{s.t.} \quad c_i^t x + d_i \geq g_i \ , \ i = 1,\dots,r \qquad (2)$$

$$d_i \geq 0 \ , \ i = 1,\dots,r$$

$$A x \leq b \ ,$$

where g_i, $i = 1,\dots,r$, represents the aspiration level (goal) for objective i,

d_i, $i = 1,\dots,r$, stands for the shortfall with respect to g_i,

C_j, $j = 1,\dots,k$, denotes the goals assigned to priority class j, and

p is the order of the L_p-norm used (typically $p = 1$ or $p = \infty$).

In a substantial proportion of goal programming applications reported in the literature a supposed solution to (1) is determined on the basis of a single set of aspiration levels and associated weighting factors, i.e. the decision maker is actively involved only once, at the outset of the analysis, and then merely presented with the solution of model (2). A number of authors have argued that results obtained in this way could be rather arbitrary, since without a prior exploration of the set of feasible alternatives the specification of appropriate goals and weights is a very difficult task (e.g. Zeleny and Cochrane 1973; Morse 1978; Zeleny 1981). Viewed from a slightly different perspective a more far-reaching criticism can be levelled at such an approach: Apart from trivial cases in which the solution obtained satisfies each of the aspiration levels set, the decision maker is not provided with any information which helps him to decide whether to accept the solution presented to him or whether to attempt somehow to find a better solution.

This same criticism also holds true essentially for applications where the decision maker is actively encouraged to experiment with different combinations of aspiration levels and/or weighting factors. While he will clearly obtain a larger set of potential solutions from which to make a final choice, the repeated use of model (2), as such, does not necessarily help him to form a rationale for deciding when to terminate the search for improved solutions. In making this decision he may therefore have to rely on his intuition or resort to setting an arbitrary limit on the number of iterations to be carried out.

It is suggested here that information about the trade-offs implied by the solutions obtained can guide the decision maker in determining whether to end the search or not. More concretely, it is proposed to provide him with information about the set of weighting vectors $\lambda = (\lambda_1,\ldots,\lambda_r)^t$ for which the additive weighting model

$$\begin{aligned} \max \quad & \sum_{i=1}^{r} \lambda_i \, c_i^t \, x \\ \text{s.t.} \quad & A\,x \leqq b \end{aligned} \tag{3}$$

would lead to the same solution as produced by the goal programming formulation (2). The ratios λ_i/λ_j, $i,j = 1,\ldots,r$, $i \neq j$, can clearly be interpreted as trade-offs between the respective objectives. A comparison with the trade-offs the decision maker is willing to make, therefore, provides a simple means of testing whether the current solution may be acceptable.

The basic idea of using a trade-off analysis of this kind as part of a MODM procedure is certainly not a new one (cf. Kornbluth 1974), but it has received only very little attention in connection with reference point approaches. The reference point procedure proposed by Wierzbicki (1979a, 1979b) comprises a rudimentary form of such an analysis. The approach, in its most widely applied version (the computer package DIDASS, see Grauer (1983)), uses the following formulation:

$$\begin{aligned} \min \quad & -\min \left[\rho \min_{i=1,\ldots,r} d_i \, , \, \sum_{i=1}^{r} d_i \right] - \varepsilon \sum_{i=1}^{r} d_i \\ \text{s.t.} \quad & c_i^t\, x - d_i/w_i = g_i \, , \; i = 1,\ldots,r \\ & A\,x \leqq b \end{aligned} \tag{4}$$

where g_i and w_i, $i = 1,\ldots,r$, stand for (as in (2) above) the goal for objective i and the associated (cardinal) weighting factor,

d_i, $i = 1,\ldots,r$, represents the weighted deviation (in either direction) from goal i,

ρ is an arbitrarily chosen coefficient greater than or equal to r,
ε is a (usually small) positive constant.

The method is put forward as a tool for exploring the feasible region, i.e. the idea of experimenting with different aspiration levels etc. is fundamental to the approach. At each iteration the decision maker is presented with both the solution of (4) and the optimal values of the dual variables associated with the first r constraints of (4), i.e. the shadow prices of the aspiration levels specified. These immediately give rise to a weighting vector λ which can be interpreted, in the sense outlined above, as a set of trade-offs that is compatible with the current solution. However, as the following simple example illustrates, knowledge of only a single such vector - out of a possibly very large set - may not be of much assistance to the decision maker.

Assume a two-variable problem where the objective functions to be considered are

$$f_1(x) = (1,2)\,x \quad \text{and} \quad f_2(x) = (2,1)\,x$$

and the constraints are given by

$$\begin{bmatrix} -1 & 1 \\ 0 & 1 \\ 1 & 3 \\ 3 & 1 \end{bmatrix} \begin{bmatrix} x_1 \\ x_2 \end{bmatrix} \leqq \begin{bmatrix} 1 \\ 4 \\ 18 \\ 30 \end{bmatrix} , \; x_1, x_2 \geqq 0 .$$

Moreover, assume that the decision maker specifies aspiration levels of, say, $g_1 = 16$ and $g_2 = 25$ with weights of $w_1 = w_2 = 1$. If this problem is tackled using model (4) (with any value of $\rho \geqq 2$) the solution is $x^* = (9,3)$ - which is also the point where both f_1 and f_2 attain their maximum over the feasible region. As the constraint relating to g_1 is not active at this point, the dual leads to weights of $\lambda_1 = 0$ and $\lambda_2 = 1$, but the weighting model (3) clearly produces the solution (9,3) with any non-negative combination $(\lambda_1, \lambda_2) \neq (0,0)$. In other words, the single weighting vector derived from the dual does not show the decision maker that the solution obtained is actually compatible with any trade-off ratio λ_1/λ_2 between f_1 and f_2.

This example is, of course, a rather extreme one as the objective functions involved assume their maximum at the same point, but the basic argument applies equally to cases where the objectives are truly conflicting. If the coefficient of x_2 in f_1, for instance, were 5 instead of 2, then the maximum of f_1 would lie at the point (6,4). Assuming that the decision maker chooses aspiration levels of $g_1 = 27$ and $g_2 = 25$ with $w_1 = w_2 = 1$, the solution of (4) is again $x^* = (9,3)$ and the dual also yields the same weighting factors as before, i.e. $\lambda_1 = 0$, $\lambda_2 = 1$. The complete set of weighting vectors which lead to that solution, however, is given by $\Lambda = \{(\lambda_1, \lambda_2) \,|\, 1/3 \leqq (\lambda_1 + 2\lambda_2)/(5\lambda_1 + \lambda_2) \leqq 3\}$.

3. THE PROPOSED PROCEDURE

The procedure suggested requires the decision maker to state explicitly the trade-offs he is prepared to make. However, he is not required to provide one single vector, but merely upper and lower bounds on the acceptable trade-off ratios between any two of the objectives. More precisely, the procedure, at a given solution x^* of the reference point approach used, consists of the following steps:

Step 1: Determination, from the dual of the model employed, of a vector λ^0 for which the additive weighting model (3) produces the solution x^*.

Step 2: Computation (via multi-parametric sensitivity analysis based on λ^0) of the complete set of weighting vectors λ which lead to the solution x^*, i.e. determination of the linear inequalities which define the set $\Lambda = \{\lambda |$ model (3) has the solution $x^*\}$.

Step 3: Specification, by the decision maker, of lower and upper limits (l_{ij} and u_{ij}) on the trade-off ratios λ_i/λ_j, $i,j = 1,\dots,r$, $i > j$. (At later iterations of the reference point procedure the decision maker need only consider whether he wants to change any of the limits previously specified.)

Step 4: Consistency check of the information provided by the decision maker, i.e. feasibility test of the system of linear constraints defined by the intervals specified in step 3:

$$\lambda_j l_{ij} \leq \lambda_i \ , \ \lambda_j u_{ij} \geq \lambda_i \ , \ i,j = 1,\dots,r \ , \ i > j \tag{5}$$

If no feasible solution exists step 3 has to be repeated.

Step 5: Test for joint solutions of (5) and the set of inequalities obtained in step 2.

The results of step 5 can be presented to the decision maker in various forms. It may be sufficient to inform him whether joint solutions of the two systems of constraints exist or not. On the other hand, it requires little additional computational effort to carry out more detailed analyses of the relationships between the respective feasible sets.

4. AN EXAMPLE

The following numerical example is intended to illustrate the procedure. The problem assumed involves four decision variables and three objectives. The latter are given by

$f_1(x) = (1,2,-2,1)\,x$, $f_2(x) = (2,1,3,-0.5)\,x$, and $f_3(x) = (-1,2,2,3)\,x$,

and the feasible region is defined by the constraints

$$\begin{bmatrix} -1 & 1 & 2 & -1 \\ 0 & 1 & 1 & 0.5 \\ 1 & 3 & 0.5 & 2 \\ 3 & 1 & 1 & -0.5 \end{bmatrix} \begin{bmatrix} x_1 \\ x_2 \\ x_3 \\ x_4 \end{bmatrix} \leq \begin{bmatrix} 4 \\ 6 \\ 18 \\ 30 \end{bmatrix} \quad , \ x_1,\dots,x_4 \geq 0 \ .$$

Assume that by some reference point approach the solution $x^* = (9.12,\ 0,\ 4.32,\ 3.36)$ has been obtained. Details of the method used in arriving at this solution are of relevance only in as far as they can have an influence on the results of step 1 of the analysis, the computation of an initial weighting vector λ^0. This vector, however, is of no significance for the results of subsequent steps. As can easily be checked, $\lambda^0 = (1,1,1)$

fulfils the required conditions.

Step 2 of the procedure calls for the determination of the set Λ, consisting of all weighting vectors λ for which model (3) yields the solution x^*. By applying the simplex method to model (3) with $\lambda = \lambda^0$ the inequalities defining Λ can be obtained directly from the final tableau (see Kornbluth 1974). Here one has the following conditions:

$$\begin{bmatrix} -1.2 & 0.4 & 2.0 \\ -2.52 & 2.44 & 2.2 \\ 1.12 & -0.64 & 0.8 \\ -0.04 & 0.88 & -0.6 \end{bmatrix} \begin{bmatrix} \lambda_1 \\ \lambda_2 \\ \lambda_3 \end{bmatrix} \geqq 0 ,$$

$$\lambda_1, \lambda_2, \lambda_3 \geqq 0 , (\lambda_1, \lambda_2, \lambda_3) \neq (0, 0, 0) .$$

The third step of the analysis requires the active involvement of the decision maker. He is asked to set lower and upper bounds on the trade-off ratios acceptable to him. This might produce the following constraints:

$$\lambda_1/\lambda_2 \geqq 2 \qquad ,\text{i.e. } \lambda_1 - 2\lambda_2 \geqq 0$$

$$\lambda_1/\lambda_2 \leqq 5 \qquad ,\text{i.e. } -\lambda_1 + 5\lambda_2 \geqq 0$$

$$\lambda_1/\lambda_3 \geqq 1 \qquad ,\text{i.e. } \lambda_1 - \lambda_3 \geqq 0$$

etc.

As the decision maker might not be consistent in his replies (he could, for instance, conceivably stipulate that $\lambda_2/\lambda_3 \leqq 1/3$, which directly contradicts the limits set above), the system of inequalities obtained is next checked for feasibility. If it is found to be infeasible, the decision maker is asked to reconsider the limits given.

In the final stage of the analysis the inequalities obtained in the second and third steps are combined and the complete system checked for feasibility. If no feasible solution of this system exists than the trade-offs implied by x^* are inconsistent with the decision maker's conceptions in this respect so that further iterations of the reference point procedure are necessary.

5. SUMMARY AND CONCLUSIONS

An attempt has been made to demonstrate how reference point methodologies for tackling MODM problems may be combined with procedures based on the concept of weighting the objectives involved. A concrete approach has been described. The only additional information demands which this approach places upon the decision maker in excess of what is required in the usual reference point procedures is a set of bounds on the trade-offs he is prepared to make between any two of the objectives. The main benefit of the approach suggested is seen in the fact that it provides the decision maker with an additional perspective from which he can evaluate potential solutions to his problem. It may thus be of greater assistance to him in the task of constructing a rationale for the final choice.

REFERENCES

Grauer, M. (1983). A Dynamic Interactive Decision Analysis and Support System (DIDASS) - User's Guide. Working Paper WP-83-60. International Institute for Applied Systems Analysis, Laxenburg, Austria.

Ignizio, J.P. (1976). Goal Programming and Extensions. Lexington Books, Massachussetts.

Kornbluth, J.S.H. (1974). Duality, Indifference and Sensitivity Analysis in Multiple Objective Linear Programming. Operational Research Quarterly, 25(4):599-614.

Lee, S.M. (1972). Goal Programming for Decision Analysis. Auerbach, Philadelphia, Pennsylvania.

Lewandowski, A., and Grauer, M. (1982). The Reference Point Optimization Approach - Methods of Efficient Implementation. IIASA Collaborative Proceedings Series Vol. CP-82-S12. International Institute for Applied Systems Analysis, Laxenburg, Austria:353-376.

Morse, J.N. (1978). A Theory of Naive Weights. In S. Zionts, Multiple Criteria Problem Solving. Lecture Notes in Economics and Mathematical Systems No. 155. Springer, Berlin:384-401.

Wierzbicki, A.P. (1979a). The Use of Reference Objectives in Multiobjective Optimization - Theoretical Implications and Practical Experience. Working Paper WP-79-66. International Institute for Applied Systems Analysis, Laxenburg, Austria.

Wierzbicki, A.P. (1979b). A Methodological Guide to Multiobjective Optimization. Working Paper WP-79-122. International Institute for Applied Systems Analysis, Laxenburg, Austria.

Zeleny, M. (1981). The Pros and Cons of Goal Programming. Computers and Operations Research, 8(4):357-359.

Zeleny, M., and Cochrane, J.L. (1973). A Priori and A Posteriori Goals in Macroeconomic Policy Making. In J.L. Cochrane and M. Zeleny (Eds.), Multiple Criteria Decision Making. University of South Carolina Press, Columbia, South Carolina:373-391.

A VISUAL INTERACTIVE METHOD FOR SOLVING THE MULTIPLE-CRITERIA PROBLEM

Pekka Korhonen and Jukka Laakso
Helsinki School of Economics, Helsinki, Finland

1. INTRODUCTION

In this paper we propose an interactive method for solving multiple criteria decision problems with convex constraints and a pseudoconcave and differentiable utility function. The general framework of our method is similar to that of the so-called GDF method (Geoffrion, Dyer and Feinberg 1972). However, the Frank-Wolfe algorithm used by Geoffrion et al. does not operate solely with efficient solutions. Since comparisons between inefficient solutions may not seem relevant from the decision maker's point of view, we use a modified gradient projection method instead of the Frank-Wolfe algorithm. However, instead of the gradient vector we use **reference directions** that reflect the decision maker's preferences, as suggested by Andrzej Wierzbicki (1980), instead of trying to estimate the gradient. The reference directions are projected on the efficient surface and an interactive line search is performed. The values of the objectives on the efficient surface are displayed for the decision maker's evaluation both numerically and graphically.

If the decision maker cannot find a feasible point at which his utility is higher than at the current point, we check whether certain sufficient conditions for optimality are fulfilled or not. If not, an improved feasible solution can always be found. The sufficient conditions are also necessary conditions, if the feasible region is defined by linear inequalities. They are a generalization of the optimality conditions for extreme solutions used by Zionts and Wallenius (1983).

In the next section and in section 3 we present the details of our method. The fourth section contains discussion.

2. THE ALGORITHM

Let us consider the following problem:

$$\max u(\mathbf{q}) \tag{1}$$

$$\text{subject to } \mathbf{q} \quad Q = \{ \mathbf{f}(\mathbf{x}) \mid \mathbf{x} \in X \},$$

where $\mathbf{f}(\mathbf{x}) = (f_1(\mathbf{x}), f_2(\mathbf{x}), \ldots, f_r(\mathbf{x}))$ is a vector whose elements are the objective functions, u is the decision maker's (unknown) utility function, $\mathbf{x}$ is a decision vector and X is the set of feasible decisions. Without loss of generality we assume that all the objective functions are to be maximized. In addition, we assume that X is a convex, compact set and u is differentiable and pseudoconcave on X. Moreover, each function f_i is assumed to be concave. The set of feasible and **efficient** vectors, Q^*, is defined as follows:

$$Q^* = \{\mathbf{q} \mid \mathbf{q} \in Q \text{ and } \mathbf{q} \text{ efficient} \} \tag{2}$$

The outlines of the algorithm are as follows.

Step 0. Find an arbitrary efficient solution $\mathbf{q}^0 = \mathbf{f}(\mathbf{x}^0)$, $\mathbf{x}^0 \in X$. Let k=1.

Step 1. Give a reference point $\mathbf{d}^k$ and find an efficient solution $\mathbf{p}^k$ that solves the problem $\min D^1(\mathbf{p}^k, \mathbf{d}^k)$

$$\text{subject to } \mathbf{p}^k \in Q^*,$$

where D^1 is a distance function.

Step 2. Find the set Q^k of efficient vectors $\mathbf{q}$ that solve the problem

$$\min \ D^2(\mathbf{q}, \mathbf{z})$$

$$\text{subject to } \mathbf{z} = t\mathbf{p}^k + (1-t)\mathbf{q}^{k-1}, \ \mathbf{q} \in Q^*,$$

as t is increased from zero to infinity.
D^2 is a distance function that is not necessarily identical to D^1.

Step 3. Find the most preferred solution $\mathbf{q}^k$ in Q^k.

Step 4. If $\mathbf{q}^{k-1} = \mathbf{q}^k$ check the optimality conditions. If the conditions are true, stop; $\mathbf{q}^k$ is an optimal solution. Else put k=k+1 and go to step 1.

In step 0 the first efficient solution can be determined using any convenient method. For instance, Wierzbicki's reference point approach will presumably generate a very good starting point. It does not matter whether the initial solution $\mathbf{q}^0$ is an extreme point or not. The only requirement is that $\mathbf{q}^0$ belongs to the efficient set Q^*.

Step 1 is carried out in the spirit of Wierzbicki's reference point approach, too. For minimizing the **distance** between the reference point and the corresponding efficient solution, an achievement (penalty) scalarizing function is defined and maximized (minimized), as Wierzbicki has suggested. A particular objective function that will generate efficient solutions is the weighted Chebysev norm, which can be expressed as follows:

$$s(\mathbf{d},\mathbf{q}) = \max\{w_i\}, \quad w_i = \begin{cases} (d_i-q_i)/\,|d_i|, & \text{if } d_i \neq 0 \\ -\infty & \text{otherwise,} \end{cases} \tag{3}$$

where $\mathbf{d} = (d_1,d_2,\ldots,d_r)$ is the reference point given by the decision maker and $\mathbf{q} = (q_1,q_2,\ldots,q_r)$ is the corresponding feasible solution. If this function is minimized the resulting efficient solution $\mathbf{q}$ has one convenient property: the relations between its components are the same as those of the vector $\mathbf{d}$, if the line connecting $\mathbf{d}$ and the origin traverses through the efficient surface. In other words, units of measurement are irrelevant.

Step 2 is the point of departure from the original reference point approach towards the GDF method. Instead of concentrating merely on the efficient **points** that are "close" to the decision maker's reference objectives, an entire efficient **curve** connecting two efficient points is examined. This is clearly a more efficient way of scanning the efficient surface: if $\mathbf{q}'$ and $\mathbf{q}''$ are both efficient solutions and $\mathbf{q}'$ is preferred to $\mathbf{q}''$, one is inclined to believe that there is a feasible point $\mathbf{q}^*$ that is preferred to $\mathbf{q}''$ and satisfies the following equation:

$$\mathbf{q}^* = P\left[\, t\mathbf{q}'' + (1-t)\mathbf{q}' \,\right], \quad t \geq 0 \tag{4}$$

where P is a projection operator.

The values of the objective functions on the curve defined by equation (4) are presented to the decision maker and he is asked to select the most preferred point. If the efficient surface can be represented with linear inequalities and $\mathbf{q}'$ and $\mathbf{q}''$ are both on the same facet, the above procedure is completely analogous with line search in nonlinear programming with linear constraints. A line search is required in the GDF method as well, but all the points on the line to be searched are not necessarily efficient.

However, there is no reason to restrict the line search to the feasible points on the line defined by (4). Indeed, we might make more rapid progress if we were able to "peek around the corner", i.e. extend our line search to the **projection** of the entire half-line (4). If the set of feasible decisions X is defined by a set of linear inequalities and all the objective functions f_i are linear, the projection of the line defined by (4) can be computed using parametric linear programming and the unweighted Chebysev norm as the objective function to be minimized. Again, we can make use of Andrzej Wierzbicki's approach. First, we set up the following problem:

$$\min \left[\max (z_i - q_i) \right] \qquad (5)$$

subject to

$$\mathbf{z} = t\mathbf{p}^k + (1-t)\mathbf{q}^{k-1}$$

$$\mathbf{q} = \mathbf{f}(\mathbf{x}), \quad \mathbf{x} \in X, \quad \mathbf{z} = (z_1, z_2, \ldots, z_r)$$

The above problem can be converted to a linear programming problem, provided the set X is defined by linear inequalities and f_i is linear for all i. The equivalent linear program will read as follows:

$$\min y \qquad (6)$$

subject to

$$\mathbf{z} = t\mathbf{p}^k + (1-t)\mathbf{q}^{k-1}$$

$$y \geq z_i - q_i, \quad i = 1,2,\ldots,r$$

$$\mathbf{q} = \mathbf{f}(\mathbf{x}), \quad \mathbf{x} \in X$$

As parameter t in problem (6) is increased from zero to infinity, we obtain an efficient curve emanating from point $\mathbf{q}^{k-1}$ and traversing to the boundary of the efficient surface. This can be done using any commercial LP code with parametric linear programming.

The unweighted Chebysev norm has been chosen the objective function in problem (5) mainly on the grounds that the resulting parametric linear programming problem is easy to solve as only the right hand side vector of the problem needs to be parametrized.

Geoffrion et al. suggested the use of a graphical representation of the objectives as a possible method for solving the step-size problem as early as 1972. However, to our knowledge a computer implementation of this approach has been nonexistent so far. We have implemented the line search procedure described above for Apple III microcomputer. The values of the objectives along the feasible curve to be examined are plotted on the screen using a distinct colour for each objective. The cursor can be moved to any point on the line and the corresponding numerical values of the objectives are displayed simultaneously. The graphics give the decision maker an overview of the behaviour of the objectives along an efficient curve. At the same time he can have recourse to exact numerical information.

So far, every step of the algorithm has been rather straightforward with little theoretical content. It is step 4 that is the most complicated part of our algorithm and it deserves a section of its own.

3. OPTIMALITY CONDITIONS

In this section, we limit our attention to problems with linear constraints and linear objective functions. To put it differently, the efficient surface can be represented with a set of linear inequalities.

Let us suppose that in step 4 $\mathbf{q}^{k-1} = \mathbf{q}^k$. That is to say, the direction $\mathbf{p}^k - \mathbf{q}^{k-1}$ projected on the efficient surface is **not** a direction of improvement. The obvious thing to do in such a case is to try the opposite direction. This requires very little extra work: just repeat step 2 with the modification that t is **decreased** from zero to **minus** infinity. After that step 3 is executed in the usual manner. Alternatively, t can be varied from minus to plus infinity in the first place if so desired.

If an adequate number of directions are examined systematically, an improved solution can always be found, if $\mathbf{q}^k$ is not an optimal solution. This fact is presented formally in the following theorem.

Theorem. Let $\mathbf{q}^*$ be a feasible solution and $\mathbf{d}^1, \mathbf{d}^2, \ldots, \mathbf{d}^p$ a set of vectors in IR^r that define the cone

$$C = \{\mathbf{q} \mid \mathbf{q} = \mathbf{q}^* + \sum a_i \mathbf{d}^i,\ a_i \geq 0\},$$

which is the cone spanned by the set of constraints that are active at $\mathbf{q}^*$. (Note that each vector $\mathbf{d}^i$ is a feasible direction and Q^* C.) Further, let us assume that u is a pseudoconcave and differentiable function, and that

$$u(\mathbf{q}^*) \geq u(\mathbf{q}^* + a_i \mathbf{d}^i) \quad \text{for all} \quad a_i \geq 0 \text{ and } i=1,2,\ldots,p.$$

Then $\mathbf{q}^*$ is an optimal solution.

Proof. Assume that there is a feasible solution $\mathbf{q}^+ \varepsilon Q^*$ such that $u(\mathbf{q}^+) > u(\mathbf{q}^*)$. From the assumptions that u is a differentiable function, and that $u(\mathbf{q}^*) \geq u(\mathbf{q}^* + a_i\mathbf{d}^i)$ for all $a_i \geq 0$ and $\mathbf{d}^i$, $i=1,2,\ldots,p$, it follows that

$$\nabla u(\mathbf{q}^*)\cdot\mathbf{d}^i \leq 0 \text{ for all } i \text{ (see, e.g., Zangwill (1969), p. 24)}$$

Because the vector $(\mathbf{q}^+ - \mathbf{q}^*)$ is a feasible direction, it can be expressed as

$$\mathbf{q}^+ - \mathbf{q}^* = \sum w_i\mathbf{d}^i \ , \ w_i \geq 0 \quad \forall i=1,2,\ldots,r.$$

Since u was assumed to be pseudoconcave and

$u(\mathbf{q}^+) - u(\mathbf{q}^*) > 0$, it follows that

$\nabla u(\mathbf{q}^*)\cdot(\mathbf{q}^+ - \mathbf{q}^*) > 0$, because $\nabla u(\mathbf{q}^*)\cdot(\mathbf{q}^+ - \mathbf{q}^*) \leq 0$ would imply

$u(\mathbf{q}^+) \leq u(\mathbf{q}^*)$ according to the definition of pseudoconcavity.

Hence, $\nabla u(\mathbf{q}^*)\cdot \sum w_i\mathbf{d}^i > 0$, which is a contradiction. This implies that $\mathbf{q}^*$ is a locally optimal solution. Because u is assumed to be pseudoconcave and the set of feasible solutions is a convex, compact set, $\mathbf{q}^*$ is also a globally optimal solution.

Thus, we have proved that in the case where all the constraints and objectives are linear, we can always find a feasible direction of improvement, provided the current solution is not an optimal one.

4. DISCUSSION

The greatest merits of our method presented in this paper are that it is relatively easy to implement and very convenient to use. We neither assume the utility function to be linear nor deal with inefficient solutions. In fact, in steps 1, 2 and 3 we need not make **any** assumptions whatever concerning the properties of the utility function. The decision maker is free to examine any part of the efficient surface he pleases, i.e. he is not confined to evaluating only extreme solutions.

We have tacitly assumed that it is relatively easy for the decision maker to indicate which solution he likes best, once he is presented with a set of alternatives. If this is not the case, our method cannot tell the decision maker what he likes and what he doesn't like! But if our assumption were true, it would imply among other things that bicriteria problems are almost trivially simple: only one iteration is required for finding a globally optimal solution to any bicriteria problem, be the utility function what it may.

The performance of our method will no doubt depend very much on how good the decision maker is at specifying reference directions that lead to improved solutions. If the user is not familiar with the problem, he may have difficulty in specifying directions that result in rapid progress of the algorithm. In this case it may be wise to use random directions insted of user-specified reference directions. One advantage of using random directions is that the user does not have to think of some "reference objectives" every time he wants to evaluate a new set of efficient, possibly improved solutions. Specifying reference directions at every iteration may be a hard task, if the number of objectives is large. In addition, the user may specify his reference points in a biased manner, which prevents him from making any progress to speak of. Using random directions in conjunction with user-specified reference directions will probably be an efficient strategy in many cases.

The fact that the consistency of the decision maker's behaviour is not checked during the process may cause the algorithm to cycle. On the other hand, it may be a merit, too. After each iteration the decision maker is still free to return to the parts of the efficient surface he has examined already. The alternatives are not limited by his previous choices. This is no doubt a very useful feature if one just wants to find out what sort of outcomes are feasible and does not necessarily want to attain an "optimum". However, consistency of the decision maker's behaviour can be checked using results presented by Korhonen, Wallenius and Zionts (1983), if desired.

We believe that the method presented in this paper is a very powerful one in solving practical problems. It is very easy to use, it is not based on too restrictive assumptions, and it has a firm theoretical basis.

REFERENCES

Dyer, J. S. (1972), "Interactive Goal Programming," Management Science, Vol. 19, No. 1, pp. 62-70.

Geoffrion, A. M., Dyer, J. S. and Feinberg, A. (1972), "An Interactive Approach for Multi-Criterion Optimization, with an Application to the Operation of an Academic Department," Management Science, Vol. 19, No. 4, pp. 357-368.

Haimes, Y. Y., Hall, W. A. and Freedman, H. T. (1975), Multiobjective Optimization in Water Resources Systems, The Surrogate Worth Trade-off Method, Elsevier, New York.

Korhonen, P. and Laakso, J. (1983), "A Visual Interactive Method for Solving the Multiple Criteria Problem," Working Papers, F-57, Helsinki School of Economics.

Korhonen, P., Wallenius, J. and Zionts, S. (1983), "Solving the Discrete Multiple Criteria Problem Using Convex Cones," Working Paper No. 498 (Revised), SUNY at Buffalo.

Nakayama, T., Takeguchi, T. and Sano, M. (1983), "Interactive Graphics for Portfolio Selection," in Hansen, P. (ed.): Essays and Surveys on Multiple Criteria Decision Making, Springer-Verlag, New York.

Nijkamp, P. and Spronk, J. (1980), "Interactive Multiple Goal Programming: An Evaluation and Some Results," in Fandel, G. and Gal, T. (eds.): Multiple Criteria Decision Making Theory and Application," Springer-Verlag, New York.

Oppenheimer, K. R. (1978), "A Proxy Approach to Multi-Attribute Decision Making," Management Science, Vol. 24, No. 6, pp. 675-689.

Steuer, R. E. (1976), "Multiple Objective Linear Programming with Interval Criterion Weights," Management Science, Vol. 23, No. 3, pp. 305-316.

Wierzbicki, A. (1980), "The Use of Reference Objectives in Multiobjective Optimization," in Fandel, G. and Gal, T. (eds.): Multiple Criteria Decision Making Theory and Application, Springer-Verlag, New York.

Zangwill, W. (1969), Nonlinear Programming: A Unified Approach, Prentice-Hall, Englewood Cliffs, N.J.

Zionts, S. and Wallenius, J. (1976), "An Interactive Programming Method for Solving the Multiple Criteria Problem," Management Science, Vol. 22, No. 6, pp. 652-663.

Zionts, S. and Wallenius, J. (1983), "An Interactive Multiple Objective Linear Programming Method for a Class of Underlying Nonlinear Utility Functions," Management Science, vol. 29, No. 5, pp. 519-529

Zoutendijk, G. (1976), Mathematical Programming Methods, North-Holland Publishing Company.

ON THE IMPLEMENTATION OF THE INTERACTIVE SURROGATE WORTH TRADE-OFF (ISWT) METHOD

Kyösti Tarvainen

Institute of Mathematics, Helsinki University of Technology, Helsinki, Finland

1. INTRODUCTION

People who are not familiar with the multicriteria optimization theory often deal with multicriteria problems in the following way. One objective is taken as a single criteria to be optimized and some limits are set for the values of the other objectives. That is, the other objectives are treated as constraints in an ordinary optimization problem. After the optimization, a trade-off analysis may be carried out with respect to the active constraints. That is, the level of an active constraint -- the limit of an objective -- is changed a little and the optimization is done again to see how much the leve of the optimized objective will change.

In many cases, the limits for all criteria but one are set by others. Fo example, for a company, the goverment may have set minimum wages, pollution limits and so on, so that the company is left with an ordinary programming problem. Sometimes companies do a trade-off analysis to get, e.g., the pollution standard lowered; that is, a company calculates how much the economical result would improve if the pollution limit would be raised by a certain amount.

The way of handling a multicriteria problem by the constraint approach seems to be very informative and reliable approach to solve multicriteria problems. A suggestion to formalize this approach to obtain a multicriteria optimization algorithm was made by Chankong and Haimes (1978). They called the derived scheme the Interactive Surrogate Worth Trade-off Method. In this paper, the ISWT method is derived in a slighty different way in Section 2, which results in a version of the method that is faster in convergence and perhaps more convenient for the decision maker. An example is given in Sectio 3.

2. DERIVATION OF THE ISWT METHOD

2.1. Mathematical Problem Formulation

We will consider the following multicriteria problem:

$$\min \quad (f_1(x),\dots,f_n(x)) \tag{1}$$

$$\text{subject to} \quad g(x) \leqslant 0, \tag{2}$$

where $x \in R^N$, $f_i : R^N \to R$ $(i=1,\ldots,n)$, $g: R^N \to R^m$.

A main mathematical assumption made later concerns the existence of trade-offs. This assumption usually implies that the f_i and g_i functions are differentiable and that the feasible region specified by Eq. (2) is compact.

Furthermore, it is assumed that, for the decision maker solving the above problem, there exists an underlying (but not known) differentiable utility function.

2.2 The Constraint Problem

At the beginning, the decision maker is asked to specify an objective with respect to whose values he is flexible; that is an objective that does not have any sharp limit under which the values of the objective are satisfactory and above which limit the values are unsatisfactory (note: we are minimizing). Let us renumerate the objectives so that this objective is f_1. The objective f_1 will be taken as a primary objective for the constraint problem. This selection will be explained later.

The decision maker is then asked to specify a desirable upper bound, denoted by ε_i^1, for each other objective f_i $(i=2,\ldots,n)$.

Given this information, the following optimization problem is solved:

$$\min f_1(x) \tag{3}$$

$$\text{subject to} \quad f_i(x) \leqslant \varepsilon_i^1, \qquad i = 2,\ldots,n, \tag{4}$$

$$g(x) \leqslant 0. \tag{5}$$

Let this problem have a unique solution x^1. Then, x^1 and the corresponding objective vector $(f_1(x^1),\ldots,f_n(x^1))$ are Pareto optimal (for the properties of the above problem, see Chankong and Haimes 1983).

In a typical case, all objectives conflict so much that the inequalities in Eq. (4) are binding at x^1. If this would not be the case for an ε_k^1, let us, for the following trade-off calculations, respecify $\varepsilon_k^1 = f_k(x^1) - e$, where e is a small positive number so that the solution x^1 of the constraint problem does not change considerably.

2.3 The Trade-offs

The objective vector $f^1 \triangleq (f_1(x),\ldots,f_n(x))$ given by the above optimization is a starting point given to the decision maker. In addition, local information about the alternatives around f^1 is given in a form of trade-offs. It is assumed here that we have trade-offs, not only total trade-offs (for trade-off concepts, see Chankong and Haimes 1983).

The trade-off between the objectives f_1 and f_i $(i=2,\ldots,n)$ at f^1, denoted by λ_{1i}^1, is easily obtained, for example, by solving the problem given by Eqs. (3),...,(5) with $(\varepsilon_i^1 - e_i)$ instead of ε_i^1 (e_i is a small number). If the corresponding change in f_1 is df_1, then, approximately, $\lambda_{1i}^1 = df_1/e_i$.

In some cases, we get the trade-offs as dual variables in the optimization algorithm. If the constraint (5) is treated via the augmented Lagrang technique, it is also useful to treat the constraints (4) with this techniqu whereby the trade-offs are obtained at the same time.

Trade-offs as marginal rates may be difficult to grasp by a decision maker. The trade-off information should, therefore, be presented in an incremental form. That is, instead of giving λ^1_{1i} a phrase like the following can be used: "If the objective f_i is improved by Δf_i, then the objective f_1 will be deteriorated by $\lambda^1_{1i}\Delta f_i$."

The increment Δf_i (i=2,...,n) should be about the size of the changes that are relevant to consider in f_i in the problem. This is often clear to the analyst from the context; if not, the decision maker is asked to give this information.

2.4. The Decision Maker's Response to the Trade-offs

Given the objective vector $f^1 = (f_1(x^1),\ldots,f_n(x^1))$ and the trade-off information around this point, there are certainly many possibilities to elicit the deciosion maker's response to this information. Chankong and Haimes propose that the decision maker gives a number between -10 and 10 for each trade-off indicating how much the decision maker prefers the trade-off in question. Chen and Wang propose that the decision maker only specifie whether he wants to lower or higher the objectives or leave unchanged (Chen and Wang 1983).

In our experiments, the following verbal questioning has worked well. Given the trade-off information between the objectives f_1 and f_i in a form such as "If you win Δf_i in f_i, you will loose $\lambda^1_{1i}\Delta f_i$ in f_1, and viceversa", the decison maker is asked to answer verbally in one of the following ways:

	W^1_{1i}	
"I am much in favor of increasing f_i by Δf_i"	2	
"I am slightly in favor of increasing f_i by Δf_i"	1	
"I cannot say; doesn't matter"	0	(6)
"I am slightly in favor of decreasing f_i by Δf_i"	-1	
"I am much in favor of decreasing f_i by Δf_i"	-2	

In the column on the right are numbers which are attached to these statements. The numbers are explained in the next section.

The above questioning is done for the (n-1) calculated trade-offs. Note that here we ask a question about a specific increment (Δf_i) in f_i, not about the change of f_i in general.

2.5 Changing the Levels of Objectives

After the decision maker's response, new values for the levels of objectives are determined based on the following reasoning.

Consider theoretically the multicriteria problem at hand as an optimization problem of the underlying utility function in the $f_2\cdots f_n$ space (the associated f_1 values are determined as solutions of the problems (3),...(5), where the $f_2,\ldots,f_n$ values are constraints).

In addition to the $f_2\cdots f_n$ space, we also consider its dimensionless counterpart, the $f'_2\cdots f'_n$ space, where $f'_i = f_i/\Delta f_i$ (i=2,...,n; the Δf_i's are defined above).

In the last section, we associated with each f_i (i=2,...,n) a number W^1_{1i} (called surrogate worth), which codifies the decision maker's willingness to trade-off the objectives f_i and f_1. It is evident that every time the decision maker is slightly in favor of a change (W^1_{1i} = 1 or -1), the absolute change in the underlying utility function is approximately the same. We can always scale the utility function so that this change is 1. That is, in this case (W^1_{1i} = 1 or -1), and naturally in the case where W^1_{1i} is zero, the W^1_{1i}'s express approximate changes in the underlying utility function.

In the case where W^1_{1i} = 2 or -2, we will also use the W^1_{1i} value as an approximation of the change of the underlying utility function when f_i is increased by Δf_i and f_1 is decreased by $\lambda^1_{1i}\Delta f_i$. We will discuss this assumption in a moment.

With this reasoning, the gradient of the underlying utility function in the $f'_2\cdots f'_n$ space is, thus, $(W^1_{12},\ldots,W^1_{1n})$. The corresponding line in the $f_2\cdots f_n$ space, in which the utility function increases fastest, is, then, in a parameter form, $\{ (tW^1_{12}\Delta f_2,\ldots,tW^1_{1n}\Delta f_n) \mid t \geqslant 0 \}$.

The information elicited so far from the decision maker only specifies this gradient direction. Therefore, some points in this line with corresponding f_1 values are presented to the decision maker. That is, objective vectors of the following generic form are presented to the decision maker ($t_i = t_1, t_2,\ldots$):

$$(f_1(t_i),\ f_2(x^1) + t_iW^1_{12}\Delta f_2,\ \ldots\ ,f_n(x^1) + t_iW^1_{1n}\Delta f_n) \tag{7}$$

where $f_1(t_i)$ is determined as a solution of the problem given by Eqs. (3),.., (5) when the other objectives are held as constraints.

The decision maker selects a value of t_i (that is, a t_i where the utility function reaches its maximum). The corresponding objective vector is denoted by f^2. This completes the first iteration, and the procedure is restarted at f^2 with trade-off calculations.

In the above, a rather arbitrary value (W^1_{1i} = 2 or -2) was selected for the "much in favor"-statesments. Extensive experimentation would probably suggest another number. But we are always increasing the utility function anyway; and it is good to have more than two absolute values (0 and 1) for the W^1_{1i}'s. On the other hand, the values -2,-1,0,1,2 are probably sufficient: for example, in the case n = 3, we have 12 possible gradient directions on the f_2f_3 plane.

2.6 Convergence of the Scheme

It is clear from the derivation of the scheme that we are always attempting to increase the underlying utility function. So, we should at leas end up with a local maximum. A more mathematical proof of the convergence uses trade-offs (not their discretized counterparts, as above) along the lines of Chankong (1977).

However, as pointed out by Nakayama et. al (1982) in a similar context, the use of finite changes may cause the scheme stop before the maximum of the utility function is achieved.

The discretization of trade-offs naturally always causes some losses in the optimization of the utility function. The f_1 objective plays a central role here; all other objectives are traded against it. Therefore, f_1 should be selected in the above mentioned way. In other words, the utility function should not be highly nonlinear with respect to f_1 , because high nonlinearity implies larger errors in discretization.

To illustrate this point, assume that f_1 has a limit f_1' above which its values are highly unsatisfactory and under which its values are all very sati factory. Assume we are in the iteration at an objective vector, where the value of f_1 , f_1'', is slightly less than f_1' so that all positive f_1 increment of the discretized trade-offs causes f_1 to exceed the limit f_1'. This would imply that f_1 is not increased. On the other hand, if f_1'' is highly satisfactory, f_1 would not be decreased at the expense of other objectives. So, in this case, the algorithm would stop. However, it is quite possible that we are not close to the preferred solution (it may be clear to the decision maker that he would trade-off the $f_2,\ldots,f_n$ objectives).

2.7 Summary of the ISWT Scheme

STEP 1. Ask the decision maker to specify one objective with respect to which he is flexible. Denote this objective by f_1.

Ask the decision maker to specify desirable limits ε_i for other objectives.

Ask the decision maker to specify increments Δf_i $(i=2,\ldots,n)$ which are small but still relevant to consider.

STEP 2. Solve the optimization problem (3),...,(5), and generate the associated trade-offs.

STEP 3. Interact with the decision maker to obtain worth values W_{1i}^1 (6). If all W_{1i}^1's are zero, stop.

STEP 4. Generate new alternatives (7), and let the decision maker select one Repeat the procedure from Step 2 on.

3. AN EXAMPLE

The following time allocation problem for the entire college period for M.Sc. has been used by students at the Helsinki University of Technology (an original version is credited to Haimes and Mike Corey). The objectives are:

f_1 = leisure time (hours in a week)

f_2 = learning, measured by GPA (0...5, 5 best)

f_3 = net earnings (Fmk in a month)

f_4 = extension of study time (years)

The decision variables are:

x = hours per week spent with studies
y = hours per week spent in part-time work
z = extension in years of the study time

The systems equations are:

$$f_1 = 91 - x - y \tag{8}$$

$$f_2 = a/(1 + bEXP(-cx(1 + z/5))) \tag{9}$$

$$f_3 = 86y \tag{10}$$

$$f_4 = z \tag{11}$$

In Eq. (8), "91" stands for the weekly available time that is left after sleeping and domestic chores. In Eq. (9), a, b and c are parameters of the learning curve (in this example, a = 4.5, b = 3.5, c = 0.05). The extension of the study time for M.Sc. is counted from 5th year and above. In the Finnish university system, it is possible to study at one's own pace. In Eq. (10), "86" converts weekly working hours into a monthly net salary (1 Fmk equals 0.2 US-dollars).

The following table shows one typical run of the ISWT method in a condensed form . Information given by the decision maker and numbers attached to his statesments are underlined. The ISWT method usually converges in a couple of iterations as shown here.

TABLE 1 A run of the ISWT method.

Step 1. Flexible objective: $\underline{f_1}$

Limits: f_2 = $\underline{4}$ grade points

f_3 = $\underline{1500}$ Fmk

f_4 = $\underline{0}$ years

Increments: Δf_2 = $\underline{0.1}$ grade points

Δf_3 = $\underline{100}$ Fmk

Δf_4 = $\underline{0.1}$ years

Step 2. f_1 = 6.5 hours, f_2 = 4 grade points, f_3 = 1500 Fmk, f_4 = 0 years

λ_{12} = 4.6 hours/0.1 grade points

λ_{13} = 1.2 hours/100 Fmk

λ_{14} = 1.3 hours/0.1 years

Step 3. $W_{12}^1 = \underline{-2}$

$W_{13}^1 = \underline{-2}$

$W_{14}^1 = \underline{2}$

Step 4.

T	leisure time	grade	earn.	ext.
0	6.5	4	1500	0
1	11.6	3.96	1350	0.1
2	16.5	3.93	1200	0.2
3	21.1	3.89	1050	0.3
4	25.5	3.85	900	0.5
5	29.7	3.81	750	0.6
6	33.7	3.77	600	0.7
7	37.6	3.73	450	0.9
8	41.4	3.7	300	1
9	45	3.66	150	1.1
10	48.5	3.62	0	1.3

T = 2

Step 2. f_1 = 16.5 hours, f_2 = 3.93 grade points, f_3 = 1200 Fmk, f_4 = 0.2 yea

λ_{12} = 3.8 hours/0.1 grade points, λ_{13} = 1.2 hours/100 Fmk,

λ_{14} = 1.2 hours/0.1 years

Step 3. $W_{12}^2 = \underline{0}$, $W_{13}^2 = \underline{-2}$, $W_{14}^2 = \underline{1}$

Step 4.

T	leisure time	grade	earn.	ext.
0	16.5	3.93	1200	0.2
1	18.6	3.93	1080	0.3
2	20.6	3.93	960	0.3
3	22.7	3.93	840	0.4
4	24.7	3.93	720	0.5
5	26.7	3.93	600	0.5
6	28.8	3.93	480	0.6
7	30.8	3.93	360	0.6
8	32.7	3.93	240	0.7
9	34.7	3.93	120	0.8
10	36.7	3.93	0	0.8

T = 4

Step 2. f_1 = 24.7 hours, f_2 = 3.93 grade points, f_3 = 720 Fmk, f_4 = 0.5 year

λ_{12} = 3.6 hours/0.1 grade points, λ_{13} = 1.2 hours/100 Fmk,

λ_{14} = 1.0 hours/0.1 years

Step 3. $W_{12}^3 = \underline{0}$, $W_{13}^3 = \underline{0}$, $W_{14}^3 = \underline{0}$. (stop)

4. REFERENCES

Chankong, V. (1977). Multiobjective Decision Making Analysis: The Interactiv Surrogate Worth Trade-off Method (Ph.D. Dissertation). Systems Engineer ing Department, Case Western Reserve University, Cleveland, Ohio.

Chankong, V., and Haimes, Y. Y. (1978). The Interactive Surrogate Worth Trade-off (ISWT) Method for multiobjective Decision Making. In S. Ziont (Ed.), Multicriteria Problem Solving. Springer, New York.

Chankong, V, and Haimes, Y. Y. (1983). Multiobjective Decision Making: Theor and Methodology. North-Holland, New York.

Chen, Ting, and Wang, Bai-lin (1983).An Interactive Method for Multiobjective Decision Making. Preprints of the IFAC/IFORS Symposium on Large Scale Systems. Warsaw, Poland, July 1983, pp. 86-91.

Nakayama, H., Takeguchi, T, and Sano, M. (1982). Interactive Graphics for Portfolio Selection. The Fifth International Conference on MCDM, Mons, Belgium, August 9-13, 1982.

IV. APPLICATIONS OF INTERACTIVE DECISION ANALYSIS

MULTICRITERIA DECISION ANALYSIS TO AID BUDGET ALLOCATION

K. Légrády[1], F.A. Lootsma[1], J. Meisner[2] and F. Schellemans[3]
[1] *Department of Mathematics and Informatics, Delft University of Technology, Delft, The Netherlands*
[2] *Royal Dutch/Shell Research Laboratories, Department of Mathematics and Systems Engineering, Amsterdam, The Netherlands*
[3] *Energy Research Council, The Hague, The Netherlands*

1. INTRODUCTION

The Energy Research Council of the Netherlands (with 18 members representing government agencies, research institutes, universities, industries trade unions, consumer organizations, and environmental groups) has been established by the Minister of Economics and the Minister of Science, 28 January 1980, to draw up, among other things, energy-research plans for several years ahead. A major task of the Council is to advice the Ministers on the allocation of the available budget to various energy technologies.

The Council has invited us to apply multi-criteria decision analysis, first, to identify and to weigh the relevant criteria, second, to rate the energy technologies, and finally, to compute a package of projects with maximum total weight. The underlying idea is, of course, that the preliminary discussions and the confrontation with the calculated results will eventually enhance the consensus in the Council.

This paper presents our experiences, so far, with two pairwise-comparison methods in the field of multi-criteria analysis: the Bradley-Terry (1952) method and the method of Saaty (1980) using logarithmic regression. Various methodological questions had to be considered again: the collection and the scaling of human judgement, the sensitivy of the calculated results, and the treatment of the budget constraints. In addition, we also concerned ourselves with the features of a decision support system for multi-criteria analysis.

2. CRITERIA AND ALTERNATIVES

The energy problem of the Netherlands is briefly characterized by abundant supply of natural gas, high dependence on natural gas and oil imports, and strong public opposition against nuclear energy.

In preceding years, the Council formulated four criteria for the evaluation of a research plan. The experiments with multi-criteria analysis led to a reformulation of the criteria; moreover, two new ones were added to the set. The energy technologies, the alternatives being considered for possible research support, were finally reviewed on the basis of their possible contribution to

1. the security of energy supply;
2. the energy efficiency;
3. the social acceptability;
4. the creation of an innovation-based industry;
5. the energy management (in the long term);
6. the establishment of a high-level scientific activity.

These criteria had to be ranked and rated according to their impact on the national economy.

The Council was concerned with the following energy-technology areas:

1. energy saving;
2. oil and gas;
3. coal;
4. uranium;
5. solar energy;
6. wind energy;
7. biomass energy;
8. geothermal energy;
9. supporting technologies.

Some areas have been subdivided but a further hierarchization was felt to be unnecessary (at least for the time being). The energy technologies under consideration (a total of 23) will be shown in the tables 3 and 4.

3. METHODS OF PAIRWISE COMPARISON

In a method of pairwise comparison, stimuli (criteria, alternatives, for example) are presented in pairs to one or more referees (decision makers). The basic experiment is the comparison of two stimuli S_i and S_j by a referee who must choose one of them; we usually say that the referee _prefers_ the stimulus he chooses. Suppose that there are N referees; let α_{ij} denote the number of referees preferring S_i over S_j, then $\alpha_{ji} = N - \alpha_{ij}$. We assume that the stimuli S_i have respective values V_i on a numerical scale; the objective of the experiments is to estimate these values.

In the Thurstone (1927) model, the perceived value X_i of S_i, averaged over the referees, is taken to be normally distributed with mean V_i and variance σ^2; the X_i are supposed to be equi-correlated with correlation coefficient ρ. In order to approximate the V_i, we take α_{ij}/N to be an estimate of

$$P(X_i - X_j \geq 0) = P\left(\frac{(X_i-X_j) - (V_i-V_j)}{\sigma\sqrt{2(1-\rho)}} \geq \frac{-(V_i-V_j)}{\sigma\sqrt{2(1-\rho)}}\right) .$$

Setting the multiplicative constant $\sigma\sqrt{2(1-\rho)}$ arbitrarily to 1, we estimate the difference of V_i and V_j by the value β_{ij} such that

$$P(Z \geq - \beta_{ij}) = \alpha_{ij}/N ,$$

where Z denotes a normally distributed variable with zero mean and variance 1. Estimates $\bar{v}_i$ of the weights V_i are now obtained by minimizing the sum of squares

$$\sum_{i<j} (\beta_{ij} - v_i + v_j)^2 .$$

The estimates are not unique: there is an additive degree of freedom since we have only considered differences of stimuli.

In the Bradley-Terry (1952) model, we take α_{ij}/N to be an estimate of the preference for S_i over S_j, which is written as $V_i/(V_i+V_j)$; it is assumed that the V_i are positive and sum to unity. The maximum-likelyhood function used to find estimates $\bar{v}_i$ of the V_i is given by

$$L = C(\prod_{i=1}^{n} v_i^{a_i})/(\prod_{i<j} (v_i+v_j)^N) , \tag{1}$$

where C denotes a constant, and

$$a_i = \sum_{j=1}^{n} \alpha_{ij} .$$

Maximization of lnL subject to the normalization constraint ($\Sigma\ v_i = 1$) yields the $\bar{v}_i$ (for further details, see David (1963)).

An obvious extension of the above models is to consider the case that some referees sometimes abstain from giving their preference: then we merely replace N by N_{ij}, the number of comparisons between S_i and S_j.

In the priority theory of Saaty (1980), gradations in the comparative judgement are easily handled. First, we consider the case of one referee who is requested to estimate the ratio V_i/V_j by a positive number denoted as r_{ij}; we assume again that the V_i are positive and sum to unity. Equality of the stimuli S_i and S_j is expressed by setting $r_{ij} = 1$. If S_i is believed to be somewhat stronger, much stronger, ... than S_j, then r_{ij} is accordingly given a value higher than 1 (the numerical scale is discussed in sec. 5). Of course, we have $r_{ij} < 1$ if S_i is felt to be weaker than S_j, and normally the judgement satisfies the reciprocal condition

$$r_{ij} \cdot r_{ji} = 1 .$$

Finally, we set the diagonal elements r_{ii} (i = 1, ..., n) to 1. This completes the assignment of values by exactly one decision maker who estimates each pair of decision factors. When we are dealing with a decision-making committee, and allow for the possibility that some members sometimes abstain from giving their opinion, we proceed as follows. We let δ_{ij} stand for the number of estimates of V_i/V_j obtained in the committee, and r_{ijk} ($k = 1, \ldots, \delta_{ij}$) for the k-th estimate of V_i/V_j. We approximate the vector $V = (V_1, \ldots, V_n)$ by the <u>normalized</u> vector $\bar{v}$ which minimizes

$$\sum_{i<j} \sum_{k=1}^{\delta_{ij}} (\ln r_{ijk} - \ln v_i + \ln v_j)^2 =$$

$$= \sum_{i<j} \sum_{k=1}^{\delta_{ij}} (y_{ijk} - x_i + x_j)^2 ,$$

where $y_{ijk} = \ln r_{ijk}$ and $x_i = \ln v_i$. Now, observing that $y_{ijk} = -y_{jik}$ and $\delta_{ij} = \delta_{ji}$, we can write the associated normal equations as

$$x_i \sum_{\substack{j=1\\ j\neq i}}^{n} \delta_{ij} - \sum_{\substack{j=1\\ j\neq i}}^{n} \delta_{ij}\, x_j = \sum_{\substack{j=1\\ j\neq i}}^{n} \sum_{k=1}^{\delta_{ij}} y_{ijk} . \tag{2}$$

These equations are dependent (they sum to the zero equation). Taking the vector $\bar{x}$ to denote a particular solution of (2), we can write the components of the general solution as $\bar{x}_i + \eta$, with arbitrary η, and we approximate V_i by

$$\bar{v}_i = \exp(\bar{x}_i+\eta) / \sum_{i=1}^{n} \exp(\bar{x}_i+\eta) = \exp(\bar{x}_i) / \sum_{i=1}^{n} \exp(\bar{x}_i) \quad .$$

We note in passing that there is an explicit solution $\bar{x}$ to (2) with components

$$\bar{x}_i = \frac{1}{n} \sum_{j=1}^{n} y_{ij}$$

in the case that $\delta_{ij} = 1$ for each factor pair; then we approximate V_i by the normalized geometric row mean

$$\bar{v}_i = \sqrt[n]{\prod_{j=1}^{n} r_{ij}} \Big/ \sum_{i=1}^{n} \sqrt[n]{\prod_{j=1}^{n} r_{ij}} \quad .$$

It is worth noting that an overall ranking and rating of the stimuli is impossible (both mathematically and in practice) if the stimuli can be split up into a number of disjunct groups without mutual (intergroup) comparisons.

Obviously, Saaty's method with logarithmic regression has certain advantages over the Bradley-Terry method (solution of a linear system only to find the values V_i, gradations in the comparative judgement possible), but it remains questionable how the gradations should be expressed on a numerical scale.

4. THE EVALUATION PROCEDURE

We are dealing with a decision problem where m alternatives $A_1,\ldots,A_m$ must be ranked and rated in the presence of n possibly conflicting criteria $C_1,\ldots,C_n$. In the first step, we approximate the values p_i of the respective criteria C_i, $i = 1,\ldots,n$, by weights $\bar{\alpha}_i$ calculated via a pairwise-comparison method. In the second step we judge the performance of the alternatives $A_1,\ldots,A_m$ under each of the criteria separately. When criterion C_i is under consideration, we approximate the values q_{ij} of the A_j, $j = 1,\ldots,m$, by weights $\bar{\beta}_{ij}$ calculated via the same pairwise-comparison method. Obviously, the performance ratio q_{ij}/q_{ik} of the alternatives A_j and A_k under criterion C_i is approximated by the ratio $\bar{\beta}_{ij}/\bar{\beta}_{ik}$. We want to obtain final scores $\bar{s}_j$ and $\bar{s}_k$ for A_j and A_k, such that $\bar{s}_j/\bar{s}_k$ estimates their overall performance ratio. When the computed weights $\bar{\alpha}_1,\ldots,\bar{\alpha}_n$ happen to be equal ($\bar{\alpha}_i = 1/n$), an appropriate expression would be

$$\frac{\bar{s}_j}{\bar{s}_k} = \sqrt[n]{\prod_{i=1}^{n} \frac{\bar{\beta}_{ij}}{\bar{\beta}_{ik}}} \quad ,$$

that is, the computed $\bar{\alpha}_i$ appear exponentially. Generalizing this, we set

$$\frac{\bar{s}_j}{\bar{s}_k} = \prod_{i=1}^{n} \left(\frac{\bar{\beta}_{ij}}{\bar{\beta}_{ik}} \right)^{\bar{\alpha}_i} .$$

Hence, the final scores can be defined by

$$\bar{s}_j = \prod_{i=1}^{n} (\bar{\beta}_{ij})^{\bar{\alpha}_i} , \quad j = 1, \ldots, m .$$

Using first-order approximations and the normalization of the $\bar{\alpha}_i$ $(i = 1,\ldots,n)$, we can easily find

$$\bar{s}_j = \exp[\sum_{i=1}^{n} \bar{\alpha}_i \ln \bar{\beta}_{ij}] \simeq$$

$$\simeq 1 + \sum_{i=1}^{n} \bar{\alpha}_i \ln \bar{\beta}_{ij} \simeq$$

$$\simeq 1 + \sum_{i=1}^{n} \bar{\alpha}_i (\bar{\beta}_{ij} - 1) = \sum_{i=1}^{n} \bar{\alpha}_i \bar{\beta}_{ij} . \quad (3)$$

This is a well-known result: multiplying the weights $\bar{\beta}_{ij}$ of alternative A_j by the weights $\bar{\alpha}_i$ of the criteria C_i $(i = 1, \ldots, n)$ and adding the products, is the traditional method to obtain the final scores $\bar{s}_j$ $(j = 1,\ldots,m)$. These numbers can be used to rank and to rate the alternatives, but we have the impression that checking for inconsistencies is more important than anything else in actual applications of the method. The user can readily detect cyclic judgements and underlying controversies in a committee. He can also solve the weights $\bar{\alpha}_i$ from (3) by estimating (a holistic approach) the final scores $\bar{s}_j$ and the performance weights $\bar{\beta}_{ij}$, whereafter he may consider whether the $\bar{\alpha}_i$ so obtained reflect his preferences.

5. MAGNITUDE SCALING

Saaty's original scale as shown in Table I (with intermediate values 2,4,6,8 assigned to r_{ij} in cases of doubt between two adjacent qualifications

TABLE 1 Saaty's scale for pairwise comparison

S_i	equal impact somewhat more impact much more impact dominance absolute dominance	S_j	r_{ij}	1 3 5 7 9

has a number of disadvantages. First, it is not easy to maintain the transitivity property

$$r_{ik} = r_{ij}\, r_{jk} ,$$

which is plausible because

$$\frac{V_i}{V_k} = \frac{V_i}{V_j} \cdot \frac{V_j}{V_k} .$$

If, for instance, S_i has somewhat more impact than S_j, and S_j somewhat more than S_k, so that both r_{ij} and r_{jk} are set to 3, then the assignment of 9 to r_{ik}, implying absolute dominance of S_i over S_k, is mostly felt to be out of proportion. A geometric scale with powers of a suitable base number is more appropriate. Second, the Saaty scale is rather short. Magnitude scaling of words and phrases expressing grades of approval or disapproval has shown that the response range (the ratio of the extreme stimuli) can easily be up to 100 (see, for instance, Lodge (1981)). Saaty's scale allows a response range of 9 only. Hence, we have employed a few geometric scales based on powers of e and 10. In our experiments, we distinguished five different cases.

TABLE 2 Numerical Scales

Case	Scale					
I	Saaty	1	2	3	. . . .	9
II	Geometric	1	$e^{1/2}$	e	. . . .	e^4
III	Geometric	1	$10^{1/4}$	$10^{1/2}$	. . . .	10^2
IV	Geometric	1	e	e^2	. . . .	e^8
V	Bradley-Terry	$\frac{1}{2}$	1	1	. . . .	1

Note. A sound argument for the above-named transitivity property can be obtained from psycho-physical experiments, demonstrating that the response $\psi(s)$, the impression of brightness of light, loudness of sound, etc., is a power function of the stimulus s because the ratio $\psi(ks)/\psi(s)$ depends on the positive number k only (Roberts (1980)). Hence, the scale value r_{ij} may be considered as an approximation of $(V_i/V_j)^{\alpha}$, with an unknown power α. In our study, we have not pursued the determination of α. Instead, we concentrated on the sensitivity of the calculated results when various scales are employed.

6. RANKING AND RATING OF ENERGY TECHNOLOGIES

In our preliminary experiments, eight members of the Energy Research Council made pairwise comparisons of the criteria by using the documents as shown in Figure 1. They were requested to consider the randomly generated pairs of criteria, and to tick their judgement in a box or on the separating line. Qualifications like "dominance" and "absolute dominance" were felt to be unnecessary; the judgement ranged from "much higher" to "much lower" impact. We assigned numerical values to the qualifications according to the scales of case I-IV (see also Table 3). In case V, the Bradley-Terry method, we interpreted "much higher" and "somewhat higher" impact as a preference for the first-named criterion.

```
R.E.O.-project

Mr.

=========+
  FOR    |   Compare the impact of the following pairs of CRITERIA and
 OFFICE  |   mark the appropriate box.
USE ONLY |
         |                  | has     | has ABOUT |   has     |
         |                  |SOMEWHAT |  EQUAL    | SOMEWHAT  |
    +----+         | has    | HIGHER  | impact as | LOWER     |  has    |
1-4|   4 |         | MUCH   | impact  +---+   +---+ impact    |  MUCH   |
    +----+         | HIGHER |  than       |   |     than      | LOWER   |
         |         | impact +-----------+ |   | +-----------+ impact  |
         |         |                    | |   | |                       |
56 78    |         +--------------+     | |   | |    +------------------+
|| ||    |                        |     | |   | |    |
VV VV    |                        V     V V   V V    V
    +===+                         +---+---+---+---+---+
3- 2|   |   Social Acceptabili    |   |   |   |   |   | Energy Efficiency
    +===+                         +---+---+---+---+---+
2- 5|   |   Energy Efficiency     |   |   |   |   |   | Long-term Contribu
    +===+                         +---+---+---+---+---+
4- 2|   |   Innovation-based I    |   |   |   |   |   | Energy Efficiency
    +===+                         +---+---+---+---+---+
4- 3|   |   Innovation-based I    |   |   |   |   |   | Social Acceptabili
    +===+                         +---+---+---+---+---+
2- 6|   |   Energy Efficiency     |   |   |   |   |   | High-level Scienti
    +===+                         +---+---+---+---+---+
1- 2|   |   Security of Energy    |   |   |   |   |   | Energy Efficiency
    +===+                         +---+---+---+---+---+
5- 6|   |   Long-term Contribu    |   |   |   |   |   | High-level Scienti
    +===+                         +---+---+---+---+---+
5- 3|   |   Long-term Contribu    |   |   |   |   |   | Social Acceptabili
    +===+                         +---+---+---+---+---+
1- 6|   |   Security of Energy    |   |   |   |   |   | High-level Scienti
    +===+                         +---+---+---+---+---+
4- 6|   |   Innovation-based I    |   |   |   |   |   | High-level Scienti
    +===+                         +---+---+---+---+---+
1- 5|   |   Security of Energy    |   |   |   |   |   | Long-term Contribu
    +===+                         +---+---+---+---+---+
3- 1|   |   Social Acceptabili    |   |   |   |   |   | Security of Energy
    +===+                         +---+---+---+---+---+
1- 4|   |   Security of Energy    |   |   |   |   |   | Innovation-based I
    +===+                         +---+---+---+---+---+
5- 4|   |   Long-term Contribu    |   |   |   |   |   | Innovation-based I
    +===+                         +---+---+---+---+---+
3- 6|   |   Social Acceptabili    |   |   |   |   |   | High-level Scienti
    +===+                         +---+---+---+---+---+
```

FIGURE 1. Computer-generated Form for Pairwise Comparison

The resulting weights, and particularly the rank numbers of the criteri inspire confidence in the geometric scales II and III, for which reasonable arguments have been brought forward in sec. 5. The geometric scale IV is too long, and the Bradley-Terry method, case V, does not employ all the information which is available. Nevertheless the shift in the results remains moderate.

For the pairwise comparison of the energy technologies under the six criteria separately, we have adopted a simplified procedure because the complete task would be unfeasible. Each of the REO participants concentrated on 12 energy technologies only; they made a controlled selection so that the whole set of 23 technologies was still reasonably covered. Gradation of their judgement was not requested; effectively, the participants followed the mode of operation for the Bradley-Terry method, stating their preference for one of the two technologies, or indifference. Returning to Saaty's method we interpreted "preference" as "somewhat higher impact", and used the values 3, 2.72, 3.16, and 7.39 respectively.

TABLE 3. Weights and Rank Numbers of Criteria and Alternatives under Various Scales.

Scales	Qualifications	I. Saaty 1-9		II. Geometric $1-e^4$		III. Geometric 1-100		IV. Geometric $1-e^8$		V. Bradley Terry	
Scale Values	Equal impact	1		1		1		1		0.5	
	Somewhat higher impact	3		2.72		3.16		7.39		1	
	Much higher impact	5		7.39		10		54.6		1	
	Dominant	7		20.1		31.6		403		1	
	Absolutely dominant	9		55		100		2981		1	
Weights of Criteria	Security of Energy Supply	24.5	1	24.9	2	26.1	2	32.1	2	30.3	1
	Energy Efficiency	13.0	4	12.9	4	12.3	4	8.6	4	8.8	4
	Social Acceptability	9.3	6	8.8	6	7.9	6	4.0	6	5.4	6
	Innovation-based Industry	18.6	3	18.7	3	18.8	3	18.1	3	17.9	3
	Long-term Contribution	24.1	2	25.2	1	26.4	1	32.7	1	30.2	2
	High-level Science	10.4	5	9.4	5	8.5	5	4.6	5	7.4	5
Weights of Energy Technologies	Energy Saving in Industry	5.4	4	5.3	4	5.4	4	5.8	4	5.4	5
	Energy Saving in Houses	6.1	2	5.9	2	6.3	2	8.6	2	12.7	2
	Energy Saving in Traffic	3.6	19	3.7	19	3.5	19	2.6	20	1.9	21
	Energy Saving in Remaining	5.3	5	5.2	5	5.3	5	5.3	6	6.6	4
	Oil and Natural Gas	4.2	11	4.3	11	4.3	11	4.4	9	4.0	10
	Coal Winning	4.5	9	4.6	8	4.7	7	5.5	5	4.8	6
	Coal Combustion	4.3	10	4.4	10	4.4	10	4.7	8	4.2	9
	Coal Gasification	5.5	3	5.5	3	5.6	3	6.8	3	6.6	3
	Coal, Odd Materials	3.9	14	3.9	14	3.9	14	3.4	13	3.0	13
	Uranium Thermal Reactor	4.2	12	4.2	12	4.2	12	4.0	12	3.6	11
	Uranium Fission Cycle	4.7	7	4.6	7	4.7	8	4.7	7	4.4	7
	Uranium Breeder	7.0	1	6.8	1	7.3	1	11.1	1	14.1	1
	Uranium Nuclear Fusion	3.7	17	3.7	18	3.6	18	2.9	17	2.9	14
	Solar Energy, Thermal	3.7	18	3.7	17	3.6	17	2.9	18	2.7	16
	Solar Energy, Electrical	4.6	8	4.5	9	4.5	9	4.2	11	3.5	12
	Wind Energy, Decentralized	3.5	20	3.6	20	3.4	20	2.7	19	2.2	19
	Wind Energy, Centralized	3.8	15	3.9	15	3.8	15	3.3	15	2.7	15
	Biomass Energy	3.7	16	3.8	16	3.7	16	2.9	16	2.4	18
	Geothermal Energy	2.8	23	3.0	23	2.8	23	1.8	23	1.3	23
	Electricity Production	3.4	21	3.5	21	3.4	21	2.5	21	2.1	20
	Thermal Energy Storage	4.0	13	4.0	13	3.9	13	3.4	14	2.7	17
	System Analysis	3.3	22	3.4	22	3.2	22	2.4	22	1.6	22
	Switching Systems	4.8	6	4.8	6	4.7	6	4.4	10	4.3	8

The resulting weights (the final scores) and the rank numbers of the energy technologies are also displayed in Table 3. Again, there is a promising robustness, not only in the cases I-III (as one might expect), but also in the cases III-V (with widely disparate scales).

7. BUDGET ALLOCATION

The final scores of the energy technologies can be used, not only as a basis for discussion in the Council, but also as a tool for the allocation of the research budget. Suppose that an investment level p_j has been given for the j-th technology; let $\bar{s}_j$ denote its final score. The problem to be solved is the simple knapsack problem of maximizing the total benefit

$$\sum_j \bar{s}_j x_j$$

subject to the budget constraint

$$\sum_j p_j x_j \leq B,$$

with zero-one decision variables x_j. We have calculated an optimal package of technologies for the cases I-V and for three values of the total budget B. The results displayed in Table 4 demonstrate again the promising robustness, which is necessary for a workable tool in decision analysis. Sensitivity to the scale and the method is only revealed when deep cuts are made in the required budget. Obviously, the cheaper projects are more likely to be selected than the expensive ones.

There are various possible extensions of the problem formulation: financial support of the technologies at distinct investment levels (a minimum and a desired level with intermediate steps), a budget allocation over several periods, the addition of capacity constraints, etc. Basically, the criteria are conflicting objectives, so that we are running up against a multi-objective integer-programming problem.

8. CONCLUDING REMARKS

At the time of writing, the Energy Research Council is subject to a major reorganization. We have noticed that multi-criteria analysis triggered deep-going discussions about the criteria; the final scores of the technologies and the allocation of the budget are still on the agenda.

It is our impression that Saaty's method with logarithmic regression is sufficiently robust for practical purposes. The scale sensitivity remains within reasonable limits. Further advantages are that human judgement can be given with certain gradations, and that it can also be used by a single decision maker. An extension, that has been dropped from consideration here, is to use fuzzy numbers with triangular membership functions (Laarhoven and Pedrycz (1982)) in order to model the fuzziness of human judgement; this also provides a useful type of sensitivity analysis.

TABLE 4. Allocation of Research Budget to Energy Technologies under Scales I-V.
An asterisk marks the technologies which are dropped because of the budget limitation.

Total budget		300					350					400				
Investment levels	Scale	I	II	III	IV	V	I	II	III	IV	V	I	II	III	IV	V
Energy Saving in Industry	40	*	*	*	*		*	*	*	*	*					
Energy Saving in Houses	30															
Energy Saving in Traffic	10															
Energy Saving in Remaining	10															
Oil and Natural Gas	3															
Coal Winning	10															
Coal Combustion	35					*										
Coal Gasification	25															
Coal, Odd Materials	25				*											
Uranium Thermal Reactor	50	*	*	*	*	*	*	*	*	*	*	*	*	*	*	*
Uranium Fission Cycle	25															
Uranium Breeder	50	*	*	*												
Uranium Nuclear Fusion	25				*	*										
Solar Energy, Thermal	10															
Solar Energy, Electrical	10															
Wind Energy, Decentralized	10															
Wind Energy, Centralized	20					*										
Biomass Energy	10															
Geothermal Energy	10					*										
Electricity Production	5															
Thermal Energy Storage	10															
Systems Analysis	10															
Switching Systems	5															
Total Investment	438	298	298	298	298	298	348	348	348	348	348	388	388	388	388	388

ACKNOWLEDGEMENT

It is a pleasure to acknowledge Dr. G. Patterson (Shell International, London) and Dr. L. Phillips (Decision Analysis Unit, London School of Economics) for their excellent comments and suggestions. We are most grateful to Mr. F. Vos (Delft University of Technology) for his dedicated, competent programming effort.

REFERENCES

[1] Bradley, R.A., and Terry, M.E., The Rank Analysis of Incomplete Block Designs. I. The Method of Paired Comparisons. Biometrika 39, 324-345, 1952.

[2] David, H.A., The Method of Paired Comparisons. Griffin, London, 1963.

[3] Laarhoven, P.J.M. van, and Pedrycz, W., A Fuzzy Extension of Saaty's Priority Theory. Report 82-21, Dept. of Maths. and Infs., Delft University of Technology, Delft, Netherlands, 1982. To appear in Fuzzy Sets and Systems.

[4] Lodge, M., Quantitative Measurement of Opinions. Sage Publications Inc., Beverly Hills, California, USA, 1981.

[5] Roberts, F.S., Measurement Theory. Addison-Wesley, Reading, Mass., USA, 1979.

[6] Saaty, Th.L., The Analytic Hierarchy Process, Planning, Priority Setting, Resource Allocation, McGraw-Hill, New York, 1980.

[7] Thurstone, L.L., A Law of Comparative Judgement. Psychol. Rev. 34, 273-286, 1927. Psychophysical Analysis. Am. J. Psychol. 38, 368-389, 1927. The Method of Paired Comparisons for Social Values. J. Abnorm. Soc. Psychol. 21, 384-400, 1927.

INVESTMENT AND FINANCIAL PLANNING IN A GENERAL PARTNERSHIP

Heinz Isermann
Faculty of Economic Science, University of Bielefeld, Bielefeld, FRG

ABSTRACT

The paper presents an interactive decision support system in order to distribute cash dividends from the investment and finance activities of the firm to the partners of the firm according to their individual time preferences. We first introduce a basic multiple objective investment and finance planning model and indicate that several well-known models of investment and financial planning are members of the same class of compromise models for our basic multiple objective model. We then introduce an interactive decision support system for the indivudual as well as the collective decision process.

1. INTRODUCTION

A partnership is an voluntary association of two or more persons for the purpose to manage and share profits (or losses) in a business enterprise. In a general partnership each partner is a general partner whose liability is not limited to the amount contributed to the firm as capital. We shall assume that each general partner takes part in the investment and financial planning of the firm and that each partner participates from the total cash dividend payments according to his proportional share in the firm's capital. As a partnership can be regarded a voluntary aggregation of persons doing business under a common name, the structure of the collective decision process will be keyed to a fair compensation among the general partners with regard to their individual time preferences. Thus we desist from majority or coalition concepts in the course of the collective decision process.

In Section 2 we shall formulate a multiple objective investment and financial planning model where the arguments of the objectives are the anticipated dividend payments to all owners of the firm.

A class of compromise models which includes the prominent compromise models discussed in the finance literature is presented in Section 3. In Section 4 we outline a decision support system for an individual decision maker to plan the investment and finance acitivities and the anticipated dividend payments according to his individual time preference. This decision support system will then be utilized in the course of a collective decision process. The decision support system for the collective decision process will be the topic of Section 5.

2. THE BASIC MODEL

In order to formulate the basic multiple objective investment and finance model we shall apply the following notation:

a_{ti} : net cash flow obtainable from one unit of investment or finance project i at time t ($i = 1,\dots,I$; $t = 1,\dots,T$), where $a_{ti} > 0$ denotes an inflow of cash and $a_{ti} < 0$ denotes an outflow of cash

b_t : amount of cash made available from projects outside this planning model and from other sources at time t

d_{ji} : amount of the j-th scarce material required by one unit of project i ($j = 1,\dots,J$)

d_j : total amount of the j-th scarce material

x_i : number of units of project i to be undertaken

x : vector of the finance and investment activities to be undertaken, $x = (x_1,\dots,x_I)'$

c_i : upper bound imposed on x_i

y_t : cash dividend to be paid to the owner(s) at time t

y : vector of cash dividends, $y = (y_1,\dots,y_T)'$.

There is widespread agreement in the literature on finance (cf. Albach (1962), Baumol-Quandt (1965), Bernard (1969), Hax (1964), Manne (1968), Weingartner (1963, 1966)) that the anticipated dividend payments to the owner(s) of the firm are the arguments of the appropriate objective in the planning of a firm's productive investment and financing policy. As for each $t = 1,\dots,T$ higher dividend payments are preferred to lower dividend payments the general objective will be to

$$\begin{array}{l}\text{maximize } y_1\\ \quad\vdots\\ \text{maximize } y_T\end{array}$$

which will be denoted by

$$\text{"max" } y = (y_1,\dots,y_T)'. \tag{1}$$

Achievement of these T objectives is limited by the following set of restrictions. For $t = 1,\dots,T$ we assume a liquidity requirement which says that the sum of the firm's outflow of cash for the investment and finance projects to be undertaken and the cash dividend to be paid to the owner(s) at time t is equal to the amount of cash made available from projects outside this planning model and from other sources. Then, the general form of the cash balance restrictions will be

$$-\sum_{i=1}^{T} a_{ti}\, x_i + y_t = b_t \qquad \text{for } t = 1,\dots,T. \tag{2}$$

We also assume a general scarce material restriction of the form

$$\sum_{i=1}^{T} d_{ji}\, x_i \leqq d_j \qquad \text{for } j = 1,\ldots,J \tag{3}$$

This restriction is, of course, merely illustrative. In a particular application, an investment and financial planning model could have many restrictions of this type. For example, there could be a set of restrictions for each of a number of scarce materials, or, for a given such material, there could be different restrictions in different periods. Moreover, we impose an upper bound on the number of units of each investment and finance project i (i = 1,...,I) to be undertaken:

$$x_i \leqq c_i \qquad \text{for } i = 1,\ldots,I. \tag{4}$$

Finally, it is required that all of the variables be greater than or equal to zero. Thus, we add the following requirements:

$$x_i \geqq 0 \text{ for } i = 1,\ldots,I; \quad y_t \geqq 0 \text{ for } t = 1,\ldots,T. \tag{5}$$

Throughout this paper we assume that the investment and finance activities of the basic model include lending activities at some positive lending rate of interest from time t to time t+1 and borrowing activities at some positive borrowing rate of interest from time t to time t+1 for all t = 1, ...,T-1.

In summary, then, our basic investment and finance model requires the "maximization" of the cash dividend vector $y = (y_1,\ldots,y_T)'$, subject to the constraints specified above, i.e.

"max" y

s.t. (2) - (5) (BM)

By "maximizing" the cash dividend vector y we want to determine all efficient cash dividend vectors y^*. Let x^* be a feasible investment and finance program for (BM) and y^* the corresponding cash dividend vector. Then y^* is an *efficient* cash dividend vector for (BM), if and only if, there exists no feasible investment and finance program x" for (BM) such that the corresponding cash dividend vector y" satisfies $y'' \geqq y^*$ and $y'' \neq y^*$. Let Y denote the set of all feasible cash dividend vectors and Y^* denote the set of all efficient cash dividend vectors for (BM). Y^* contains (infinitely) many efficient cash dividend vectors. Thus additional information about the time preference of the investor(s) is necessary in order to select a *compromise* cash dividend vector $\hat{y}$ from Y^*.

Several compromise models have been proposed (cf. e.g. Bernard (1969), Hax (1964), Weingartner (1966)) which assume that the investor is able and willing to specify his time preference in such a way that his preference system can be *represented* by a scalar-valued preference function which is to be maximized.

3. A CLASS OF COMPROMISE MODELS

The most prominent compromise models belong to a class of compromise models of the following form:

$$\max \quad \phi_p(y) = \left(\sum_{t=1}^{T} (\alpha_t \, y_t)^p \right)^{1/p}$$

$$\text{s.t.} \quad (2) \; - \; (5) \qquad\qquad (CM_p)$$

with $p \neq 0$, $\alpha_t > 0$ for all $t = t,\ldots,T$.

For $p = +\infty$ and $\alpha_t = 1$ $(t = 1,\ldots,T)$ we obtain (cf. Isermann (1974))

$$\phi_\infty(y) = \max_t \; \{y_t\}$$

$$= y_T \, ,$$

i.e. a compromise objective function which represents the terminal wealth. Thus the compromise model $(CM_{+\infty})$ provides for the maximization of the terminal wealth of the investment and finance program.

For $p = -\infty$ and $\alpha_t = 1$ $(t = 1,\ldots,T)$ the general compromise objective function ϕ_p assumes the form (cf. Isermann (1974))

$$\phi_{-\infty}(y) = \min_t \; \{y_t\}.$$

In the compromise model $(CM_{-\infty})$ an investment and finance program is to be determined such that the annuity is maximized. Instead of maximizing a vector of cash dividends which are equal at each point of time t a different time pattern of the cash dividends is readily attained by assigning different values to the respective α_t $(t = 1,\ldots,T)$. Let e.g. $\alpha_t := (1+K)^{t-1}$ $(t = 1, \ldots,T)$, then the optimal vector of cash dividends $\hat{y}$ will have the structure: $\hat{y}_t = (1+K)^{t-1} \; \hat{y}_1$ $(t = 1,\ldots,T)$.

In order to determine an optimal solution for $(CM_{-\infty})$ we can apply the following linear program

$$\max \; v$$

$$\text{s.t.} \; (2) - (5) \qquad\qquad (CM^*_{-\infty})$$

$$\alpha_t \; v \leqq y_t \qquad (t = 1,\ldots,T).$$

For $p = 1$ and $\alpha_t > 0$ with $\dim(\alpha_t) = \dfrac{1 \text{ unit cash in } t^* = 1}{1 \text{ unit cash in } t}$

we obtain the compromise function

$$\phi_1(y) = \sum_{t=1}^{T} \alpha_t \; y_t,$$

which represents the total present value of the finite stream of dividend payments. By applying the compromise model (CM_1) we determine a cash dividend vector $\hat{y}$ with maximal present value.

If we assign to α_t dim $(\alpha_t) = \frac{\text{1 unit cash in T}}{\text{1 unit cash in t}}$ $\phi_1(y)$ represents the terminal value of y.

The construction of a compromise model is based on the fundamental assumption that the decision maker is able and willing to represent his valuation system by means of a compromise function. As this preference function - by assumption - comprehends the complete information on the investor(s)' time preference, the selection of an efficient compromise cash dividend vector can be performed via a solution procedure for the respective mathematical programming problem.

Our own experiments support the hypothesis that the formation of the decision maker's valuation system is neither complete nor definite at the beginning of the decision process. Rather the formation of the decision maker's implicit valuation system *develops* in the course of the decision process (cf. e.g. Dinkelbach-Isermann (1980)) and it was observed in our experiments that the formation process of the decision maker's valuation system is attended by consecutive modifications of one or more objectives. Moreover, even in the case that the decision maker's valuation system complies with the requirements which are necessary in order to represent the valuation system by means of a preference function, it does not seem necessary to demand full information on the decision maker's valuation system. In other words: The compromise models presume information on the decision maker's valuation system which he is unable to provide or which is mainly redundant.

4. OUTLINE OF AN INTERACTIVE DECISION SUPPORT SYSTEM

The process of goal formation and decision making can be characterized as a cognitive process of information processing. Thus the structure of a decision support system has to consider the decision maker's specific needs for information on the efficient cash dividend vectors of the underlying multiple objective investment and finance model as well as his specific ability to express partial information about his implicit valuation system. Comparative evaluation of some interactive approaches are e.g. reported in Dyer (1973) amd Wallenius (1974). Our findings which partly differ from the reproted results lead to conjecture that problem-specific as well as decision-maker specific aspects should determine the structure of an interactive decision support system.

For these and other reasons interactive decision support systems have been developed which provide an interactive dialogue between the decision maker and the computer. The basic technique of the interactive procedures is to elicit partial information from the decision maker about his valuation system and to provide partial information on the criteria configuration of the underlying multiple objective decision model. Thus in the course of an interactive procedure the decision maker articulates partial information on his valuation system which leads to some progress with respect to the selection of a compromise cash dividend vector while a numerical procedure provides a suggested cash dividend vector which has been generated on the basis of the partial information provided by the decision maker so far. The interactive procedure terminates with the selection of a compromise cash dividend vector by the decision maker or the outcome that the multiple objective investment and finance model does not provide an efficient cash dividend vector, which is accepted by the decision maker.

We propose a modified version of the STEM method (cf. Benayoun - de Montgolfier-Tergny-Laritchev (1971)). In order to introduce into the structure of the proposed interactive decision support system, we shall first assume that only *one* investor owns the firm and that he wants to determine a compromise cash dividend vector. The following notation will be applied:

ℓ: index of the current stage of the interactive decision process ($\ell = 1,2,\ldots$)

$\tilde{y}_t^{\ell}$: current lower bound on the cash dividend y_t which has been fixed by the decision maker in the course of the first (ℓ-1) stages of the interactive decision process.

$D^{(\ell)}$: index set of those cash dividends y_t, for which the decision maker has not yet specified a lower bound $\tilde{y}_t^{(\ell)}$ up to the (ℓ-1)th stage of the interactive decision process. ($D^{(1)} = \{1,2,\ldots,T\}$).

The interactive decision support system is outlined as follows:

Step 1: Initialization

Step 2. In order to generate an efficient cash dividend vector proposal for the decision maker determine an optimal solution $(x^{(\ell)}, y^{(\ell)})$ for the linear program

$$\max \quad w + \varepsilon \sum_{t=1}^{T} y_t$$

$$\text{s.t.} \qquad (2) \; - \; (5) \qquad\qquad (LP)$$

$$w - y_t \leqq 0 \text{ for all } t \in D^{(\ell)}$$

$$y_t \geqq \tilde{y}_t^{(\ell)} \quad \text{for all } t \in \{1,\ldots,T\} \setminus D^{(\ell)}.$$

with ε being a sufficiently small but positive scalar.

Present the efficient cash dividend vector $y^{(\ell)}$ to the decision maker.

Step 3. If $\ell = 1$ go to Step 5; otherwise go to Step 4.

Step 4. Does the investor want to modify one or more lower bounds $\tilde{y}_t^{(\ell)}$ $t \in \{1,\ldots,T\} \setminus D^{(\ell)}$ in order to provide for more attractive values for the cash dividends y_t ($t \in D^{(\ell)}$)? If "yes", go to Step 9. If "no", go to Step 5.

Step 5. Does the investor accept the cash dividends $y_t^{(\ell)}$ for all $t = 1,\ldots,T$? If "yes", go to Step 12. If "no", go to Step 6.

Step 6. Does the investor accept for at least one $t \in D^{(\ell)}$ the cash dividend $y_t^{(\ell)}$? If "yes", go to Step 7. If "no", go to Step 13.

Step 7. The investor is asked to specify $\tilde{y}_t^{(\ell)} < y_t^{(\ell)}$ for at least one $t \in D^{(\ell)}$ which imposes a lower bound on y_t.

Step 8. Actualize $D^{(\ell)}$ and the program (LP) of Step 2 and to to Step 11.

Step 9. The investor is asked to reconsider the lower bounds $\tilde{y}_t^{(\ell)}$ and specify actualized values for $\tilde{y}_t^{(\ell)}$ $(t \in D^{(\ell)})$.

Step 10. Actualize the program (LP) of Step 2.

Step 11. Set $\ell := \ell+1$ and go to Step 2.

Step 12. The investment and finance program $x^{(\ell)}$ yields a compromise cash dividend vector $y^{(\ell)}$. Stop.

Step 13. The multiple objective investment and finance model does not provide a compromise cash dividend vector for the investor. Stop.

5. AN INTERACTIVE COLLECTIVE DECISION SUPPORT SYSTEM

We shall now consider the case that $K > 1$ decision makers participate in a collective decision process. Let us first introduce the notation:

k : index of the decision makers $(k = 1,\ldots,K)$;

$\alpha_k^{(1)}$: proportional share of the k-th decision maker in the general partnership $(0 < \alpha_k^{(1)} < 1, \sum_{k=1}^{K} \alpha_k^{(1)} = 1)$;

m : index of the current stage of the collective decision process $(m = 1,2,\ldots)$;

$\Lambda^{(m)}$: index set of the decision makers who are involved in the m-th stage of the collective decision process, $(\Lambda^{(1)} = \{1,\ldots,K\})$.

The principal conditions for the collective decision process are the following:

1. Let the k-th decision maker individually determine an investment and financial plan x^* according to his individual time preference, where y^* is the corresponding vector of the total stream of dividend payments. Then in the course of the collective decision process the k-th decision maker will realize a vector of cash dividend payments $\bar{y}^k$ such that $\bar{y}^k \geqq \alpha_k^{(1)} y^*$.

2. For the total vector of cash dividend payments $\bar{y} = \sum_{k=1}^{K} \bar{y}^k$ $\bar{y} \in Y^*$ has to hold.

3. If in the course of the collective decision process $\bar{y} \notin Y^*$, each decision maker k who participates in the collective decision process participates from the additonal dividend payment potential according to his relative share.

At the beginning of each stage of the collective decision process the decision makers involved in the collective decision process determine simultaneously an individual compromise cash dividend vector $\bar{y}^k$ in the course of an interactive decision process as outlined in Section 4. As the k-th decision maker holds a proportional share of $\alpha_k^{(1)}$ of the general partnership, he can make his disposition with respect to his proportional share of the total cash dividend payments. Thus in order to generate an efficient cash dividend vector proposal for the k-th decision maker ($k \in \Lambda^{(m)}$), program (LP) of Step 2 of the interactive decision support system for an individual decision maker obtains the form

$$\max w + \varepsilon \sum_{t=1}^{T} y_t$$

$$\text{s.t.} \quad (3) - (5) \qquad\qquad (LP_k)$$

$$-\sum_{i=1}^{I} a_{ti} x_i + y_t = b_t^{(m)} \qquad (t = 1,\dots,T)$$

$$w - \alpha_k^{(m)} y_t \leqq 0 \qquad \text{for all } t \in D^{(\ell)}$$

$$\alpha_k^{(m)} y_t \geqq \tilde{y}_t^{(\ell)} \qquad \text{for all } t \in \{1,\dots,T\} \setminus D^{(\ell)}.$$

with $b_t^{(1)} := b_t$. The expressions $b_t^{(m)}$ and $\alpha_k^{(m)}$ $(m = 2,3,\dots)$ will be defined in the sequel. Let x^*, y^*, w^* be an optimal solution for (LP_k) such that $\bar{y}^k := \alpha_k^{(m)} y^*$ has been accepted as a compromise dividend vector by the k-th decision maker ($k \in \Lambda^{(m)}$).

If each decision maker has determined his individual compromise cash dividend vector $\bar{y}^k$ $(k = 1,\dots,K)$ the resulting vector of the total cash dividend payments is $\bar{y} = \sum_{k=1}^{K} \bar{y}^k$. $\bar{y}$ is a convex combination of efficient cash dividend vectors and may not be efficient. In order to test the efficiency of $\bar{y}$ we apply the following efficiency test program:

$$\max w + \varepsilon \sum_{t=1}^{T} u_t$$

$$\text{s.t.} \quad (3) - (4) \qquad\qquad (TP)$$

$$\left.\begin{aligned} -\sum_{i=1}^{I} a_{ti} x_i + u_t &= b_t - \bar{y}_t \\ u_t &\geqq 0 \\ w - u_t &\leqq 0 \end{aligned}\right\} \qquad (t = 1,\dots,T).$$

Let $\hat{x}$, $\hat{w}$, $\hat{u} = (\hat{u}_1,\dots,\hat{u}_T)'$ be an optimal solution for (TP). If $\hat{u} = 0$, our current $\bar{y} = \sum_{k=1}^{K} \bar{y}^k$ is efficient for (BM). The collective decision process terminates. If, however, $\hat{u} \neq 0$ our current $\bar{y}$ is not efficient for (BM) but $\bar{y} + \hat{u} \in Y^*$. Thus all decision makers involved in the collective decision process can improve their current cash dividend vector. It is proposed to distribute the additional stream of cash dividend payments such that $\bar{y}^k_{new} := \bar{y}^k_{old} + \alpha_k^{(m)} \hat{u}$ $(k \in \Lambda^{(m)})$.

Now we have to distinguish 3 cases:

(i) Each decision maker $k \in \Lambda^{(m)}$ accepts the actualized cash dividend vector $\bar{y}^k$. Then the collective decision process terminates as the resulting total vector of cash dividend payments is efficient.

(ii) At least one decision maker $k \in \Lambda^{(m)}$ accepts the actualized cash dividend vector $\bar{y}^k$. We actualize $\Lambda^{(m)}$, i.e. k is excluded from $\Lambda^{(m)}$, if the k-th decision maker has accepted the actualized $\bar{y}^k$, and start a new stage of the collective decision process:

Let m := m+1.

The expressions $b_t^{(m)}$ and $\alpha_k^{(m)}$ in (LP_k) are defined as follows:

$$b_t^{(m)} := b_t^{(1)} - \sum_{\substack{k=1 \\ k \notin \Lambda^{(m)}}}^{K} \bar{y}_t^k \qquad (t = 1,\dots,T) \tag{6}$$

$$\alpha_k^{(m)} := \begin{cases} \alpha_k^{(1)} \Big/ \sum_{k \in \Lambda^{(m)}} \alpha_k^{(1)} & \text{for each } k \in \Lambda^{(m)} \\ 0 & \text{for each } k \notin \Lambda^{(m)} \end{cases} \tag{7}$$

(iii) No decision maker $k \in \Lambda^{(m)}$ accepts the actualized cash dividend vector $\bar{y}^k$. We start a new stage of the collective decision process:

Let m := m+1.

The expressions $b_t^{(m)}$ and $\alpha_k^{(m)}$ in (LP_k) are defined as follows:

$$b_t^{(m)} := b_t^{(1)} - \sum_{\substack{p=1 \\ p \neq k}}^{K} \bar{y}_t^p \qquad (t = 1,\dots,T)$$

$$\alpha_k^{(m)} := \begin{cases} 1 & \text{for each } k \in \Lambda^{(m)} \\ 0 & \text{for each } k \notin \Lambda^{(m)} \end{cases}$$

All decision makers $k \in \Lambda^{(m)}$ determine simultaneously a new compromise cash dividend vector $\bar{y}^k$.

Let $\bar{y} = \sum_{k=1}^{K} \bar{y}^k$. In this case it may happen that $\bar{y} \notin Y$.

In order to test the feasibility and efficiency of $\bar{y}$ we apply the following lexicographic linear program (Isermann (1982)):

$$\text{lex max} \begin{bmatrix} - z - \varepsilon \sum_{t=1}^{T} v_t \\ w + \varepsilon \sum_{t=1}^{T} u_t \end{bmatrix}$$

$$\text{s.t.} \quad (3) \quad - \quad (4) \qquad \text{(LTP)}$$

$$- \sum_{i=1}^{I} a_{ti} \, x_i - v_t + u_t = b_t - \bar{y}_t$$

$$\left. \begin{array}{r} v_t \geqq 0 \\ z - v_t \geqq 0 \\ u_t \geqq 0 \\ w - u_t \leqq 0 \end{array} \right\} \quad (t = 1,\dots,T)$$

Let $\hat{x}$, $\hat{w}$, $\hat{z}$, $\hat{u}$, $\hat{v} = (\hat{v}_1,\dots,\hat{v}_T)'$ be an optimal solution for (LTP). If $\hat{v} = 0$ and $\hat{u} = 0$, our current $\bar{y} = \sum_{k=1}^{K} \bar{y}^k$ is efficient for (BM) and the collective decision process terminates. Let $\hat{v} \neq 0$ or $\hat{u} \neq 0$. Then it is proposed to distribute the total cash payments $(\hat{u} - \hat{v})$ to the decision makers involved in the collective decision process in the following way

$$\bar{y}^k_{new} := \bar{y}^k_{old} + \alpha_k^{(1)} (\hat{u} - \hat{v}) \Big/ \sum_{k \in \Lambda^{(m)}} \alpha_k^{(1)} .$$

The actualized cash dividend vectors $\bar{y}^k$ $(k \in \Lambda^{(m)})$ are presented to the decision makers and the collective decision process is continued in the described mode.

REFERENCES

Albach, H. (1962). Investition und Liquidität. Gabler-Verlag, Wiesbaden.

Baumol, W.J. and Quandt, R.E. (1965). Investment and discount rates under capital rationing - A programming approach. The Economic Journal, 75: 317 - 329.

Benayoun, R., de Montgolfier, J., Tergny, J. and Laritchev, O. (1971). Linear programming with multiple objective functions: STEP method (STEM). Mathematical Programming 1: 366 - 375.

Bernard, R.H. (1969). Mathematical programming models for capital budgeting - A survey, generalization, and critique. Journal of Financial and Quantitative Analysis, 4: 111 - 158.

Dinkelbach, W., and Isermann, H. (1980). Resource allocation of an academic department in the presence of multiple criteria - Some experience with a modified STEM-method. Computers and Operations Research, 7: 99 - 106.

Dyers, J.S. (1973). An empirical investigation of a man-machine-interactive approach to the solutions of the multiple-criteria problem. In J. Cochrane and M. Zeleny (Eds.), Multiple Criteria Decision Making, 202 - 216. University of South Carolina Press, Columbia, S.C.

Hax, H. (1964). Investitions- und Finanzplanung mit Hilfe der linearen Programmierung. Zeitschrift für betriebswirtschaftliche Forschung, 16: 430 - 446.

Isermann, H. (1974). Lineare Vektoroptimierung. Regensburg.

Isermann, H. (1982). Linear lexicographic optimization. OR-Spektrum, 4: 223 - 228.

Manne, A.S. (1968). Optimal dividend and investment policies for a self-financing business enterprise. Management Science, 15: 119 - 129.

Wallenius, J. (1974). Comparative evaluation of some interactive approaches to multicriterion optimization. Management Science, 21: 1387 - 1396.

Weingartner, H.M. (1963). Mathematical programming and the analysis of capital budgeting problems. Prentice Hall, Englewood Cliffs, N.J.

Weingartner, H.M. (1966). Criteria for programming investment project selection. The Journal of Industrial Economics, 15(1): 65 - 76.

A MULTIOBJECTIVE EXPERT SYSTEM FOR SUPPLIERS OF OUT-OF-THE-MONEY OPTIONS

Joel N. Morse
Loyola College, Baltimore, Maryland, USA

ABSTRACT

The proliferation of telecommunications and computing capability has sparked speculation about dispersing work. The electronic cottage industry approach has potential in the area of office and professional services. This paper proposes that certain functions of a centralized financial market can be decentralized. To relocate an element of an information processing system, its functions as well as its linkages must be duplicated. For that purpose, we draw on the theories of multiple criteria decision making (MCDM), artificial intelligence, and finance.

On the trading floors of the world's options exchanges, people called market-makers provide liquidity; when a buyer cannot find a seller, or a seller cannot find a buyer, these functionaries sometimes fill that void by trading for their own account. The physically grueling work of transacting on the exchange floor is often delegated to lower level employees. These people act with supervision from senior people, or perhaps with a set of decision rules formulated by the suppliers of capital.

This paper will attempt to outline the features of an automated, remotely-sited system that emulates the market-making function which is normally performed on the site of centralized options exchanges. To make the task less formidable, I will concentrate on one very specialized market-making function, namely supplying uncovered out-of-the money options. The system is intended to promote useful communication between man and computer. Although it would be presumptuous to say that the system can learn, it can decide to query a human when certain conditions are present. From these situations, a richer array of decision rules will develop.

I. INTRODUCTION

An option is the right, but not the obligation, to purchase a specified asset at a specific price. The institutional details, as well as the mathematical valuation theories can be found in any modern finance text (see, for a particularly careful exposition, Chapter 16 of Sharpe [1978]). Options exchanges exist in Canada, the U.S.A., Europe and Asia. The contracts, known as puts and calls, are associated with wide variety of underlying assets. Among these are common stock, market indices, gold, foreign currencies, various futures contracts, and several fixed income securities.

Purchasers of options seek speculative potential or the safety of hedging. Or they may be involved in a complex series of transactions involving both options and securities. Suppliers (i.e. sellers) of options are similarly motivated. In addition, it is possible to generate a stream of income by performing this economic function on a regular basis. This paper will outline the design of a system for managing the portfolio of such an economic agent, who could be a market-maker on the exchange floor or an investor located elsewhere. In either case, the agent could be a firm or an individual. I will identify and address the particular concerns of the supplier of uncovered out-of-the-money options. This is a well-defined market segment currently of interest to market-makers, investment advisory firms, brokerage houses and sophisticated individual investors.

II. UNCOVERED OUT-OF-THE-MONEY OPTION WRITING

In this section I will cover the terminology and the particular requirements of this chosen market niche. Some of this is available in depth in modern finance texts, such as Sharpe [1978]. Less documented parts of this information set have been gleaned from actual market participation. The supplier (or seller) of an option contract is called a <u>writer</u>. For the privilege of receiving the option <u>premium</u>, the writer must present evidence that he has the financial ability to deliver the asset covered by the option contract. For the <u>covered</u> writer, this is demonstrated by ownership of the asset. For the <u>uncovered</u> writer, this is accomplished by posting <u>margin</u>, which is normally in the form of cash or U.S. Treasury Bills. The rules for computing margin requirements are complex, and will be dealt with later. Options are of two types, <u>puts</u> and <u>calls</u>. A call is the right to buy an asset under specified conditions. A put is the right to sell. The writer of an option is said to be <u>short</u> that option. Thus, his benefit is precisely the opposite of someone who is <u>long</u> (i.e. owns) an asset. The call writer gains when the underlying asset moves down. The put writer gains when the underlying asset moves up.

The short option position also benefits from the passage of time, since an option is a wasting asset. In addition, any decrease in prevailing interest rates favors the writer. The terms of the option contract specify a price at which the underlying asset will be transfered, at the request of whoever holds the option (i.e. the long position). That price is called the <u>strike</u> price. When the <u>market</u> price of an underlying asset is the same as the strike price, the option is <u>at-the-money</u>. When the market price exceeds the strike price, a call is <u>in-the-money</u>, and a put is <u>out-of-the-money</u>. When the market price is lower than the strike price, the call is out-of-the-money, and the put is in-the-money. When options are <u>deeply</u> (i.e. extremely) out-of-the-money, they sell for very low prices, since the probability of profitable exercise is very low. Because of institutional features, namely margin rules and commissions, writing these options is not particularly profitable for the covered writer. However, it can be quite profitable for uncovered writers. A specialized group of market participants has recognized this potential. This paper addresses their needs.

III. OBJECTIVES, CONSTRAINTS AND CONCERNS

In this section, I will try to explain more of the workings of uncovered option writing. Although there are objectives and constraints, certain concerns do not fit naturally into this framework. We will see that this leads to a natural extension of what at first appears to be a mathematical programming problem.

The objective of our system is clearly to maximize the stream of option premia received. Specifically, we want to maximize the quotient z , where

$$z = \frac{\text{premium received}}{\text{margin requirement}}$$

That margin requirement, for equity (i.e. stock) options, is 30% of the market price of the stock, plus (or minus) the number of points that the option is in (or out of) the money, subject to a $250 minimum. The premium itself may be applied to the margin requirement. The calculations for non-equity options are somewhat different. It is this return on margin, or return on capital employed, which motivates our option writer. Let us turn now to his constraints.

The most obvious danger to an uncovered option writer is the risk of exercise. In addition to transacting at a price that represents an immediate loss, both a buy-side and a sell-side commission must be absorbed. Control of this risk is accomplished by imposing a constraint on the standard deviation of the stock price. In less formal terms, the option writer recognizes that the stream of premia received will turn into losses unless his portfolio is constructed from a list of stocks of suitable risk. Since there is a positive correlation between z and the volatility (normally measured as a standard deviation) of the underlying security, formulating this constraint involves assessing the option supplier's risk tolerances; it may also be necessary to distinguish between policies for efficient and inefficient markets.

Whether the approach is mathematical or intuitive, it is demonstrably possible to manage the risk described above. For example, by prescribing a sufficiently wide corridor between market price and striking price, and by constructing a partially hedged diversified portfolio including both puts and calls, the exercise risk can be fine-tuned. A subtle risk of far greater concern is the volatility of the writer's margin requirement. As described above, margin is computed as a function of both the stock price and the corridor between that market price and the strike price. Thus, the variance of the margin to be posted is a function of the variance on the assets on which the portfolio of options is written.

The Options Clearing Corporation, and in turn the writer's broker or clearing agent, mark the portfolio to market on a daily basis. When the underlying securities fluctuate to the extent that the posted margin is insufficient, a <u>margin call</u> is issued. At this point, the option writer must put up more cash or Treasury bills, or he must reverse some of his short positions. In other words, he can reduce his margin requirement, by buying back, or <u>covering</u> some of the options he has written.

The most obvious defense is to maintain a reserve fund from which these margin calls could be met. Since this reduces the number of options which can be written, this strategy has a positive opportunity cost; it is only one of several strategies that must be considered at each decision iteration.

The process of <u>portfolio construction</u> must include an acute awareness of this risk of margin variability. This is accomplished by the following constraints:

1) Hold down the number of options written so that a non-negative free cash balance is maintained;

2) As in the classic Markowitz portfolio problem, the writer must strive to diversify the elements in his portfolio; he must seek low pairwise correlations among the holding period returns of the underlying assets.

3) We will define a target, or desired level of margin volatility for the portfolio. To achieve it, various mixtures of individual options will be evaluated, keeping in mind our maximand z.

The difficulty of building these constraints will be discussed in a later section.

In this portfolio construction phase, it is necessary to be aware of certain financial costs of portfolio revision, or updating. As described above, one way to meet a margin call is to cover a portion of the short options. The release of margin is governed by the rules discussed earlier, with a few exceptions. I call this process portfolio unwinding. There is an inter-relationship between the premium paid to cover the options, the margin released, the commission paid to transact, and the bid-asked spread. These latter two are very significant, in a percentage sense. The commission can be as high as ten percent of the option premium. A typical bid-asked spread is 1/8 - 1/4. In dollar terms, this is $12.50 bid (what a party will pay for the option) and $25.00 asked (what a seller wants) per contract. Even these spreads widen when a writer wants to transact in volume in a thin options series. If you were to write an option on Monday at 1/4, and be forced to reverse that trade on Tuesday, you would have shrunk your capital, in one day, by over half of the premium you originally sought by writing that option.

Portfolio unwinding is to be minimized under any successful expert system. But it will be necessary as capital markets fluctuate. Should the option writer unwind by covering high-priced or low-priced options? Should he cover a few options which tie up large amounts of margin, or instead cover many options, each of which ties up a small amount of margin. An acceptable path through this network of choices is a formidable task.

Let us now relax the assumption that the portfolio is constructed de novo. In fact, a portfolio of short options usually already exists during all but the initial run of the system. Typcially, free credit balances become available for use for two reasons. First, market movements in the underlying assets may release funds. Second, option expirations take place every month. For a portfolio that was diversified over time, each of these inevitable expirations generates funds to be used for option-writing. Then a set of options must be added to the existing portfolio, in accord with our notions of diversification, margin volatility for the portfolio, and all the other features previously described. Thus the term portfolio revision includes both portfolio unwinding and portfolio updating.

In section IV we will discuss this investment activity in terms of mathematical programming, expert systems and artificial intelligence.

IV. MATHEMATICAL PROGRAMMING AND EXPERT SYSTEMS

At first glance, the objectives and constraints of Section III would appear amenable to formulation as a mathematical programming problem. The programming problem would be to maximize z, subject to the several stated constraints. Alternatively, a large master problem could be formulated, with sub-systems which were not necessarily of a programming format. For example, various modules of computer code could calculate the margin requirements for each candidate option, calculate the standard deviation of the underlying asset, and gather all necessary price data automatically from machine-readable financial databases. Part of the problem could be solved by quadratic programming methods, or more direct routes such as those suggested in Morse [1982, 1983] or Karney, Morse and Ben-Israel [forthcoming]. Since the constraints I have elaborated are intimately involved with the preference structure of the option supplier, it could be profitable to express them as multiple objectives. In that case, the natural paradigm would be multiobjective mathematical programming (Zeleny, [1982]).

Rather than subject the reader to an avalanche of notation and equations, I will move directly to the shortcomings of this type of approach. The heading for Section III included the word concern because the issues that are relevant to the option writer are not really constraints as that word is used in mathematical programming. They are extremely transitory, difficult to assess and redolent with information feedback mechanisms. The concerns lead to price and volatility discovery. They can lead to increases or decreases in the amount of capital the investors devote to the option selling operation. As time passes, the investors' experiences with option exercise or margin calls may lead to a new multiattribute utility function.

Here are some examples. During the summer of 1982, the z ratio (recall that this is the premium divided by the margin requirement) for Cities Service Corporation was extremely high by historical standards. This was due to swirling rumors of a takeover attempt. This presented the option writer with an exceptional opportunity for high return on investment, given an historical standard deviation for that stock. But expert intervention was required (either human or artificial intelligence) to project a new judgmental volatility based on the particular bidding war occurring that summer. In such cases, the model's normal sensitivities must factor in some consciousness of the gambler's ruin problem. An example of a feedback loop is that some option market participants used a volatility that was implied (via the option pricing equations) by the observed option premia. This, however, was itself unstable, and the problem became very unstructured. There even was a spillover effect to the prevailing option premia for Getty Oil and Mesa Petroleum.

Another important feature of an option management system is the stimulus and direction it can provide for associated fundamental research. When the volatility computing module observes that the volatility for certain assets is going up, the investment group is often alerted to seek information which may not yet be fully reflected in asset prices (for a study of information contained in option premia see Beckers [1981]). In a more technical sense, as thinness, which is a lack of liquidity and widening bid-asked spreads, appears in various sectors of the options markets, new strategies for portfolio unwinding will be tested.

The difficulty with the mathematical programming approach is that its very rigid structure causes some information to be discarded, some to be damaged, and some to be linked by modeling rather than financial insights.

Artificial intelligence (AI) and expert systems (ES) may offer an attractive expansion of the above model. Numerous articles (for example, Alexander [1982], Nau [1983], Business Week [1981a, 1981b], Manage Today [1982], and Datamation [1980]) tout the power and insight of these systems in a time of ever more powerful computers. Nau [1983, p. 68] describes the "propagation of constraints" method of AI. In this approach, the solution is successively bounded by an ever-increasing set of constraints. Some of them are initially built into the system. Others are implied by fellow constraints. Still others are learned during interaction with changing markets and human operators.

In their Society of Minds theory (a ready summary is Fortune [1982]), Minsky and Papert propose an approach for AI. They believe that natural minds employ distinct but communicating agents. Every agent governs an aspect of human behavior. To extend this concept to computer-based expert systems, one imagines modules of code. Some of these are "doers," and address functional areas, decision modes, or information searches. Other modules are "critics" which compare and check the effectiveness of the "doers." Finally, a set of "censors" actually turns off the doers that the censors determine to be unnecessary or draining elements of the system. This outlook, because of the fresh modeling design that it implies, may hold promise for an option writing system, as well as for other automated trading systems.

V. SUMMARY AND DIRECTION OF FUTURE RESEARCH

There is some risk that AI and ES have become facons de parler. These fashionable concepts take a tremendous programming effort before they become operational in any one field. In the area of man-machine dialog, or in other communications taks, scientists are deriving intelligent principles of language design and comprehension. However, in the area of allocation, design (such as CAD/CAM) and decision models, the progress is evolutionary rather than revolutionary.

Just as mathematical programming approaches generate alternatives and then search that space, AI and ES methods attempt that same task. Mathematical programming tactics exploit the structure that is often evident in the mathematical representation of the problem. The AI/ES methodology seeks to reduce problem complexity by using the structure of much less formal representations. By defining a limited domain of discourse, these systems save work by intelligent (i.e. non-routine) branching rules and calls for human interaction. Naturally, there are more various strategies that prove efficient in each applications area. Unlike mathematical programming, there are few rules that can be generalized. AI/ES has probably been reasonably successful because modern computers have become so powerful that brute force methods are economically feasible.

This paper has outlined a computer-based system for an economic agent who supplies uncovered out-of-the-money options. The terminology, the objectives, the constraints and concerns, as well as the institutional environment of this agent have been discussed. These items were placed in a mathematical programming framework. Next, several organizational principles from the fields of artificial intelligence and expert systems were proposed as extensions which might do a better job of meeting the needs of this decision problem.

The development of an operational model that combines human input, optimization modules and an AI/ES macro model awaits a serious commmitment by an option-writing individual or group.

References

Alexander, Tom, "Computers on the Road to Self-Improvement," Fortune, June 14, 1982, pp. 148-160.

Beckers, Stan. "Standard Deviations Implied in Option Prices As Predictors of Future Stock Price Variability," Journal of Banking and Finance, Vol. 5, 1981, pp. 363-381.

Karney, D. F; Morse, J. N. and Ben-Israel, A. Untitled, forthcoming.

Morse, J. N. "Portfolios With Stochastic Betas: Theory and Heuristics for a Mixed Integer Quadratic Programming Problem," in Grauer, M.; Lewandowski, A.; and A. Wierzbicki (eds), Multiobjective and Stochastic Optimization, International Institute of Applied Systems Analysis, Vienna, Austria, 1982, pp. 235-250.

Morse, J. N. "Banking in a Volatile World" Setting Country Lending Limits," in Pierre Hanson (ed.) Essays and Surveys on Multiple Criteria Decision Making, Lecture Notes in Economics and Mathematical Systems, No. 209, Springer - Verlag, Berlin, 1983, pp. 269-279.

Nau, Dana S. "Expert Computer Systems," Computer, February 1983, pp. 63-85.

Sharpe, William F. Investments, Prentice-Hall, Inc., Englewood Cliffs, N.J., 1978, 2nd edition.

Zeleny, Milan. Multiple Criteria Decision Making, McGraw-Hill Book Company, NY, 1982.

"AI Comes of Age," Datamation, Oct. 1980, p. 48.

"AI - Computers That Think More Like Human Experts," Business Week, pp. 50-1, July 6, 1981a.

"5th Generation: Computers That Think," Business Week, December 14, 1981b, Yasaki, Edward K., pp. 94-96.

"5th Generation Computer," Manage Today, Dec. 1982, p. 97.

A MULTIPLE-LAYER MODEL FOR ECONOMIC–ENVIRONMENTAL–ENERGY POLICY ANALYSIS

Wim Hafkamp[1] and Peter Nijkamp[2]
[1] *Department of Economics, University of Amsterdam, Amsterdam, The Netherlands*
[2] *Department of Economics, Free University, Amsterdam, The Netherlands*

1. INTRODUCTION

Economic-environmental-energy modelling has become increasingly complicated over the last decade. Systems-theoretic concepts, optimal control models and multidisciplinary analyses have become necessary tools for environmental-economic-energy analyses. There is a strong tendency towards more integrated policy analysis, in which economic - environmental - energy aspects are brought together in one coherent framework of a spatial context (see Lakshmanan and Nijkamp, 1980). This tendency towards integrated modelling is mainly caused by the fact that the post-war economic growth paradigm intertwined with technological, scientific and educational progress and rising population numbers, has neglected the social and ecological dimensions of this process and hence has led to a serious threat for the man-made and natural environment. This development does not only take place in the developed countries, but also in the Third World countries, especially in those areas where a rapid industrial expansion is not accompanied by monetary resources for environmental protection. Integrated planning and policy models are essentially necessary means to restore the balance in favour of more emphasis on environmental dimensions (cf. also Guldman and Shefer, 1981).

In this paper we will attempt to develop an integrated approach to regional-economic-environmental-energy policy analysis by discussing the Triple-Layer Model (TLM) (see Hafkamp and Nijkamp, 1982, and Hafkamp, 1983). It will be shown that recently developed interactive, integrated economic-environmental-energy policy models appear to provide a promising perspective for an integrated environmental policy analysis. Two elements are central in these approaches, viz. efficient solutions for conflicting objectives and interactive strategies among analysts and policy-makers. The operationality of the TLM will be illustrated by presenting also some empirical and illustrative results for the Netherlands.

2. INTERACTIVE MULTIPLE OBJECTIVE PROGRAMMING MODELS

In this section, a brief introduction to interactive multiobjective decision analysis will be given, as this approach makes up one of the foundation stones of the abovementioned TLM. Interactive decision analysis is one of the fruitful results of modern high speed computer technology. This approach to decision analysis aims at including in a stepwise manner various political (or subjective) considerations in formal optimizing models characterized by multiple policy objectives. After a specification of conflicting objectives and the identification of a feasible (not necessarily the most desirable) compromise solution, a set of additional policy desires (for instance, minimum achievement levels, reference points, or aspiration levels) may be introduced so as to find a new feasible compromise solution that is more satisfactory.

Interactive approaches have several advantages: a closer involvement of actors in the choice process, a procedural view of planning, a 'satisficing' instead of an optimizing behaviour, a greater flexibility by means of simulation experiments or scenario analyses, and a greater potential for practical applications (especially because no policy weights have to be specified). The majority of these interactive approaches are based on a reference point optimization technique, in which an attempt is made at minimizing the discrepancy between a series of points on the efficiency frontier and a reference point. It has to be added that especially procedural interactive policy analyses may be very helpful tools in policy negotiations on conflicting issues.

Fortunately, in the field of mathematical programming and mathematical economics, in recent years much work has been undertaken to formulate operational optimization procedures for problems with multiple objectives (see among others, Keeney and Raiffa, 1976; Cohon, 1979; Rietveld, 1980, and Nijkamp and Spronk, 1981). At present, there is a whole spectrum of different multiobjective methods available, both in the field of *continuous* programming analysis (see, e.g. Nijkamp, 1979) and in the field of *discrete* plan and project evaluation methods (see, e.g. Voogd, 1982).

Many problems in an integrated policy analysis do not require an unambiguous solution that represents once and for all *the* optimal state of the system concerned: compromise strategies appear to prevail. In the light of the process character of many decision problems, an interactive policy analysis may therefore, be a reasonable and operational approach. This approach is usually composed of a series of steps based on a systematic exchange of information (based on computer experiments) between decision-makers and analysts. Such interactive approaches are normally characterized by the following pair of steps:

- the analysts propose meaningful and feasible (trial) solutions on the basis of a well-defined compromise procedure.
- the decision-makers respond to each (trial) solution by indicating in which respect (i.e., in regard to which effects) the proposed compromise is still unsatisfactory (given their views on minimum achievement levels, etc.).

These pairs of steps are then successively repeated, until after several computer experiments, a final satisfactory compromise solution has been identified . As mentioned before, a large number of interactive models has recently been developed (see among others, Rietveld, 1980 and Spronk, 1981).

Interactive policy analyses based on multiobjective programming methods have already demonstrated their meaning in various policy problems, also in a macro-economic context. They may be regarded as having many significant advantages compared to traditional optimization methods (see Nijkamp, 1980 and Spronk, 1981).

In the present paper, only one specific interactive policy method will be dealt with, viz. the method of displaced ideals (see Zeleny, 1976 and Nijkamp, 1980). It is a method which needs no explicit information on the trade-offs between objectives expressed by the decision-makers in the procedure. If they are presented with a possible solution to the multi-objective problem, they only need to choose an objective which has to be improved in the next iteration of the procedure. Fig. 1 contains a concise presentation of the stages of this optimization procedure.

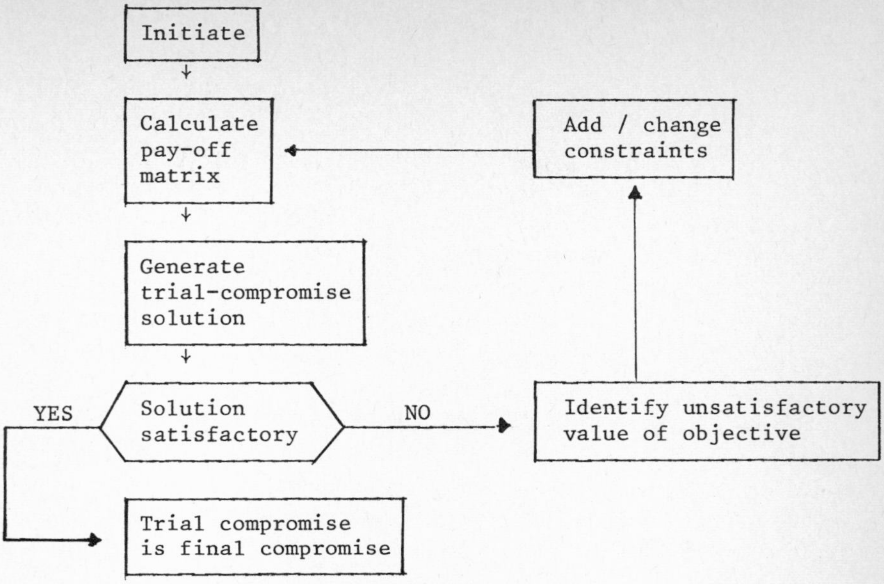

FIGURE 1 Stages of an interactive optimization procedure.

More details regarding this method can be found in Hafkamp and Nijkamp (1982).

3. A TRIPLE-LAYER MODEL (TLM)

TLM is a model of a spatial system where economic, environmental and socio-political aspects are integrated. The spatial elements implies that the system is analyzed at the level of regions interacting with the national level. Consequently, TLM is a national-regional economic environmental model. TLM is a result of projecting a complex reality on three mutually interacting parallel layers:

- an economic layer
- an employment layer
- an environmental layer

Several elements in human (individual or collective) behaviour can thus be depicted in three submodels, according to their respective different aspects and consequences (an extensive description of TLM can be found in Hafkamp, 1983).

The operational version of the TLM is built up by means of 3 modules:

- *an economic module*; this is a national-regional economic model of the (Dutch) economy. It is the result of coupling the so-called Secmon-model to a multi-regional input-output model of five Dutch regions. The Secmon-model has been developed by Driehuis (1978). It is primarily developed as a simulation model of the Dutch economy which analyses long-term effects of various alternative economic policies. Main goal variables included in this model are: inflation, unemployment, economic growth and current accounts. Main policy instruments are: taxes and public expenditure, monetary instruments, exchange rate, wages and price control, and labour market policy.

The relationships between the components of the economic module are described by means of 10 sub-models:

- production (based on a multiregional input-output table)
- final demand (consumption, investment, public expenditure and exports)
- imports (final products, raw materials and manufacturing inputs)
- production capacity
- labour market (various demand and supply categories)
- wages and prices
- income
- government expenditure
- social insurances
- monetary systems

- *a labour market module*; this describes employment (supply and demand) in all regions and sectors. The demand for labour is analyzed through the production structure; gross production, capacity and capacity use in capital - intensive sectors, as well as import substitution constitute major elements in this module. Supply of labour is analyzed through wages, prices and growth of income. Also demographic data play an important role on the supply side.

- *an environmental module* describes 3 aspects of environmental quality:
  - i. Emission of air pollutants caused by:
    - a. combustion of fossil fuels
    - b. process emissions, etc.
  - ii. Concentration of air pollutants (via diffusion)
  - iii. Reduction of emission by:
    - a. saving energy, selective growth, etc.
    - b. alternative choices of energy sources
    - c. anti-pollution technology.

Pollution of water and soil is not taken into account here, neither is any attention paid to the phenomenon of synergetic effects. The following pollution categories are taken into account: sulphur dioxide, nitrogen oxides and dust particles.

The choice of energy source also has an important influence on the emission of air pollutants. For example: SO_2 emissions in the Netherlands decreased drastically after a large-scale introduction of natural gas, but since a switch back to coal or oil took place, a drastic increase occurred. Especially the shift of electricity producers from natural gas to oil, coal or nuclear energy and the further exploration and introduction of alternative energy sources (solar energy, wind, etc.) are of great importance to environmental quality.

4. EMPIRICAL RESULTS

In the present section, results based on an empirical application with 3 objectives (production, employment and environmental quality) will be presented. The results serve only as illustrative outcomes, as they refer to the period from which the data are taken (1970-1977). Furthermore, they are not yet entirely realistic because regional sectoral production volumes are allowed to vary widely around their starting values.

The information given per iteration in the tables has been limited to the values of objectives on a national and on a regional level. In addition, for the sake of simplicity, the procedure has been modified for this occasion by optimizing objectives at a *national* level (which reduces the number of optimizations per iteration) and - after identification of an unsatisfactory objective value - adding (or changing) constraints on the *regional* objectives.

Pay-off Matrix

Optimisation of Variable:	Production (10^9 Dfl)	Employment (10^6 man-years)	Environmental Quality	Compromise
National Production	283.430	280.719	279.366	282.947
National Employment	2.722	2.895	2.698	2.824
Environmental Quality	82.348	85.204	79.505	80.244
Production, Region 1	34.420	29.667	24.563	32.709
" " 2	50.127	57.501	40.419	50.786
" " 3	72.742	61.008	63.259	61.858
" " 4	69.319	59.462	79.529	70.137
" " 5	56.820	73.081	71.594	67.454
Employment, Region 1	.314	.305	.218	.303
" " 2	.442	.624	.377	.495
" " 3	.748	.622	.604	.657
" " 4	.682	.582	.832	.690
" " 5	.533	.760	.663	.676
Env.Quality, Region 1	8.656	7.041	6.807	6.919
" " 2	8.282	14.112	8.138	11.592
" " 3	36.613	20.475	20.524	20.484
" " 4	12.366	16.392	15.522	14.168
" " 5	16.428	27.183	28.466	27.179

Table 1 . Results of the first interactive optimisation procedure; iteration no. 1 (Reproduced with kind permission of the publishers from an article by the authors in R. Stäglin (Ed.), International Use of Input-Output Analysis, Vandenhoeck and Ruprecht, Göttingen, 1982, pp. 175-198.)

Pay-off Matrix

Optimisation of Variable:	Production (10^9 Dfl)	Employment (10^6 man-years)	Environmental Quality	Compromise
National Production	283.308	280.588	281.205	285.899
National Employment	2.823	2.890	2.823	2.849
Environmental Quality	84.326	85.200	80.020	80.591
Production, Region 1	35.147	29.773	30.423	33.437
" " 2	51.020	49.494	50.442	48.896
" " 3	63.700	63.584	64.157	63.498
" " 4	68.702	66.935	70.254	69.437
" " 5	64.737	70.800	65.928	76.656
Employment, Region 1	.303	.303	.303	.303
" " 2	.495	.510	.495	.497
" " 3	.657	.657	.657	.669
" " 4	.690	.690	.690	.690
" " 5	.676	.727	.676	.687
Env.Quality, Region 1	6.708	7.034	6.939	5.134
" " 2	14.070	14.072	8.191	11.743
" " 3	20.495	20.486	20.487	20.503
" " 4	15.960	16.456	17.305	16.070
" " 5	27.091	27.151	27.096	27.139

Table 2. Results of the interactive optimisation procedure; iteration no. 2
(Reproduced with kind permission of the publishers from an article by the authors in R. Stäglin (Ed.), International Use of Input-Output Analysis, Vandenhoeck and Ruprecht, Göttingen, 1982, pp. 175-198.)

Pay-off Matrix

Optimisation of Variable:	Production (10^9 Dfl)	Employment (10^6 man-years)	Environmental Quality	Compromise
National Production	283.185	281.130	281.335	282.491
National Employment	2.823	2.865	2.823	2.847
Environmental Quality	80.520	80.591	80.090	80.411
Production, Region 1	32.434	30.954	29.203	30.491
" " 2	52.097	48.149	51.756	49.342
" " 3	63.504	64.985	63.631	62.385
" " 4	69.166	67.185	70.609	72.427
" " 5	65.983	69.855	66.134	68.027
Employment, Region 1	.303	.303	.303	.303
" " 2	.495	.495	.495	.495
" " 3	.657	.657	.657	.657
" " 4	.690	.690	.690	.690
" " 5	.676	.717	.676	.699
Env.Quality,Region 1	5.134	5.134	5.134	5.134
" " 2	11.743	11.743	11.316	11.743
" " 3	20.403	20.503	20.503	20.503
" " 4	16.018	16.070	16.070	15.894
" " 5	27.120	27.139	27.065	27.135

Table 3 . Results of the interactive optimisation procedure; iteration no. 3
(Reproduced with kind permission of the publishers from an article by the authors in R. Stäglin (Ed.), International Use of Input-Output Analysis, Vandenhoeck and Ruprecht, Göttingen, 1982, pp. 175-198.)

The first step of the analysis was the identification of a first compromise solution (Table 1). After the first iteration, employment was taken to be the objective which needed to be raised most urgently. Therefore, the compromise values of regional employment were added to the constraint set as lower bounds on employment. As a result, national employment was raised in the next iteration, though apparently not all regional employment variables were necessarily increased in value (Table 2).

For the last iteration the compromise values of the regional environmental quality indicators in the second iteration were added to the constraint set. From Table 3, it can be seen that the values of objectives showed very little variation across the columns of the pay-off matrix. Clearly in this way the consequences of many policy decisions, of various policy preferences or of various policy scenario's can easily be identified.

5. CONCLUDING REMARKS

The interactive multiobjective approaches to integrated economic-environmental decision-making in a spatial system presented and applied in the previous sections, have several advantages over traditional approaches:

- They reflect the process character of complex economic-environmental policy problems; they constitute learning aids for policy-makers as well as for modelers.
- They emphasize an active role of policy-makers in specifying and solving choice problems, *inter alia* by making policy objectives and trade-offs more explicit.
- They are able to take into account the variety and the conflicting nature of policy options or criteria without requiring a prior specification of weights.
- They provide an integrative framework for eliminating less relevant alternatives and for choosing consistent compromise solutions.

REFERENCES

Cohon, J.L. (1978). Multiobjective Programming and Planning. Academic Press, New York.

Driehuis, W. (1978). Een Sectoraal Model t.b.v. de Analyse van de Nederlandse Economie op Lange Termijn (SECMON). Dept. of Economics, University of Amsterdam (mimeographed).

Guldman, J. and Shefer, D. (1980). Industrial Location and Air Quality Control. Wiley, New York.

Hafkamp, W. and Nijkamp, P. (1982). Towards an Integrated National-Regional Environmental-Economic Model, Environmental Systems and Management S. Rinaldi et al. (Eds.), North-Holland Publ. Co, Amsterdam: 653-664.

Hafkamp, W. (1983). Triple Layer Model. Dissertation, Dept. of Economics, Free University, Amsterdam.

Keeney, R. and Raiffa, H. (1976). Decisions with Multiple Objectives. Wiley, New York.

Lakshmanan, T.R. and Nijkamp, P. (1980). Economic-Environmental-Energy Interactions. Martinus Nijhoff, Boston.

Nijkamp, P. (1979). Multidimensional Spatial Data and Decision Analysis. Wiley, Chichester.

Nijkamp, P. (1980). Environmental Policy Analysis. Wiley, Chichester.

Nijkamp, P. and Spronk, J. (1981). Multicriteria Analysis: Operational Methods. Gower, Aldershot.

Rietveld, P. (1980). Multiple Objective Decision Methods and Regional Planning. North-Holland Publ. Co, Amsterdam.
Spronk, J. (1981). Interactive Multiple Goal Programming. Martinus Nijhoff, Boston.
Zeleny, M. (1976). The Theory of Displaced Ideal, Multiple Criteria Decision Making. M. Zeleny (Ed.), Springer Berlin: 153-206.
Voogd, H. (1983). Multicriteria Evaluation for Urban and Regional Planning. Pion, London.

SIMULATION OF AN INTERACTIVE METHOD SUPPORTING COLLECTIVE DECISION MAKING USING A REGIONAL DEVELOPMENT MODEL

Zenon Fortuna[1] and Lech Krus[2]

[1] *International Institute for Applied Systems Analysis, Laxenburg, Austria and Institute of Automatic Control, Technical University of Warsaw, Warsaw, Poland*

[2] *Systems Research Institute of the Polish Academy of Sciences, Warsaw, Poland*

1. INTRODUCTION

This paper deals with a computerized interactive system which supports the making of collective decisions in a gaming framework. The basic idea of the system was proposed by Wierzbicki (1982), although several modifications have also been tested. The system has been implemented for a simple decision problem concerning the allocation of funds for regional development.

2. THE DECISION PROBLEM AND ITS INTERPRETATION

We assume that there are two decision makers, each of whom has two objectives. Their models can be described as follows:

Decision maker 1:

$$g_1 = g_1(x_1, x_2) \rightarrow \max \quad \text{(net production)}$$

$$g_2 = g_2(x_1, x_2) \rightarrow \max \quad \text{(consumption level)}$$

subject to

$$x_{1l} < x_1 < x_{1u} ,$$

where x_2 is a given value (fixed by the second player).

Decision maker 2:

$$g_3 = g_3(x_1, x_2) \rightarrow \max \quad \text{(net production)}$$

$$g_4 = g_4(x_1, x_2) \rightarrow \max \quad \text{(consumption level)}$$

subject to

$$x_{2l} < x_2 < x_{2u} ,$$

where x_1 is a given value (fixed by the first player). The decision variables for the first and second decision makers are denoted by x_1 and x_2 , respectively, and are constrained to lie in the rectangle defined by the values x_{1l}, x_{1u}, x_{2l}, x_{2u}. The problems of the decision makers are assumed to be interrelated.

This decision problem can be studied in more detail using a practical example. We shall consider a problem taken from the Notec Project, a study of integrated development in the Notec region carried out jointly by the Systems Research Institute of the Polish Academy of Sciences and IIASA. The final report of the Notec Project is given in Albegov and Kulikowski (1980). The project involved the construction of a system of models, one of which is a regional development model (RDM).

Relatively high rural-to-urban migration, particularly among people of working age, is one of the main features of the Upper Notec region. This causes changes in the distribution of the labor force and influences production and consumption processes significantly. The RDM (see Krus, 1981) describes these processes in an aggregate way, taking the migration into account. In this paper the RDM is reformulated as a problem of allocation of funds between capital expenditure and aggregate consumption in rural and urban areas.

One expert (decision maker) is considered to be responsible for the rural part of the region, and another for the urban areas. Each allocates his given budget Z_i between capital expenditure z_i and aggregate consumption z_{i+2}, $i=1,2$, trying to achieve his two objectives: maximum net production and maximum consumption level.

The net production is described by the relation:

$$y_i = r_i \, y_i(\alpha_{0i}) z_i(\alpha_{1i}) \ ,$$

where y_i is the size of the labor force, z_i represents capital expenditure, and r_i, α_{0i}, α_{1i} are known positive parameters.

The labor force is a function of the migration rate m :

$$y_i = y_i(m) \ ,$$

where the coefficient m is assumed to be the ratio of the net migration to the population in the rural area.

The consumption level (see also Kulikowski, 1981) is defined as a function (i) of expenditure in the aggregate consumption sphere (in a centrally planned economy this sphere includes all services supported by the government, such as education, health care and cultural services), (ii) of the wage fund (which depends on capital expenditure), and (iii) of demographic factors (in particular, the migration rate). Thus the function may be written as follows:

$$U_i = U_i(z_{i+2}, z_i, m) \ .$$

The rural-urban migration flow links the two parts of the region, and is assumed to be a result of unequal consumption levels in these areas. The migration rate has been econometrically estimated to be a function of the consumption ratio:

$$m = f(U_1/U_2) \ .$$

Software elaborated within the RDM model takes given values of $z_1=Z_1-x_1$, $z_3=x_1$, $z_2=Z_2-x_2$, $z_4=x_2$ and uses them to compute the values of the objectives, i.e., the net production $g_1=Y_1$ and the consumption level $g_2=U_1$ in the rural area; the net production $g_3=Y_2$ and the consumption level $g_4=U_2$ in the urban area.

The above description of the model allows us to interpret the decision problem defined in this section in terms of the RDM.

3. INTERACTIVE SYSTEM

3.1. Assumptions

The interactive system is considered to be a tool available to support the decisions of experts trying to solve the problem presented in the previous section. These experts are treated as players in a game. It is assumed that each of them has his own private utility function (unknown to the other players) based on maximized objectives. For each player, the system generates a function which scalarizes his objectives. At every step of the game, each player obtains information on the Nash equilibrium calculated with respect to the scalarizing functions, and can test any neighborhood of this equilibrium.

Using this information, the player expresses his preferences in the space of his objectives. It is assumed that he does this according to his private utility. The scalarizing functions are then modified and the procedure is repeated.

3.2. Structure of the Procedure

The procedure can be structured as follows:

Step 1. Choose the scalarizing functions from the assumed family of functions, e.g.,

$$s_1 = s_1(g_1, g_2, p_1)$$

$$s_2 = s_2(g_3, g_4, p_2) ,$$

where vectors p_1, p_2 contain parameters, e.g., reference points g_r and scaling points g_s.

Step 2. Compute the Nash equilibrium for s_1 versus s_2, finding the objective vector g_n.

Step 3. (DIALOG)

3a. Ask player 1 to change his parameters (e.g., the reference points g_{r1} and g_{r2}). Ask him to select the best solution from those actually tested.

3b. Repeat this procedure for player 2.

Step 4. Modify parameters p_1 and p_2 on the basis of the solutions selected by the players.
Repeat steps 1-4.

The exchange of information that occurs at step 3 of the procedure is illustrated in Fig. 1. In essence, the players supply values of the parameters p_1 and p_2 and obtain the Nash solutions g_n . The values of the objectives for given decision variables are calculated using the RDM, which is linked to the decision support system (DSS).

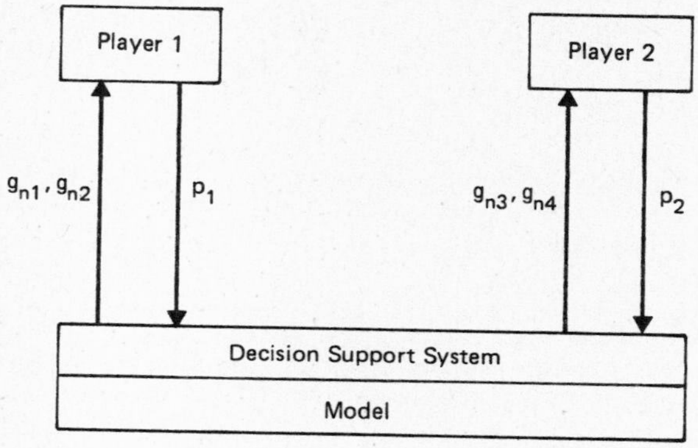

FIGURE 1 Exchange of information between the players and the decision support system.

3.3. Details and Comments

The above procedure has been modified in various ways: different scalarizing functions have been assumed, different methods for computing the Nash equilibria have been used, and the parameters of the scalarizing functions have themselves been modified in different ways. The results obtained on testing these modified procedures are summarized below.

Scalarizing functions. The following forms of the scalarizing function were tested:

$$s_1 = s_1(g_1, g_2, p_1)$$

$$= - \left\{ 0.5 \left[\left(\frac{g_{s1}-g_1}{g_{s1}-g_{r1}} \right)^p + \left(\frac{g_{s2}-g_2}{g_{s2}-g_{r2}} \right)^p \right] \right\}^{1/p} \tag{1}$$

$$s_1' = s_1'(g_1, g_2, p_1) = - \log |s_1| , \tag{2}$$

where $p_1 = \{g_{r1}, g_{r2}, g_{s1}, g_{s2}\}$. The above formulas are given for player 1; analogous equations can be constructed for player 2.

We observed that the algorithms computing the Nash equilibrium diverged when we used form (2). This is because this function does not preserve concavity for certain concave functions g_1 and g_2 . A simple example has been found for which the function is not concave with respect to variables x_1 and x_2 .

General concavity of function (1) can be proven, and this formula was used in the final version of the DSS. The power p was set equal to 20, but other tests were successfully carried out for p up to 80. It is however necessary to reduce the size of the terms raised to a power, dividing (or multiplying) them by properly chosen powers of 2. Without such "scaling" the computed value of the scalarizing function may be very inaccurate and/or overflow may appear.

Computation of Nash equilibria. Two methods have been used to compute Nash equilibria. The first version of the algorithm utilized the MINOS/ Augmented system because nonlinear constraints appeared in the formulation of the Nash conditions. Unfortunately, due to the linearization of these constraints, the convergence of MINOS became dependent on the starting points and the chosen values of the accuracy parameters. This means that MINOS could not be used as part of the DSS without "manual" control of convergence.

Eventually we chose a scaled steepest-descent-like method. The solutions are obtained iteratively, using quadratic approximations of the original scalarizing functions. The method is general but directly applicable to problems with "rectangle" constraints.

A more detailed analysis of the problem of calculating the game equilibria can be found in the description of the GEDASS system (Fortuna, 1984).

Modification of the scalarizing functions. Two approaches to the problem of modifying the parameters of the scalarizing functions were tested:

(a) Automatic choice of parameters p_1 and p_2 combined with simple truncation of the feasible rectangle.

(b) Direct choice based on the decisions of the players.

We shall first consider approach (a). In Step 3 (DIALOG) the player investigates the neighborhood of the actual solution g_n and then informs the system which objective he would like to take higher values (e.g., g_2). Because each solution g_n is the Pareto solution for each player (due to the form of the chosen scalarizing function), the system assumes that the original value of the other objective (in our case, g_1) can be taken as an upper bound for this objective in future manipulations.

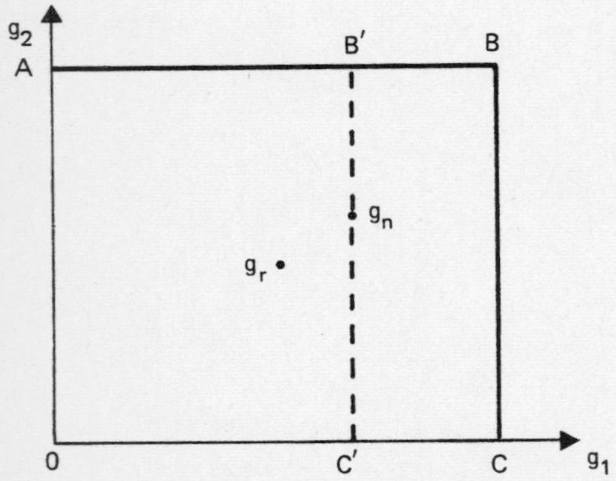

FIGURE 2 Simple truncation of the feasible rectangle.

Consider the example presented in Fig. 2. Here the rectangle ABCO, which represents the feasible region in the space of the objective values $g_1 - g_2$, is truncated to AB'C'0 after the player has indicated that the value of objective g_2 should be increased. The parameters of the scalarizing function were calculated in the following way:

-- The reference point g_r is equal to the geometrical center of the feasible rectangle (the point g_r in Fig. 2).
-- The scaling point g_s was chosen in two different ways; in the first version it was assigned a fixed large value (outside the original rectangle ABCO) while in the second version this large value changed when the rectangle was truncated.

We found both versions very inefficient, with very slow convergence due to saturation effects. Simple examples were eventually found which explain this effect. Thus, the whole method involving automatic choice of parameters is not very efficient.

Now let us consider approach (b), which requires direct choice of parameters. This means that the value of the reference point selected by the player after examining the neighborhood solutions is used in the subsequent iteration without any modification.

This method of parameter selection has the following features:
-- It allows the player to correct bad solutions assumed in earlier steps due to inconsistent decisions in DIALOG. Version (a) above did not allow such correction and one mistake could cut off the region containing the proper Nash solution.
-- The method is linearly convergent if the influence of the other player is sufficiently small (it is possible to evaluate the rate of convergence from the size of the derivatives), and if the accuracy of maximization of the player's own utility function is not decreasing.
-- If a player gives inconsistent answers there is a possibility of cycling, which may mean jumping over the region of feasible solutions. This is certainly one of the weaknesses of the method. In version (a) the truncation of the feasible region prevents such cycling or jumping.

4. EXAMPLE

The system was tested a number of times with human players who took decisions according to their own personal preferences, as well as with players simulated through utility functions. In the example considered here, these utility functions were of the form:

Player 1:

$$u_1 = A_1 \times g_1^{\alpha_1} \times g_2^{\beta_1} ,$$

where $\alpha_1/\beta_1 = 1.809$.

Player 2:

$$u_2 = A_2 \times g_3^{\alpha_2} \times g_4^{\beta_2} ,$$

where $\alpha_2/\beta_2 = 2.356$.

Note that the ratio of α and β coefficients defines the direction of a ridge in the space of objectives. The ridge increases with increasing objectives. Figure 3 presents the sequence of Nash equilibrium points obtained in six consecutive iterations.

The Nash points converge relatively quickly to the ridges of the utility functions of the players. The ridges are represented by lines on the figures, and describe the players' preferences between the objectives of maximum net production and maximum consumption level.

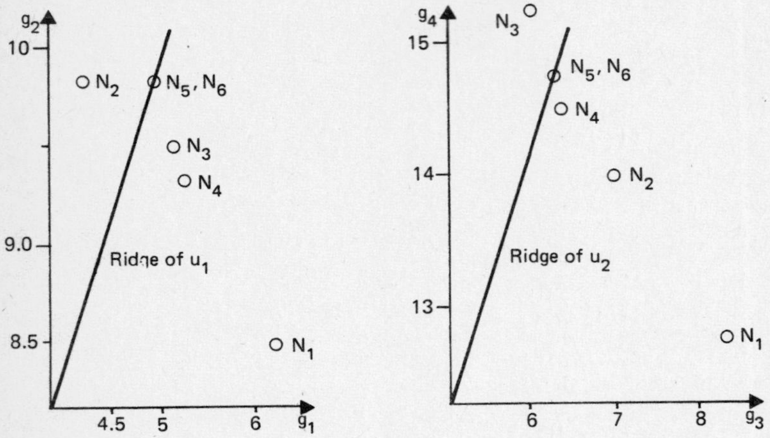

FIGURE 3 Sequence of Nash points obtained in six consecutive iterations.

5. IMPLEMENTATION

In addition to carrying out numerical experiments which demonstrate the properties of the procedure, we also prepared a program package which simulates a game between two players, using the computer as an interactive tool.

Only the nonlinear and linearized versions of the RDM model have as yet been included in the system. However, the players may prepare their own simple FORTRAN procedure to compute the values of their objective functions, allowing the system to be applied to other models.

The system allows work from remote terminals, thus providing a better simulation of independent negotiations. The system of programs is constructed on two levels:

-- The upper-level program computes temporary Nash solutions, sends the results to the players, receives their new reference points and the selected best solutions.
-- The lower-level (local) program provides "user-friendly" communication with each player and prepares messages for the upper-level program.

REFERENCES

Albegov, M. and Kulikowski, R. (Eds.) (1980). Proceedings of Joint Task Force Meeting on Development Planning for the Notec (Poland) and Silistra (Bulgaria) Regions. CP-80-9. International Institute for Applied Systems Analysis, Laxenburg, Austria.

Fortuna, Z. (1984). GEDASS - Game Equilibria Decision Analysis and Support System. Working Paper, International Institute for Applied Systems Analysis, Laxenburg, Austria (forthcoming).

Fortuna, Z. and Krus, L. (1984). Interactive Negotiations: An Example based on a Regional Development Model (Notec Case Study). Collaborative Paper, International Institute for Applied Systems Analysis, Laxenburg, Austria (in preparation).

Krus, L. (1981). An interactive regional development model (IRDM). In Albegov and Kulikowski (1980).

Kulikowski, R. (1981). Modeling methodology for the Notec case study. In Albegov and Kulikowski (1980).

Wierzbicki, A.P. (1982). An Idea of the Interactive Method Supporting Collective Decisions. An informal description of the game system. International Institute for Applied Systems Analysis, Laxenburg, Austria (unpublished).

A MULTIOBJECTIVE OBSERVATION NETWORK DESIGN PROCEDURE AND ITS APPLICATION IN HYDROLOGY AND MINING

Ferenc Szidarovszky

Department of Mathematics and Computer Science, University of Horticulture, Budapest, Hungary

1. INTRODUCTION

In geosciences a large set of data has to be usually collected and its structure has to be examined. In many applications, the observations are very expensive. In the mining industry drillhole data are used for exploration, and in underground hydrology water well data are analysed for monitoring water quality parameters. The data examined in these applications are usually spread out in space or /and time, and they are considered as realizations of certain regionalized variables.

The theory of regionalized variables has been developed by Matheron /1957, 1971/.

During the last few years increasing attention has been given to the application of this theory in various fields of applied sciences. For example, in hydrology the works of Delhomme /1978/, Gombolati and Volpi /1979/, Carrera et al /1983/; in mining the books of David /1977/, Journel and Huijbregts /1978/; in soil mechanics the paper of Webster and Burgess /1980/ are noteworthy. On the theoretical basis developed by Matheron a sequence of estimation processes have been developed which are called kriging in honour of Krige /1951/ who first proposed a special regression procedure to mining problems. The different variants of kriging give an optimal, unbiased, linear estimate under quite general assumptions. By using kriging, not only the estimates of the natural phenomena can be obtained, but the uncertainty of the estimates can also be characterized by the estimation variances.

In this paper we shall introduce a special minimization procedure to determine the optimal locations of the measurement points which minimizes the estimation variances. This is a typical multiobjective programming problem, since in applied sciences usually more parameters are simultaneously estimated.

2. AN OUTLINE OF KRIGING

Let D denote a subset of a finite dimensional Euclidean space and let Z/x/ be a random variable for all $x \in D$. Then Z/./ can be considered as a random function. Function Z/./ is called an intrinsic random function, if

$$/a/ \quad E\left[Z/x+h/ - Z/x/\right] = 0; \qquad /1/$$

$$/b/ \quad Var\left[Z/x+h/ - Z/x/\right] = 2\gamma/h/ \qquad /2/$$

for all $x, x+h \in D$. Function $\gamma/./$ is called the variogram.

Let V denote a bounded subset of D, and define the average value of Z/./ on V by the relation

$$\overline{Z}/V/ = \frac{1}{|V|}\int_V Z/x/dx, \qquad /3/$$

where $|V|$ is the measure /length, area, or volume/ of V. Assume that a relization of the random function Z/./ has been measured in k distinct points $x_1, x_2, \ldots, x_k$ and let $Z_1, Z_2, \ldots, Z_k$ denote these measurements. In using kriging the average value $\overline{Z}/V/$ is estimated by the linear estimator

$$Z^* = \sum_{j=1}^{k} \lambda_j Z_j \qquad /4/$$

where the unknown coefficients $\lambda_1, \ldots, \lambda_k$ are determined in the following way /Journel and Huijbregts, 1978/.

Introduce the folloing rotations:

$$\gamma_{ij} = \gamma/x_i - x_j/, \quad \gamma_{vj} = \frac{1}{|V|}\int_V \gamma/x_j - x/dx, \quad \gamma_{vv} =$$

$$= \frac{1}{|V|^2}\int_V\int_V \gamma/x-x'/dxdx',$$

$$\underline{\underline{A}}_k = \begin{pmatrix} 0 & 1 & 1 & \cdots & 1 \\ 1 & \gamma_{11} & \gamma_{12} & \cdots & \gamma_{1k} \\ \vdots & \vdots & \vdots & & \\ 1 & \gamma_{k1} & \gamma_{k2} & \cdots & \gamma_{kk} \end{pmatrix}, \quad \underline{\lambda}_k = \begin{pmatrix} \mu \\ \lambda_1 \\ \vdots \\ \lambda_k \end{pmatrix}, \quad \underline{\gamma}_k = \begin{pmatrix} 1 \\ \gamma_{v1} \\ \vdots \\ \gamma_{vk} \end{pmatrix}, \qquad /5/$$

then the kriging coefficients can be obtained by solving the linear equations

$$\underline{\underline{A}}_k \underline{\lambda}_k = \underline{\gamma}_k, \qquad /6/$$

and the variance of the estirator /4/ is given by

$$Var /x_1,\ldots,x_k/ = \underline{\gamma}_k^T \underline{\lambda}_k - \gamma_{vv} , \qquad /7/$$

which is called the estimation variance.

Before introducing the network design procedure, some basic properties of kriging will be discussed.

a/ Assume first that a new observation point x_{k+1} is included into the kriging process. Then an additional row and column is added to matrix $\underline{\underline{A}}_k$, and one additional component should be added to vectors $\underline{\lambda}_k$ and $\underline{\gamma}_k$. For solving the new kriging equation we do not need to repeat the entire computations /which needs $0/k^3/$ operations/, because the well known numerical technique known as "inversion by blocks" /Szidarovszky and Yakowitz, 1978/ can be applied in this case. As it is known, it requires only $0/k^2/$ operations. Observe furthermore that the new estimation variance is smaller than that based on only k observation points.

b/ Assume next that the point x_k is dropped from kriging. Then the solution of the new kriging system can be solved by the method "inversion by blocks" which requires only $0/k^2/$ operations, and the new estimation variance is larger than that based on the original k observation points.

c/ It can be verified that the above properties also hold for cokriging, when the average values of the intrinsic random functions $Z_1/./,\ldots,Z_m/./$ are simultaneously estimated on the sets $V_1,\ldots,V_m$, where some of the functions $Z_i/./$ or sets V_i may be identical. In this general case relation

$$\overline{Z}_i/V_i/ = \frac{1}{|V_i|} \int_{V_i} Z_i/x/dx \qquad /8/$$

defines the average values, and let

$$Var_i/x_1,\ldots,x_k/ \qquad /9/$$

denote the estimation variance in estimating $\overline{Z}_i/V_i/$ for $i=1,\ldots,m$. In the case of cokriging the kriging system and estimation variances have to be modified so that the elements of matrix $\underline{\underline{A}}_k$ and vectors $\underline{\lambda}_k$, $\underline{\gamma}_k$ are replaced by smaller dimensional matrices and vectors, respectively.

3. THE MULTIOBJECTIVE OBSERVATION NETWORK DESIGN MODEL

Assume again that $V_i \subseteq D$ for $i=1,\dots,m$, and $Z_i/./$ are intrinsic random functions defined on D. Let $\overline{Z}_i/V_i/$ denote the average values of functions $Z_i/./$ on V_i. Assume furthermore that the kriging estimation process has been applied for estimating the average values $\overline{Z}_i/V_i/$ on the basis of the existing data points $/x_i, Z_1/x_i/,\dots,Z_m/x_i//$, and the estimation variances are not satisfactory small. Then the estimation variances, that is, the uncertainty of the estimators can be improved by performing further measurements and repeating the kriging process with the increased number of data points. The question arises now can be stated as follows. How to select the additional measurement points so that the estimation variances will be as small as possible?

The mathematical model of this problem can be formulated in the following way. Let $x_1,\dots,x_k$ denote the existing observation points and assume that further n points should be selected from the finite set $T = \{ t_1,\dots,t_N \}$ of alternatives. Then our problem is equivalent to the m-objective minimization problem:

$$\text{minimize} \quad Var_i/x_1,\dots,x_k, t_{i_1},\dots,t_{i_n}/ \quad /i=1,\dots,m/$$

$$\text{subject to} \quad t_{i_1},\dots,t_{i_n} \in T . \qquad /10/$$

In hydrologic applications, the set T of alternatives is given e.g. by the existing water wells, while in mining exploration it has to be specified on the basis of prior geological informations known about the region under consideration.

The single-objective version of this problem has been earlier discussed by Szidarovszky /1983 a/, and a special multiobjective approach has been introduced by Szidarovszky /1983 b/. These special methods were applied in underground hydrology by Carrera et al /1983/.

The solution of problem /10/ can be solved by a special branch and bound procedure which is a simple generalization of the algorithm presented e.g. is Szidarovszky /1983 b/.

4. CASE STUDY IN HYDROLOGY

In our first numerical example a subregion of the river basin of the Tajo river /Spain/ is investigated. This river basin has been investigated earlier by Carrera and Szidarovszky /1983/.

Two variables are considered, $Z_1/x/$ denotes log-transmissivity and $Z_2/x/$ denotes the water quality measured by the TDS. It is also assumed that monitoring water quality is important only in a subset of the subregion. The whole subregion is denoted by V_1 and the subset for monitoring water quality is denoted by V_2.

The variogram for log-transmissivity is given as

$$\gamma_1/h/ = \begin{cases} 0 & \text{if } |h| = 0 \\ 0.08+0.1 \,/\frac{3}{2} \cdot \frac{h}{40.0} - \frac{1}{2} \cdot /\frac{h}{40.0}/^3/ & \text{if } 0 < |h| < 40.0 \\ 0.18 & \text{if } |h| \geq 40.0 \,, \end{cases}$$

and the variogram for water quality is given as

$$\gamma_2/h/ = \begin{cases} 0 & \text{if } |h| = 0 \\ 1.0+4.0/\frac{3}{2} \cdot \frac{h}{12.0} - \frac{1}{2} \cdot /\frac{h}{12.0}/^3/ & \text{if } 0 < |h| < 12.0 \\ 5.0 & \text{if } |h| \geq 12.0 \end{cases}$$

The correlation between log-transmissivity and water quality is very law, they are assumed to be independent. Two measurement points are considered, and the eight candidates for additional observation points have been selected as the locations of the existing water wells in the close neighborhood of V_1 and V_2. Their locations are given in Figure 1.

The multiobjective branch and bound procedure has been applied for these data. Three selections are efficient, they are presented in Table 1. If the weighting method is used, then the "best" solution depends on the weights selected. In this case the composite objective

$$\alpha \, Var_1 + /1-\alpha/ \, Var_2$$

is minimized. The results are summarized in Table 2.

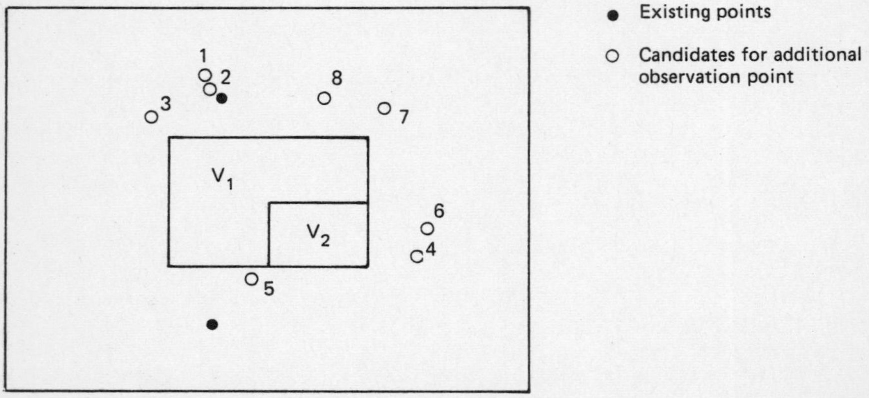

Figure 1 Existing and candidate observation points

Table 1. Efficient solutions

selection	Var_1	Var_2
t_3, t_4, t_5, t_8	0.0319	2.7618
t_3, t_4, t_5, t_7	0.0322	2.7600
t_4, t_5, t_7, t_8	0.0326	2.7532

Table 2 "Best" solution as function of α

	"best" selection
$0 \leqq \alpha < 0.92$	t_4, t_5, t_7, t_8
$\alpha = 0.92$	t_4, t_5, t_7, t_8 and t_3, t_4, t_5, t_8
$0.92 < \alpha \leqq 1$	t_3, t_4, t_5, t_8

The details of applying another multiobjective programming technique for solving this problem, are not discussed in this paper.

5. CASE STUDY IN MINING

In our second numerical example a test case used by a major mining software vendor is investigated. Figure 2 shows the existing 59 drillhole locations and the 10 candidate drillhole sites for additional drilling. The drillhole data represented the average grade /%/. Two blocks are considered, they are shown in Figure 3 and it is assumed that the block grades for these blocks should be estimated with minimal estimation variances.

On the basis of the existing drillhole data the block grades has been estimated as

$$Z_1^* = 0.023846 \approx 2.38\ \% \text{ and } Z_2^* = 0.010204 \approx 1.02\ \%,$$

and the estimation variances are obtained as

$$Var_1 = 0.000804 \quad \text{and} \quad Var_2 = 0.000383.$$

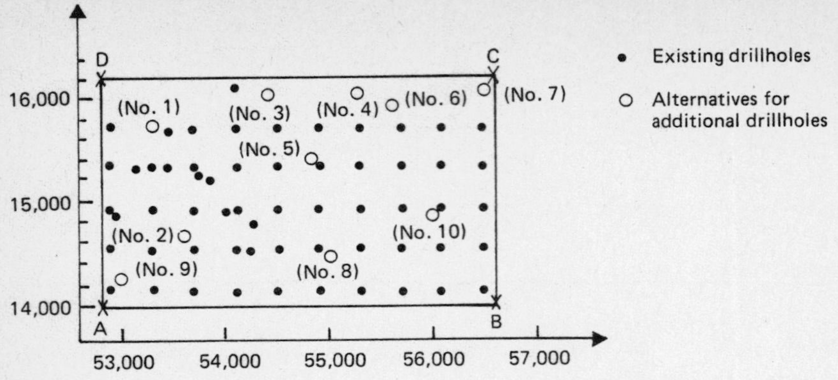

Figure 2 Existing and candidate drillhole sites

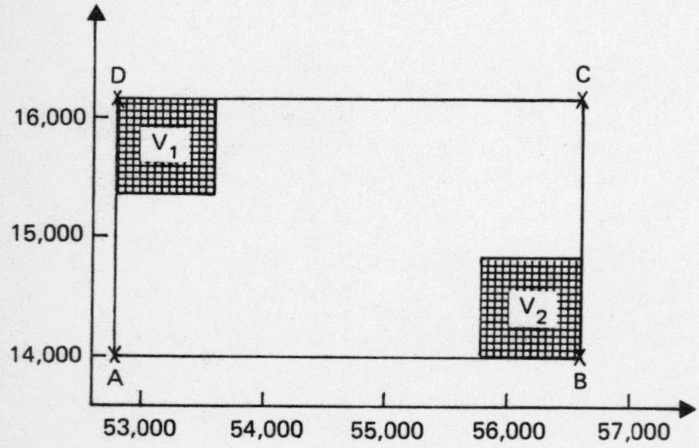

Figure 3 Blocks for estimating block grades

The optimal locations of five additional drillhole sites have been determined from the ten alternatives. The weighting method has been selected again. If equal weights / $\alpha = 0.5$/ are chosen, then the "best" selection is as follows:

t_2, t_3, t_4, t_5, t_6 with estimation variances

$\mathrm{Var}_1 = 0.000718$ and $\mathrm{Var}_2 = 0.000306$

If $\alpha = 1$ is selected, then t_1, t_2, t_3, t_5, t_8 is the "best" choice, and if $\alpha = 0$ then the best choice is given as $t_4, t_5, t_6, t_8, t_{10}$.

Finally we remark, that this case study has been earlier investigated by Szidarovszky /1983 a/.

References

Matheron,G. /1957/ Theorie lognormale de l'enchantillonnage systematique des gisements. _Ann. Mines,_ 577.

Matheron,G. /1971/ The theory of regionalized variables and its applications. _Cahiers du CMM,_ Fasc. no.5. ENSMP, Paris

Delhomme,J.P. /1978/ Kriging in the hydrosciences. _Advances in Water Resources,_ 1/5/,251.

Gambolati,G. and G. Volpi /1979/ Groundwater contour mapping in Venice by stochastic interpolation, 1. Theory. _Water Resources Research,_ 15/2/, 281.

Carrera, J.,E. Usunoff and F. Szidarovszky /1983/ Optimal observation network design for ground water management: application to the San Pedro River Basin, Arizona. Submitted for publication.

David, M. /1977/ _Geostatistical ore reserve estimation._ Elsevier, Amsterdam, 364.

Journel A.G. and Ch.J. Huijbregts /1978/ _Mining geostatistics._ Academic Press, New York, London, 600.

Webster, R. and T.M. Burgess /1980/ Optimal interpolation and isaritmic mapping in soil properties, III. changing drift and universal kriging. _J. of Soil Sci,_ 31, 505.

Krige, D.G. /1951/ A statistical approach to some basic mine valuation problems on the Witwatersrand. _J. Chem, Metall. Min. Soc. S. Afr.,_ 52, 119.

Szidarovszky F. and S. Yakowitz /1978/ _Principles and procedures of numerical analysis._ Plenum, New York.

Szidarovszky F. /1983 a/ Optimal observation network in geostatistics and underground hydrology. _Appl. Math. Modelling,_ 7, 25-32.

Szidarovszky F. /1983 b/ Multiobjective observation network desing for regionalized variables. To be published in _International Journal of Mining Engineering._

Carrera, J. and F. Szidarovszky /1983/ Numerical comparison of network design algorithms for regionalized variables. Accepted for publication.

ANALYSIS OF REGIONAL WATER POLICIES IN OPEN-CAST MINING AREAS – A MULTICRITERIA APPROACH

S. Kaden
International Institute for Applied Systems Analysis, Laxenburg, Austria

1. INTRODUCTION

Within the Institutions and Environmental Policies Program at IIASA, a project is underway which focuses on concepts, procedures, and methods in the area of resource and environmental policy analysis and design with special regard to groundwater management and protection strategies.

The research concentrates on the following generic issues that dominate virtually all problems in environmental and natural resource policy design. First, these problems always involve controversy among interest groups. Second, even for each of these groups it is difficult or impossible to select a single criterion for appraising alternative courses of action. Not all objectives concerning human health and fundamental environmental equilibria can be translated into Dollar and Cents. Third, uncertainty and imprecision due to limited understanding, data base and predictive capabilities are common.

One objective of this project is the development of relatively simple policy-oriented methods and computerized procedures that can assist in addressing the above-mentioned generic issues. Thereby, the project team is working with, and attempting to synthesize experience from national studies concerned with environmental and resource policies carried out in several National Member Organization (NMO) countries. One of these studies is the Analysis of Regional Water Policies in Open-Cast Mining Areas undertaken in collaboration with institutes in the GDR. The study is directed at the development and implementation of methods and models for analyzing the *use of water resources and environmental problems in open-cast mining areas*. Conflicts caused by open-cast lignite mining in middle and eastern Europe, in particular in the GDR, FRG, CSSR, USSR, and Poland, are one of the conspicuous examples for interactions in socio-economic-environmental systems with special regard to groundwater and surface water.

2. PROBLEM DESCRIPTION

In the GDR, more than two-thirds of the total output of primary energy is based on lignite extracted exclusively by strip mining. The annual output of lignite amounts to more than 250 million tons/annum. Thereby it is necessary to pump out 1.5 billion m^3/annum water for dewatering of the open-cast mines. For 1990, a coal output of about 300 million tons/annum is planned; the rate of mine water pumping is estimated at about 2 billion m^3/annum. The stable runoff of the GDR runs to 9 billion m^3/annum. That means that the amount of mine-water is about 20% of the stable runoff (see, for instance, Luckner et el. 1982). Hence in the mining area itself the water resources system is mainly determined by the lignite mining.

The impact of mining upon water resources creates significant environmental and resources use conflicts between different users in such regions. The most important interest groups are mining, municipalities, industry, in many cases located downstream, and agriculture. The activities of each of these interest groups modify the water resources system, as well as the conditions for resources use by other groups. Figure 1 gives a general view of the interdependencies between the water users and water resources subsystems in mining areas. Recreation and environmental protection also represent conflicting users.

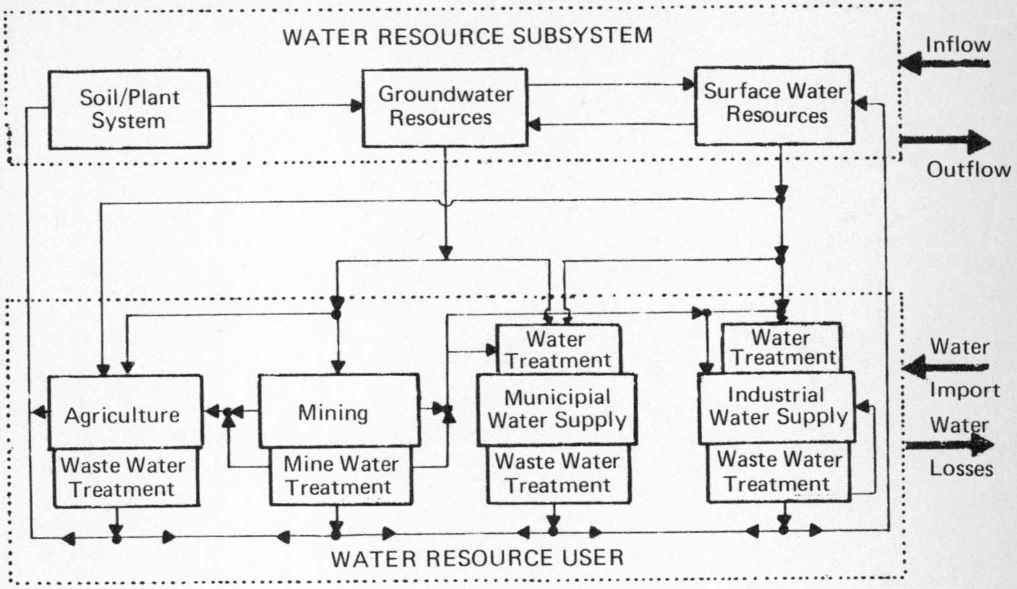

Figure 1. Interdependencies between water users and water resources subsystems in mining areas.

Under the typical hydrogeological conditions in lignite mining areas, mine dewatering becomes a significant cost and energy factor. The amount of water to be pumped exceeds ten to one hundred times the output of coal [m^3]! That means a considerable part of the energy produced by lignite is used for dewatering the mine itself. Since the mines are about 40 to 60 meters deep (sporadically 100 meters or more) large regional cone-shaped groundwater depressions are formed. One of the consequences is that the wells for municipal water supply are becoming dry. Hence the objective "*satisfying drinking water supply in a certain quality and quantity*" conflicts with the mining objective "*lowering the groundwater table in given areas in a given time*". Management/technological alternatives are, for instance, the limitation of groundwater depression areas with the help of side walls, switch to alternative water supply sources (e.g. surface water, water transfer from other regions, reuse of mine water, etc.).

There are also water quality problems caused by mining. Mine drainage water characteristically contains both high quantity of suspended and dissolved solids, particularly iron and sulphate ions resulting from the oxidation of ferrous sulphide in the host rocks. Chloride concentrations may also be high because of connate water trapped within the sedimentary rocks. Commonly the conspicuous quality problems are connected with mine spoils. For example, in the Lusatia area in the GDR, sulphate concentrations up to 700 mg/l have been estimated in the drainage water of spoils, Starke (1980). Polluted mine water may effect downstream water yields significantly.

In general, the water resources and environmental problems in mining areas include long-term planning (management) and short-term control aspects. They are embedded in a hierarchical policy-making process with interdependent policy makers. For *short-term control* problems the policy makers as well as the environmental subsystems can be assumed independent. Based on the different time characteristics of the water resources subsystem, above all the significant retardation in the system due to the groundwater flow, these problems usually can be solved separately for the different water resources subsystems (considering other subsystems as constraints). A lot of efficient methods for modeling of these subsystems exist. The *long-term planning* pinpoints the general targets, thereby setting up the margins for short-term control activities. It is characterized by significant interdependencies in the socioeconomic environmental system and policy-making process and it will be the main focus of our study. The planning horizon is 30-50 years. The time interval to be adopted for analysis may vary from month to year. The area affected by open-cast lignite mines amounts to some 10,000 km^2.

The above described problems elucidate the importance of effective management alternatives and means of regulating the interactions within the socio- economic-environmental system. Mathematical, computerized methods and models as methods for multiobjective decision analysis are a necessary and useful tool.

The choice of a suitable test area determines both the theoretical and the practical value of the study, therefore *the first research topic* of the study is a detailed analysis of the socio-economic-environmental processes in the test area.

As *the second research topic*, suitable submodels for these processes will be developed. *The third research topic* is the choice and development of the mathematical and computer framework for a policy-oriented interactive decision support model system.

The fourth research topic will be the development of an approach for the integration of the decision support model system in the policy making process.

The final (fifth) research topic will be the use of the developed methods and models for policy design in the test area.

3. METHODOLOGICAL APPROACH

3.1 Integration of the Decision Support Model System into the Policy-Making Process

The policy-making analysis for regulating the dynamics of the socio-economic-environmental system of the type discussed in this paper requires consideration of a complex hierarchical socio-economic system with multiple interdependent interest groups or decision-makers having different preferences. A simplified structure of this hierarchy is illustrated in Figure 2. We assume that for long-term planning purposes we can neglect lower levels like factories, mines, etc., and consider only a two-level system as in Figure 3. Three types of interactions between the interest-groups will be considered.

The first type involves a regulating body. We assume the following sequence of decision-making in this structure. First, the regulating body chooses its policies (required production levels, etc.), and then the lower level elements knowing these policies, with their own goals in mind, choose their behaviour. The general problem for this structure lies in the analysis and/or determination of regionally rational policies capable of coordinating the activities of the lower level interest groups to achieve a sustainable long-term development of the whole system.

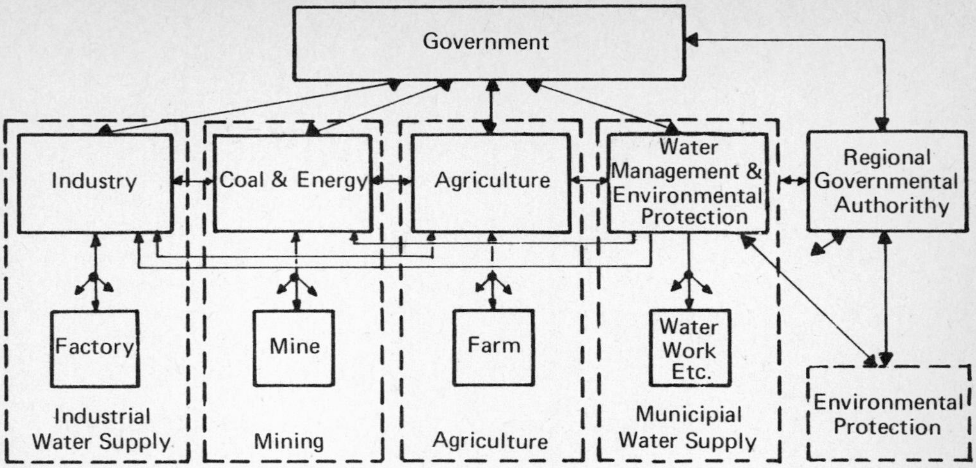

Figure 2. Schematic policy-making process in mining areas.

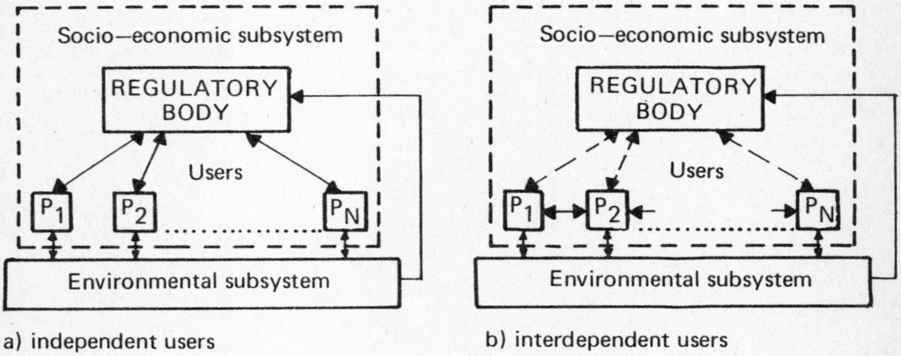

Figure 3. Idealized two-level policy making system.

The following approach (see Hughes et al. 1983), based on a two-stage decomposition of the problem, can be used: *The first stage* of the analysis based on this approach is directed towards generating scenarios of the potentially rational development of the system under study.

At the second stage this scenario serves as a "target" scenario, and the analysis at this stage is concerned with the search for those feasible regulatory policies that can provide for the development of the whole system along the lines specified by the scenario obtained at the first stage, considering the interests and reactions of users.

In the second type of interactions in the policy-making process we neglect the regulating body and we look for a cooperative behaviour of multiple decision makers. Finally, the third type is concerned with analyzing the system from the viewpoint of a separate interest group.

A decision support model system is needed, having a high flexibility which allows its use for the above mentioned types of interactions in the policy-making process.

3.2 DECISION SUPPORT MODEL SYSTEM

3.2.1 Conception

The following general goals should be considered:

- The model must integrate the essential interactions between, both, the socioeconomic subsystem (water users) and the environmental subsystem (water resources system).
- The model must fit in the policy-making process, that means it has to reflect the goals and policy-making reality of the policy-makers in mining areas. Therefore interactive and user-friendly systems are needed.

It is reasonable to assume that common surface water-supply models which are based on the stochastic simulation of inputs (streamflow) and the deterministic simulation of water usage (considering the priorities of certain users), will form the basis for the proposed model. Such models found extensive practical application in the GDR for long-term planning purposes (see, for example, Kozerski 1981). These models combine stochastic inputs with deterministic simulation using the Monte-Carlo method.

Figure 4 characterizes the practical application of the long-term water management models. Management/technological alternatives have to be included

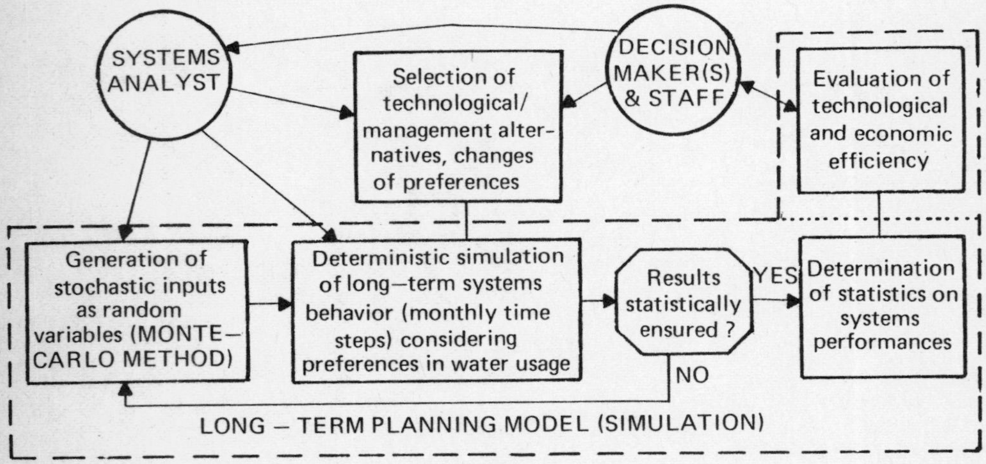

Figure 4. Typical long-term water management approach.

exogenously. The decision-makers perform the analysis by evaluating the economic and technical efficiency of the fixed alternatives, and by selection of new alternatives, occasionally through changes in priorities. Without conflicting interest groups this is a helpful tool. In the case of multiple objectives or decision-makers, the exogenous selection of rational alternatives is very difficult, often impossible.

The further development of this approach toward a decision support model-system for the socio-economic-environmental processes in mining areas necessitates the integration of submodels for all water resources subsystems and the integration in, or combination with, normative models for a partial automatized choice of scenarios or selection of technological/management alternatives.

The main difficulties implementing these models evolve from the dynamic, and at the same time uncertain systems behaviour. To avoid these difficulties the following two level model systems may be used:

- time-discrete multiobjective model for planning periods (one to five years), aggregating long-term decisions and objectives;
- simulation model for the monthly systems behaviour in the planning period using stochastic input simulation and deterministic allocation of water resources between users (with given priorities).

Figure 5 characterizes in a simplified way, the application of this approach. Based on an exogenous selection of fundamental technological/management alternatives by the decision makers, the choice of scenarios for the planning period can be done with the help of an appropriate time-discrete multiobjective model used interactively. For estimation of the parameters of the multiobjective model and the verification of its results, the simulation model with stochastic inputs capturing monthly system behaviour will be used. For the model system characterized in Figure 5 an effective multiobjective model is needed, the use of DIDASS (Grauer 1983) based on the reference point approach (Wierzbicki 1983) is presumed.

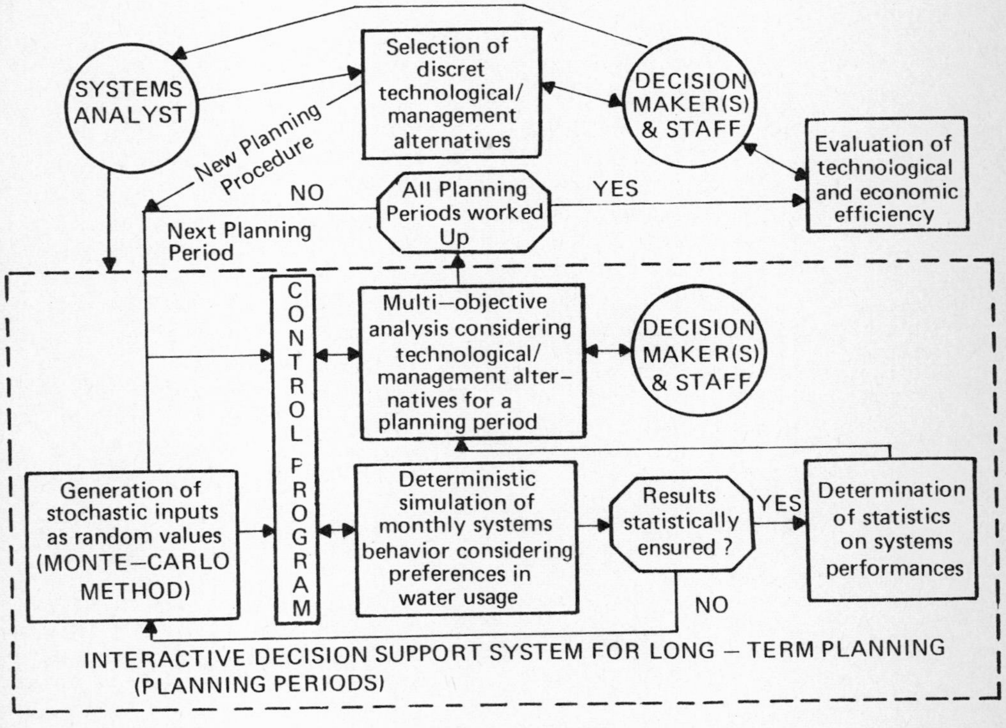

Figure 5. Two-level approach for long-term planning.

3.3 The Use of DIDASS

To test the possibilities of DIDASS a schematized, simplified test area has been chosen, which is characterized in Figure 6.

The test region is characterized by a deep open-pit mine, located near a river. The main impacts on the water resources system are:

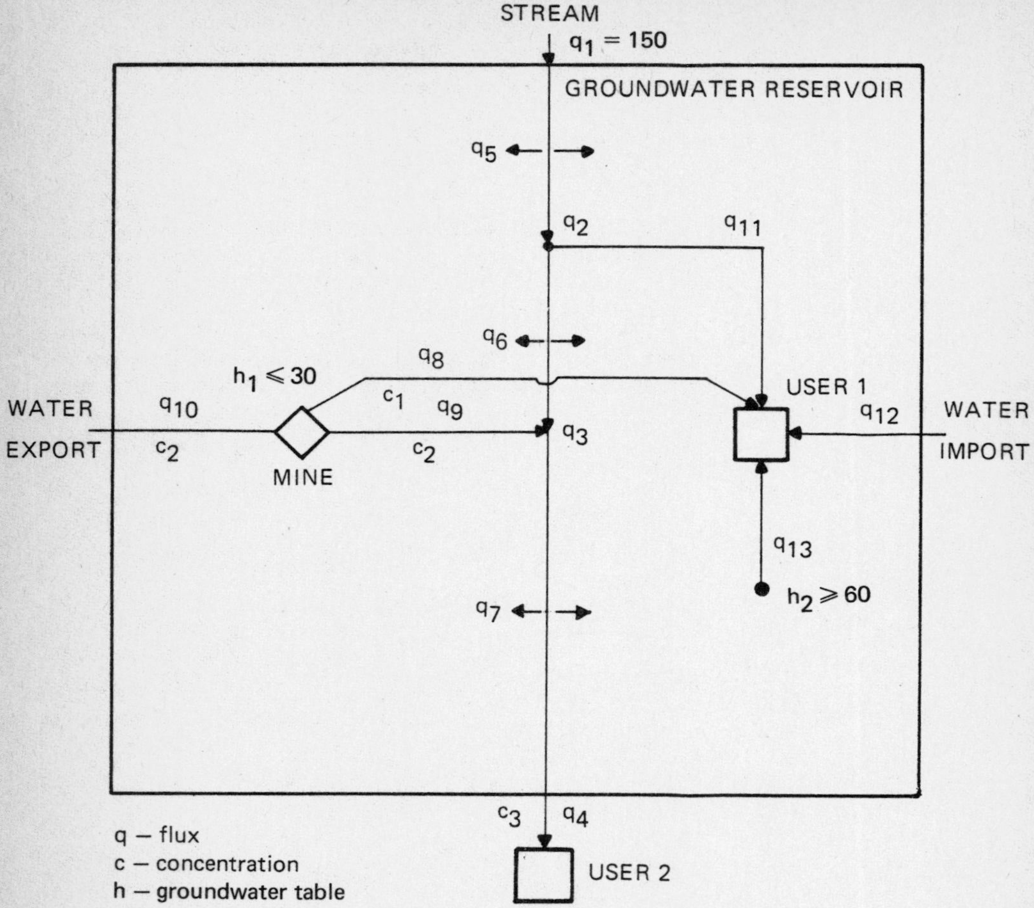

Figure 6. Schematized test region for the use of DIDASS.

- regional lowering of groundwater table which essential effects the river flow (infiltration losses) as well as a groundwater-waterwork in this region;
- high mineralized mine drainage water which is needed for river flow augmentation but effects the downstream water use.

Possible technological alternatives are for instance:

- water import for water supply and/or flow augmentation
- export of high mineralized water
- selective mine drainage
- treatment of high mineralized water

The following nonlinear static model has been used for first test runs:

Objective functions

Minimizing deviation between water supply and demand

$obj1 = 1000-(q_8+q_{11}+q_{12}+q_{13})$ USER 1

$obj2 = 1000-q_4$ USER 2

Minimizing costs for mine drainage

$obj3 = 2q_8+q_9+1.5q_{10}$

Minimizing costs for water supply

$obj4 = (1.0+0.01\cdot c_1)\cdot q_8+1.5q_{11}+q_{12}+q_{13}$ USER 1

$obj5 = 0.01\cdot q_4\cdot c_3$ USER 2

Constraints

Flux balance for river sections

$150-q_5-q_2=0 \quad q_2-q_6-q_{11}-q_3 = 0 \quad q_3+q_9-q_7-q_4 = 0$

Groundwater tables (response functions)

$$30 > h_1 = 50-0.5(q_9+q_{10})-0.1q_8-0.01q_{13}+0.001(q_9^2+q_{10}^2)$$
$$+0.0002q_8^2+0.1q_5+0.3q_6+0.2q_7$$

$$60 < h_2 = 80-0.2q_{13}-0.1(q_8+q_9+q_{10})+0.01q_5+0.02q_6+0.03q_7$$

Bank filtration

$$q_5 = 27 -20 \exp(-0.01(q_8+q_9+q_{10})-0.001q_{13}+0.002q_6+0.01q_7)$$

$$q_6 = 22.2-20 \exp(-0.02(q_8+q_9+q_{10})-0.002q_{13}+0.001q_5+0.001q_7)$$

$$q_7 = 44.2-40 \exp(-0.02(q_8+q_9+q_{10})-0.005q_{13}+0.001q_5+0.002q_6)$$

Mineralization

$c_1 > 100+0.1q_8 \quad c_2 > 200+0.2(q_9+Q_{10}) \quad c_3\cdot q_4 < c_2\cdot q_9$

Bounds

$0 \le q_i \le 200,\ i = 1,13 \quad c_i \ge 0,\ i = 1.3 \quad c_1 < 500 \quad c_2 < 1000 \quad c_3 < 200$

The results of some test runs are summarized in the Appendix. Based on different reference points and scaling factors efficient solutions have been computed.

REFERENCES

Grauer, M. (1983). A Dynamic Interactive Decision Analysis and Support System (DIDASS) User's Guide. WP-83-60. International Institute for Applied Sysrems Analysis, Laxenburg, Austria.

Hughes, T.C., Orlovsky, S., and Narayanan, R. (1983). Salinity Management by Use of Low Quality Water. WP-83-18. International Institute for Applied Systems Analysis, Laxenburg, Austria.

Kozerski, D. (1981). Rechenprogrammsystem GRM als verallgemeinertes Langfristbewirtschaftungsmodell (Computer program systems as a generalized long-term management model). Wasserwirtschaft/Wassertechnik Berlin: 31(11)390-394 and 31(12)415-419 (in German).

Luckner, L., and Hummel, J. (1982). Modelling and Prediction of the Quality of Mine Drainage Water Used for the Drinking Water Supply in the GDR. First International Mine Water Congress, Budapest, Hungary.

Starke, W. (1980). Nutzung von Grubenwasser der Braunkohlentagebaue zur Trinkwasserversorgung (Utilization of lignite-mine drainage water for municipal water supply). Wasserwirtschaft/Wassertechnik, Berlin: Vol. 30, No.11, pp.386-388 (in German).
Wierzbicki, A.P. (1982). A Mathematical Basis for Satisficing Decision Making Mathematical Modelling USA 3:391-405 (Reprint in IIASA RR-83-7).

APPENDIX. DIDASS - Test runs

	u	r	s	e	r	s	e	r	s	e
obj. 1.	581.0	581.0	1	815.0	900.0	1	875.0	900.0	7	849.0
obj. 2	800.0	800.0	1	902.0	900.0	1	919.0	900.0	6	923.0
obj. 3	0.0	0.0	1	172.0	100.0	1	80.0	100.0	5	73.0
obj. 4	82.0	82.0	1	253.0	200.0	1	169.0	200.0	1	230.0
obj. 5	0.0	0.0	1	145.0	100.0	1	105.00	100.0	2	102.00
q_2				127.3			129.7			129.0
q_3				73.1			72.3			71.6
q_4				98.5			80.8			77.3
q_5				22.7			20.3			22.0
q_6				21.4			20.2			21.1
q_7				42.6			40.5			42.0
q_8				92.5			44.9			78.3
q_9				68.0			49.0			47.7
q_{10}				0.0			20.0			17.4
q_{11}				32.8			37.2			27.1
q_{12}				30.5			0.0			0.0
q_{13}				29.4			42.6			37.8
c_1				109.2			104.5			105.2
c_2				213.6			213.8			213.0
c_3				147.4			129.7			131.4

u = utopia point, r = reference point, s = scale, e = efficient point.

DECISION SUPPORT VIA SIMULATION FOR A MULTIPURPOSE HYDROENERGETIC SYSTEM

F. Breitenecker and A. Schmid
Institute of Applied Mathematics, Technical University of Vienna, Vienna, Austria

ABSTRACT

A program package for the simulation of a hydro-energetic multipurpose system consisting of dams, reservoirs, rivers and pumps is implemented within a hybrid simulation language. The aim of the program is to support decisions about the operation ot these systems in an interactive and practical way. Few commands allow to define and examine the model automatically. Documentation can be done by usual features of the simulation language.

1. INTRODUCTION

A hydro- energetic system consisting of dams. pumps, reservoirs and rivers can be modelled by a set of nonlinear differential equations. The multipurpose profits of the system can be analysed by different cost functionals (section 2).

At the Hybrid Computation Centre of the Technical University Vienna a program package for the simulation of this model is implemented within a simulation language. The simulation package is realized in "supermacro"-technique: one or only few commands which are added to the commands of a (hybrid) simulation language activate and perform the simulation. Consequently the definition of the model equations is done automatically according to the input of the user (number of dams, connections between dams).

A lot of preprogrammed functions allow to choose between different natural inflows and between different inflows and outflows (control strategy). The values of the cost functionals representing the multipurpose profits can be compared directly using another (preprogrammed) module. The implementation is described in section 3. Section 4 deals with a simple example describing a hydro- energetic system consisting of three dams.

2. MATHEMATICAL MODEL OF A HYDRO- ENERGETIC SYSTEM

In this section a deterministic continuous model for the simulation of a hydro- energetic multipurpose system is described. Such a system may consist of rivers, reservoirs, power-plants, water users and pumps.

To get a model which can be implemented with reasonable effort, it is necessary to make some simplyfying assumptions:

1) All the pumps and water- users take the water directly out from the reservoirs and give it back there, too.
2) River- plants are only situated at the outlets of the reservoirs.
3) Evaporation losses and water quality are neglected.

4) Water inflows and the demands of users are assumed to be statistically known.

Due to the above assumptions the system is described by state equations for the reservoirs, which are obtained by the continuity principle (⟨4⟩,⟨6⟩,⟨8⟩)

$$s_i(t) = z_i(t) - a_i(t)$$

$$s_{i,min} \leq s_i(t) \leq s_{i,max}, \qquad i = 1,\dots,n \tag{1}$$

with $s_i(0)$ given and time $t \in [0,T]$.

There $s_i(t)$, $z_i(t)$, $a_i(t)$ denote storage, inflow and outflow of the i-th reservoir, n the number of reservoirs and T the end of the simulation interval. The storage of each reservoir is limited by $s_{i,min}$ and $s_{i,max}$.

The inflow $z_i(t)$ consists of four parts, namely of natural inflow, inflow from upstream reservoirs, inflows from pumping (k pumps) and from users (m users):

$$z_i(t) = y_i(t) + \sum_j u_{ij}(t-t_{i,oj}) + \sum_k p_{ik}(t-t_{p,ik}) + \sum_m e_{il}(t-t_{e,im}) \tag{2}$$

There $y_i(t)$, $u_{ij}(t)$, $p_{ik}(t)$ and $e_{im}(t)$ denote the natural inflow, the inflow coming from upstream j-th reservoir, the pumped inflow from the k-th pump and the inflow from the k-th pump and the inflow from the m-th user respectively. The quantities $t_{u,ij}$, $t_{p,ik}$, $t_{e,im}$ characterize time- delays.

The outflow $a_i(t)$ consists of three parts through the outlet of the reservoir:

$$a_i(t) = \sum_j v_{ij}(t) + \sum_k q_{ik}(t) + \sum_m f_{im}(t) \tag{3}$$

There $v_{ij}(t)$, $q_{ik}(t)$ and $f_{im}(t)$ denote the outflow to the j-th reservoir, the outflow to the k-th pump and the outflow to the m-th user.

Consequently inflows (2) and outflows (3) are related by the following equations:

$$u_{ij}(t-t_{u,ij}) = \sum_j v_{ij}(t) \tag{4.a}$$

$$p_{ik}(t-t_{p,ik}) = q_{jk}(t) \tag{4.b}$$

$$e_{il}(t-t_{e,im}) = r_m f_{jm}(t) \tag{4.c}$$

In (4.a) one has to summarize only over these values of the index j, if the j-th reservoir is upstream of the i-th reservoir. Equation (4.b) characterizes, that the k-th pump takes water from the j-th reservoir and gives it back to the i-th reservoir with the time delay $t_{p,ik}$. Equation (4.c) describes, that the l-th user takes water from the j-th reservoir and gives it back only in parts to the i-th reservoir with a time delay $t_{e,im}$, where r_m $(0 \leq r_m \leq 1)$ measures, how much water is given back.

In this model (1) - (4) all the variables are bounded technically, the variables v_{ji}, y_{ji} and f_{ji} are the controls and the s_i characterize the state of the system.
Consequently an implementation of the model should allow to study the reactions of the system to the application of different controls.
This aim makes it necessary to define measures for the quality for the operation of the system.
Those measures are due to the purpose of the system and are modelled as follows:

$$c_{en} = \int_0^T b_p(t) \sum_i c_i h_i(t) \sum_j v_{ij}(t)\,dt \rightarrow \max \tag{5a}$$

describes the benefit of energy production. There $b_p(t)$ is a price coefficient function, the constant c_i includes the efficiency of the plant of the i-th reservoir. The effective head $h_i(t)$ of the i-th power plant depends on the actual volume and on the geometry of the i-th reservoir ([9]).
The cost functional

$$c_{fl} = \int_0^T \sum_i (s_{i,max} - s_i(t))\,dt \rightarrow \max \tag{5b}$$

should be maximized, if the flood control is very important. From the point of the recreational use the "contrary cost" functional

$$c_{re} = \int_0^T \sum_i (s_i(t) - s_{i,min})\,dt \rightarrow \max \tag{5c}$$

is to be maximized.
Also other cost functionals describing e.g. the benefits of withdrawal of water of the costs of pumping can be considered ([4],[8]).

3. IMPLEMENTATION OF THE SIMULATION PACKAGE

The model (1) - (3) of the hydro- energetric system together with the equation (5) modelling the multipurpose profits is implemented as simulation package on the Hybrid Computer of the Technical University Vienna within the (hybrid) simulation language HYBSYS.
HYBSYS has been developed at the Hybrid Computation Centre of the Technical University Vienna. It provides model declaration and problem investigation in a simple and hardware- independent manner ([10],[11]). If analog integration is choosen as integration algorithm, HYBSYS performs automatically the problem set-up using an autopatch system and automatic online scaling ([2]).
HYBSYS is supported by the hybrid time- sharing system MACHYS developed at the Hybrid Computation Centre of the Technical University Vienna ([7]), too.
The simulation package is implemented in "supermacro"-technique ([3]). The concept of supermacros, developed in conformity with the CSSL-Standard 1968 ([12]) and with the proposals for the new CSSL-Standard 1981 ([5]), can be implemented in parts within HYBSYS ([3]).
A supermacro is a special kind of a macro of a simulation language, which performs

a) definition of the model equations according to the input of the user

b) specification of "methods" describing useful actions which can be done with the model
c) initialization or initialization and performance of experiments using the defined model and the defined "methods".

A supermacro can be implemented within HYBSYS as macro in overlay technique: a user- written FORTRAN- subroutine describes all actions of the macro (change of parameters, simulation run, etc.), the name of the subroutine is an additional command to HYBSYS commands. So an arbitrary complex (preprogrammed) action can be invoked by a single command.
The HYBSYS- supermacro HYDRO simulates the hydroenergetric system (1) - (5) (fig 1).
Invoking the supermacro by the command HYDRO first the equations (1) - (5) are defined automatically according to the input of the user: in dialogue the user types in the number of reservoirs, pumps, users, followed by the connections.
After the problem set- up the macro displays the actions, which can be done now ("methods") and performs them conditionally.

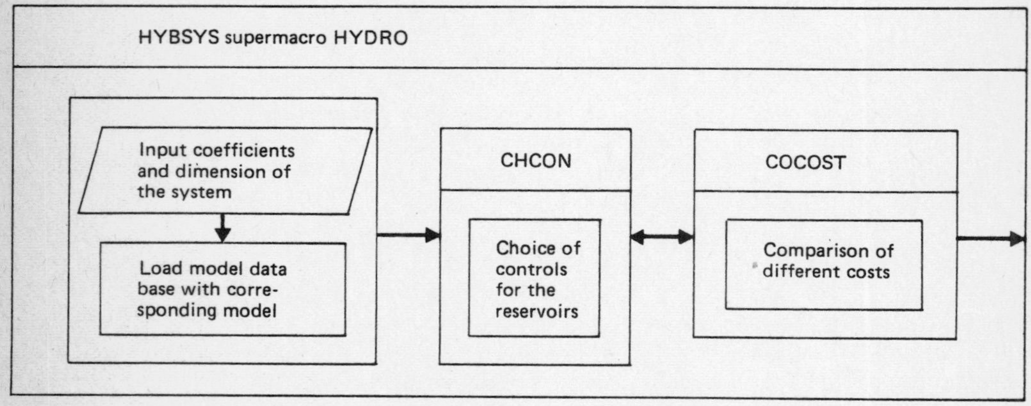

Fig.1: HYBSYS- supermacro HYDRO

The submacro CHCON allows to define and change point by point the values of natural inflows and of the controls.
The submacro COCOST reads out the usually different values of the cost functionals (5). These submacros can be activated also independently from the supermacro HYDRO.
Simulation runs, displays and plots are performed by usual HYBSYS commands.

4. EXAMPLE

In this section a characteristic (small) example is described, which consists of three reservoirs, two rivers and a water user (fig 2). Only for the water user a time delay is taken into account. This yields to the following system equations:

$$s_1 = y_1 - u_{13}$$
$$s_2 = y_2 - u_{23} - e_{12}$$
$$s_3 = u_{13} + u_{23} + r_1 e_{12}(t-t_{e,12}) - a_3$$

where r_1 is the percentage of the water returned by the user and all the other variables are functions of time t, $t \in [0,T]$. As simulation horizon a time T of two years was chosen, starting in October.

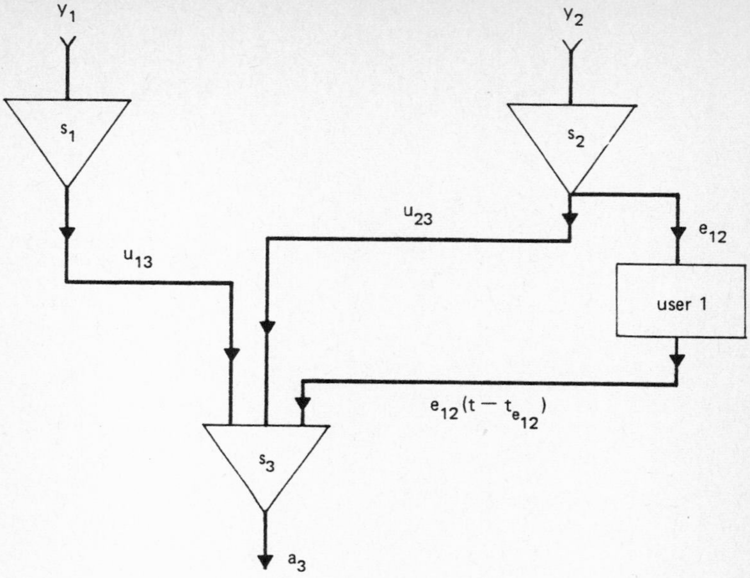

Fig. 2: Hydro- energetric system with three reservoirs

The input data for y_1,y_2 and r_1 were taken from statistical reports, ([1]), while the controls a_3, u_{13}, u_{23},(e_{12}) were implemented felxibly, so that one could apply all his experience with such systems. Activating the supermacro HYDRO, the model equations are set up on the hybrid computer. Performing CHCON allows to define the natural inflows and the controls (fig. 3, fig.4). The plots are generated by the usual HYBSYS- PLOT- command (PLOT Y1,Y2; PLOT U12,U23,A3), fig.5 (PLOT E21,DE21) shows the value of water taken by the user (E21) and given back with time-delay (DE21); fig.6 shows the contents of the reservoirs (s_1,s_2,s_3).

The values of the benefits can be computed by activating COCOST, fig. 7 shows their values over time: the benefit of flood control is very high, the benefit of energy production increases monotonely, the benefit of recreation use seems to approach a maximal value and to decrease for $T > 24$.
Furthermore the final values of the benefits can be observed in dependency of different (parametrized) operation rules for the system which is shown in fig.8. So this simulation package seems to be a powerful tool to study the behaviour of a multipurpose hydro-energetric system and to decide about its best operation in a multiobjective sense.

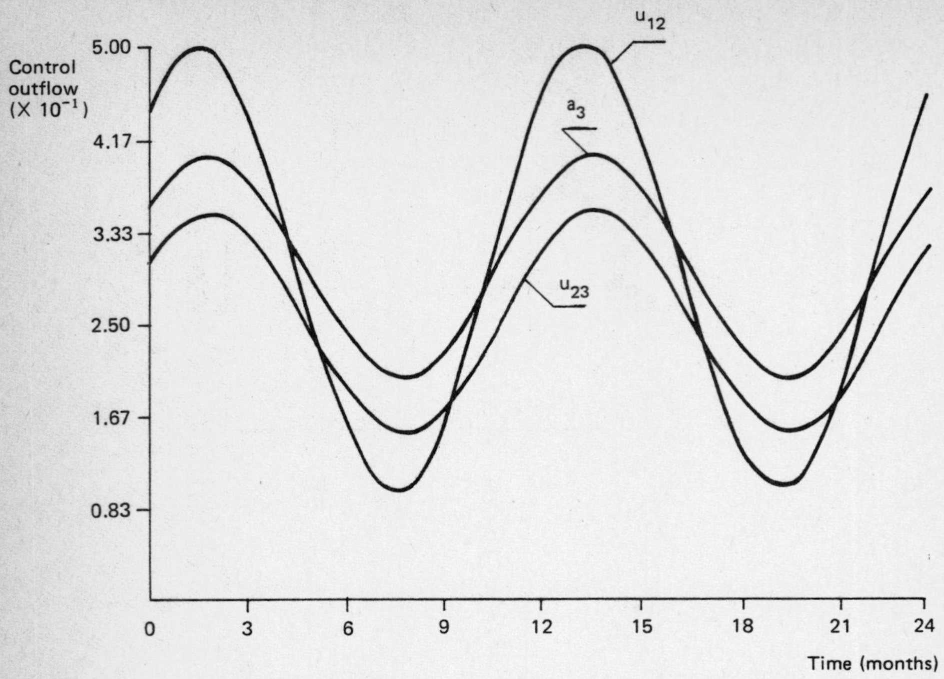

Fig.3: Natural inflows to the reservoirs

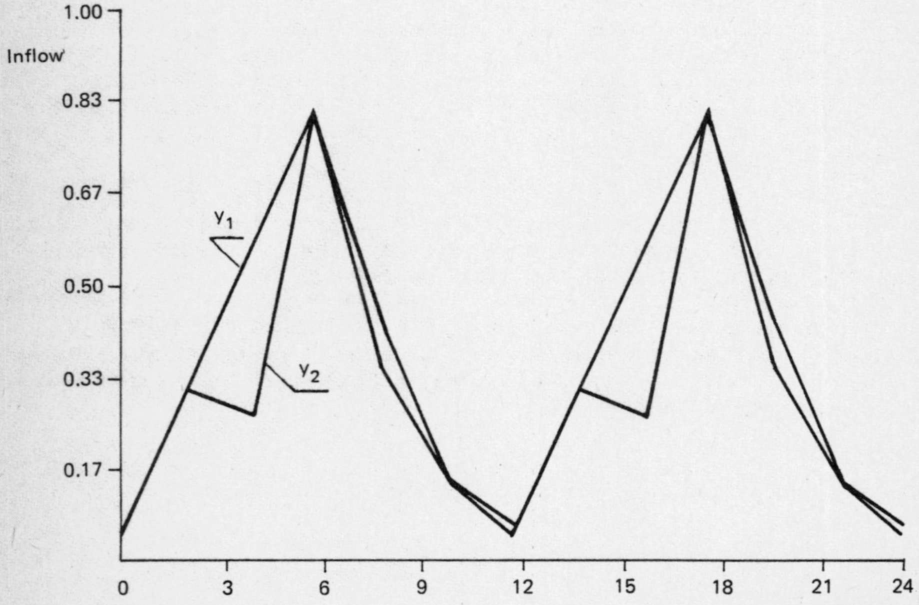

Fig.4: Controls: Outflows of the reservoirs

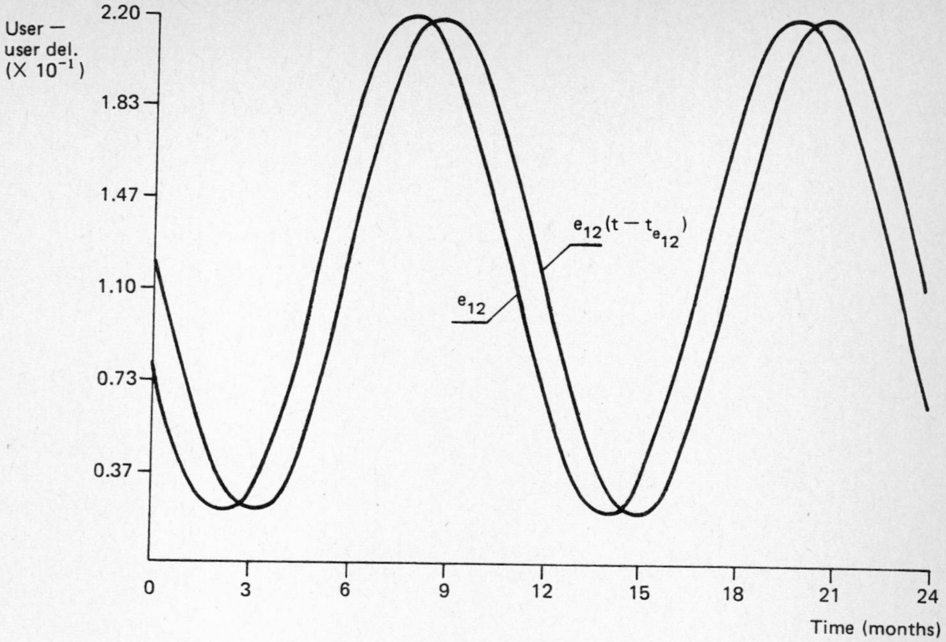

Fig. 5: Water taken and given back by the user

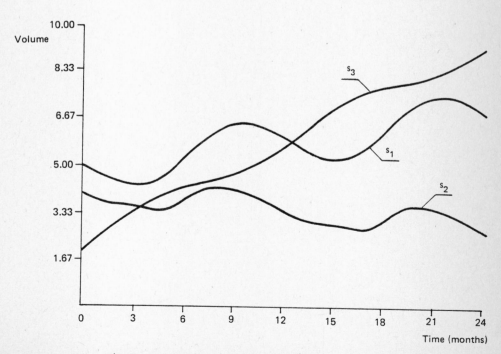

Fig. 6: Contents of the reservoirs

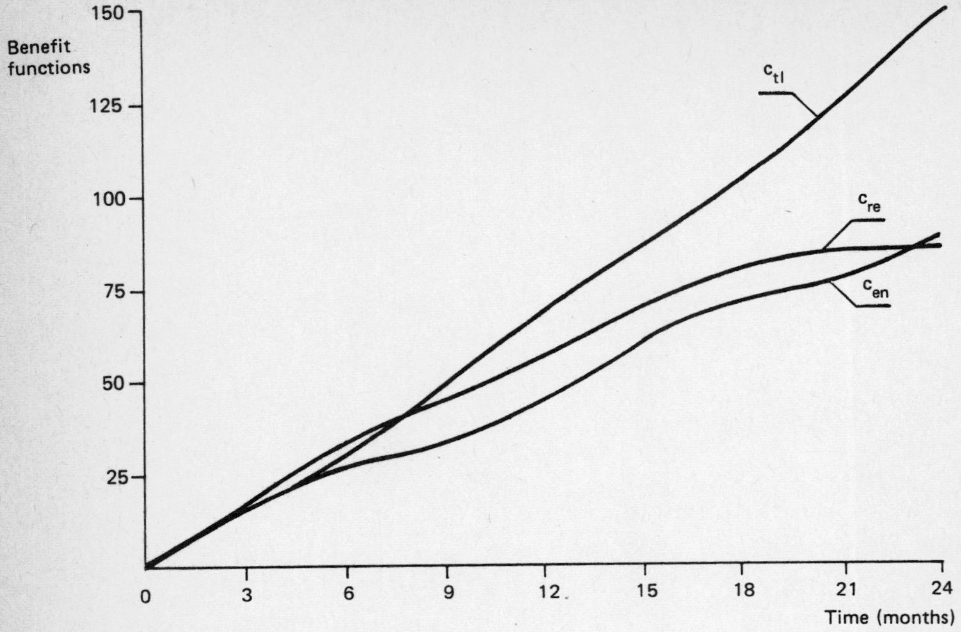

Fig.7: Benefits

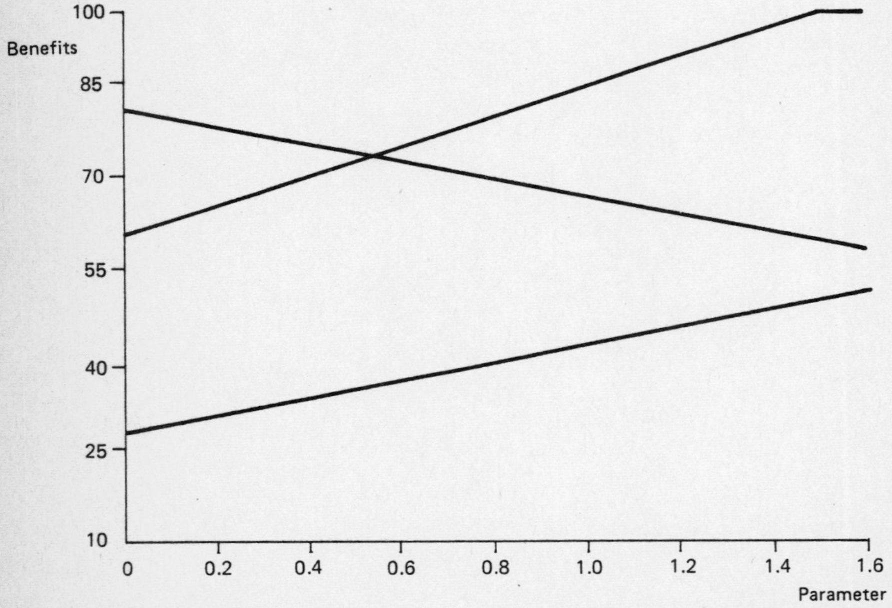

Fig.8: Final benefits depending on a parametrized set of operation rules

LITERATURE

[1] ALLINGER G. et al.: Taschenbuch der Wasserwirtschaft, 5. Auflage, Verlag Wasser und Boden, Hamburg 1971

[2] BERGER F., SOLAR D.: The autopatch system at the Technical University Vienna.Proc.Int.Conf.on Simulation, Lyon, France 1981

[3] BREITENECKER F.: The concept of supermacros in today's and future simulation languages. Mathematics and Computers in Simulation, to appear 1983.

[4] EDELMANN H., THEILSTEFJE E.K.: Optimaler Verbundbetrieb in der elektrischen Energieversorgung. Springer Verlag, Berlin, Heidelberg, New York 1974.

[5] HAY J.L., CROSBIE R.E., NAROTAM M.D.: Outline proposals for a new standard for continuous system simulation language (CSSL 81). TC3-IMACS Simulation Software Committee Newsletter no.11 (1982).

[6] JAMSHIDI M., HEIDARI M.: Application of Dynamic Programming to Control Khuzestan Water Resources Systems. Harward University Press, Cambridge Mass. 1972.

[7] KLEINERT W., BERGER F., STALLBAUMER H., WITTEK E.: The hybrid system MACHYS at the Technical University Vienna. Informatik-Fachbericht 56 (1982), Springer-Verlag, 234-241.

[8] O'LAOGHAIRE, HIMMELBLAU D.M.: Optimal Expansion of Water Resources Systems. Academic Press, New York - London, 1974.

[9] SCHMID A., TROCH I.: Zur optimalen Bewirtschaftung von hydroenergetischen Systemen mit Mehrfachnutzung. RT 28 (1980), 395-403.

[10] SOLAR D.: HYBSYS User Manual. Hybrid Computation Centre, Technical University Vienna, 1981.

[11] SOLAR D., BERGER F., BLAUENSTEINER A.: Interactive Simulation software for a hybrid multiple- user system. Informatik-Fachbericht 56 (1982), Springer, 257-265.

[12] STRAUSS J.C. et al.: The SCi continuous system simulation language CSSL. Simulation 9 (1967), 281 - 303.

MULTIOBJECTIVE ANALYSIS OF FORESTRY MANAGEMENT MODELS USING THE GENERALIZED REACHABLE SET METHOD

A.V. Lotov and H.M. Stolyarova
Computing Center of the USSR Academy of Sciences, Moscow, USSR

1. INTRODUCTION

Regions with a significant wood-processing industry based on the presence of large local supplies of wood will necessarily experience a gradual reduction in forest reserves. A point may be reached at which there is a conflict between the industrial demand for raw materials and the need to reduce felling volume. This may eventually have to be resolved by importing timber into the region to supply the wood-processing industry with raw materials. It is clear that a more rational method of forestry management should be sought.

To increase the efficiency of forest management we developed the idea of a forest plantation. On these forest plantations trees are planted and grown in some optimal fashion and then felled. Mathematical methods should provide the optimal growing strategy as well as an effective felling policy. This paper is concerned with the development of an effective felling policy of this type. We assume that the forest growth strategy (that is, the method of planting, care of the forest, thinning etc.) has already been formulated and implemented. We are concerned only with a policy for felling and replanting trees on various parts of the plantation. Furthermore, we assume that an adequate mathematical model of forest growth is available. Using this model decision makers and experts can forecast the consequences of different policies.

It should be stressed that there are many objectives involved in any decision on the use of forest reserves. There is a conflict between demand for forest products at the present time and future demand. Moreover, the state of the forest is very important, especially at the end of the planning period. Thus, the formulation of an effective felling and replanting policy is a multiobjective problem.

The models which provide an accurate description of the processes of forest growth are very complicated and thus simplified models must be used to formulate policies; these policies are then checked in simulation experiments. Within the framework of a simulation system (Moiseev, 1981), decision makers and experts can employ a wide range of operational research methods (simulation, optimization, game theory, informal techniques) to address multiobjective problems, using the hierarchical array of models of the system under study.

This paper presents a new approach to multiobjective problems based on the so-called generalized reachable set (GRS) method of investigating controlled systems (Lotov, 1980, 1981a). The first papers dealing with this method were published in the early seventies (Lotov, 1972, 1973a,b). The basic idea of the GRS approach is to construct a set of all combinations of aggregated variables which are reachable (or accessible) using feasible combinations of the original variables of the model. This is called the generalized reachable set. When used in multiple-criteria decision making, the GRS approach employs an explicit representation of the set of all accessible objective values. Unlike other multiobjective methods, the GRS approach is based on linear inequality techniques. This approach was developed at the Computing Center of the USSR Academy of Sciences and has already been applied to several problems (see, for example, Bushenkov et al., 1982; Moiseev et al., 1983).

Here we present the first application of the GRS approach to controlled systems described by partial differential equations. The applicability of the GRS approach to problems of this type has already been proven (Lotov, 1981b). The problem studied in this paper is rather simple, but it clearly demonstrates the potential of the GRS approach.

2. STATEMENT OF THE PROBLEM

We shall consider a forest plantation of total area S. We assume that the state of the plantation at time t can be described in terms of the area $x(t,\tau)$ occupied by forest of age τ. The age distribution of the forest is the main variable in the model. The dynamics can be described by the following equation:

$$\frac{\partial x(t,\tau)}{\partial t} + \frac{\partial x(t,\tau)}{\partial \tau} = -u(t,\tau),\ t \in (t_0,t_1),\ \tau \in (0,\tau_{max}) \ , \tag{1}$$

where $u(t,\tau)$ are the areas of forest of age τ felled at time t and τ_{max} is the maximum age of trees. The system operates over some time interval $[t_0,t_1]$. The initial age distribution of trees is taken to be

$$x(t_0,\tau) = \phi(\tau) \ , \ \tau \in [0,\tau_{max}] \ , \tag{2}$$

where $\phi(\tau)$ is the area occupied by forest of age τ at time t_0. It is clear that $\int_0^{\tau_{max}} \phi(\tau)d\tau \le S$.

In the model it is assumed that felled areas are immediately replanted with new trees in accordance with

$$x(t,0) = \int_0^{\tau_{max}} u(t,\tau)d\tau \ , \ \ t \in [t_0,t_1] \ . \tag{3}$$

The control variable $u(t,\tau)$ satisfies the following constraints:

$$0 \le u(t,\tau) \le x(t,\tau) \ . \tag{4}$$

The dependence of the output of wood on the age of the forest is described by the function $\beta(\tau)$, which characterizes the volume of timber obtained from unit area of forest of age τ. This curve is presented in Fig. 1.

The overall performance of the plantation is evaluated on the basis of the following performance indices:

$$f_1(t) = \int_0^{\tau_{max}} \beta(\tau)u(t,\tau)d\tau \ , \ t \in [t_0,t_1] \tag{5}$$

$$f_2(\tau) = x(t_1,\tau) \ , \ \tau \in [0,\tau_{max}] \ . \tag{6}$$

Function $f_1(t)$ describes the total quantity of timber obtained from the plantation at time t. Function $f_2(\tau)$ characterizes the state of the plantation at the end of the planning period t_1.

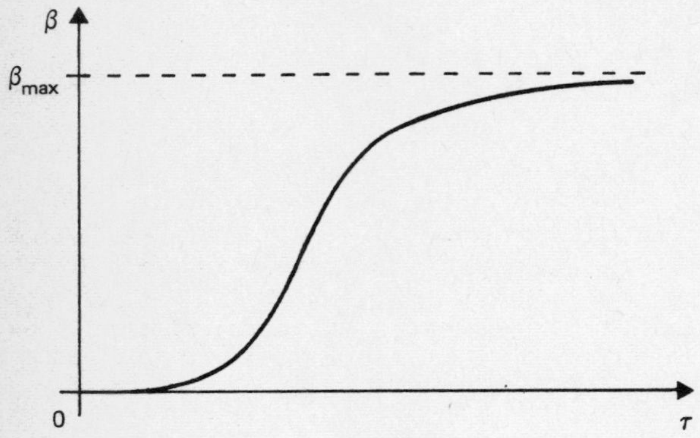

FIGURE 1 The function $\beta(\tau)$, which characterizes the volume of timber obtained from unit area of forest of age τ.

3. INVESTIGATION OF MULTIOBJECTIVE PROBLEMS USING THE GENERALIZED REACHABLE SET APPROACH

The general idea of the GRS approach is as follows. Let the mathematical model of the system under study be

$$y \in G \subset Y \ , \tag{7}$$

where Y is a linear topological space of variables y and G is the set of feasible variables y. We will not specify the nature of the space Y at present. Let the set G be nonempty. In models of controlled systems there are many variants of variables y satisfying (7). Let the mapping $F : Y \rightarrow V$ describe new aggregated variables:

$$f = F y \ , \tag{8}$$

where V is also a linear topological space. The set $G_f = F(G)$, i.e.,

$$G_f = \{f \in V : f = Fy \ , \ y \in G\} \ , \tag{9}$$

is called the generalized reachable set (GRS). This set represents all variants of aggregated variables f which can be "reached" or "accessed", i.e., can be obtained by means of (8) using feasible variables y. The GRS approach has been developed for convex sets G and linear continuous mappings F.

The GRS approach may be used for various purposes: for evaluation of the possibilities of controlled systems (Lotov, 1981b; Moiseev et al., 1983), for aggregation of economic models (Lotov, 1982), and for coordination of economic models (Lotov, 1983). It can also be effectively applied to multiple-criteria decision making (MCDM). If we treat $f \in V$ as the performance indices (objectives), the mapping F defines the consequences of each decision or alternative y. The set G_f in this case is the set of all accessible objective values.

The approximate construction of the GRS is carried out as follows. We shall approximate the model (7) by the finite-dimensional model

$$y^* \in G^* \subset R^n , \qquad (10)$$

where R^n is an n-dimensional linear space and G^* is a polyhedral set, i.e.,

$$G^* = \{y^* \in R^n : Ay^* \leqq B\} .$$

We approximate $f \in V$ by the finite-dimensional objective vector $f^* \in R^m$, while the mapping (8) is approximated by $F^* : R^n \to R^m$, i.e.,

$$f^* = F^* y^* , \qquad (11)$$

where F^* is an m×n matrix. The GRS for model (10) with mapping (11) is defined as

$$G_f^* = \{f^* \in R^m : f^* = F^* y^* , \ Ay^* \leqq B\} . \qquad (12)$$

The set G_f^* is used to approximate G_f, and can be constructed in the explicit form:

$$G_f^* = \{f^* \in R^m : Df^* \leqq d\} . \qquad (13)$$

To construct G_f^* in the form (13), that is, to construct the matrix D and the vector d, we use linear inequality techniques. If the graph of the mapping F^* is defined as

$$Z = \{z \equiv \{y^*, f^*\} \in R^{n+m} : f^* = F^* y^*, \ Ay^* \leqq B\} , \qquad (14)$$

then the set G_f^* is an orthogonal projection of the set Z described by the system of linear equalities and inequalities on R^m. To construct the projection we can use methods for excluding variables in systems of linear inequalities (convolution of systems of linear inequalities). The first convolution method was introduced by Fourier (1829) and was later modified by Motzkin et al. (1953) and Chernikov (1965). These methods and alternative convolution methods complemented by methods for removing inactive inequalities have been implemented in the program system POTENTIAL (Bushenkov and Lotov, 1980), which constructs the set G_f^* in the form (13).

The GRS approach as applied to MCDM problems belongs to the class of *generating methods* of interactive decision making (Cohon, 1978; Hwang et al., 1980). In contrast to preference-oriented methods based on a formal procedure that should lead the decision maker (DM) to a solution of the problem, generating methods present the set of all efficient points in objective space to the DM. Generating methods provide the DM with information on the possibilities of the system under study. The nonformalized process of choosing a compromise between competing objectives is then left to the DM. Methods of this type have a clear advantage if the DM has no consistent preference or if the concept of the DM is only a convenient abstraction (for example, if the decision is reached by compromise between a group of decision makers, each with his or her own different goals).

Generating methods can vary in the manner in which they present the efficient set. There are four main groups of generating methods (Cohon, 1978): weighting methods, constraint methods, multiobjective simplex methods, and noninferior set estimation methods. The generalized reachable set (GRS) approach discussed here has two main features that distinguish it from the methods listed above. First of all, this method can be used to construct the entire set of reachable objective values of the system, the efficient set being part of its boundary. The second distinguishing feature of the approach lies in its use of linear inequality techniques rather than the optimization techniques usually employed in multiobjective methods.

The display mechanism in generating methods usually provides the DM with various two-dimensional projections and cross-sections (slices) of the efficient set. When the set G_f^* has been constructed, it takes only a few seconds to display selected slices of the set to the DM, so it is possible to present about 100 two-dimensional pictures to the DM in a relatively short time. Our experience shows that this number is sufficient for a proper understanding of the structure of a convex set in five-to-ten-dimensional space.

The GRS approach has several advantages over other generating methods of interactive decision making. Firstly, it is easier to imagine a convex set (the GRS) than a nonconvex efficient set. Secondly, it is easier to construct two-dimensional slices for a set presented in the form (13) than for an efficient set given by individual points. Thirdly, in many cases the DM may be interested not only in the efficient set, but also in dominated points. The use of linear inequality techniques rather than optimization techniques in a generating method seems quite natural since optimization is related to the search for individual points rather than for an entire set.

4. ANALYSIS OF THE FORESTRY MODEL

The original model (1)-(6) is approximated by its finite-dimensional analogue. The period covered by the investigation is divided into T steps (decades). All the trees are distributed into τ^m groups. Trees less than ten years old belong to the first group, trees 10-20 years old to the second, and so on. Let x_τ^t be the area occupied by trees of the τ-th group at the end of the t-th decade, where $\tau=1,2,\dots,\tau^m$; $t=1,2,\dots,T$. Let x_τ^0 , $\tau=1,2,\dots,\tau^m$, be some initial age distribution. Then the main equation of the model is a difference approximation of (1), i.e.,

$$x_{\tau+1}^t = x_\tau^{t-1} - u_\tau^t , \qquad (15)$$

where $t=1,2,\dots,T$, $\tau=1,2,\dots,\tau^m - 1$, and u_τ^t is the area occupied by trees in age group τ felled during period t. All of the trees in group τ^m are assumed to be felled:

$$u^t_{\tau^m} = x^{t-1}_{\tau^m} \;, \quad t=1,2,\ldots,T \;. \tag{16}$$

The initial and boundary conditions are:

$$x^0_\tau = \phi_\tau \;, \quad \tau=1,2,\ldots,\tau^m \;, \tag{17}$$

$$x^t_1 = \sum_{\tau=1}^{\tau^m} u^t_\tau \;, \quad t=1,2,\ldots,T \;. \tag{18}$$

The restrictions on the control variables are:

$$0 \le u^t_\tau \le x^{t-1}_\tau \;, \quad t=1,2,\ldots,T \;; \; \tau=1,2,\ldots,\tau^m - 1 \;. \tag{19}$$

The performance indices (objectives) are based on the quality of timber obtained in each decade:

$$f^t_1 = \sum_{\tau=1}^{\tau^m} \beta_\tau u^t_\tau \;, \quad t=1,2,\ldots,T \;. \tag{20}$$

as well as the final state of the forest:

$$f^\tau_2 = x^t_\tau \;, \quad \tau=1,2,\ldots,\tau^m \;. \tag{21}$$

Given the values of T and τ^m, the coefficients β_τ, and the initial age distribution ϕ_τ, it is possible to study the system by constructing the GRS in the space of objectives f^t_1 , $t=1,2,\ldots,T$, and f^τ_2 , $\tau=1,2,\ldots,\tau^m$. The DM can then analyze the situation and come to a decision by studying the displayed slices and projections of the GRS.

The GRS for model (15)-(21) was constructed for various values of T and τ^m, for various functions β_τ and initial conditions ϕ_τ. It is clearly impossible to present here the hundreds of projections and slices obtained during the investigation, and for this reason we shall illustrate the analysis using a simple example for which it is possible to construct the GRS in analytical form.

Let τ^m=8, T=8, and let β_τ=1 for τ=5,6,7,8. We shall assume that trees in the first four age groups are not felled. In this case it is possible to construct the GRS in the form (13) for the parametric function ϕ_τ. In objective space $\{f^t_1,\ t=1,2,\ldots,8 \;;\; f^\tau_2,\ \tau=1,2,\ldots,8\}$, the GRS has the following form:

$$f^k_2 = f^{9-k}_1 \;, \quad k = 1,2,\ldots,5$$

$$f_2^k \le f_1^{9-k} \ , \ k=6,7,8$$

$$\sum_{t=1}^{k} f_1^t \ge \sum_{\tau=1}^{k} \phi_{9-\tau} \ , \ k=1,2,\ldots,7$$

$$\sum_{t=1}^{k} f_1^t \le \sum_{\tau=6-k}^{8} \phi_\tau \ , \ k=1,2,\ldots,5 \tag{22}$$

$$\sum_{t=2}^{6} f_1^t \le S - f_2^8$$

$$f_1^3 - f_1^8 \le f_2^6$$

$$\sum_{\tau=1}^{8} f_2^\tau = S$$

$$f_1^t \ge 0 \ , \ t=1,2,\ldots,8$$

$$f_2^\tau \ge 0 \ , \ \tau=1,2,\ldots,8 \ .$$

In this case the GRS is a polyhedral set in 16-dimensional space and is given by six equalities and 33 inequalities.

If the DM is interested in a scalar index of the final state of the forest, say,

$$f_2 = \sum_{\tau=5}^{8} \beta_\tau f_2^\tau$$

(which describes the potential timber production for the period T+1), rather than in a detailed description of the final state (given by f_2^τ, $\tau=1,2,\ldots,\tau^m$), then it is possible to construct the GRS in nine-dimensional space $\{f_1^t,\ t=1,2,\ldots,8\ ;\ f_2\}$. In this case the GRS is described by:

$$\sum_{t=1}^{k} f_1^t \ge \sum_{\tau=1}^{k} \phi_{9-\tau} \ , \ k=1,2,\ldots,8$$

$$\sum_{t=1}^{k} f_1^t \le \sum_{\tau=6-k}^{8} \phi_\tau \ , \ k=1,2,\ldots,5$$

$$\sum_{t=k+1}^{k+5} f_1^t \le S \ , \ k=1,2,3 \tag{23}$$

$$f_2 + \sum_{t=5}^{8} f_1^t = S$$

$$f_2 \ge 0 \ , \ f_1^t \ge 0 \ , \ t=1,2,\ldots,8 \ .$$

In other words, the GRS is described by one equality and 24 inequalities. Some projections of the GRS described by equations (23) are represented in Figs. 2 and 3 (they are also projections of GRS (22)).

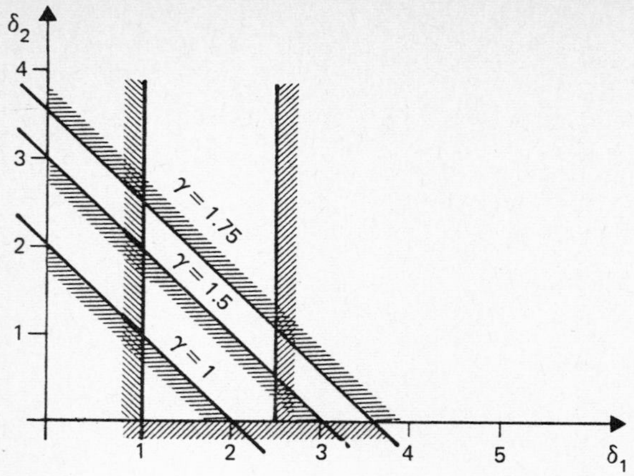

FIGURE 2 A projection of the generalized reachable set described by eqns. (23).

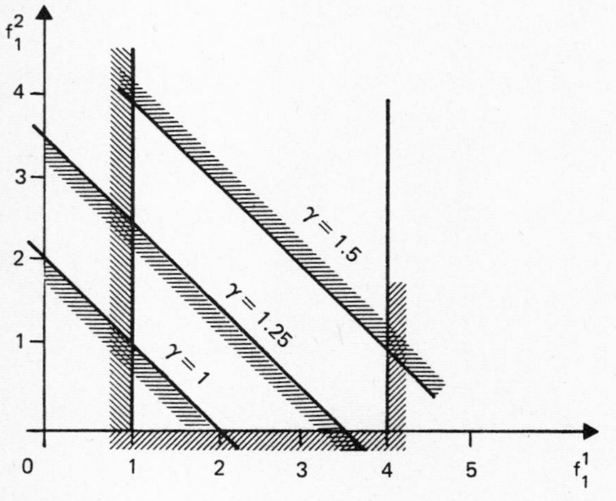

FIGURE 3 A projection of the generalized reachable set described by eqns. (23).

The projections given in Figs. 2 and 3 refer to a particular case with a uniform initial age distribution, i.e., $\phi_\tau \equiv 1$ (the total area of the plantation is taken to be 8), and with equal areas x_τ^t for the first four and last four age groups, i.e., $x_1^T = x_2^T = x_3^T = x_4^T = 2-\gamma$, $x_5^T + x_6^T + x_7^T + x_8^T = 4\gamma$, where $1 \le \gamma \le 2$.

It is also assumed that felling in the first and second decades is the same: $f_1^1 = f_1^2 = \delta_1$; an analogous assumption is made for the third and fourth decades: $f_1^3 = f_1^4 = \delta_2$. The set of reachable values of δ_1 and δ_2 (for different values of γ) is illustrated in Fig. 2. We can see that only one inequality depends on γ. If $\gamma > 1.75$, the set of reachable values of δ_1 and δ_2 is empty. If $\gamma = 1.75$, the set coincides with the segment $\delta_1 + \delta_2 = 3.5$, $1 \le \delta_1 \le 2.5$.

Let us now consider Figure 3, which shows the set of reachable values of f_1^t , t=1,2 , assuming that $f_1^3 = f_1^4 = 2 - \gamma$. If $1 \le \gamma \le 1.5$, this set is non-empty; if $\gamma > 1.5$, the set is empty.

Of course, Figs. 2 and 3 alone cannot give a full picture of the nine-dimensional set (23)--to do this it would be necessary to investigate about 100 slices and projections. The DM can obtain this information in an interactive dialogue with the computer. He may also wish to consider the super-aggregated performance indices ψ_1 and ψ_2 , which represent timber production for the first and last 40 years, i.e.,

$$\psi_1 = \sum_{t=1}^{4} f_1^t \quad , \quad \psi_2 = \sum_{t=5}^{8} f_1^t \; .$$

The GRS in objective space $\{\psi_1, \psi_2, f_2\}$ can be described simply as:

$$
\begin{aligned}
& f_2 + \psi_2 = S \\
& \psi_1 \ge \sum_{\tau=5}^{8} \phi_\tau \\
& \psi_1 + \psi_2 \ge S \\
& \psi_1 \le S \\
& \psi_1 + \psi_2 \le S + \sum_{\tau=3}^{8} \phi_\tau \\
& \psi_1 + \psi_2 \le S + \sum_{\tau=3}^{6} \phi_\tau + \sum_{\tau=4}^{8} \phi_\tau \; .
\end{aligned}
\tag{24}
$$

The projection of set (24) on the plane $\{\psi_1, \psi_2\}$ is given in Fig. 4 for the case $\phi_\tau \equiv 1$. Since the values of ψ_2 and f_2 satisfy the equation $f_2 + \psi_2 = S$, it is possible to calculate f_2 from ψ_2 .

Now let us consider another initial distribution of tree ages: $\phi_1=3$, $\phi_2=3$, $\phi_3=0$, $\phi_4=0$, $\phi_5=1$, $\phi_6=1$, $\phi_7=0$, $\phi_8=0$. The projection of set (24) on the plane $\{\psi_1, \psi_2\}$ is given in Fig. 5. This allows the DM to first make a decision in terms of ψ_1, ψ_2, f_2, and then proceed to an analysis of the problem in terms of f_1^t, $t=1,2,\ldots,8$, and f_2^τ , $\tau=1,2,\ldots,8$, where ψ_1, ψ_2, f_2 are fixed.

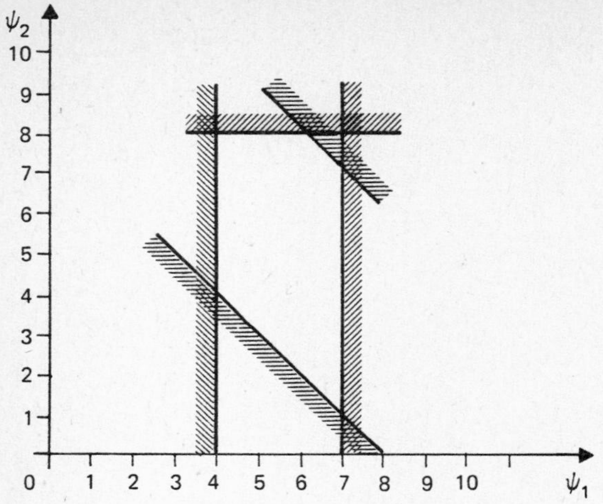

FIGURE 4 The projection of set (24) on the plane $\{\psi_1,\psi_2\}$ for the case $\phi_\tau=1$, $\tau=1,2,\ldots,8$.

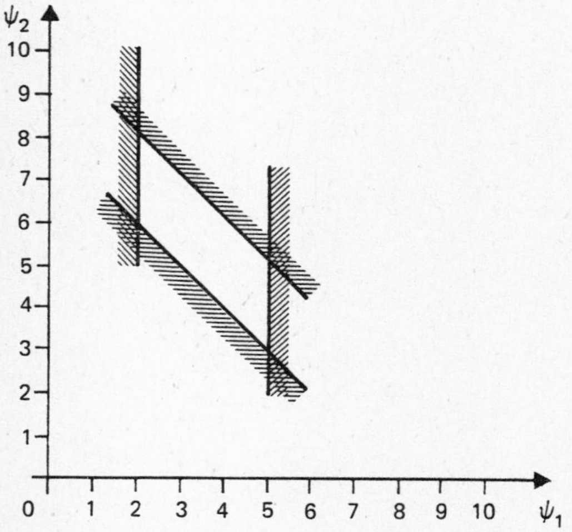

FIGURE 5 The projection of set (24) on the plane $\{\psi_1,\psi_2\}$ for the case $\phi_1=3$, $\phi_2=3$, $\phi_3=0$, $\phi_4=0$, $\phi_5=1$, $\phi_6=1$, $\phi_7=0$, $\phi_8=0$.

The example presented in this paper gives a general idea of the GRS method. In more complicated models the system of inequalities describing the GRS is very bulky, so that the GRS can be investigated only through the display of projections and slices.

5. CONCLUSION

The GRS approach provides the DM with a general understanding of the sets of accessible and efficient points for rather simplified models of the system under study. On the basis of this information the DM can identify his goal (aspiration level) in objective space. The next step in the decision-making procedure is the construction of a decision which will lead to the achievement of the goal. This can be done by means of preference-oriented multiobjective methods. We have found that the most convenient preference-oriented method for use in conjunction with the GRS approach is the reference objective method developed by Wierzbicki and others (Wierzbicki, 1979; Lewandowski, 1982; Grauer, 1983). For this reason we have included the reference objective method in the POTENTIAL program system, in the form given by Lewandowski (1982). The joint application of the methods has proved to be very successful.

ACKNOWLEDGMENTS

This study was performed as part of the work of the Soviet-Finnish Technical Working Group on Operations Research. The authors are grateful to Professor Olavi Hellman (University of Turku, Finland) and to Professor Alexander Schmidt (Computing Center of the USSR Academy of Sciences, Moscow), the joint coordinators of the Soviet-Finnish Technical Working Group on Operations Research.

REFERENCES

Bushenkov, V.A. and Lotov, A.V. (1980). Methods and algorithms for linear systems analysis based on the construction of generalized reachable sets. USSR Computational Mathematics and Mathematical Physics, 20(5).

Bushenkov, V.A., Ereshko, F., Kindler, J., Lotov, A., and de Maré, L. (1982). Application of the generalized reachable sets method to water resources problems in southwestern Skåne, Sweden. WP-82-120. International Institute for Applied Systems Analysis, Laxenburg, Austria.

Chernikov, S.N. (1965). Convolution of finite systems of linear inequalities. USSR Computational Mathematics and Mathematical Physics, 5(1).

Cohon, J.L. (1978). Multiobjective Programming and Planning. Academic Press.

Fourier, J.B. (1829). Solution d'une question particulière du calcul des inégalités. Nouveau bulletin des sciences par la Société philomathique de Paris, p. 99.

Grauer, M. (1983). A dynamic interactive decision analysis and support system (DIDASS). WP-83-60. International Institute for Applied Systems Analysis, Laxenburg, Austria.

Hwang, C.L., Paidy, S.R., Yoon, K., and Masud, A.S.M. (1980). Mathematical programming with multiple objectives: A tutorial. Computers and Operations Research, 7(1-2).

Lewandowski, A. (1982). A program package for linear multiple criteria reference point optimization. WP-82-80. International Institute for Applied Systems Analysis, Laxenburg, Austria.

Lotov, A.V. (1972). A numerical method of constructing attainability sets for a linear system. USSR Computational Mathematics and Mathematical Physics, 12(3).

Lotov, A.V. (1973a). An approach to perspective planning in the absence of a unique objective. In Proceedings of the Conference on "Systems

Approach and Perspective Planning" (May 1972). Computing Center of the USSR Academy of Sciences, Moscow (in Russian).

Lotov, A.V. (1973b). A numerical method of studying the optimal time continuity in linear systems and the solution of the Cauchy problem for Bellman's equation. USSR Computational Mathematics and Mathematical Physics, 13(5).

Lotov, A.V. (1980). On the concept of generalized reachable sets and their construction for linear controlled systems. Soviet Physics Doklady, 25(2).

Lotov, A.V. (1981a). Reachable sets approach to multiobjective problems and its possible application to water resources management in the Skåne region. WP-81-145. International Institute for Applied Systems Analysis, Laxenburg, Austria.

Lotov, A.V. (1981b). On the concept and construction of generalized accessibility sets for linear controllable systems described by partial differential equations. Soviet Physics Doklady, 26(11).

Lotov, A.V. (1982). Aggregation as approximation of generalized reachable sets. Proceedings of the Academy of Sciences of the USSR, 265(6) (in Russian).

Lotov, A.V. (1983). Coordination of economic models with the help of reachable sets. In Mathematical Methods for Analyzing the Interaction between Industrial and Regional Systems. Nauka, Siberian division (in Russian).

Moiseev, N.N. (1981). Mathematical Problems of Systems Analysis. Nauka, Moscow (in Russian).

Moiseev, N.N., Aleksandrov, V.V., Krapivin, V.F., Lotov, A.V., Svirezhev, Yu.M., and Tarko, A.M. (1983). Global models, the biospheric approach (theory of noosphere). CP-83-33. International Institute for Applied Systems Analysis, Laxenburg, Austria.

Motzkin, T.S. et al. (1953). The double description method. In Contributions to the Theory of Games. Princeton University Press, Vol. 2.

Wierzbicki, A.P. (1979). The use of reference objectives in multiobjective optimization. WP-79-66. International Institute for Applied Systems Analysis, Laxenburg, Austria.

A MULTIOBJECTIVE PROCEDURE FOR PROJECT FORMULATION – DESIGN OF A CHEMICAL INSTALLATION

H. Górecki[1], J. Kopytowski[2], T. Ryś[3] and M. Żebrowski[1]

[1] *Institute for Control and Systems Engineering, Academy of Mining and Metallurgy, Cracow, Poland*

[2] *Institute for Industrial Chemistry, Warsaw, Poland*

[3] *Systems Research Department of the Institute for Control and Systems Engineering and of the Institute for Industrial Chemistry, Cracow, Poland*

1. INTRODUCTION

Industrial Development is a Strategic Management Decision Area which can be looked upon as a chain of hierarchical decision problems.

As an output from a Decision Analysis on a given higher level comes formulation of problem (or most often set of problems) to be analysed and solved on the lower level. Such process is continued on down the hill levels. Appropriate feedback links assure a possibility of verification of problems formulated on the higher level.

This common sense approach however general may easily be accepted both by theory and by practitioners. It also seems to be a natural field for application of Multiobjective Interactive Decision Analysis.

But the picture becomes less bright when one looks into reality. They are various factors affecting logic and smoothness of operation of such a decision system. Three of them are of the fundamental importance. First is the long time which elapses before a sequence of decision cycles on various levels can be performed. This stems from the nature of the development decision processes that are evolving for many years1/.

Second is also a feature of the "nature of the system" and this is sometimes a very big qualitative difference between objects of analysis and methods used even on neighboring levels. Therefore we may speak about problem of communication and understanding between various levels. Third factor which is here the last but far from being least it is the problem of methodology or rather lack of methodology. This would be twofold:

- a problem of methodology for solving particular problems on a given level which is equivalent to formulating problems for sublevels down the hierarchy,

---

1/ So called industrial development cycle which includes periods of research, design, investment and production covers for various branches of the chemical industry from approx. 10 to 35 years.

- a problem of "overall methodology" which could help to integrate whole system.

While impacts from first and second factor cannot be influenced directly since they form a core of the area investigated and come from its nature, the real job can be done in the field of methodology. In particular a methodology for project formulation for the design of an industrial installation would be a good example.

In this paper we concentrate on project formulation stage. This stems, from an experience gained in the research on development strategy of industrial structure in the chemical industry. Development strategy deals with rather large areas covering whole branches of the industry called Production Distribution Areas (or PDAs) and can be described by specially devised models called PDA models. Nevertheless the basic element for development in such a PDA is a (eventually proposed for investment) chemical installation. The problem is how to devise and formulate a design task of such a new chemical plant which would be in a natural agreement with the development strategy designed for the whole PDA. The process of design of a development strategy for PDA is to be carried out as a process of quest for concordance between available technologies and resources that are critical for the development (see Górecki et.al./1980/). This is to be continued down through several levels with narrowing field of the quest, while accuracy and number of details of the analysis are supposed to be growing. It is our intention to show the very nature of such a decision analysis process which is aimed at generating development alternatives for the process industry.

The next section gives a general view of the problem. Levels are distinquished and their respective activities described showing basic inputs, outputs and interactions as well as feedbacks. This is done to show how from such a multistage activities evolves a project formulation as an opening to the design of a chemical installation.

In the section 3 a new more general formulation of the problem of quest for concordance is described this time it is aimed at assuring a homogenous approach for all levels involved and for interface between the levels. This is done through formal description of the criteria and their properties. This properties can be used for the appropriate choice of criteria and for establishing preferences within a chosen set. Following section is devoted to more detailed description of the last level which is the project formulation level. A real life example is also given to illustrate the point.

2. PROBLEM OF GENERATING CONCORDANT DEVELOPMENT ALTERNATIVES

We should now look more closly into problems of generating concordant development alternatives in order to reveal applicability of the Interactive Decision Analysis. This will anable us to show the main point of our paper it is importance of methodology of project formulation, and to describe our attempt to propose such a methodology. It would be displayed as an integral part of a much broader decision activity.

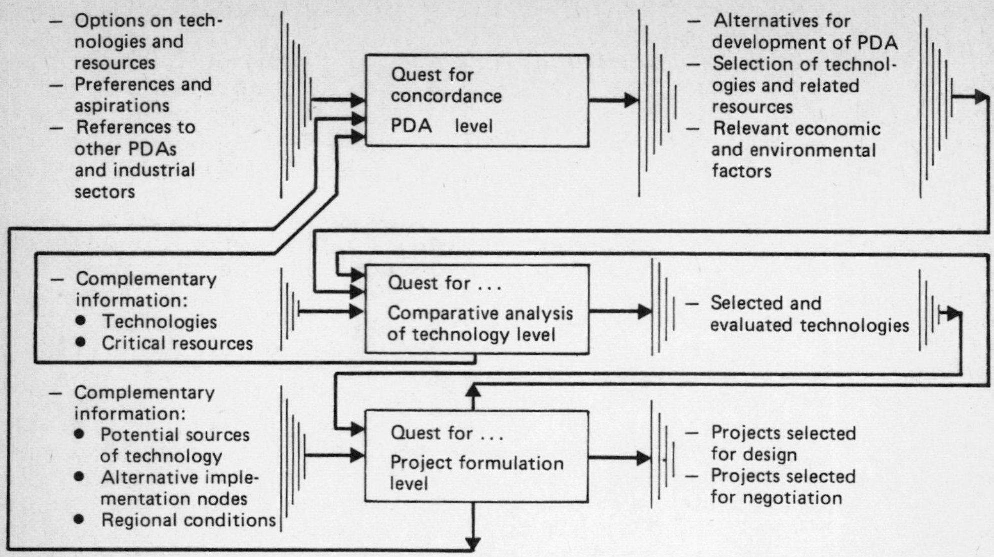

Fig. 1. Process of generating concordant Development Alternatives on Three Levels as Multiobjective decision Analysis.

On the Fig. 1 there is shown a process of generating concordant industrial development alternatives. It integrates our earlier findings obtained in the course of research on this subject (see Borek et.al. /1978/ , Dobrowolski et.al. /1982/, Dobrowolski et.al. /1983/, Kopytowski et.al. /1981/). There can be distinquished three levels of an interactive decision analysis:

1. Production Distribution Area level,
2. Comparative Analysis of technology level,
3. Project formulation level.

On each level activity is aimed at finding concordance between available resources and corresponding technologies.

In the considerations below we do not intend to repeat our earlier findings. These will be used as a reference. Intention here is however such an interpretation and explanation of a decision process (see Fig. 1) which is relevant and important for the project formulation.

To accomplish this let us try to lay down what is necessary and what is to be made known in order to formulate a project for the chemical installation. This will be simplified only to main lines.

They are basically three directions of approaching the problem:

- first is from raw materials to products,
- second is opposite: from products to raw materials,
- third would be a combination of the above.

In the first case the question is how could we best process raw materials that are available?

In the second case it would be - how to obtain demanded products? And naturally the third would be equivalent to a question: how could we best obtain demanded products from the given array of raw materials?

Chained to those would be naturally questions about availability levels of raw materials and range of demand as well about other resources, necessary for production such as energy, manpower; terms of trade also bring in a specific set of factors.

Analysis structured along above questions or those similar to them seems to be an obvious professional rule in design and its marketing: those projects should be initiated which provide not only a good design in strictly technical terms. Design must produce technologies and installations well fitted to demand steming from true not apparent trajectory of the industrial development.

Here a circle closes: we come back to the problem of industrial development and problem of fitting project formulation to it. It is not at all a simple procedure of fulfilment of clients will. Only then design may become what it should be: a creative act in decision activities for development.

An important factor in this considerations is, mentioned already, a long time span of industrial development cycle.

It makes interactions between project formulation (and consequently design) and a development strategy formulation even more important, since resulting impacts last for many years and can be corrected with proportionally long delays.

We may now look again at Fig. 1 and this time interpret it not only for its meaning as one representing idea of interactive methodological steps, but at the some time a conceptual view of model of the complex development process. An ideal methodology would be such which would enable for control of the process. It means change it from a process of development into the decision process of development.

The first level to be considered is level of PDA (Fig. 1) or Production Distribution Area. The concept of a PDA and its model was developed since some years (see Borek et.al. /1978/, Dobrowolski et.al. /1982/, Dobrowolski et.al /1983/), similar models are also finding their way both in research and applications (see Kendrick et.al. /1978/, Sophos et.al. /1980/).

An appropriate methodology was worked out for handling PDA models aimed at generating development alternatives for PDA (see Dobrowolski et.al. /1983/). By a definition it considers a PDA development problem as problem of quest for concordance. Let us briefly lay down what comes out of a PDA level from the project formulation point of view.

PDA represents a whole branch of an industry and therefore for the whole set of technologies it contains (model describes existing and potentially available plants) a problem of quest is to be solved. We leave for the next section a discussion of criteria for evaluation of optimum, concordant solution. The heart of the matter in the case of a PDA can be described exactly in terms of questions we have just formulated when analysing what has to be known in order to formulate the project. This time however we deal not with single case (of a raw material, technology or product) but with the whole strongly interlinked set of technologies, including flows of appropriate raw materials, products and intermidiates. For such a network, a balance of production and distribution is established.

Levels of flows and capacity utilisation are described and corresponding to the state of network amounts of ordinary and critical resources are calculated. These include amounts of investment, energy, labor etc.

For the purpose discussed here, from a PDA level we obtain a list of technologies which, for a given development thesis (it is within conditions and goals of a given development scenario), are feasible and should be taken for further investigation. Basic conditions for their mode of operation are also specified. With this preselected list we may continue analysis. This should be done in two directions:

- first for creating a feedback to PDA level,
- second to further select and deepen knowledge for project formulation.

Second level (see again Fig. 1) deals with problem of quest for concordance at the stage of a comparative study of technologies. We can characterise this case very briefly however without diminishing its importance. It is very similar to the case of a PDA but this time a structure of a PDA is limited to the technologies for obtaining same product from various raw materials, or containes technologies for processing same raw material. Case study of methanol production from various resources such as crude oil, natural gas, coal etc. serves as a good example (see Dobrowolski et.al. /1983/). From this stage more details are known, some additional estimates such us demands for construction materials, land and hardware can also be obtained.

3. PROBELM OF QUEST FOR CONCORDANCE

The problem of quest of concordance was formulated and studied in our research both from methodological and formal point of view (see Górecki et.al. /1982/, Dobrowolski et.al. /1983/). There we aim at another insight of this key issue in decision making process for development. As was shown above it is performed on various levels as well as through interactions between these levels.

The key point is the choice of criteria and their respective preference for a decision maker.

It is this choice that settles a question about quantified transformation of a development thesis, aspirations, preferences etc. - it is "soft" elements of the decision process into "hard" elements - it is quantities of resources and relevent industrial structure as well as expected gains.

Choice of criteria is very much open to the invention, knowledge and experience of a decision maker and later can be verified through methodological steps. Through solving problem of preference of criterial functions within initially assumed set, decision maker can review his primary choice and modify it. The fundamental importance of this choice underlines the indispensible role of a decision maker. Therefore application of any theoretical tools in order to improve and ease a decision process is a matter of a great responsibility. It is to be made clear to a decision maker what are exactly limits of theory, its advantages and drawbacks. What can be achieved and what can be neglacted or missed?

They are two basic factors which have to be considered and compromised if preference of criteria is to be settled[2/].

First is intensity factor and second is a robustness factor.

Let F be a criteria under consideration and u be resources available.

For the simplest one dimentional case:

$$F \in R^1 \;;\; u \in R^1$$

intensity

$$S = \frac{dF}{du} \tag{1}$$

while z represents a disturbance where $z \in R^1$ then

$$\text{robustness} \quad R = \left(\frac{dF}{dz}\right)^{-1} \tag{2}$$

For the case of a linear model z represents in the model changes in matrix coefficients or in the right hand side coefficients. Robustness analysis can be in such case helped through post optimal analysis. This illustrates how theoretical properties of a model could be used in selection and evaluation of criteria.

While selecting and evaluating criteria decision maker takes into account those that are most intensive and most robust.

Let us discuss properties of criterial functions F starting from simplest form of F and then generalising results.

Let $c \in R^1$ represent total available amount of a critical resource.

If an amount $u \in R^1$ of the resource c would be consumed it would produce gain $g(c,u) \in R^1$, and would deplete c by $h(c,u) \in R^1$. Total gain $F(c) \in R^1$ which could be obtained may be found from Bellmans (1961) procedure:

$$F(c) = \max_u \left\{ g(c,u) + F[c-h(c,u)] \right\} \tag{3}$$

under assumption that:
$h(c,u) \geqslant 0$ and is sufficiently small with respect to c , and assuming that derivative $F'(c) > 0$ (at least at the start of the process) eq.(3) can be approximated by the following:

$$F\ c = \max_u \left\{ g(c,u) + F(c) - h(c,u)F'(c) + \ldots + \right\} \tag{4}$$

This leads to the following formula for the approximated optimal strategy:

$$F'(c) = \max_u \left[\frac{g(c,u)}{h(c,u)}\right] \tag{5}$$

The above formula shows that in the process of development the suboptimal strategy is one which assures maximum gain from

2/ Due to space limitations the time factor is not discussed here. Naturally the more important with respect to time would be these criteria which persist their significance over assumed time horizon.

a unit of the resource.

It is very fortunate that this formula is in agreement with approach applied by experienced practitioners.

The above generalised for a multidimentional case:

$$\underline{c} \in R^n \;,\; \underline{u} \in R^n \;,\; \underline{h}(\underline{c},\underline{u}) \in R^n \;,$$

$$F(\underline{c}) \in R^1 \;,\; g(\underline{c},\underline{u}) \in R^1 \;,$$

formula (3) may be written as follows:

$$F(\underline{c}) = \max_{\underline{u}} \left\{ g(\underline{c},\underline{u}) + F[\underline{c} - \underline{h}(\underline{c},\underline{u})] \right\} \tag{6}$$

and

$$F(\underline{c}) = \max_{\underline{u}} \left\{ g(\underline{c},\underline{u}) + F(\underline{c}) - \mathrm{grad}_{\underline{c}}^T \, F(\underline{c}) \underline{h}(\underline{c},\underline{u}) \right\} \tag{7}$$

finally suboptimal strategy will be given by:

$$\mathrm{grad}_{\underline{c}}^T \, F(\underline{c}) \min_{\underline{u}} \underline{h}(\underline{c},\underline{u}) = \max_{\underline{u}} g(\underline{c},\underline{u}) \tag{8}$$

Further generalisation can be obtained for case where:

$$\underline{c} \in R^n \;,\; \underline{u} \in R^n \;,\; h(\underline{c},\underline{u}) \in R^n$$

$\underline{F}(\underline{c}) \in R^m$, $\underline{g}(\underline{c},\underline{u}) \in R^m$, and formula (3) will have form:

$$\underline{F}(\underline{c}) = \max_{\underline{u}} \left\{ \underline{g}(\underline{c},\underline{u}) + \underline{F}[\underline{c} - \underline{h}(\underline{c},\underline{u})] \right\} \tag{9}$$

which leads to suboptimal strategy:

$$\mathrm{Jac}\, \underline{F}(\underline{c}) \min_{\underline{u}} \underline{h}(\underline{c},\underline{u}) = \max_{\underline{u}} g(\underline{c},\underline{u}) \tag{10}$$

for multiobjective, multiresource development problem.

4. PROJECT FORMULATION

4.1. The problem

As explained in previous sections decision process attains level of project formulation after a complex analysis of various factors and their interdependencies. In fact the results of this analysis stand for "initial conditions" when process of quest of concordance enters the stage of project formulation.

Let us enumerate knowledge gained so far and describe the "initial conditions".

This can be done in the following manner:

There is a demand for production of a product P on the assumed level (or within certain range). P can be obtained from a raw material(s) M - available on the certain level (or within certain range). Preference list of technologies chosen for this purpose is known. From this follows also knowledge about relevant production capacities, consumption coefficients etc.

Informations that can be obtained from a comparative study were already mentioned (for more detail, see Dobrowolski et.al.

/1983/, Górecki et.al. /1982/).

There also should be known a sensivity of the development alternative of the higher level to the changes of the values of the respective parameters of the considered technology.

At this moment additional information has to be supplied for a project to be formulated. This concerns informations about regional and environmental conditions about potential sites for the installation, information about constraints and preferences on energy supplies, investment rates etc. For each technology in case this additional knowledge is assumed, specifically a process data from existing plants may serve as a reference.

Some of the above parameters may be not stated explicite when problem is formulated. For example a production capacity may be left open. This seems surprising but may happen when raw material availability due to regional conditions or goverment policy is more restrictive then a technology itself. In such a case production level of a product P as well as raw material demand M which stem from previous stages are not treated as constraints (or objectives). Simple comparison of results may be carried out after a lower level (it is project formulation) analysis is completed.

The above information is to be confronted with the information previously obtained in order to clarify any contradictions. If necessary feedback channels have to be activated as was discussed when Fig. 1 was described.

The above knowledge is to be transformed into a model. This model is to enable a decision maker for a multiobjective analysis of a particular technology with the assumptions and conditions which were implied by results of previous analysis and its further modifications due to additional information.

An important issue at this stage of analysis is finding a source for acquiring the technology in trade.

They are two basic possibilities of acquiring a technology:
- through own design,
- through technology transfer it is via negotiating a contract.

At this stage both should be considered on equal basis with help of the practically same model.

In the real case discussed below only one alternative is completly covered namely the one which assumes acquiring a technology through own design. The remaining one was discussed in detail in another paper (see Górecki et.al. /1983/) it has to be underlined however that the main body of procedures applied is the same in both cases.

4.2. Real life example

A scope

The case presented here is a real life one. It was simplified, however without altering elements significant both from technological and design point of view. The example was chosen due to its fair generality, and since it represents wide range of chemical installations as well as a process type technologies. Owing to its specific features it can also be described by a simple, understandable model which enables to show a flexibility of structure or alternative configurations of a technical system as expressed in terms of resources involved.

Object of a potential project

Technological scheme of the process is shown on the Fig. 2. The character of the process offers a possibility of assembling a whole set of installations each with different values of process parameters. Specific tradeoffs between process parameters are sustained of course and that creates a zone for design or as we would rather say the zone for multiobjective project formulation procedure.

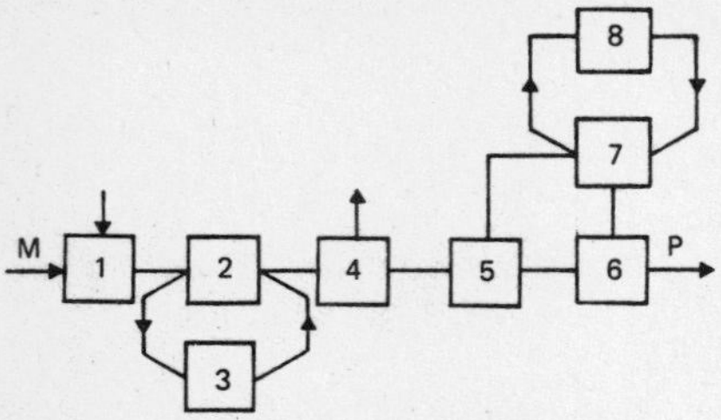

Fig. 2. Technological scheme of the installation: 1 - heating section; 2 - 1-st step reaction section; 3 - cooling cycle; 4 - condensation-absorption section; 5 - splitting section; 6 - purification section; 7 - 2nd step reaction section; 8 - cooling cycle 2.

In the process shown on the Fig. 2. its main characterizing parameter is the conversion level c . The maximum conversion is 100 %. At lower levels of conversion the fraction which was not transformed into final product P is again transformed in second reactor (unit 7) also closed in closed cycle (unit 8). Lower the conversion level c of the raw material M into product P a more powerful units (numbered 4 - 8) are necessary for the process, allowing however, for some reduction of hardware used in the first stage (units 2 and 3). At lower conversion level higher becomes energy consumption but at the same time lowers raw material consumption.

It is assumed that some data describing dependence of consumption of raw material M, energy E and investment I on the conversion level c are available. This empirical data can be approximated analytically:

$$M(c) = 0,000018\ c^2 + 0,0016\ c + 0,556 \tag{11}$$

$$E(c) = \frac{641,23}{c + 49,12} \tag{12}$$

$$I(c) = \frac{510}{c + 41,67} \tag{13}$$

Practically to stay in agreement with reality one has to assume a certain deviations from this characteristics which can be considered to be "ideal".

To describe criterial function one should start from finding a simplified unit cost of production of a final product P. Simplified unit cost (measured in [m.u/Mg]) would be:

$$B(c) = \alpha M(c) + \beta E(c) + \gamma I(c) \tag{14}$$

where

α = 50000 [m.u/Mg] - price of raw material M;

β = 2310[m.u/10^9J] - price of energy E;
γ = 2000[1/Mg] - depreciacion coefficient calculated for the period of 10 years, and assumed average production capacity of 50000 Mg/year.

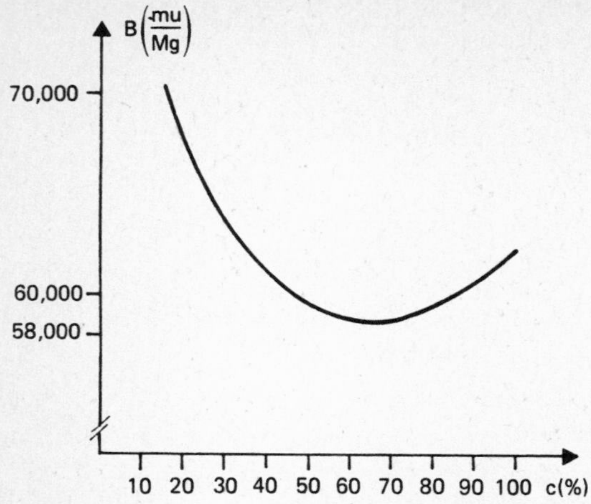

Fig. 3. Value of unit cost of production as a function of conversion level c .

Fig. 3 shows dependence of B(c) on conversion level c for the ideal functions of M(c), E(c) and I(c). The unit cost is at minimum for c = 65% which is B(65) = 59339,89[m.u/Mg] and for the c = 15% at its highest: B(15) = 70300[m.u/Mg].

In the case discussed here they were following constraints. due to domestic policy there was given a guaranty for availability of energy amounting to the level corresponding to technology run at conversion c = 100%. Since raw material M would have to be imported and it is an energy carier itself then authorities´ policy allowed for additional supply of energy under the condition that for a saving of 0,1[Mg/Mg] 1,75 · 10^9 [J/Mg] increase in energy consumption would be covered. This policy can be expressed by the following equation:

$$E(c) \leqslant E(100) + \xi(M(100) - M(c)) \qquad (15)$$

where ξ = 1,75[10^9 J/Mg], E(100) = 4,3[10^9 J/Mg] and M(100) = = 0,9[Mg/Mg]. The above condition can be satisfied by $c \in [20,100]$.

Second constraint came from bank policy. Bank was ready to provide a minimum, low interest credit at the level 3,6 · 10^9 [m.u] which corresponds to lowest investment (for c = 100 %). Any higher credit was to be accepted under the condition that unit cost of production would be lowered according to the following rule.

For each saving of a magnitude of 1000[m.u] from unit production cost, of B(100) = 62133[m.u] and additional credit of 0,5 · 10^9[m.u] could be made available. This in fact ment that bank imposed constraint of effectiveness of investment setting it above certain acceptable level:

$$I(c) \leqslant I(100) + \delta(B(100) - B(c)) \qquad (16)$$

where
$I(100) = 3,6 \quad \delta = 0,5 \cdot 10^{-3}$ and
$B(100) = 62133$
This can be satisfied for $c \in [55,100]$. Therefore, constraints narrow down a set of possible solutions to the technological structures which belong to the range $c \in [55,100]$. It contains global minimum of function B, at c = 65%. This is an important assignation in project formulation.

The above procedures complete problem of one criterion analysis. It has to be underlined that all forms of criteria used are of a general type devised in section 3, where criterial functions were discussed.

Conditions for project formulated so far are to certain extent inflexible. To find degree of acceptable flexibility more then one criterion should be admitted in the analysis. The simplest in this case would be to add as a criterion investment level I(c) therefore a multiobjective problem would be:

$$B(c) \rightarrow \min , \quad I(c) \rightarrow \min \tag{17}$$

with constraints remaining unchanged.

Solution to this problem yields to Pareto compromise (Fig.4

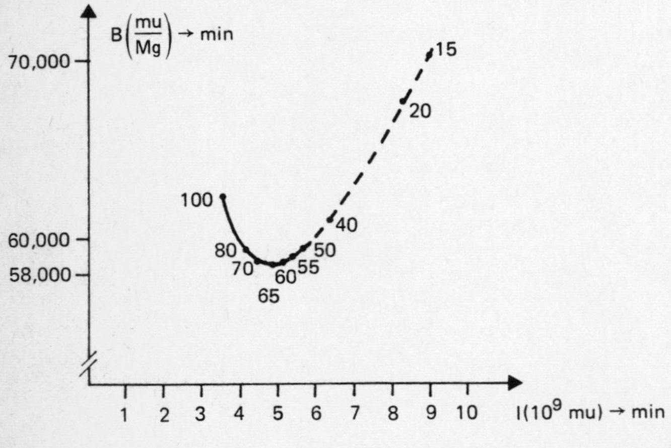

Fig. 4. Pareto compromise solution: B - unit cost, I - investment.

5. CONCLUDING REMARKS

Our basic thesis that project formulation goes far beyond the strict limits of design was confirmed in view of our research and experience as was displayed in the paper. It resulted in creating a basic methodology which shows the way how to synthetise knowledge indispensable for project formulation. It is to be done along a decision process of an industrial development. Moreover it makes a project formulation an integral part of such a decision process.

It is very important to realise that philisophy and approach presented are to far extent independent from the type of economy. Form or set of criteria may be different but general fromework and mechanism as well as multilevel structure would remain. The following rule has to be accepted: prior to design an understanding of development phenomena and relevant behaviour of industrial structure is indispensable and has to result in project formulation.

We feel obliged to mention at the and that a very important inspiration to our work came from a management system which was initiated by the chemical industry (see Kopytowski et.al./1972/) relativly long ago - in early seventies. However it was based on teams of experts not an algorithms and computers its very pragmatic core was in agreement with philosophy which led us to the approach and conclusions presented here.

6. REFERENCES

Bellman,R. (1961). Adaptive Control processes: a guided tour. The Rand Corporation Princetown New Jersey. Princetown Univ. Press.

Borek,A., Dobrowolski,G., and Żebrowski,M. (1978). GSOS - a Growth Strategy Optimization System for the Chemical Industry. In Advances in measurement and Control - MECO-78, Vol. 3, Acta Press, pp. 1128-1131.

Dobrowolski,G., Kopytowski,J., Lewandowski,A., and Żebrowski,M. (1982). Generating Efficient Alternatives for Development of the Chemical Industry. Collaborative Paper, CP-82-54, International Institute for Applied Systems Analysis, Laxenburg, Austria.

Dobrowolski,G., Kopytowski,J., Wojtania,J., and Żebrowski,M. (1983). Alternative Routs from Fossil Resources to Chemical Feedstocks. Identification, Methodological Approach and the Case of Methanol. Research Report delivered for print: International Institute for Applied Systems Analysis, Laxenburg, Austria.

Górecki,H. (1981). Problem of Choice of an Optimal Solution in a Multicriterion Space. Proceedings of the VIIIth Triennial World IFAC Congress, 24-28 August, Kyoto, Japan, pp.106-110.

Górecki,H., Dobrowolski,G., Kopytowski,J., and Żebrowski,M. (1982). The Quest for a Concordance Between Technologies and Resources as a Multiobjective Decision Process. In M.Grauer, A.Lewandowski, and A.P.Wierzbicki, Multiobjective and Stochastic Optimization. Conference proceedings, CP-82-512. International Institute for Applied Systems Analysis, Laxenburg, Austria.

Górecki,H., Kopytowski,J., and Żebrowski,M. (1983). Negotiating Agreements, Multiobjective Approach. Paper presented at the IFAC Workshop on SWIIS - Supplemental Ways for Improving International Stability. Sept. 13-15, 1983, Laxenburg, Austria.

Kendrick,D.A., and Stoutjestijk,A.J. (1978). The Planning of Industrial Investment Programs. Vol. 1. A Methodology. Published by Johns Hopkins University Press for World Bank Research Publications.

Kopytowski,J., Bertish,W. (1972). ALPHA - System for Evaluation and Planning of Investment in the Chemical Industry. Internal Report (in Polish). Prosynchem Design Office. Gliwice, Poland.

Sophos,A., Rotstein,E., and Stephanopolous,G. (1980). Multiobjective Analysis in Modelling the Petrochemical Industry. Chemical Engineering Science, Vol. 35, No 12, pp. 2415-2426.

APPENDICES

INTERNATIONAL WORKSHOP ON
INTERACTIVE DECISION ANALYSIS AND
INTERPRETATIVE COMPUTER INTELLIGENCE

Laxenburg, 20-23 September, 1983

PROGRAM

Tuesday, 20 September

Opening Session and Introduction
Prof. V. Kaftanov, Deputy Director of IIASA

SESSION 1: METHODS, CONCEPTS AND EXPERIENCES I (Chairman: S. Zionts)

A. Wierzbicki	Interactive Decision Analysis and Interpretative Computer Intelligence
M. Grauer, A. Lewandowski and A. Wierzbicki	DIDASS - Theory, Implementation and Experiences
F.A. Lootsma, K. Légrády, J. Meisner and F. Schellemans	Multicriteria Decision Analysis to Aid Budget Allocation

SESSION 2: METHODS, CONCEPTS AND EXPERIENCES II (Chairman: M. Peschel)

F. Forgó	Multiple-Criteria Analysis: A Game-Theoretic Approach
M. Vlach	Levitin-Miljutin-Osmolovski Conditions for Local Pareto Optimality
P. Korhonen and J. Laakso	A Visual Interactive Method for Solving the Multiple-Criteria Problem
S. Zionts and J. Wallenius	Recent Developments in Our Approach to Multiple-Criteria Decision Making
A. Lotov	Generalized Reachable Set Approach to MCDM Problems

Wednesday, 21 September

SESSION 3: METHODS AND TECHNIQUES I (Chairman: J. Wallenius)

T. Matsuda	Interactive Decision Analysis as a Distributed Decision-Support System
K. Tarvainen	On the Implementation of the Interactive Surrogate Worth Trade-Off (ISWT) Method
H. Nakayama and Y. Sawaragi	Satisficing Trade-Off Method for Multiobjective Programming

M. Sakawa	Interactive Fuzzy Decision Making for Multiobjective Nonlinear Programming Problems
E. Jaquet-Lagreze	PREFCALC, an Interactive Method to Assess Additive Value Functions

SESSION 4: METHODS AND TECHNIQUES II (Chairman: H. Nakayama)

F. Seo and M. Sakawa	Fuzzy Assessment of Multiattribute Utility Functions
R.E. Steuer	Operating Conditions Pertaining to the Interactive Weighted Tchebycheff Procedure

On-Line Demonstration of Interactive MCDM Methods

K.-H. Elster	On Some Computational Experience with the Solution of Vector Optimization Problems
E. Bischoff	A Posteriori Trade-Off Analysis in Reference Point Approaches

Thursday, 22 September

SESSION 5: METHODS AND TECHNIQUES III (Chairman: P. Nijkamp)

J. Guddat and K. Wendler	On Two Dialogue Algorithms for Vector Optimization Based on Parametric Optimization
P. Serafini	Dual Relaxation and Branch-and-Bound Interactive Techniques for Multicriteria Optimization
C. Carlsson	Handling Conflicts in Fuzzy Multiple-Criteria Optimization
M. Grauer	Interactive Multiple-Criteria Stochastic Programming - A Feasibility Study
N. Sugihara and M. Ichikawa	The Systems Approach and Contingency View in Managerial Behavior and Management Organization

SESSION 6: METHODS AND APPLICATIONS I (Chairman: F. Szidarovszky)

M. Peschel and F. Breitenecker	Interactive Structure Design and Simulation of Nonlinear Systems from the Multiobjective Viewpoint Using the Lotka-Volterra Approach

P. Nijkamp and W. Hafkamp	An Operational Multicomponent Multi-actor Policy Model for Economic-Environmental Scenarios
H. Isermann	Investment and Financial Planning in a General Partnership - A Case Study of Intertemporal Collective Optimization
Z. Fortuna and L. Krus	Simulation of an Interactive Method Supporting Collective Decision Making as Applied to a Regional Development Model
V. Mazurik	On a Dialogue System for Solving Optimization Problems

Friday, 23 September

SESSION 7: METHODS AND APPLICATIONS II (Chairman: C. Carlsson)

F. Szidarovszky	A Multiobjective Observation Network Design Procedure and Its Applications in Hydrology and Mining
S. Kaden	Regional Water Policies in Open-Cast Mining Areas of the GDR - A Multicriteria Approach
J. Morse	A Multiobjective Expert System for Suppliers of Out-of-the-Money Options
F. Breitenecker and A. Schmid	Decision Support Using Standard Simulation Software as Applied to a Multipurpose Hydroenergetic System
H. Górecki, M. Żebrowski and T. Ryś	A Multiobjective Procedure for Project Formulation - Design of a Chemical Installation

Final Discussion and Closing Session

LIST OF CONTRIBUTORS

Dr. E.E. Bischoff
International Institute for
Applied Systems Analysis
Schlossplatz 1
A-2361 Laxenburg
Austria

and

Department of Management
Science
University College of Swansea
Swansea SA2 8PP
UK

Dr. F. Breitenecker
Institute of Applied Mathematics
Technical University of Vienna
Gusshausstr. 27-29
1040 Vienna
Austria

Professor C. Carlsson
Department of Business Administration
Åbo Academy
Henriksgatan 7
20500 Åbo 50
Finland

Professor F. Forgó
Institute of Mathematics
and Computer Science
Karl Marx University of Economics
Dimitrov ter. 8
1093 Budapest
Hungary

Dr. Z. Fortuna
International Institute for
Applied Systems Analysis
Schlossplatz 1
A-2361 Laxenburg
Austria

and

Institute of Automatic Control
Technical University of Warsaw
ul. Nowowiejska 15/19
00-665 Warsaw
Poland

Professor H. Górecki
Institute of Control and
Systems Engineering
Al. Mickiewicza 30
30-053 Cracow
Poland

Dr. M. Grauer
International Institute for
Applied Systems Analysis
Schlossplatz 1
A-2361 Laxenburg
Austria

and

Department of Systems Engineering
Technical University of Leuna-
Merseburg
Otto-Nuschke-Str.
42 Merseburg
GDR

Professor J. Guddat
Department of Mathematics
Humboldt University
Unter den Linden 6
1086 Berlin
GDR

Dr. W. Hafkamp
Department of Economics
Free University
P.O. Box 7161
1007 MC Amsterdam
The Netherlands

Professor M. Ichikawa
Faculty of Business Administration
Kyoto Sangyo University
Kamigamo-Motoyama, Kita-Ku
Kyoto
Japan

Professor H. Isermann
Faculty of Economic Science
University of Bielefeld
P.O. Box 8640
4800 Bielefeld 1
FRG

Dr. S. Kaden
International Institute for
Applied Systems Analysis
Schlossplatz 1
A-2361 Laxenburg
Austria

and

Institute for Water Management
Schneller Str. 140
119 Berlin
GDR

Dr. J. Kopytowski
Institute for Industrial
Chemistry
ul. Rydygiera 8
01-793 Warsaw
Poland

Professor P. Korhonen
Helsinki School of Economics
and Business Administration
Runeberginkatu 14-16
00100 Helsinki
Finland

Dr. L. Krus
Department of Large-Scale Systems
Theory
Systems Research Institute
Newelska 6
01447 Warsaw
Poland

Dr. J. Laakso
Helsinki School of Economics
and Business Administration
Runeberginkatu 14-16
00100 Helsinki
Finland

Ms. K. Légrády
Department of Mathematics and
Informatics
Delft University of Technology
Julianalaan 132
2628 BL Delft
The Netherlands

Dr. A. Lewandowski
Institute of Automatic Control
Technical University of Warsaw
ul. Nowowiejska 15/19
00-665 Warsaw
Poland

Professor F.A. Lootsma
Department of Mathematics and
Informatics
Delft University of Technology
P.O. Box 356
2600 AJ Delft
The Netherlands

Dr. A. Lotov
Computing Center of the USSR Academy
of Sciences
Vavilova St. 40
Moscow
USSR

Dr. V. Mazurik
Computing Center of the USSR Academy
of Sciences
Vavilova St. 40
Moscow
USSR

Mr. J. Meisner
Royal Dutch/Shell Research Laboratory
Badhuisweg 3
1031 CM Amsterdam
The Netherlands

Professor J.N. Morse
Finance Department
Loyola College
4501 N. Charles St.
Baltimore, Maryland 21210
USA

Professor H. Nakayama
Department of Applied Mathematics
Konan University
8-9-1 Okamoto, Higashinada
658 Kobe
Japan

Professor P. Nijkamp
Department of Economics
Free University
P.O. Box 7161
1007 MC Amsterdam
The Netherlands

Professor M. Peschel
Division of Mathematics
and Cybernetics
GDR Academy of Sciences
Otto-Nuschke-Str. 22-23
108 Berlin
GDR

Dr. T. Ryś
Institute for Control and Systems Engineering
Academy of Mining and Metallurgy
Al. Mickiewicza 30
30-053 Cracow
Poland

Professor M. Sakawa
Department of Systems Engineering
Faculty of Engineering
Kobe University
Rokko Nada
Kobe 657
Japan

Professor Y. Sawaragi
The Japan Institute of Systems Research
4 Ushinomiya-cho,
Yoshida, Sakyo
Kyoto 606
Japan

Mr. F. Schellemans
Energy Research Council
Ministry of Economic Affairs
Herengracht 9
2511 EG The Hague
The Netherlands

Dr. A. Schmid
Institute of Applied Mathematics
Technical University of Vienna
Gusshausstr. 27-29
1040 Vienna
Austria

Professor F. Seo
Kyoto Institute of Economic Research
Kyoto University
Yoshida-Honmachi
Sakyo-Ku
Kyoto 606
Japan

Professor P. Serafini
Department of Mathematics, Computer and Systems Sciences
University of Udine
Via Mantica 3
33100 Udine
Italy

Professor R.E. Steuer
Department of Quantitative Business Analysis
University of Georgia
Athens, Georgia 30602
USA

Dr. H.M. Stolyarova
Computing Center of the USSR Academy of Sciences
Vavilova St. 40
Moscow
USSR

Professor N. Sugihara
Faculty of Business Administration
Kyoto Sangyo University
Kamigamo-Motoyama, Kita-Ku
Kyoto
Japan

Professor F. Szidarovszky
Department of Computer Science and Mathematics
University of Horticulture
Villanyi ut. 29-35
1118 Budapest
Hungary

Dr. K. Tarvainen
Department of Mathematics
Helsinki University of Technology
Otakaari 1
02150 Espoo
Finland

Professor M. Vlach
Department of Operations Research and Computer Science
Faculty of Mathematics and Physics
Charles University
Sokolovska ul. 83
18600 Prague 8
Czechoslovakia

Professor J. Wallenius
Department of Economics and Management
University of Jyväskylä
Seminaarinkatu 15
Jyväskylä 10
Finland

Dr. K. Wendler
Department of Mathematics
Humboldt University
Unter den Linden 6
1086 Berlin
GDR

Professor A. Wierzbicki
International Institute for
Applied Systems Analysis
Schlossplatz 1
A-2361 Laxenburg
Austria

and

Institute of Automatic Control
Technical University of Warsaw
ul. Nowowiejska 15/19
00-665 Warsaw
Poland

Dr. M. Żebrowski
Institute for Control and Systems
Engineering
Academy of Mining and Metallurgy
Al. Mickiewicza 30
30-053 Cracow
Poland

Professor S. Zionts
School of Management
State University of New York
at Buffalo
Buffalo, N.Y. 14214
USA

THE INTERNATIONAL INSTITUTE FOR APPLIED SYSTEMS ANALYSIS

is a nongovernmental research institution, bringing together scientists from around the world to work on problems of common concern. Situated in Laxenburg, Austria, IIASA was founded in October 1972 by the academies of science and equivalent organizations of twelve countries. Its founders gave IIASA a unique position outside national, disciplinary, and institutional boundaries so that it might take the broadest possible view in pursuing its objectives:

To promote international cooperation in solving problems arising from social, economic, technological, and environmental change

To create a network of institutions in the national member organization countries and elsewhere for joint scientific research

To develop and formalize systems analysis and the sciences contributing to it, and promote the use of analytical techniques needed to evaluate and address complex problems

To inform policy advisors and decision makers about the potential application of the Institute's work to such problems

The Institute now has national member organizations in the following countries:

Austria
The Austrian Academy of Sciences

Bulgaria
The National Committee for Applied Systems Analysis and Management

Canada
The Canadian Committee for IIASA

Czechoslovakia
The Committee for IIASA of the Czechoslovak Socialist Republic

Finland
The Finnish Committee for IIASA

France
The French Association for the Development of Systems Analysis

German Democratic Republic
The Academy of Sciences of the German Democratic Republic

Federal Republic of Germany
The Max Planck Society for the Advancement of Sciences

Hungary
The Hungarian Committee for Applied Systems Analysis

Italy
The National Research Council

Japan
The Japan Committee for IIASA

Netherlands
The Foundation IIASA–Netherlands

Poland
The Polish Academy of Sciences

Sweden
The Swedish Council for Planning and Coordination of Research

Union of Soviet Socialist Republics
The Academy of Sciences of the Union of Soviet Socialist Republics

United States of America
The American Academy of Arts and Sciences

Vol. 157: Optimization and Operations Research. Proceedings 1977. Edited by R. Henn, B. Korte, and W. Oettli. VI, 270 pages. 1978.

Vol. 158: L. J. Cherene, Set Valued Dynamical Systems and Economic Flow. VIII, 83 pages. 1978.

Vol. 159: Some Aspects of the Foundations of General Equilibrium Theory: The Posthumous Papers of Peter J. Kalman. Edited by J. Green. VI, 167 pages. 1978.

Vol. 160: Integer Programming and Related Areas. A Classified Bibliography. Edited by D. Hausmann. XIV, 314 pages. 1978.

Vol. 161: M. J. Beckmann, Rank in Organizations. VIII, 164 pages. 1978.

Vol. 162: Recent Developments in Variable Structure Systems, Economics and Biology. Proceedings 1977. Edited by R. R. Mohler and A. Ruberti. VI, 326 pages. 1978.

Vol. 163: G. Fandel, Optimale Entscheidungen in Organisationen. VI, 143 Seiten. 1979.

Vol. 164: C. L. Hwang and A. S. M. Masud, Multiple Objective Decision Making – Methods and Applications. A State-of-the-Art Survey. XII, 351 pages. 1979.

Vol. 165: A. Maravall, Identification in Dynamic Shock-Error Models. VIII, 158 pages. 1979.

Vol. 166: R. Cuninghame-Green, Minimax Algebra. XI, 258 pages. 1979.

Vol. 167: M. Faber, Introduction to Modern Austrian Capital Theory. X, 196 pages. 1979.

Vol. 168: Convex Analysis and Mathematical Economics. Proceedings 1978. Edited by J. Kriens. V, 136 pages. 1979.

Vol. 169: A. Rapoport et al., Coalition Formation by Sophisticated Players. VII, 170 pages. 1979.

Vol. 170: A. E. Roth, Axiomatic Models of Bargaining. V, 121 pages. 1979.

Vol. 171: G. F. Newell, Approximate Behavior of Tandem Queues. XI, 410 pages. 1979.

Vol. 172: K. Neumann and U. Steinhardt, GERT Networks and the Time-Oriented Evaluation of Projects. 268 pages. 1979.

Vol. 173: S. Erlander, Optimal Spatial Interaction and the Gravity Model. VII, 107 pages. 1980.

Vol. 174: Extremal Methods and Systems Analysis. Edited by A. V. Fiacco and K. O. Kortanek. XI, 545 pages. 1980.

Vol. 175: S. K. Srinivasan and R. Subramanian, Probabilistic Analysis of Redundant Systems. VII, 356 pages. 1980.

Vol. 176: R. Färe, Laws of Diminishing Returns. VIII, 97 pages. 1980.

Vol. 177: Multiple Criteria Decision Making-Theory and Application. Proceedings, 1979. Edited by G. Fandel and T. Gal. XVI, 570 pages. 1980.

Vol. 178: M. N. Bhattacharyya, Comparison of Box-Jenkins and Bonn Monetary Model Prediction Performance. VII, 146 pages. 1980.

Vol. 179: Recent Results in Stochastic Programming. Proceedings, 1979. Edited by P. Kall and A. Prékopa. IX, 237 pages. 1980.

Vol. 180: J. F. Brotchie, J. W. Dickey and R. Sharpe, TOPAZ – General Planning Technique and its Applications at the Regional, Urban, and Facility Planning Levels. VII, 356 pages. 1980.

Vol. 181: H. D. Sherali and C. M. Shetty, Optimization with Disjunctive Constraints. VIII, 156 pages. 1980.

Vol. 182: J. Wolters, Stochastic Dynamic Properties of Linear Econometric Models. VIII, 154 pages. 1980.

Vol. 183: K. Schittkowski, Nonlinear Programming Codes. VIII, 242 pages. 1980.

Vol. 184: R. E. Burkard and U. Derigs, Assignment and Matching Problems: Solution Methods with FORTRAN-Programs. VIII, 148 pages. 1980.

Vol. 185: C. C. von Weizsäcker, Barriers to Entry. VI, 220 pages. 1980.

Vol. 186: Ch.-L. Hwang and K. Yoon, Multiple Attribute Decision Making – Methods and Applications. A State-of-the-Art-Survey. XI, 259 pages. 1981.

Vol. 187: W. Hock, K. Schittkowski, Test Examples for Nonlinear Programming Codes. V. 178 pages. 1981.

Vol. 188: D. Bös, Economic Theory of Public Enterprise. VII, 142 pages. 1981.

Vol. 189: A. P. Lüthi, Messung wirtschaftlicher Ungleichheit. IX, 287 pages. 1981.

Vol. 190: J. N. Morse, Organizations: Multiple Agents with Multiple Criteria. Proceedings, 1980. VI, 509 pages. 1981.

Vol. 191: H. R. Sneessens, Theory and Estimation of Macroeconomic Rationing Models. VII, 138 pages. 1981.

Vol. 192: H. J. Bierens: Robust Methods and Asymptotic Theory in Nonlinear Econometrics. IX, 198 pages. 1981.

Vol. 193: J. K. Sengupta, Optimal Decisions under Uncertainty. VII, 156 pages. 1981.

Vol. 194: R. W. Shephard, Cost and Production Functions. XI, 104 pages. 1981.

Vol. 195: H. W. Ursprung, Die elementare Katastrophentheorie. Eine Darstellung aus der Sicht der Ökonomie. VII, 332 pages. 1982.

Vol. 196: M. Nermuth, Information Structures in Economics. VIII, 236 pages. 1982.

Vol. 197: Integer Programming and Related Areas. A Classified Bibliography. 1978 – 1981. Edited by R. von Randow. XIV, 338 pages. 1982.

Vol. 198: P. Zweifel, Ein ökonomisches Modell des Arztverhaltens. XIX, 392 Seiten. 1982.

Vol. 199: Evaluating Mathematical Programming Techniques. Proceedings, 1981. Edited by J.M. Mulvey. XI, 379 pages. 1982.

Vol. 200: The Resource Sector in an Open Economy. Edited by H. Siebert. IX, 161 pages. 1984.

Vol. 201: P. M. C. de Boer, Price Effects in Input-Output-Relations: A Theoretical and Empirical Study for the Netherlands 1949–1967. X, 140 pages. 1982.

Vol. 202: U. Witt, J. Perske, SMS – A Program Package for Simulation and Gaming of Stochastic Market Processes and Learning Behavior. VII, 266 pages. 1982.

Vol. 203: Compilation of Input-Output Tables. Proceedings, 1981. Edited by J. V. Skolka. VII, 307 pages. 1982.

Vol. 204: K. C. Mosler, Entscheidungsregeln bei Risiko: Multivariate stochastische Dominanz. VII, 172 Seiten. 1982.

Vol. 205: R. Ramanathan, Introduction to the Theory of Economic Growth. IX, 347 pages. 1982.

Vol. 206: M. H. Karwan, V. Lotfi, J. Telgen, and S. Zionts, Redundancy in Mathematical Programming. VII, 286 pages. 1983.

Vol. 207: Y. Fujimori, Modern Analysis of Value Theory. X, 165 pages. 1982.

Vol. 208: Econometric Decision Models. Proceedings, 1981. Edited by J. Gruber. VI, 364 pages. 1983.

Vol. 209: Essays and Surveys on Multiple Criteria Decision Making. Proceedings, 1982. Edited by P. Hansen. VII, 441 pages. 1983.

Vol. 210: Technology, Organization and Economic Structure. Edited by R. Sato and M. J. Beckmann. VIII, 195 pages. 1983.

Vol. 211: P. van den Heuvel, The Stability of a Macroeconomic System with Quantity Constraints. VII, 169 pages. 1983.

Vol. 212: R. Sato and T. Nôno, Invariance Principles and the Structure of Technology. V, 94 pages. 1983.

This series reports new developments in mathematical economics, economic theory, econometrics, operations research, and mathematical systems, research and teaching – quickly, informally and at a high level. The type of material considered for publication includes:

1. Preliminary drafts of original papers and monographs
2. Lectures on a new field or presentations of a new angle in a classical field
3. Seminar work-outs
4. Reports of meetings, provided they are
   a) of exceptional interest and
   b) devoted to a single topic.

Texts which are out of print but still in demand may also be considered if they fall within these categories.

The timeliness of a manuscript is more important than its form, which may be unfinished or tentative. Thus, in some instances, proofs may be merely outlined and results presented which have been or will later be published elsewhere. If possible, a subject index should be included. Publication of Lecture Notes is intended as a service to the international scientific community, in that a commercial publisher, Springer-Verlag, can offer a wide distribution of documents which would otherwise have a restricted readership. Once published and copyrighted, they can be documented in the scientific literature.

Manuscripts

Manuscripts should be no less than 100 and preferably no more than 500 pages in length. On request, the publisher will supply special paper with the typing area outlined and essentials for the preparation of camera-ready manuscripts. Manuscripts should be sent directly to Springer-Verlag Heidelberg or Springer-Verlag New York.

Springer-Verlag, Heidelberger Platz 3, D-1000 Berlin 33
Springer-Verlag, Tiergartenstraße 17, D-6900 Heidelberg 1
Springer-Verlag, 175 Fifth Avenue, New York, NY 10010/USA
Springer-Verlag, 37-3, Hongo 3-chome, Bunkyo-ku, Tokyo 113, Japan

ISBN 3-540-13354-2
ISBN 0-387-13354-2